DATE DUE

In an Age of Experts

In an Age of Experts

THE CHANGING ROLE OF
PROFESSIONALS IN POLITICS AND
PUBLIC LIFE

• STEVEN BRINT •

PRINCETON UNIVERSITY PRESS

PRINCETON, NEW JERSEY

Library of Congress Cataloging-in-Publication Data

Brint, Steven G.
In an age of experts : The changing role of professionals
in politics and public life / Steven Brint.
p.   cm.
Includes bibliographical references and index.
ISBN 0-691-03399-4 (CL)
1. Professions—Social aspects—United States.   2. Middle class—United States.
3. Intellectuals—United States.   I. Title.
HT687.B75   1994   305.5′53—dc20   93-50578   CIP

This book has been composed in Sabon

Princeton University Press Books are printed on acid-free paper and meet the guidelines for
permanence and durability of the Committee on Production Guidelines for Book
Longevity of the Council on Library Resources

Printed in the United States of America

1 3 5 7 9 10 8 6 4 2

• *FOR MY PARENTS* •

• C O N T E N T S •

• A C K N O W L E D G M E N T S •

THIS BOOK has a long history, and I have a number of people to thank for help along the way. Christopher Jencks, Jerome Karabel, and Ann Swidler helped me to get started by expressing interest in the original idea—which was to investigate versions of the "new class" theory using survey data. James Davis kept me moving along with computer funds and words of advice, and he later brought me back to Harvard for a year of wonderfully uninterrupted number-crunching. Charles Derber also enabled me to continue to work on the quantitative side of the investigation, while at the same time providing constant theoretical stimulation during the year I spent as coordinator of his research project on professionals for the National Institute of Mental Health.

In the drafts of this book, my thinking only gradually moved away from concerns about the "new class" to concerns about professions in the structure of social stratification. I have Eliot Freidson primarily to thank for that subtle but meaningful change in direction, and for much else. As an intellectual guide, I owe Seymour Martin Lipset a similarly large debt for ways of thinking about the intersection of social stratification and the political order.

I have received a large share of encouragement from colleagues and friends. For this encouragement and for helpful discussions and comments, I would like to thank Jerome Karabel, Paul DiMaggio, David Karen, Kevin Dougherty, David Swartz, David Stark, Ann Swidler, Wendy Griswold, Frederick Weil, Ivan Szelenyi, William Schwartz, Kathleen Gerson, Wolf Heydebrand, Caroline Persell, Dennis Wrong, Terence Halliday, Charles Perrow, Walter Powell, Jonathan Rieder, Christopher Rootes, Lennard Svensson, Carl Levy, Michèle Lamont, Roger Waldinger, John Mollenkopf, Matthew Drennan, Norman Fainstein, Saskia Sassen, Michael Macy, Alexander Hicks, Rogers Brubaker, Terry Clark, Richard Hamilton, Jill Quadagno, John Campbell, Robert Jenkins, David Williams, Burton Bledstein, Magali Sarfatti Larson, Randall Collins, Michael Schudson, Lewis Coser, Charles Kadushin, Sheldon Rothblatt, Andrew Abbott, William Roy, Neil Fligstein, Jeff Manza, Eliot Krause, Alan Wolfe, Deborah Davis, Juan Linz, Stanton Wheeler, and Robert Kuttner. I wish that I had been able to take all of their good advice.

Critics are an acquired taste, but in the process of scholarship they are often more helpful than friends. For criticism that proved particularly useful to me at various stages in the process of writing this book, I would like to thank Paul Starr, Michael Harloe, and Bruce Kimball. The most difficult task, of course, is to combine encouragement and criticism in an equitable way. At an early stage of the project, Daniel Bell provided both in good measure and set a standard in many other ways.

I have been aided in my work by research support from the Social Science Faculty Research Fund and the A. Whitney Griswold Fund at Yale University and by a grant from the Spencer Foundation. Participation in the Social

Science Research Council's Committee on New York City helped me to formulate ideas about the political economy of professions. A fellowship year awarded by Yale helped me to complete the quantitative research for the book. I have also been fortunate for the opportunity to present parts of my research at colloquia and research seminars at New York University, the Social Science Research Council, Yale University, Harvard University, the Center for European Studies at Harvard, the University of Pennsylvania, UCLA, and the University of California, Berkeley.

Several graduate students from Yale worked on the project as research assistants. I would like to thank Susan Kelley, Bill Cunningham, Francesca Polletta, Leif Haase, Dan Ryan, Bill Preston, Corey Robin, and Iverson Griffin for their good work. I would like to thank Merle Sprinzen, Cheri Minton, and Nancy Williamson for computer assistance, and Terry Miller and Robin Whittington for help in the preparation of the manuscript. I would also like to thank my editor at Princeton, Mary Murrell, for her encouragement, and for her many useful suggestions.

In the writing of this book, my family has been a great support, particularly my sweet and sassy children, Juliana and Benjamin, and my beautiful, strong-minded, and talented wife, Michele Salzman. Like everyone else, my parents waited patiently for the book to achieve the form I wanted for it. I dedicate this book with much love to them.

S.B.
New Haven, Connecticut
August, 1993

In an Age of Experts

Introduction: Professionals and the Character of American Democracy

THIS is a book about the people we call *professionals*—about their social standing, their work, their beliefs and values, and their politics. Ultimately, therefore, it is a book about the uses of trained intelligence in American society and about the relationship of the educated middle class to the larger society and political order.

For the last thirty years, the professional stratum has proven a particular puzzle to social scientists. Very little consensus exists except on one point: the number of people categorized as "professionals" by census bureaus throughout the developed world has been growing in a dramatic fashion. In the United States before World War II, for example, only one percent of all employed people were college-educated and classified by the Census Bureau as "professional, technical, and kindred" workers. Today, the comparable group is twelve times as large.

I define members of the "professional middle class" as people who earn at least a middling income from the application of a relatively complex body of knowledge. Professional services can involve teaching, healing, advocating in court, building, designing, accounting, researching, or any one of a number of other activities requiring advanced training in a field of learning and nonroutine mental operations on the job. Not surprisingly, professionals are the most highly educated of all strata; their education now typically extends beyond the baccalaureate. Usually, professionals are considered to be distinct from business executives and managers, another relatively well educated group, in so far as they are not primarily engaged in the administration of enterprises.[1] The professional middle class, therefore, includes most doctors, natural scientists, engineers, computer scientists, certified public accountants, economists, social scientists, psychotherapists, lawyers, policy experts of various sorts, professors, at least some journalists and editors, some clergy, and some artists and writers.

For some, like the sociologist Daniel Bell, the professions are heralds of a new kind of "post-industrial" society in which formal knowledge becomes an ever more important resource in both economic development and social problem solving.[2] Here professionalism is most often thought of as providing a self-directing dignity and ethical tone to intellectually demanding work. For others, like the historian Laurence Veysey, the professions are a mere concatenation of occupations, sharing little more than a loose-fitting label and higher-than-average educational requirements (requirements that are often regarded as quite arbitrary).[3] Here the *ideology* of professionalism is usually considered to mask the increasing differentiation of the powerful and the powerless among the college-educated.

Whatever their views on professions as an element of the social structure, a good many observers do find professionals to be increasingly visible in public life. One recent commentator, Barbara Ehrenreich, has noted that the authorities who dominate discussions in the public arena are "all members of this relatively privileged group": "When we see a man in work clothes on the screen, we anticipate some grievance or, at best, information of a highly local or anecdotal nature. On matters of general interest or national importance, waitresses, forklift operators, steamfitters—that is, most 'ordinary' Americans—are not invited to opine."[4] Others have shown that as the professions have advanced, labor unions have retreated as centers of political influence. Where the proportion of the work force enrolled as union members has slipped to under 20 percent in recent years,[5] membership in professional associations has grown from 7 to 16 percent in the last quarter century.[6] Similarly, between 1960 and 1980, at a time of rapid growth in the Washington "pressure community," professional associations tripled their percentage representation among all interest organizations (from 5 to 15 percent), while union representation dwindled from 10 to 3 percent.[7]

In spite of their visibility in public life, the political preferences of professionals remain very much in dispute. Once considered among the solidly conservative elements of American society,[8] the professions are now sometimes depicted as the source of a new kind of class conflict in which "knowledge-based" professional elites engage in a half-hidden, half-open conflict with "profit-oriented" business owners and executives for power and status in the advanced societies. It is a theory that has aroused the fears of such conservative political thinkers as Irving Kristol and Kevin Phillips, the hopes of such liberal thinkers as Alvin Gouldner and Barbara Ehrenreich, and the analytical interest of a wide range of social scientists, from Seymour Martin Lipset to Pierre Bourdieu, and historians, from Robert Wiebe to Harold Perkin and Sheldon Rothblatt.[9] In the view of the "new class" theorists, the main lines of class division have become inverted in advanced societies like the United States, with the most consequential conflicts occurring between articulate, intellectually oriented professionals and property-owning business people, rather than between capital and labor. For many of these theorists, the leading edge of "new class" dissent can be found in and around the universities, where an enlarged vision of human life stands in contrast to the economistic consideration of human beings as "human resources." Others, eschewing the "new class" theory, find in professionals a group with a tendency to play the role of social balance wheel, moderating the more extreme passions and interests of democratic politics.[10] Still others continue to find in them a generally conservative, business-oriented middle class.[11]

In this book, I will attempt to resolve some of the puzzles that have grown up around the professional stratum by looking at professions and professionalism as historically evolving sociological forms. This rethinking is based on an examination of the history of professions as a form of organization and status category, and on an examination of the development of expert labor in the American economy. In this respect, my study is very much in the Weberian tradition of sociology, a tradition that emphasizes the historical development of meaningful forms of social life.

My analysis will focus on two important outcomes of recent historical changes: first, the triumph of the idea of professionals as agents of formal knowledge over the older idea of professionals as "trustees" of socially important knowledge; and, secondly, the splintering of the professional stratum along functional, organizational, and market lines. Politically, these changes have led, I will argue, to a polarization of views *within* the professional stratum, rather than to a separation of professionals from other social classes and strata. The 10–15 percentage point differences that separate highly educated professionals and high-income business people on most political issues, while certainly of interest, are dwarfed by the differences separating the liberal and conservative wings of the professional stratum.

A third change that I will emphasize is demographic and compositional. Both the explosive growth and the changed compositional mix in the professions have had important effects on the political views of professionals, though in opposite directions. In many professional occupations, a growing number of practitioners has stimulated an aggressive search for new economic opportunities, a situation encouraging more market-oriented attitudes and more conservative political outlooks on issues related to the economy. At the same time, the professions are now composed of a more diverse population mix, and this new diversity has supported an opposite movement—toward greater liberalism—on social issues related to tolerance and majority-minority relations.

PROFESSIONS IN THE AGE OF "COLLECTIVE MOBILITY"

The modern professions are the product of a dynamic era of white-collar professionalization encompassing roughly the century between 1860 and 1960. The period can be characterized as one in which a great many white-collar occupations—from engineers to social workers—sought "collective mobility" through efforts to emulate the "established professions" of medicine, law, theology, and the professoriat.[12] The main actors in this movement were the leaders of the professional associations, who sought to raise the status and standards of their occupations' activities. New markets for specialized labor provided the essential grounds out of which emerging professions developed. The universities conferred the essential mark of professional status by allowing some occupations to enter their gates and by refusing others' claims to require formal and advanced training. Engineers were readily accepted but business managers were for many years excluded. State governments provided special protections for many professions by adopting licensing requirements, and they provided critical legitimating recognition for all professions and would-be professions by recognizing a larger public interest in competent performance of many jobs requiring formal academic training.

New markets controlled by people with formal academic training legitimated and regulated by the state—these are the social structural coordinates out of which the modern professional stratum developed. Yet, as a prism of common experience, the professions during this period are best thought of as a *form of collective organization,* as a *status category,* and as representing a coherent *ideology.*

The professions, alone among occupations, rely on higher education as a requisite for access to markets. This institutional fact has created conditions for a certain number of common powers and privileges, the most widespread of which has been autonomy in relation to how work is to be accomplished. Part of the strength of occupational organization in the professions grew out of a common emphasis on credentialing and voluntary memberships in the professional associations, and part was based on the successful institutionalization of occupational authority as an alternative to managerial hierarchy. In this sense, the professions represented, as Eliot Freidson has argued, an *occupational principle* of authority, based on ties to universities and organizations of practitioners. This occupational principle serves as an alternative to the more common *administrative principle* of organization, based on hierarchical authority.[13] All professionalizing occupations sought to establish at least a substantial degree of occupational self-governance and therefore a substantial limitation in the allowable range of managerial control of work activities. When university professors during the Progressive era, men such as Richard Ely and E. A. Ross, insisted on the incompetence of managerial authorities to decide on questions of intellectual quality, they struck the first blows for the occupational principle of authority over the managerial principle in bureaucratic organizations.[14]

With organization came new conceptions of status. The social creation of expectations concerning professional life involved both popular and more explicitly sociological understandings. Folk expectations about professional status oscillated—and still do—between an upper-middle-class pole, emphasizing the combination of learning and high incomes typical of only the most prestigious professional occupations, and a middle-class pole, emphasizing the conjunction of a rationalist outlook, occupational competence, and middle-class respectability that could be attained by a much wider range of educated people. Sociological analyses sought to identify the structural roots of professional distinction. They also tended, however, to accept in a rather uncritical way some of the more debatable idealizations of the ethical standards and service orientation of professions[15]

The ideology of professionalism during this dynamic age centered on ideas about *community* and *authority.* I am speaking here of very specific kinds of community and authority. Community was understood as the aggregation of socially important *functions,* not as some more general kinship with members of one's country or nation. Each profession was understood to work on a single important sphere of social life—such as conflict resolution, health, design, education—and the whole of the realm of socially essential knowledge could be realized only through the aggregation of these many spheres. Authority, too, had a distinctive meaning. It was cultural, rather than social; the authority that grows out of acceptable levels of understanding—the ability to apply successfully—a body of relatively demanding knowledge.[16]

As an ideology, professionalism had both a technical and a moral aspect. Technically, it promised competent performance of skilled work involving the application of broad and complex knowledge, the acquisition of which required formal academic study. Morally, it promised to be guided by an appreciation of the important social ends it served. In demanding high levels of self-governance, professionals claimed not only that others were not technically *equipped* to judge them, but also that they could not be *trusted* to judge them.[17] The idea was expressed in classic form by the British economic historian and social critic R. H. Tawney: "[Professionals] may, as in the case of the successful doctor, grow rich; but the meaning of their profession, both for themselves and for the public, is not that they make money, but that they make health, or safety, or knowledge, or good government, or good law. . . . [Professions uphold] as the criterion of success the end for which the profession, whatever it may be, is carried on, and [subordinate] the inclination, appetites, and ambition of individuals to the rules of an organization which has as its object to promote the performance of function."[18] These functions, for Tawney and for many other advocates of the professions, were activities that embodied and expressed the idea of larger social purposes.

In this respect, the idea of professions, so intertwined with the development of modern capitalism and the modern welfare state, nevertheless showed a remarkable resonance with much older cultural and political priorities in the Anglo-American world: the idea of work in a calling, a rationalist frame of mind, collective self-governance, and high levels of self-direction in day-to-day work activities.

In its inclusiveness, the dominant model served many important functions for the emerging white-collar professions. Occupations like schoolteaching and social work with dubious technical capacities could nevertheless claim a kind of moral superiority, and they could at least look forward to further technical achievements as an important aspiration. Occupations like engineering with a more secure technical base often found it convenient to identify themselves as serving larger social purposes.

From the beginning of the period of collective mobility, however, a rival idea of professions existed in industrial organization, and it is this rival idea that has become dominant in our own time. Here the fundamental concept was of intellectual training in the service of purposes determined by organizational authorities or market forces. For professionals who saw themselves primarily as "experts" or "specialists," the issue of social contribution had little intrinsic meaning. Most often, it was assumed that social contribution could be measured, more or less unproblematically, by the market value of specialized skills. The newer kind of "expert professionalism" was in full bloom already at the 1916 celebration of the new campus of the Massachusetts Institute of Technology, when floats sponsored by the major corporations of early 20th-century America chugged down the streets of Nantasket Beach in honor of a university designed in large part to serve the technical needs of American industry. Among the newer "professions," those whose skills were most highly valued on the market had less compunction about shaking free of the precapitalist ideals of "social trustee professionalism." Throughout the period of "collective mobility," applied science and engineering provided an alternative interpretation of professionalism, one that privileged specialized skills and discounted any broader societal "responsibilities."[19]

THE TRANSFORMATION OF THE PROFESSIONAL STRATUM

As a status category, the label "professional" has, one might say, proven to be a piece of sociological material that can be refashioned periodically to suit an evolving social and cultural context. In early modern England, the professions appropriated many of the cultural ideals of the old aristocracy, especially those that contrasted sharply with the utilitarianism of the merchant classes. These included, notably, a public outlook influenced by noblesse oblige, an emphasis on character and trust, and an insistence on cultivated judgment.[20] These cultural ideals remained a meaningful part of professionalism in nineteenth- and early twentieth-century America as well, though they were less removed from the spirit of enterprise in America than they were in England. Over the last thirty years, the idea of professions as a status category has become increasingly disconnected from functions perceived to be central to the public welfare and more exclusively connected to the idea of "expert knowledge."

The presumption of professionals to speak in the name of the public good did not always enjoy an easy acceptance even during the period when social trustee professionalism had its most vigorous expression and greatest legitimacy. Expressions of professional responsibility fit uncomfortably with the spirit of both populist democracy and business entrepreneurship. To the democrat and the entrepreneur, the moral side of professionalism could seem overly genteel, unnecessarily intrusive, and inclined to purism. (Indeed, these were fair criticisms in many instances.) By contrast, expert knowledge has enjoyed a virtually unquestioned legitimacy in American culture. The applied scientific disciplines have always seemed complementary to the practical and problem-solving spirit of the people.[21] The successes of expert knowledge, moreover, are frequently spectacular—from the erection of the monumental works of modern engineering to the prolonging of life through medical science.

In contrast to social trustee professionalism, expert professionalism needed no sharp distinction from business enterprise, and it required less separation from the idea of pursuing trade for a profit. One aspect of the complex movement toward expert professionalism, therefore, involved closer associations between the major professions and business and the weakening of barriers to the pursuit of profit in openly competitive markets.

The growing connection between business and the professions can be seen unfolding over time in a series of decisions and accommodations by key institutions. One important change occurred very early, in the 1920s, when the leading universities began to accept business management as a suitable subject for professional training.[22] This incorporation of business training into the universities began to erode the status distinction between "community-oriented" professionals and "profit-oriented" business people, however much professional managers may have been counseled at first to emulate the broad social vision associated with the professions. Other important changes occurred after World War II. The postwar movement of certified public accountants into the new markets for management consulting was emblematic of the market-driven erosion of the "public welfare" legitimations surrounding professionalism. The old insistence on independence in the name of public welfare clearly no longer existed in situations where monitoring of behavior (as in the auditing function) gave way to direct assistance (as in consulting work).[23] During the 1960s and 1970s, the firm structure of professions such as law and architecture became increasingly dualistic—with the larger firms concentrating exclusively on corporate, business-related activities and the smaller firms on individuals.[24]

This movement away from social trustee professionalism occurred against the backdrop of the increasing implausibility of community-oriented ideals in various professional activities. When many professional occupations—from schoolteaching and nursing to engineering and consulting—obviously served interests defined and even directed by others, the idea of occupationally defined contributions to the public good seemed increasingly dubious to a skeptical new generation.[25]

In some measure, the very popularity of the idea of professions—the idea of status linked to learning—also helped to destroy the structural basis for the older form of professionalism. When a profession such as law grows four times as fast as the population, it is not surprising that a great many lawyers, in their struggle to make a living, treat law as a trade solely for profit. A larger factor, however, has been the uneven development of the various professional service industries. Growth in a few industries—business services such as corporate law and medicine, in particular—has substantially outpaced the Gross Domestic Product, while others have grown more slowly or even declined. As a result, partners in some corporate law firms now earn well over $1 million annually and the average doctor earns approximately $200,000 per year; while at the lower rungs of academe, the arts, the human services, and government, a large number of nominally professional people have slipped beneath the middle-class style of life that professional training once seemed to promise.[26]

The courts abandoned many of the legal protections of social trustee professionalism beginning in the late 1960s. During this period, the Supreme Court struck down the legality of standard fees for service, bans against competitive bidding, and bans on advertising. These anticompetitive practices had been justified by the special need of professions for economic security and regulatory autonomy to ensure that quality of service would not be undercut by economic competition. The Court, reflecting a changed legal philosophy as much as a changed professional environment, now began to look at the professions as commercial activities, albeit of a special type. By introducing competitive incentives, it hoped, the cost of professional services would be lowered while the quality of service improved.

In the deregulatory climate of the succeeding years, some of the remaining inhibitions to expediency were abandoned. Lawyers defeated a reform proposal in the American Bar Association that would have required forty hours of *pro bono* work to those underserved by the profession.[27] Doctors refused to prohibit referrals to clinics and other facilities in which they had a financial interest.[28] Universities liberalized policies concerning the profit-making activities of faculty.[29] Critics steeped in the older tradition of social trustee professionalism now began to complain more frequently that the professions had lost their moral bearings. They saw the new conditions as encouraging a "race to the bottom" or a "hollowness at the core," and they warned that the professions were "in danger of losing their soul."[30]

Yet it is a mark of the degree to which conditions have changed that today even people in the original fee-for-service professions rarely point to the social importance of their work as justification for social distinction. Instead, they justify differences between themselves and other people by discussing the kinds of skills involved in their work. They almost uniformly describe their work as involving broad and complex forms of knowledge, whose application requires sensitivity and judgment, but they only rarely remark on the "social importance" of their work. When colleagues and I asked a sample of Boston-area doctors, lawyers, engineers, and scientists about the meaning of their work, nearly all were well prepared to talk about the complexity and breadth of knowledge required, about their reliance on basic theory, and the difficult judgments they had to make. But only a small minority were prepared to think of their work as distinctive in relation to its importance for society. "I see no reason to think that our work is more important to society than the work of an electrician or an auto mechanic," said one life scientist, expressing the views of many. There is an appealing note of democratic egalitarianism in this statement, but in the background there is, more importantly, the triumph of expertise as a basis of distinction that requires no moral vaulting.

In our age of expert professionalism, it is virtually impossible to imagine an "interprofessional conference" such as the one convened in Detroit in 1919—halfway through the century of "collective mobility." This conference attracted hundreds of architects, chemists, dentists, doctors, engineers, nurses, and other professional people. Its stated objective was to discuss "how to liberate the professions from the domination of selfish interest . . . to devise ways and means of better utilizing the professional heritage of knowledge and skill for the benefit of society, and to create relations between the professions looking toward that end."[32]

The shift from social trustee professionalism to expert professionalism has led to a splintering of the professional stratum in relation to the market value of different forms of "expert knowledge." There is the real possibility in this split for the eventual consolidation of the professional stratum into a more exclusive status category, since "formal knowledge" implies gradations in the value, efficacy, and validity of different forms of knowledge. At a minimum, it has created the basis for significantly decreased status among the lower ranks of the professional stratum whose members lack bona fide "formal knowledge." Recent university cutbacks have tended to reinforce the splintering of the professional stratum by concentrating cuts on the lower professional (and largely female) "periphery."[33] In this process of splintering, the technical and moral aspirations of professionalism have tended to separate and to become associated, respectively, with the "core" and the "periphery" of the stratum.

Today, more clearly than ever before, a stratum of upper-level experts has become definable by the combination of marketable skills and location in resource-rich organizations, while a stratum of lower-level experts has become definable by the combination of less marketable skills and location in resource-poor organizations. These defining combinations, growing as they do out of processes of social stratification, are clearly quite different from the combination of community orientation and cultural authority that provided touchstones for the somewhat more unified and certainly more inclusive professional stratum of the past.

Indeed, the character of contemporary professionalism is thoroughly interwoven with the development of the organizations and industries that employ large numbers of professional specialists. What remains of social trustee professionalism has become associated more or less exclusively with the public and nonprofit sectors. Occasionally, it is true, a continued emphasis on social trustee professionalism is found in the private sector, particularly where issues of public trust are consequential—as in the pharmaceutical and mass media industries—and where state regulation is significant, at least in the background. Conversely, expert professionalism sometimes emerges in the public and nonprofit sectors, particularly in areas that are closely tied to technological and business interests. But, in every instance, professional development must be read, not just in occupational terms, but in relation to the development of markets for professional services and in relation to the interests of organizations that employ large numbers of professionals.

The Defining Matrix of Contemporary Professions

Because of the ever more transparent importance of markets and organizations on the development of the professional stratum, I will argue that the defining matrix of contemporary professionalism is no longer very well considered from a perspective that focuses exclusively on occupations, or relations among occupations. Rather, a more useful perspective must be at once occupation-based, organization-based, and market-based. To use a metaphor suggested by Gerhard Lenski's comparative study of social stratification,[34] contemporary professionals differ from other strata in so far as they are simultaneously "retainers," "merchants," and "priests." They are "priest-like" in their authority over secular knowledge bases. But, no less importantly, they are also merchants of the cultural and human "capital" that is their major source of mobility across and up organizational hierarchies; and, within organizations, they typically occupy positions as relatively high-ranking officials. Together, these elements define a distinctive *employment situation* for the majority of professionals. These elements of the employment situation condition what is shared by professionals, and they also define the main lines along which political and cultural differentiation occurs.

Professionals remain similar to one another in some ways. Some commonalities grow out of their special reliance on higher education, and others from their special circumstances of employment. Professionals, as compared to other groups, are, for example, particularly likely to indicate strong commitments to education and meritocracy as principles of advancement, reflecting their special reliance on education. They are also somewhat more likely than others to be sensitive to issues involving autonomy and self-direction, and they are more likely to find congenial efforts to synthesize and balance opposed political and value positions. These characteristic outlooks are related to, and conditioned by, the constant juxtaposition of freedom and constraint in professional work: the simultaneous experience of a large degree of technical control over work and, often, a significant degree of opportunity *combined with* the constraints of organizational life and the fluctuations of market demand for expert labor. Some other commonalities arise out of expectations associated with professional status: expectations for a middle-class (or, where possible, an upper-middle-class) style of life, a rationalist outlook on problem solving, and a competence and seriousness of purpose in relation to occupational activities.

If one likes, these patterns of expectation and belief can be called a common culture, although this culture is not much different from the culture of highly educated managers. The commonalities, in any event, are less important than the differences that grow out of the specific *kinds* of occupational and organizational ties that professionals have and the specific kinds of market situations in which they are located. The status culture of professionalism is, in this respect, by now a rather porous net thrown around a diverse mix of employment situations. Professionals are the ranking staff in radically different kinds of organizations; they are merchants of quite unequally valued forms of knowledge; and they are practitioners of knowledge oriented to very different social ends. For understanding the differences that separate the liberal and conservative wings of the professional stratum, the key analytic questions have to do with how professionals are distributed in the organizational life of the economy; with the means by which the relative market value of different types of professional knowledge is established; and with how professions are divided by the major spheres of social purpose they serve. In this book I will develop a disaggregated analysis of the political economy of expert labor to explore these issues.

THE OLD LIBERALISM AND THE NEW LIBERTARIANISM

The disaggregated analysis that I will develop leads to a new perspective on the politics of the professional middle class, a perspective that has little in common with the "new class" theory. The political movement of professionals has been toward greater liberalism, it is true, on social issues and, at times, in voting. However, it is the changing composition of the professional stratum that is principally behind these trends, not a rise in class feeling. Moreover, the internal divisions among professionals are larger and more important than the divisions between professionals and other classes. Both the decline of social trustee professionalism and the differentiation of professional employments have helped to reduce the coherence of the professional middle class as a force in political life.

The "new class" theorists have placed much emphasis on higher education as a force encouraging intellectual distance from "bourgeois society." But only rather weak grounds exist for thinking that the high levels of education found in the professions create a sense of distance from business values. Higher education socializes most people into the ascendant views among political elites at any given time. In the conservative climate of the recent past in the United States, high levels of education (including professional and graduate training) were associated with conservative views—at least on issues related to the economy—just as they have been associated with more liberal views during periods of reform.

Employment is more often the decisive influence on the political views of professionals. More liberal views are concentrated in the "social and cultural professions" (i.e., academe, journalism, urban planning, psychotherapy, social science, and the arts), in the human services occupations, in the public and nonprofit sectors, and among lower-income professional people—that great sea of younger college graduates mired at the lower and middle levels of corporate staff hierarchies, including the many recent casualties of "downsizing." The liberalism found in these relatively "progressive" spheres is hardly of a piece. Liberal professionals vary by the type of orientations that make up their worldviews—whether these are primarily "people-centered," "idea-centered," or "expression-centered." Because of this, professional people who nominally share "liberal views" often approach one another with a mixture of incomprehension and at least mild disdain.

The professional middle class as a whole is not at all liberal compared to the majority of Americans—at least not on issues related to the economy. At the same time, professionals are somewhat more liberal than business executives and managers. This relative liberalism, which is not decisive enough to represent an "inversion" of traditional class politics, is primarily based on a compositional oddity. Unlike all other socioeconomic strata in American society, professionals are employed more often in the government and nonprofit sectors than in the for-profit sector. It is this sectoral connection that is most consequential, not the association of professionals with intellectual activity that has so often been invoked to explain the liberal politics of professionals.

One of the striking features of the politics of professional people is the rapidity with which their views appear to change over short periods of time. Over the course of a mere fifteen years, from the later 1960s to the early 1980s, political stereotyping of highly educated professionals shifted from portraits emphasizing the idealism of a group close to the "humanistic culture" of the universities to images emphasizing the materialism and market-consciousness of a group close to the centers of economic power in urban centers. Survey data suggests an element of validity in these shifting images: no stratum changed its views as quickly between the 1960s and 1980s.

A large part of this trajectory can be explained by the issues that have been salient at different times. When social issues like civil rights and moral protest are prominent, college-educated professionals can *seem* like an "oppositional intelligentsia" because professional people tend to be relatively liberal on these kinds of issues. However, when economic issues are ascendant—as they have been more or less constantly over the last twenty years—the "new class" idea loses credibility because professional people tend to be conservative on these kinds of issues.

Some historical changes in fiscal conditions and the condition of professionals themselves have reinforced these long-standing political tendencies. In so far as the national debt has made government expansion a dubious alternative for economic renewal, even those located in the most liberal professional quarters have tended to consider themselves "postliberals" or "neoliberals" in recent years. Years of conservative ascendance combined with the increasing market orientation of the professions themselves have reinforced beliefs that economic competitiveness is an overriding priority and that improving conditions for competitiveness is at the heart of economic renewal.

While Americans, in general, moved to the right on most economic issues in the 1970s and 1980s, they moved in a liberal direction on many social issues, such as those involving the preservation of a wide domain for personal and civil freedoms and those involving the elimination of discrimination against women and members of minority groups. The survey evidence suggests that, on these issues, college-educated professionals are more liberal than people in other classes and strata. Compositional factors are once again involved. The contemporary professional stratum contains a disproportionate number of the kinds of people who nowadays tend to be outside of the more conservative moral traditions: not only better-educated people, but younger people, less religious people, and residents of cities.

In the domain of social issues, many professionals now have views that are better described as libertarian than liberal. Professionals very frequently want government to stay out of issues involving moral choices, and they even tend to take a stance in favor of community self-determination when it comes to the purposes of education and other socializing institutions. This tells us more than is immediately apparent about the character of contemporary professionalism. Very little could be as distant from the spirit of the old professionalism—with its emphasis on community stewardship and cultural authority—as this shift toward libertarian views on issues related to cultural choice and social relations. It is the political hallmark of the rise of a new "expert" stratum with strong interests in marketable knowledge and weaker concerns about the relationship between community and authority.

THE OLD PROFESSIONALISM AND THE NEW EXPERTISM

Indeed, one of the principal themes of this book is that the old connection between community and authority has been largely severed in the contemporary professional world. To be sure, a few professional occupations and a few professional spheres of activity are able to maintain something of the older outlook, either because of the extremely protected nature of their markets (as in medicine) or because of protected circumstances in the nonprofit sector (as in the case of professors at some liberal arts–oriented institutions). But those who claim knowledge-based authority increasingly eschew any claims to representing vital social or public interests. From a sociological perspective, expertise is now a resource sold to bidders in the market for skilled labor. It is no longer a resource that requires an extensive sphere of occupational judgment about purposes. Conversely, a strong community orientation separated from claims to expert authority is not uncommon in the professional periphery—it is the attitude of the helper and the populist alike. In the first case, authority is of marginal importance; in the second it is actively distrusted as a force legitimating the power of those outside the (ideally) self-determining community.

This separation of community orientation and expert authority has had, I believe, some important implications. One secret to the success of America's democratic capitalist society is how incompletely democratic and capitalist it has been. It was often argued by the social theorists of the eighteenth and nineteenth centuries—by men as different as Adam Smith and Karl Marx— that the modern age led inevitably to the triumph of capitalist entrepreneurs and of the working masses who sought to control them through the voting booth, through labor unions, and through other interest organizations. Of course, this vision has some considerable truth in it, but the truth is only partial because the theorists of the classical period largely failed to take into account the persistence of precapitalist institutions, such as universities and churches, and of the new social institutions, such as the voluntary sector and the professions, that capitalism itself helped to promote.[35]

The professions, neither democratic nor capitalist, played an important role in efforts to shape and (at times) to constrain capitalist development in relation to standards of a broader social well-being, and also in efforts to educate popular sensibilities in relation to standards of cultural authority. Ultimately constituted by markets, universities, and states, the professions nevertheless created grounds for their legitimacy on the basis of ideals—by promising to serve important functions for the broader community and to meet high standards in the performance of intellectually demanding work.

It is, of course, better to avoid an absolute sort of nostalgia for professional authority of the older type. As a generation of critics of professionalism has correctly argued, undisputed claims to representing "the public good" can lead to excesses of self-interest legitimated in the name of professional authority. There are without question innumerable examples of professional cupidity and abuse of power in the name of "the public good."[36] The older kind of professionalism also encouraged at times a dangerous arrogance based on convictions of intellectual or moral purity. This arrogance, indeed, is the threat that ties together many of the failures of professionalism—from the self-righteous anti-abortion stance of nineteenth-century doctors[37] to the failures of certain social policies such as busing[38] to the formally perfect but inhuman edifices of architectural modernism.[39]

Nevertheless, when the promise of a link between community and authority is broken, corporate and state organization loom ever larger at the upper tiers of the professional stratum, and populist distrust of authority looms larger at the lower levels. These sources of control, too, have their characteristic failings. Corporations understand their interests in terms of consumer preferences, and governments in terms of the interests of a governing coalition. Populism tends to privilege the rhetorically skilled and the emotionally comforting. No enduring conception of cultural values or the public interest is necessary in any of these cases. When social interests cannot be properly aggregated through markets or voting mechanisms, forms of control that rely on markets or votes obviously cannot be trusted to provide socially desirable outcomes.

This does not mean that the bolstering of professional elites is always desirable. In liberal societies where the dangers of authoritarianism are not great, expert professionalism may be the more useful model for some professional occupations, while social trustee professionalism may be the better model for others.[40] In many instances, postgraduate training provides a sufficient technical safeguard for the provision of professional services, while markets and states may direct the applications and character of expert knowledge in entirely acceptable ways. Most societies want engineers and agronomists whose skills are directed primarily in relation to the technical applications and innovations determined by markets and governments. A degree of danger in market and state control exists only when long-term societal interests, fundamental cultural values and traditions, or the basic requirements of a decent public life are at stake. Under these circumstances, market and state controls are likely to be less than completely sufficient and the influence of a highly cultivated, value-sensitive professional elite can be considered a potentially useful center of influence. Everyone will likely have a separate list of activities that fit the criteria I have suggested as relevant conditions for protection of the stronger forms of professional autonomy. A plausible list, in my view, would include the basic fiscal health of the state and the banking system, the natural and the built environment, the educational system, health and welfare services, the news media, the arts, and basic research. In these areas, the encouragement of democratic forms of communication between professionals and interested publics will obviously also continue to be important.

Traditionally, professional autonomy has been strengthened by many partial barriers against the influence of markets and private sector employers on the practices of professionals. The welfare state and the nonprofit sector have clearly been two of the most important of these partial shelters, in so far as they helped to guarantee that services would be provided to a broader segment of the population than would otherwise have received them. The standards and traditions of academe, the institutions of elite culture, and even the priorities of a progressive political culture have provided other kinds of partial shelters—more cultural than economic—against the domination of markets and private sector employers for those professional occupations operating primarily in the private sector.

By contrast, the recent age of expertise has been an age of relatively unrestrained consumer markets and corporate power. Where it is allowed to do so, the movement toward market and corporate power has shucked off the old barriers and restraints like a constricting skin.

AGAINST THE GRAIN

In my view, powerful social and economic forces have brought the older idea of professionalism linking social purposes and knowledge-based authority close to an end. They have helped to reconstitute the professions ever more exclusively on the basis of "applied formal knowledge," or expertise. Without a strong sense of the public and social purposes served by professional knowledge, professionals tend to lose their distinctive voice in public debate. It is in this respect that it is possible to speak of the decline of the professional middle class, in spite of the expansion of that class and the many concrete instances of important expert influence on economic and political affairs. In my view, the important issues have to do not with limiting the power of professionals—however necessary this may sometimes be—but rather with improving the capacity of professionals to work in a way that is true to the highest standards of practice, and connected, where appropriate, to long-term societal interests, important cultural values and traditions, and the requirements of a decent public life.

In emphasizing professional stratification and the decline of "social trustee professionalism," the arguments of the book run very much against the grain of the better-known characterizations of the professional stratum and its "meaning" for American society. They have particularly little in common with formulations that emphasize the increasing *power* of professionals—formulations such as "postindustrial society," "technocracy," "the new class," and the "adversary culture."

The first two of these ideas focus on the technical side of professionalism: the claim to knowledge-based authority. The idea of "postindustrialism" suggests that the growth of the professional stratum is tied to the practical value of science and to the growth of a knowledge-based service economy. Yet the growth of the professional stratum has no such singularly important sources. I will show that there are multiple sources of growth and development of the various professional occupations and professionally dominated industries, and each has its own implications for the spheres touched by it. We have certainly moved to a "post-industrial society" in two important respects. First, manufacturing is no longer as central in the economy, while services are far more central. Secondly a small stratum of "symbol specialists," to use Robert Reich's phrase, has clearly emerged as an important new elite. These real changes ought not to imply, however, that the society is now directed by the "trained intelligence" of the professional work force. This is far from true.

The related idea that the technically able increasingly make important political decisions is also fallacious. Most studies indicate that the influence of experts in policy making is of distinctly secondary importance. These experts are mainly important in the stages of policy development that precede actual decision making, and their importance is greatly diminished, even in those stages, whenever issues become politicized. Like professionals generally, policy experts are creatures of the organizational systems in which they operate. The American system of decentralized and fragmented pluralism sometimes gives the illusion of expert influence, because of its openness to multiple sources of political mobilizing, but the underlying reality is that influence is organizationally concentrated in the hands of leading interest groups and the leading politicians.

Ideas about the "new class" and the "adversary culture" of intellectuals focus not on the technical but on the moral side of professionalism: the claim to represent community interests. The "new class" theory sees intellectually oriented professionals as engaged in a sometimes hidden, sometimes open struggle for power and status in American society with the "old class" of business owners and executives. On the surface, the theory has some appeal. It is true that class conflicts often occur between relatively privileged classes, rather than between a clearly superordinate and a clearly subordinate class.[41] At first glance, the theory seems to explain everything from differences in taste and politics to the social tensions that so often arise between people who are close to the world of business and those who are close to the world of the universities and nonprofits. The social tensions between these two groups have found a secure place in the society's folklore. We have the popular residue of intellectuals' complaints about business and material riches in curt dismissals of "the man who knows the price of everything and the value of nothing," of lives "wasted in getting and spending," of "the spiritual wasteland," "the rat race," and the "air-conditioned nightmare." The businessman's contempt for "impractical" men of knowledge is found in equally flavorful retorts: "Don't trust a man who hasn't met a payroll," "Those who can't do, teach," and "If he's so smart, why isn't he rich?"[42]

Yet survey evidence indicates that even the most liberal segment of professionals—the people who would be counted as members of the "new class" in any version of the theory—are, by and large, far from unconventional in their tastes or decidedly left-of-center in their political views, and they certainly show little opposition to the basic organizing principles of a business civilization. On issues connected to the economy and economic inequality, they are usually more conservative than blue-collar workers. In part, this is because they are dependent themselves on the success of business enterprises, and in part it is because members of this putative "new class" have, at least for the time being, accepted the priorities of business.

Indeed, even those people who can legitimately be defined as intellectuals have their own defining involvements in publishing organizations and consumer markets. Let us assume that intellectuals can be defined as people who address an educated general audience on matters of political and cultural interest. I will show that, far from representing an "adversary culture," contemporary intellectuals are, in general, quite moderate in their expressed political views, reflecting the outlooks of their major audiences, and they also show rather little interest in at least the more indignant forms of social criticism. In recent years, theirs has been more a culture of particularizing refinement than of taking stances. Both the political climate and the market and organizational context of intellectual publishing have an important impact on the concerns and sympathies of intellectuals. The latter in particular create conditions that encourage intellectuals to rely on conventionalized ways of educating the sensibilities of consumers of intellectual opinion and commentary, while discouraging much of the principled stance-taking in relation to public issues that was once considered to be among the "responsibilities" of intellectuals.

ORGANIZATION OF THE BOOK

The first part of the book, "The Professional Stratum in America," provides the main analytical framework for understanding the professional stratum as it has developed over time and for understanding related issues involving the politics of the professional middle class.

Chapter 2 provides a social history of the idea of professions, emphasizing phases in the history of the term as a status category. It focuses on changes that have occurred in the shift from the older phase of societal trustee professionalism to the current phase of consolidation around the idea of marketable expertise. The following two chapters discuss professions in the contemporary American political economy, emphasizing the structural divisions that have led to the fragmentation of the professional stratum. Chapter 3 analyzes the major spheres of social purpose and the sectoral organization of the professions. Chapter 4 discusses the market value of different types of professional knowledge and different circumstances of professional practice. Both chapters draw extensively on census data and on data I have collected from the various professional associations.

In chapters 5 and 6, the focus of the book shifts to the realm of politics. In these chapters, I show how the political outlooks found among professionals are connected to their employment situations, to compositional changes in the professional stratum, and to the rise and fall of issues. Chapter 5 examines the commonalities and differences found among professionals in their cultural values and political orientation. Chapter 6 discusses the rhythms of political change among professionals over the last twenty-five years. Survey data provide the empirical foundations for the argument in both chapters.

The second part of the book is about "Experts, Intellectuals, and Professionals." The first two chapters of this second part of the book address the technical and moral sides of professionalism as these take shape in the realm of public discourse. The focus is on policy experts in chapter 7 and on intellectuals in chapter 8. In these chapters, I continue to emphasize the shaping influence of the organizational and market contexts in which professional work occurs. Empirical support for the argument in chapter 7 is based primarily on an analysis of some seventy-five case studies of patterns of influence in public-policy making. Empirical support for the argument in chapter 8 is based primarily on a content analysis of over 300 articles and reviews in leading American periodicals of intellectual opinion. Chapter 9 offers a first effort in comparative cross-national analysis of the professional middle class and middle-class politics. The chapter discusses the more state-centered context shaping the development of the professional stratum in Europe, and it compares the political outlooks of professionals in America with those of professionals in several other advanced societies. The chapter also includes a brief comparative analysis of technocracy and middle-class protest in Europe and America. The evidence in this chapter is drawn primarily from comparative-historical studies and from cross-national survey data.

The book concludes in chapter 10 with some final thoughts on the transformations of the professional stratum and on the future of intellectuals.

· PART ONE ·

The Professional Stratum in America

Professions as Organization and Status Category

THE SOCIOLOGICAL REALITY behind the familiar term "profession" is not as obvious as it may at first seem. Indeed, the historian Laurence Veysey has argued that professions are little more than "a rather random set of occupations that have historically been called that in our culture. . . . "[1] There is something quite tempting in this skeptical view, given the wide variety of usages that have grown up around the terms "profession" and "professional."[2]

However, professions do have an underlying reality. *They are both a type of organization and a type of status category.* At the same time, the ways we understand that underlying reality have changed at different historical moments with changes in the constitution of the professions. In this sense, any *realist* analysis of professions must also be *historical:* professions can be understood only as a historically developing type of social organization and as a historically changing status category.

Some commonalities grow out of reliance on the credential system and also out of what professions share in their typical employment situation. Yet the dominant picture is of consequential differences between the major and the minor professions and between types of professional status cultures. Most important, the increasing emphasis on market-valued expertise as the critical element of professional status has created grounds in recent years for a more exclusive status category.

PROFESSIONS AS A TYPE OF ORGANIZATION

In their contemporary reality, professions are, above all, a phenomenon of labor market organization. They are those occupations exercising the capacity to create exclusive shelters in the labor market through the monopolization of advanced degrees and other credentials related to higher education that are required for the attainment of the social and economic opportunities of authorized practice.

The essential characteristics of professions as a form of organization, therefore, have nothing to do with public service, ethical standards, or collegial control, however often these ideals and practices may grow up in support of the professions' claims to distinction. Instead, professions are based on the link between tasks for which a demonstrable market demand exists, training provided by the higher educational system for the performance of those tasks, and a privileged access of trained workers to the market for the demanded tasks.[3] Professionals are, therefore, people whose ties to the skills and cultures of an organized occupational group provide structure for markets for professional labor. Disciplinary training and ties out to the occupational group also provide a constraint on the hierarchical control of the organizations professionals work for.

All the major professions—from medicine and law to the scholarly professions and applied sciences—share this common denominator. Some disputed professions also do—or at lest begin to share it. For example, the master of business administration degree, in so far as it is required for access to some managerial occupations, crates a category of "professional managers." At the same time, many highly skilled and unquestionably intelligent people who compete in markets unsheltered by credentials based on advanced education do not fit the professional pattern of organization, however often they may be called "professionals." This includes most people in the arts and culture industries, as well as many people in business occupations, such as advertising and real estate.

As compared to universities, other institutions discussed by theorists of the professions—above all, the professional associations and the regulatory state—are of secondary importance in the constitution of professions. Occupational associations, after all, exist to promote the interests and to encourage the collective life of a great many nonprofessions, and they sometimes do so quite successfully. The states themselves regulate literally thousands of occupations other than professions—from cosmetologists to watchmakers.

The professional associations and the regulatory state do, however, contribute to the constitution of professions through their influence on the credentialing system.[4] Indeed, the professional associations are involved in creating the structure of university credentialing through their role in the accreditation of training programs. They also hold significant power over forms of credentialing that supplement the requirements of academic degree programs. Where certification or licensing is required for practice, the organized professions help to reproduce themselves through their privileged influence over the setting of standards for the acquisition of indispensable occupational credentials.[5]

Practitioners approved through the credential system are conventionally presumed to meet at least minimal standards of technical competence. It is on this basis that individual professionals are typically granted control over *how* their work is to be accomplished. This is the only form of control over the work process that professionals as a whole can depend upon with high probability,[6] but it is an important one. This technical autonomy creates a sphere of activity in which the individual worker, not the organizational hierarchy, is sovereign under normal conditions. It allows for the pleasures of self-direction that are clearly not open to all workers. In this respect, it is sufficient to distinguish professionals both from the bottom layers of workers and from bureaucrats (though not necessarily from skilled craft workers or "professional managers").

Professions do not necessarily hold unchallenged authority over an area of functional expertise. The extent of this authority is, instead, an important variable in helping to define the difference between the *major* and the *minor* professions. The authority of the minor professions is very often subject to overrule, either because the rigor, complexity, and/or efficacy of the knowledge base is distrusted (as in the teaching, social work, and religious professions), or because another profession ultimately directs its work (as in nursing), or for both reasons. Authority over a sphere of functional expertise is, however, the base out of which professional occupations control aspects of their work process and gain leverage in relation to administrative hierarchies. It is, therefore, important enough to be considered a characteristic of "ideal typical" professions

Levels of participation in occupational associations and occupational networks also vary between the professional occupations. Many scientists are preeminently members of their occupational specialty group, and, comparatively, only weakly identified with their employing organizations. The situation of most engineers is very much the reverse: the outward connection of engineers to one another is usually minimal in comparison to their ties to the organizations and industries in which they work. Yet collective organization maintained by members' participation in the life of the occupational group is typical of most professions, and, where it exists, it is also important. It no doubt influences the formation of stronger-than-average occupational identities among professionals.[7] It is also important in the ability of an occupational group to pursue its interests in the political arena.[8] And it can be important also in the successful resolution of jurisdictional struggles with organizational authorities and with other occupational groups.[9] It, too, can be considered a characteristic of "ideal typical" professions.

Professions are the characteristic form of the organization of middle-class labor. They provide a model even for many nonprofessions employing educated people of middle-class aspiration. Because of this, it is possible to speak of *professionalized work environments,* even in the absence of labor markets organized rigorously through the credential system. In these professionalized environments, high levels of education and an orientation to formal knowledge are typical among staff and management. The upper reaches of academic publishing and the nonprofit performing arts have long been professionalized work environments, and some other middle-class settings, ranging from substance abuse treatment facilities to specialized areas of journalism and management show signs of becoming professionalized environments in this sense.

PROFESSIONS AS A STATUS CATEGORY

Professions developed in their contemporary form as a type of social organization only in the course of the nineteenth century, but they have been a status category at least since the time of the first modern usage of the term "professions" in the early years of the eighteenth century. Indeed, the occupations that came to be called professions were associated together as high-status occupations as early as the thirteenth century.[10] The nature of the status category, however, has changed several times over the course of centuries of usage, and with these changes have come corresponding changes in the status cultures surrounding professionalism.[11] At each stage of the development of professions as a status category, new cultural elements have been overlaid on those that came before, with the older elements retaining a resonance in some quarters of the professional stratum.

It is possible to identify three major phases in the social history of the professions as a status category, and perhaps the beginnings of a fourth. I will call these four phases the "original phase," the "transitional phase," the "collective mobility phase," and the "consolidation phase," respectively. These phases have to do with conceptions of professional status by elites and by institutional authorities that have been important in conferring status. I will concentrate on the two countries, Great Britain and the United States, where professions as forms of occupational organization relatively indepen- dent of the state have been most important. The first two of the four phases are primarily relevant to the history of professions in Great Britain, but they provide an important backdrop to subsequent developments both in the United States and in Britain.

Phase One: Origins

Many professions have their origins as dignified occupations in the ancient world, but their modern history develops with their emergence from the dominance of the church and guilds in the late medieval period. The circle of high-status, learned occupations is at first quite narrowly constituted, extend- ing only to theology, law, and medicine (and, by extension, to the university teachers of these subjects, provided that they were also clergymen).[12] The upper branches of these professions became associated in the medieval univer- sities, which provided the meeting ground for learning in the form of graduate faculties. A sense of kinship among the three fields of theology, medicine, and law becomes conventional in usages of Renaissance humanists dating from the fifteenth century.[13]

The clergy were the first and preeminent profession in England and indeed throughout Europe in the medieval period. By the end of the twelfth century, the Church had "gained a considerable hold" over the country's "wealth and property" and "all forms of intellectual activity." The clergy were, above all, gatekeepers for the practice of all occupations requiring any sort of formal learning.[14] The law emerged during the second half of the twelfth century, with the establishment of a permanent court at Westminster, which encour- aged full-time "professional pleaders" to appear.[15] The precursors of the English barristers, called the serjeants, quickly monopolized the pleading function and set up apprenticeships, organized around residence halls at which the apprentices lived and took instruction. With the formal establishment of the Inns of Court as a professional association in 1400, it could be said that the law had been organized as a full-fledged secular profession. Medicine was the last of the original "learned professions" to organize. Physicians, who were in the late medieval period typically connected to the Church through universities dominated by ecclesiastics, had very little organization until the fifteenth century, apart from the guild organization of the lower branches of medicine. Indeed, physicians were a widely despised group in the fifteenth century because of the many "untrained, unskilled practitioners and quacks" who were able to practice.[16] The first significant professional organization of physicians was the Royal College of Physicians of London, founded in 1518.[17] This organization did not guarantee good practice in an era when medicine was still often barbarous in practice, but it did encourage respectability. This respectability was reinforced by the continued connection between physicians and clergy through the colleges.[18]

In the early modern period, theology, law, medicine, and higher learning gradually acquired a distinct status in British society as the "learned" (or, as it was sometimes said, the "liberal") professions. The terms themselves are probably found first in the work of Joseph Addison in 1711 and 1712, but the reality of a status-based association between the fields predates the invention of the terms.[19] These professions could lead to wealth and influence, but, particularly in the case of the clergy, they usually did not. Nevertheless, they enjoyed the "social glamour" (or, to put it more prosaically, the prestige) associated with a "classical education" and the public associations of this "gentlemanly" education with morality, intelligence, and public spirit.

It was not just a particular type of education that united these three seemingly disparate occupations. Rather, it is a very particular set of characteristics —the combination of (1) high traditional social status based on direct links to the upper classes, (2) specialized occupational tasks in the division of labor that are centrally connected to the fates of individual clients, (3) the requirements of trust and full disclosure between practitioners and their clients, and (4) (usually) significant levels of formal book learning, beginning with a classical education.

The particular kinds of services provided were clearly important. These occupations had responsibility for the vitality, the financial vitality, and the after-death "vitality" of their clients. The critical importance of these concerns to individual well-being cannot be stressed too highly. In the age of piety, these were, needless to say, all highly consequential spheres. To do their work, moreover, professionals were required to have what Everett Hughes once called "guilty knowledge"—knowledge of the diseases, impecunities, illegalities, and moral sins of these same clients.[20] These requirements further encourage the characteristic emphasis in professional culture on trust, discretion, judgment, and character—a constellation of personal traits associated, in any event, with upper-class background in Great Britain.

Of the four characteristics shared by the original professions, the element of "gentlemanly" background appears to have been decisive. These three pursuits were, at first, almost exclusively activities of the well born. High status was therefore attached to the occupations, "more perhaps because of the status of those who filled them than because of any deep respect for the skills and activities involved in their practice."[21] Indeed, while practitioners of law, physic, and divinity generally obtained a classical education in secondary schools—the characteristic status mark of the "gentleman"—through the mid-nineteenth century they learned most of what they needed for their professional work by way of apprenticeship.[22] Because of this, it cannot be argued plausibly that these original "learned" professions were based on demanding bodies of occupational knowledge, but it is without doubt true that they were founded on the traditional education of gentlemen. "The force of much that later came to be absorbed into the word 'profession' was carried in the adjective 'liberal,' which meant that the essential qualification for entry into any of these three occupations . . . was a liberal education; that is, the education of a gentleman, not of a trader or an artisan."[23]

Phase Two: Transition

Beginning in the seventh century, the circle of socially prestigious occupations stretches a little from its narrow confines to take in, at least on occasion, members of a new group of high-status and/or "learned" occupations of two types: (1) service occupations newly freed from their medieval moorings, and (2) scientific and scholarly occupations growing out of the scientific revolution. The most important of the service occupations were military officers and architects. The most important of the new learned occupations were scientists and humanist scholars.

Of course, one of the striking things about these "new" high-status occupations is how dissimilar they were to the original "liberal" professions. The "new" prestige occupations did not gain their levels of social respect from their centrality in the regulation of the individual fates of clients. Nor, by extension, did they require the high levels of trust between practitioner and client that are often required in the classical professions precisely because of this centrality in the governing of individual fates.

At the same time, each of the emerging status occupations shared at least one characteristic of the original liberal professions. Military officers, of course, do not offer an "expert service" to individual clients. Rather, their service is to the state. However, military officers were typically of gentlemanly status. Scientists and artist-scholars were "learned" without necessarily being either gentlemen (although many were) or involved in the provision of an "expert service." Architects were sometimes gentlemen, sometimes learned, but clearly always engaged in the provision of a "service based on learning," albeit not one as vital as the services provided by clerics, lawyers, and physicians.

Two of the new status occupations, military officers and architects, emerged from the breakdown of medieval institutions. The beginnings of a "professional military" can be dated from the Maurician reforms in Holland at the beginning of the seventeenth century. These included the first military academy for the formal training of officers.[24] Before long, the officer cadres in the standing armies of Europe, including those of England, were centers of "professional" careers for a dispossessed aristocracy, a (partly) self-regulating fraternity dedicated to codes of honor and service.[25] Architecture emerged also at the beginning of the seventeenth century with the breakdown of medieval traditions of building that emphasized anonymous craftsmen working to a collectively developed and often traditional design. Inigo Jones (1573–1651), widely known as the first architect in Great Britain, distinguished himself from the older type of craft architects through the formal study of Italian Renaissance design and by developing plans for execution of their own designs based on a single directing source of authority. In doing so, he introduced features of formal academic study and individuated practice that are consistent with the previously existing constitution of high-status occupations.[26]

The rise of science and secular learning was partly a result of the new spirit of investigation in Renaissance Europe, and it is also partly the result of declining church control of education.[27] So, again, the decline of traditional feudal institutions was partly responsible for the widening of the circle of professions to include new high-status occupations. In England, the first associations of learned men in the sciences and humanities, existing for social and study purposes, date also from the seventeenth century with the constitution of the Royal Society (in 1660). Further organization of scientific and learned specialties occurred in the eighteenth and early nineteenth centuries, beginning with the institution of the Society of Antiquaries (1717), the Society of Artists of Great Britain (1765), and the Royal Academy (1768).[28] Scientists had no concrete services to render, typically could not make a regular livelihood out of their work, and therefore stood in an ambiguous relation to the established "professions." On the one hand, the leading scientists (and also the leading artists and writers of the day) were eagerly welcomed into the best society. On the other hand, the activities of the majority of scientists and artists were too often impecunious and purely intellectual in spirit for these groups as occupations to be considered functionally in quite the same light as the eminently practical men of the established "professions."[29]

Thus, to say that the stratum of recognized high-status occupations began to expand in the seventeenth and eighteenth centuries is not to say that acceptance of the new occupations was complete. Qualified acceptance is evident in fields other than science and the arts. Architects, for example, were very much divided between an upper social branch, for the most part well-born and well-schooled, and a lower branch hardly different from tradesmen and builders.[30] In so far as established professionals accepted architects, this acceptance was clearly limited to the upper branch.

Indeed, the professions remained, above all, "status occupations" in Great Britain until the middle of the nineteenth century. For many commentators, the key characteristic of the professional classes at mid-century remained social exclusiveness: "It might have been thought that in England, very consciously the leader of industrial world of the early nineteenth century, the engineer would have been accorded an honored place in society. . . . [But] in a society still deeply conscious of ancient, pre-industrial traditions, the engineer could point to no very impressive social origins. . . . [Consequently] the makers of the industrial England were doubtfully on the outskirts of the professional class; certainly not unreservedly admitted within."[31]

In England particularly, the leading professional men also took on much of the cultural ambiance of the old aristocracy, an ambiance transmitted through the elite universities and reinforced in opposition to the utilitarianism and commercial outlooks of the industrial and merchant classes. In this respect, professional men stood apart from the bourgeoisie and presented an alternative ideology, one that was both more "socially responsible" than bourgeois culture and yet at least as socially distant from the lower classes. The model professional man, as the ideal was conveyed by the dons of Oxford and Cambridge, possessed the character of a "gentleman": trustworthiness, discretion, and judgment in relations with clients and associates, but also an attitude of *noblesse oblige,* a sense of responsibility for the great affairs of government and society, and a high level of cultivation in the liberal arts.[32]

This status culture was far from dominant at the lower ends of the British professional stratum, or outside of Great Britain. Naturally, at the lower ends of the professional stratum, the pursuit of a livelihood, using whatever resources might be available for the purpose, remained the chief and overriding concern.[33] In the United States, populist distrust of the special status and privileges of professionals led to a low ebb in the position of the professions during the Jacksonian period and for approximately a quarter-century thereafter.[34]

Phase Three: Collective Mobility

The complexion of the professions as a status category changed dramatically during the course of the late nineteenth century and the first decades of the twentieth. This change sometimes has been characterized as a movement from "status professionalism" (which is to say, "gentlemanly professionalism") to " occupational professionalism."[35] Because many new white-collar occupations organized successfully as professions, the period is also properly characterized as one of "collective mobility" for the upper strata of white-collar occupations.[36] Traditional status considerations continued to persist, but outside of the more traditional milieus (for example, some university humanities departments),[37] they existed largely as powerful reminders of a passing era. The new defining marks of status were increasingly based on intellectual skills tied to a socially important service. For the first time in the latter half of the nineteenth century, the professional stratum became definable by the now-familiar matrix of tasks involving specialized knowledge, requirements of high levels of formal training, tests for competent performance, regulation by professional associations, and licensing by the state. At the same time, many of the precapitalist legitimations of the professions continue, in a transformed way, during this period of capitalist expansion. The professions were very often marked as performing complex tasks vital to the public welfare and which, therefore, could not be regulated simply on the principle of *caveat emptor.*

Just as the middle and late nineteenth century is properly characterized as a dynamic period of capitalist expansion in the Anglo-American world, so too is it a dynamic period of professionalization. The two movements, indeed, are quite closely connected. New organizational forms and new technological achievements produced by capitalist enterprise called forth new professions—in engineering and other applied sciences, in accounting, in corporation law. The problems of poverty created, in large part, by a highly dynamic, but weakly regulated capitalism, also called forth new aspiring professions—in city planning, social work, public health, and, again, teaching. And finally, new wealth, also the by-product of capitalist expansion, called forth the growth or development of new cultural and consumer service professions: university teachers, journalists, curators, librarians, psychologists, and other therapists.

The gates of access to professional status were opened, in large part, because both the state and the universities were persuaded of the virtues of tested and regulated expertise in a wide range of occupations and, therefore, made it relatively easy for occupations to claim professional status by adopting the forms of professionalism. So, while the new "occupational professionalism" was, to a large degree, a product of the industrial revolution, it was not simply that. It was also a product of learned behavior on the part of aspiring white-collar occupations, by governments convinced of the civic virtues of trained expertise and professional "ethics," and by universities given to entrepreneurial expansion during a time of increasing "thirst" for specialized higher education.

Origins of Occupational Professionalism. The solicitors, the lower branch of the legal profession in Great Britain, were the first to form a professional association of national scope, but surgeons and general practitioners, the lower branches of British medicine, were the first successfully to upgrade themselves following a soon-to-be standard course of "professionalization." This course involved organizing effectively to improve standards, testing competence, weeding out (or, more properly, attempting to weed out) incompetents, and, in so doing, gaining the sanction and protection of the state.[38]

The reform movements of surgeons and provincial doctors began in the 1810s and did not fully succeed until 1858. This slow progress is, in large measure, a tribute to the tenacity of social prejudice in Great Britain.[39] Though lacking in scientific learning and public esteem,[40] the regular physicians continued to monopolize privileges in hospital appointments and elsewhere.[41] By the early 1800s, a good many of the most eminent medical men in England were, in fact, surgeons. What the surgeons lacked, more than medical qualifications, was simply social acceptability.[42]

The Medical Act of 1858 reconstituted the medical profession as a non-differentiated corporate group. It also provided, as W. J. Reader observed, the "approved pattern" for an occupation to "aspire to equal dignity" with the established professions. The act created the status of "registered medical practitioner," to be conferred on the passage of an examination conducted by an approved licensing body. Once registered, a doctor had the right to practice anywhere in England. He also had the right to practice any branch of medicine. The act also created a single body of disciplining the whole profession. The establishment and composition of this body "substantially confirmed the notion that professional men should be responsible for their own behavior."[43]

The Process of "Professionalization." Beginning at the time of agitation for medical reform in Great Britain and after the Civil War in America, the members of virtually any occupation could mobilize to gain acceptance as a "profession," provided that they had reason to think of their occupation as based on specialized knowledge and a body of formal theory; as providing services oriented to the public interest and welfare; and to think of themselves as the best judges of proper practice.[44]

Harold Wilensky's account of the ideal typical process of "professionalization" included five steps in a modal sequence: first, a group of people begins "doing full-time the thing that needs doing"; second, the group forms an association for the purposes of socializing, study, and the discussion of common problems; third, the group seeks a course of professional training, either in the universities or, less often, outside; fourth, the state is approached to protect the public interest by licensing as competent only those who have the proper qualifications; and, finally, a formal code of ethics is adumbrated to further protect the public from unscrupulous practitioners and to reinforce professional status by providing evidence of a sense of public responsibility.[45]

Many mutual advantages existed in the three-party alliance between the professional associations, the state, and the universities. The professional associations gained a degree of control over economic opportunities from these connections, and they were able to protect themselves from potential public disfavor by using state regulation and university degrees to weed out impostors and incompetents. The states, for their part, gained some promises that unethical and incompetent activity would not prevail in occupations providing significant human and technical services. And the universities found new client groups and new highly placed training markets at the time when they were experiencing an unparalleled entrepreneurial surge of activity.

The Professional Associations. Which occupations in the nineteenth century proclaimed themselves professions by forming professional associations of national scope? In broad outline, the patterns are not too different in Great

Britain and the United States, though several of the waves of organization occur some twenty years earlier in Great Britain. In England, the first tended, not surprisingly, to be law and medicine and occupations closely connected to these two original professions, such as pharmacy and veterinary science. Architecture and engineering were also early organizers. These were followed at mid-century by a flurry of scholarly and scientific societies in the 1850s and 1860s, and including the first fully established engineering society. Then in the 1870s came the mainly female "helping professions" of teaching and librarianship. And finally toward the end of the century, professional associations were formed by the new business-industrial professions (such as accounting), the new engineering specialties (such as mechanical engineering), and the new allied health professions (such as nursing and optometry). These included any new medical specialties, virtually one for "every region of the body."[46]

In the United States, there were only a few major differences in the sequence. Social relations were evidently of greater concern in the avowedly democratic, but ethnically and religiously heterogeneous, United States, as indicated by the early formation of social work and social science societies. Indeed, the "helping professions" of teaching, social work, and librarianship tended to organize before many of the scholarly and scientific disciplines. This appears to be due to a mix of status anxieties and a quasi-evangelical sense of mission in the "helping professions,"[47] and certainly it is also due to the slow development of higher learning in the scientific and scholarly fields.[48] Another notable difference in sequence is that attorneys organized rather late. This is often explained as a product of difficult-to-bridge cleavages in the profession between corporate lawyers and other attorneys.[49]

The burst of professional organization continued in the early twentieth century with a grand variety of new aspiring professions forming national associations. In the United States, these included, among others, sociologists (1905), journalists (1913), city managers (1914), city planners (1917), social workers (1921), and hospital administrators (1933), as well as many new scientific, medical, and engineering specialties.

The Regulatory State. The state was, by some measure, the more open and accommodating of the two institutions whose sanction was necessary to the new aspiring professions. Beginning with the passage of the Medical Act, professional regulation in Great Britain was centralized at the national level. Indeed, there was something like a reemergence of the ancient guild pattern, since licensing by Parliament delegated substantial control to the professional associations. In general, two qualifications for licensing were all that were necessary: a sense that the skill requirements involved in doing the work could not easily be judged by the public, and a sense that the work might vitally affect the public's health, safety, or welfare. Needless to say, a great many occupations could be said to qualify for state licensing on the basis of these considerations. Moreover, many occupations desired regulation. By requiring a training and examination program, licensing allowed for some control on the supply of producers, improved the "respectability" of the occupation in the eyes of the public, and, therefore, frequently tended to improve the economic prospects of the licensed occupation.

In the United States, the pattern was again only slightly different than in Britain. Regulation began in the 1870s, at the same time that the modern university was forming, local professional societies were coalescing into national associations, and a new dynamic phase of capitalist and industrial expansion was beginning. As in England, licensure was justified as a means of protecting the public health, safety, and welfare against unskilled and dishonest practitioners in fields requiring special training and expertise. And, as in England, regulation was eagerly welcomed and actively pursued, not by the public, but by leaders of the professionalizing occupations themselves. The Americans, however, rejected national level regulation and adopted state licensing boards, most of which were dominated by members of the regulated profession.[50]

A vast range of occupations came to be regulated by the states in conjunction with occupational associations. These occupations were in no way limited to the obvious professions, which is why state licensing and regulation does not in itself provide a very helpful guide to the institutional matrix of professionalism.[51] The professions were distinctive only in so far as they were among the first to be licensed and because educational requirements for practice were higher and examinations more demanding than for other regulated occupations.

The Universities. In America, the universities became the central arbiters of professional status during the era of collective mobility.[52] Aspiring occupations acquired professional status primarily by gaining a place in the regular curricular offerings of universities. They did so by persuading the universities that the tasks involved in their work required training in a formal body of knowledge, knowledge that was, furthermore, relevant to the performance of important services for individual clients or organizational employers.

The history of the American university during the period of its great transformation (1870–1910) is, in large measure, the history of an ambitious and visionary group of university presidents and faculty, many of them influenced by graduate study in Germany, who saw the possibility of raising the status of their institutions at the same time that they contributed to the economic and cultural development of their society. The leading university presidents of the period self-consciously saw their institutions as serving an increasing number of client groups, as taking a more direct role in public life, and moving, in particular, toward a closer connection with people of middle-class aspiration. The president of the most elite, research-oriented institution in late nineteenth-century America wrote, "It is neither for the genius nor the dunce, but for the great middle-class possessing ordinary talents that we build colleges."[53]

The key to acceptance as a profession during the period of "collective mobility" was a successful claim to testable expertise on the basis of formal knowledge, combined with the successful claim to social status arising from the conviction of an occupation's "respectability" and social importance. These are rather vague criteria, and therefore it is not surprising that formal university-level training became the authoritative guide to the boundaries of the professional world. For all intents and purposes, it is the universities that define the professions. During this period, economic power without this cultural legitimation describes the world of entrepreneurial industry and commerce, while cultural legitimation with or without economic power describes the world of "the professions."[54]

During the course of the nineteenth century, the appeal to science became a keynote and not just an accompaniment of professionalizing activity. A "scientific" base served as a prima facie argument for incorporation. Even law and management, both so clearly based on human institutions and human judgment, claimed a scientific base.[55] Social workers are exemplary of the aspiring white-collar occupations that hitched their stars to science. "Probably no single factor has contributed, or is likely to contribute, more to a growing demand for the services of social workers than the widespread character of the belief in the potentialities of science as applied to human problems. . . . [T]his growing confidence in the scientific approach has been especially evident in those aspects of life concerned with the growth and development of the individual and with human relationships."[56]

Among the liberal arts faculties, the pattern of incorporation of new disciplines brings in the pragmatically and intellectually uncontroversial scientific and engineering specialties first. Physical, chemical, and biological science were all established parts of the antebellum college, with the most important institutionalizing developments occurring in the late 1840s and early 1850s.[57] Engineering became an established part of the curiculum in many colleges in the 1860s. The social science specialties emerged at the end of the century, following the fragmenting of two pillars of the established curriculum, moral philosophy and political economy. Economics split off from political economy following the marginalist revolution of the 1860s and was taught in neoclassical form in many places by the 1890s. Political science had gained a secure status in most of the leading universities by the mid-1890s;[58] psychology by around the same time;[59] and anthropology and sociology appear to have become at least reasonably well institutionalized by the 1930s.[60]

Professional schools followed much the same course of incorporation. The three original "learned professions" developed first (together with the three auxiliary medical fields of dentistry, pharmacy, and veterinary medicine).[61] The second wave of incorporation started at the end of the nineteenth century with the founding of the first graduate architecture, business, and engineering programs. These occupations can be fairly described as practical occupations near the core of economic activity. The third wave of incorporation beginning after the turn of the century showed a much more incomplete pattern of incorporation, full of fits and starts and institutional resistances. This wave involved social and public service occupations—public health, public administration, teaching, social work, psychotherapy, and journalism.[62] From the beginning, then, predominantly female occupations and occupations connected to the welfare state showed a much slower climb to professional status, while occupations connected to large amounts of capital and advanced technology showed an earlier and swifter acceptance.

Professional Ideologies. The new professional stratum gave rise to a great variety of ideals and orientations regarding the role of knowledge in society— from a hermetic commitment to knowledge for knowledge's sake to various activist persuasions aimed at using knowledge to reform or even to revolutionize society.[63] As I have argued, the dominant form of professionalism, however, combined civic-minded *moral* appeals and circumscribed *technical* appeals: a commitment to the public welfare and high ethical standards combined with a claim to specialized authority over a limited sphere of formal knowledge. This social trustee professionalism clearly bore the imprint of the institutional alliance at the heart of the new professional stratum. From the professional associations, it took the idea of regulation by the occupational community in relation to high practice standards. From the justifications of the regulatory state, it took the idea of service in relation to the interests of public safety, convenience, and welfare. And from the departmental structure of the universities, it took the ideals of specialized expertise in a sphere of formal learning.

In the last decade of the nineteenth and the first half of the twentieth century, the ideals of social trustee professionalism were proclaimed with some regularity by the leaders of professional associations, by political leaders tied to the professional stratum, and by university officials. The leaders of the professional associations took a particularly active role in the development and transmission of professional ideology. One of the first times that the ideal took on a crystallized form was in an 1894 speech by John F. Dillon, the president of the American Bar Association. The true conception of the lawyer, said Dillon, "is that of one . . . who scorns every form of meanness or disreputable practice, who . . . masters the vast and complex technical learning and details of his profession, but who, not satisfied with this, studies the eternal principles of justice. . . . In his conception, every place where a judge sits, although the arena be a contentious one where debate runs high and warm, is yet over all a temple where faith, truth, honor, and justice abide, and he one of its ministers."[64] Such views gradually entered the scholarly literature, beginning in the 1910s and 1920s. At this time, scholars affirmed that "the three ideas involved in a profession" were "[collegial] organization, learning . . . and a spirit of public service."[65] These characterizations changed little in the main body of scholarly writings on the professions over the succeeding half-century.[66]

The origins of most modern forms of ideological tension between liberal professionals and conservative business people can be traced to the noncapitalist (if not *necessarily* anticapitalist) elements of social trustee professionalism.[67] Thorstein Veblen and John Dewey are among the most prominent of the many Progressive Era intellectuals who criticized the material and moral foundations of capitalist industry on the basis of an alternative set of "professional values." Veblen's writings lampooned the wastefulness of "conspicuous consumption" that drove the social strivings of the modern capitalist class. He derided the profligacy of capitalist speculation and greed, comparing these wasteful motives unfavorably to the sober and socially useful efficiency of engineers. He also railed against the decline of open scholarship and free inquiry in an age of business control of higher education under the aegis of "captains of erudition."[68] For Dewey, the hierarchical and narrowly specialized character of jobs in modern industrial organizations were inimical to the development of a responsibly democratic polity and to the full development of individual personality. "A democracy cannot flourish," he wrote, "where there is a narrowly utilitarian education for one class and a broadly liberal education for another. It demands a universal education in the problems of living together, one broadly humane in outlook calculated to enhance social insight and interest."[69] Ideas such as these, with their pointed sense of the limitations of business as an arena of social life and human development, remain a resource in the more liberal quarters of the professional stratum to this day.

Although social trustee professionalism remained preeminent at least through the early 1960s, it did not, as I have noted, fully control the field of ideal expressions. A second important ideal also developed during the period. This ideal of expert professionalism emphasized the instrumental effectiveness of specialized, theoretically grounded knowledge, but included comparatively little concern with collegial organization, ethical standards, or service in the public interest.

The most important source of expert professionalism[70] was the indifference of some applied science occupations to the nonmarket elements of social trustee professionalism. Expert professionalism developed principally in the engineering specialties with close ties to entrepreneurial and large-scale business and weak levels of collegial organization. The entrepreneurially minded mining engineers and the highly corporate electrical engineers showed the strongest affinities with expert professionalism and the least interest in social trustee professionalism.[71] Although engineers were not immune to the status lift they received from membership in a "profession," the self-esteem and satisfactions of professionalism "came from proficiency in an increasingly abstruse discipline," not from commitment of collective organization or from serving public purposes somehow separate from the market.[72] For expert professionals, the dictates of disciplinary principles combined with the demands of the market to provide an equitable criterion of the public interest.

At a time of dynamic growth of new professions, social trustee professionalism provided the more useful ideology for most aspiring occupations, espe-cially for those with less reliably efficacious disciplinary bases. A peaceful coexistence, moreover, prevailed between the dominant ideal of professional-ism and its more technically oriented rival. The unequivocal commitment of the leading professions to social trustee professionalism supported this peace-ful coexistence, as did the overlapping commitment of both to high standards in fields of "specialized knowledge."

Popular Definitions of Professional Status. Ordinary citizens judged profes-sions as a status category differently than did the status-conferring institutions out of which the modern professions emerged. These popular judgments were based far more on "style of life" criteria and far less on commonalities in the organization of work and training. It is important to take note of these popu-lar definitions both because they locate some consequential divisions among the professions and because they describe, in broad outline, the popular ex-pectations associated with the "culture of professionalism" that emerged in the later nineteenth century.

During the period of "collective mobility," popular definitions of profes-sional status fluctuated (as they still do) between a relatively exclusive under-standing based on occupational prestige and a relatively inclusive understand-ing based on mental outlook and habits of conduct. The first understanding of professions was limited to only a small number of particularly prestigious professions; the second was relevant to a much larger group of educated middle-class people.

Once the professions had overcome the Jacksonian distaste for distinction and had become reestablished in America, beginning in the 1870s, the origi-nal "learned professions" reassumed a prestigious position in most American communities. In the first sociological studies of occupational prestige, in the 1920s, theology, medicine, law, architecture, and college teaching ranked highest among occupations, followed by some new professions that expressed the authority of science (scientist and civil engineer). Other nominally profes-sional occupations were much less well regarded.[73] The basic outlines of this rank structure continued, with the science-based occupations advancing and ministers declining, through the 1930s and 1940s.[74]

But the idea of professions also had broader cultural connotations in the public mind. Histories of late nineteenth- and early twentieth-century Amer-ica suggest that a characteristic set of expectations—a kind of character structure—was widely associated with the professional middle class from the 1870s onward. This "culture of professionalism" emphasized the material comforts and respectability of middle-class life and an ambition in relation to career that can be considered typical of the middle classes in general. This middle-class striving was combined, however, with ideals of rationalism, men-tal concentration, self-control, and dedicated commitment to work that was the mark of a distinctively professional form of asceticism. "A person's work was more than an unrelated series of jobs and projects. . . . Work was the person: a statement to the world of his internal resources, confidence, and discipline; his active control over the intrinsic relationships of a life, his steadfast character."[75] The model professional was "self-reliant, independent, ambitious, and mentally organized." He was also highly protective of the autonomy he was granted in the name of a "specialized grasp of a meaningful universe."[76] This "culture of professionalism" provided a grid of status-linked expectations and understandings extending beyond the major professions to the broader stratum of the educated middle class.

Phase Four? The Beginnings of Consolidation

It is more difficult to perceive the contours of the present than the outlines of the past. Nevertheless, the present does appear to depart in significant ways from the era of "collective mobility."[77] In particular, the last three decades show a double movement—away from antimarket elements in professional organization and ideology, and toward a more exclusive emphasis on bona fide formal knowledge as the critical element in the constitution of professions. In so far as this is true, the professions show signs of consolidating around a narrower and more exclusive base.

Beginning in the 1960s, social trustee professionalism fell under increasing attack for its apparent lack of correspondence to the organizational realities of professional life. At the same time, a variety of forces—from the increasing importance of income as a status element in the general population to the population explosion within the professions—favored the rise of expert professionalism to a position of greater significance. Some important changes in the underlying institutional structure of professions also encouraged the new prominence of expert professionalism.

The Attack on Social Trustee Professionalism. The critique of social trustee professionalism began in earnest in the mid-1960s, and it was marked particularly by an increasing interest in the substance of professionalism over its forms. Harold Wilensky's 1964 article, "The Professionalization of Everyone?," represents a turning point. In the article, Wilensky identified several barriers to the substantive, as opposed to the purely formal, professionalization of occupations. These included organizational contexts that threaten professional autonomy and the service ideal; and forms of knowledge that are either too general and vague, or too narrow and specific.[78]

Following Wilensky, authority and autonomy at work became important substantive measures of professional jobs. Many of the human services professions, such as nursing and social work, were consigned by sociologists to "semiprofessional" status, because of their circumscribed areas of autonomy and the high levels of control of their activities exercised by organizational authorities.[79] The same was true of the more routinized technical professions, such as business accounting and computer systems programming.[80] The "wrong kind" of knowledge base also came to be seen as a disqualification for full professional standing. Prestige came from elegance, depth, and rigor; from levels of precision that allowed for meaningful judgment; and from high levels of esoteric information.[81] The more prestigious the knowledge base of a profession, the more likely it was to be considered properly professional.

The ethical and organizational claims of social trustee professionalism also came under scholarly attack. By the late 1970s, the propositions that professions were governed by high ethical standards, the norms of self-denying service in relation to a public interest, or high levels of collegial control were no longer taken seriously by most scholars. Critiques of the medical profession led the way. Eliot Freidson's *Profession of Medicine* and other similar works documented numerous examples of self-interested and self-serving behavior that contradicted professional claims to dedicated service in the public interest. They also showed how assumptions of professional competence often led to the abdication, rather than the embrace, of meaningful collegial control.[82] Claims to high ethical standards and collegial regulation were reinterpreted by some scholars as "myths" aimed at protecting the privileges of professionals.[83]

The Rise of Expert Professionalism. At the same time that social trustee professionalism came under attack for its lack of correspondence to the realities of professional life, expert professionalism grew in importance as an alternative idealization.[84] Expert professionalism implied not just the ability to make authoritative judgments and to solve problems based on disciplinary training, but also that the training and skills received were highly valued in the market for services.

In one sense, the prominence of expert professionalism grew naturally out of the sense of progress and power long associated with new technology and new intellectual tools of control. This sense of potency was augmented by the increasing role of research and development during and following World War II and the new breakthroughs that R&D had inspired. As Daniel Bell has written, "The joining of science, technology, and economics in recent years is symbolized by the phrase 'research and development.' Out of this have come the science-based industries (computers, electronics, optics, polymers) which increasingly dominate the manufacturing sector of the society. . . . [T]hese science-based industries, unlike industries which arose in the nineteenth century, are primarily dependent on theoretical work prior to production."[85] In addition to the new product technologies, new "intellectual technologies" promised control over complex systems, both natural and social. "Since 1940, there has been a remarkable efflorescence of new fields whose results apply to problems of organized complexity: information theory, cybernetics, decision theory, game theory, utility theory, stochastic processes. From these have come specific techniques . . . which are used to predict alternative optimal outcomes of different choices in strategy situations."[86]

These were the more glamorous images of experts, based on the old positivist dream of a link between theoretical reason and practical power. The appeal of the expert, however, was also the appeal of marrying empirical science and old-fashioned ingenuity to more prosaic, but still useful, applications. New medical technologies allowed doctors to diagnose and treat previously undetectable problems. Consultants could find ways to make fertilizer out of tomato waste products, contributing to growth while ending pollution, and they could find solutions to organizational problems that would allow "giants to dance."

In the more hyperbolic formulations of the age, professionals were idealized as possessors of great skills and great quantities of knowledge demanded by an increasingly complex society. These ideas misinterpreted professional activity in their haste to glorify it. The abilities that count in good professional work are not mere skills, and the capacities that are most meaningful involve something different than the retention of information. As Michael Oakeshott has observed, when we think about "the abilities denoted in the [words] engineer, Latin scholar, explorer, actor, surgeon, lawyer, army commander, physicist, teacher . . . what we are aware of is not a number of items of knowledge available for use, but having powers of specific kinds—the power of being able to solve a legal problem, or to understand a Latin inscription, or perform a surgical operation. What we know constitutes an equipment which we possess in terms of what it enables us to do or to understand."[87]

Nominally professional occupations that could not compete as "expert" occupations were naturally suspect under these circumstances. They lacked the certainty and often the competence to solve problems in the areas in which they claimed authority. "There are certain conflicts which arise in professional schools that train for education, social work, town planning, and divinity. . . . [All of these sources of conflict result from] the fact that in some sense these are not 'true' professions. . . . [t]he base of knowledge and competence with which students enter practice is not really serious, specialized knowledge."[88]

A number of social forces, in addition to the achievements of experts themselves, lay behind the rise of expert professionalism. One was the increasing tendency of Americans in the postwar years to think of occupational prestige in standard-of-living terms rather than in terms of an occupation's contributions to community well-being. By the early 1960s, Otis Duncan had created a "socioeconomic index" for occupations based on the linear combination of the percentage of incumbents at the upper ends of the educational and income distributions. As a justification for the index, Duncan noted the high correlations with other measures of prestige and also a "theoretical" justification: "[A] man qualifies himself for occupational life by obtaining an education; as a consequence of pursuing his occupation, he obtains income. Occupation, therefore, is the intervening activity linking income to education."[89]

Later studies of social standing using more sensitive instruments revealed an even larger impact of income on social standing. Using better measurements and estimation procedures, sociologists in the 1970s concluded that income dwarfed occupation and education as a determinant of status.[90] In the process of achieving social standing in late twentieth-century America, "[i]ncome is everyone's goal, and the more of it the better. Education is a first step toward its attainment—the launching platform. . . . The status attached to given schooling levels is a function of the realistic observations people make of how much money those in different educational categories actually earn."[91]

Demographic pressures were a fundamental support for the rise of expert professionalism. In this respect, the very popularity of the professions, based partly on the ideals of social trustee professionalism, created the grounds for the transformation of those ideals. The population explosion in higher education and in the professions between the 1960s and the 1980s led to a decidedly greater explicit interest in the marketability of educational resources. This greater interest in marketable qualifications fostered both a movement away from nonbusiness professions toward business-related professions and, together with the natural development of disciplines, a movement in the direction of greater specialization in virtually all professions.

The shortage of college-educated labor became a glut beginning in 1969 as college and university enrollments expanded faster than desirable job openings for the new graduates. Humanities and social science graduates were particularly hard hit, and their pay dropped sharply in the early and mid-1970s.[92] The results were a predictable movement of students away from the liberal arts, and a great increase in utilitarian motivations among all students. Liberal arts degrees declined by 15 percent in ten years beginning in 1972, while business and engineering degrees increased by 15 percent.[93] In the years between 1967 and 1987, the number of college freshmen who looked to their college experience as a way to become "very well-off financially" increased by nearly 40 percent, while the number who looked to college as a way to develop "a meaningful philosophy of life" declined by more than 40 percent.[94]

It is an old sociological principle that the higher the population density the more fervent the search for specialized market niches. This principle held true for the professions in the 1970s and 1980s. Specialization in many fields became the preferred way to avoid competition by carving out a place in a new or undersupplied market. Generalists continued to flourish in fields where the volume of business or the nature of problems were particularly irregular, but specialists became the norm elsewhere. Academe, law, medicine, and science all experienced unprecedented levels of field-level specialization in the 1970s and 1980s.[95]

As a result of these changes, even members of the more autonomous professions began to adopt expertise-based understandings of professional standing, while tending to abandon understandings based on the ideals of social trustee professionalism. The best evidence of this is found in data I collected in the early 1980s with Charles Derber and his associates from a sample of some 750 Boston-area doctors, lawyers, scientists, and engineers. When these professional people were asked to distinguish the characteristics of professionals' knowledge as compared to the knowledge possessed by skilled craft workers, they were virtually unanimous in emphasizing the breadth of matters apprehended in the professional knowledge base; the degree of judgment that professional work required; the amount of time and effort required to learn the formal knowledge involved in professional work; its complexity; and its theoretical content. However, they did not consider professional knowledge to be "more important to society" or more stringently directed by ethical codes than the knowledge of craft workers.[96] In this Boston-area sample, the class identifications of professionals were also built more on a sense of shared education and high-level expertise than on any other criteria.[97]

Institutional Change. Some evidence of consolidation—as yet rather limited—can be found at the institutional level as well. These institutional changes have been based primarily on growing judicial and practitioner opposition to antimarket elements in professional organization and to the contractionary effects of the recent fiscal problems of universities. Together, these forces have increased the already substantial role of the market as an agent of professional organization, while creating the grounds for a potential narrowing of the occupational boundaries of the professional stratum.

Anticompetitive practices have been typical of all of the more autonomous professional occupations. These practices, however inefficient from an economic perspective, provided important foundations for the sense of collegiality that pertained in these occupations, a sense of collegiality that indirectly served as a model for professional behavior in less autonomous professional occupations. The traditional method of regulation, sanctioned by the courts, involved a degree of protection from economic competition and significant levels of protection from outside political pressures. Economic protections were meant to insure that quality of service would not be compromised by price competition. Exemption from external regulatory controls was meant to protect the professions from the interference of politicians and interest groups who were not competent to judge the requirements of professional practice.

These protections began to break down in the late 1960s. At that time, the Supreme Court struck down the legality of several economic privileges enjoyed by the major professions—standard fees, bans against competitive bidding, and bans on advertising. By introducing market incentives, the Court expected that the cost of professional services would be lowered while the quality of service improved. In the deregulatory climate, market-based decisions became common in the professional associations as well. In well-publicized cases, doctors and lawyers rejected efforts to require conformity to ethical and moral standards unrecognized in the market. Doctors opposed a ban on "self-referrals"—the referral of patients to clinics and other facilities in which the referring doctor had a financial interest. Lawyers rejected a proposal to sanction five days of service a year to underserved populations. The universities, too, moved in the direction of encouraging market-oriented behaviors by liberalizing policies on the profit-making activity of faculty, and by forming partnerships with business to exploit faculty research.

While deregulation of enterprise encouraged economistic attitudes in the professions, greater regulation of performance in some professions encouraged the predominance of knowledge-based elites. Medicine, the strongest of the professions, became subject to a "massive increase" in external bureaucratic regulation, also beginning in the 1960s. The regulation included review of professional decisions by external agents, and it also mandated formal regulation by colleagues, including the proliferation of disciplinary boards. Through the new checks on competence, the importance of expertise was reinforced. In his review of the changing nature of professional regulation, Eliot Freidson concluded, "The facade of equal probity and competence no longer exists."[98]

More importantly, the universities also moved, however slightly, toward narrowing the scope of bona fide professional knowledge.[99] Budget deficits in the 1980s and early 1990s encouraged many research universities to reconsider their curricular offerings. In these reconsiderations, the less popular scholarly fields, the "softer" social sciences, the newer interdisciplinary fields, and, in particular, the more marginally situated "human services" fields experienced losses.[100] By contrast, basic science and applied business-related fields were generally unquestioned. Indeed, they often continued to grow in resources and administrative affections, as did the powerful professional schools in medicine, law, and business.[101] One study of five public research universities facing budget cuts showed that public health and education, two human services fields enrolling large numbers of women, tended to be eliminated or reduced at most of the universities studied.[102] At another public research university in the midwest, the major programs slated for cuts or elimination included social work, human nutrition, and library science.[103] The available accounts suggest that cutbacks on the "professional periphery"—the fields of lower market value and less secure specialized knowledge—were most common.

Since the universities are central in the constitution of the professional stratum, their actions have large implications for the future. Renewed budgetary difficulties would place added pressure on universities to rethink the boundaries of higher-level learning. Some of the new justifications that have been considered already involve a logic of concentration on cognitively sophisticated and high-income-producing fields consistent with other trends toward market orientation and consolidation. Resistance to such redefinitions on the basis of ideals dating from earlier periods of professional development would, of course, also be great in the event of further challenges to the curricular span reached by the research universities in the early twentieth century.

Professions in the Political Economy I:
Spheres and Sectors

TERMS SUCH AS "expertise" and "knowledge work" have well served people in the professional stratum by evoking a convincing basis for elevated status. Yet they are by no means specific enough for an adequate analysis of the situation of the professional middle class in American society. Many different kinds of "experts" exist and many distinct forces give rise to a perceived need for expert services. An obvious implication is that to understand the modern professional stratum, it is not very useful to focus exclusively on essentially contentless concepts like "expertise" and "knowledge," or to emphasize uni-causal trends like the rise of an "information economy" or a "post-industrial society."

Rather, it is necessary to discuss how people providing various kinds of "expert services" fit into the political economy and the commodity and labor markets. From this perspective, some of the key questions are "knowledge *about what?*," "knowledge *valued by whom?*," and "knowledge *valued at what level?*" In this chapter and the next, I will provide an analysis of expert services by focusing on the distinct spheres of social purpose, the organizational locations, and the market situations of professionals. In my view, these are the three major dimensions of the employment situation of expert labor in the American political economy. These dimensions also lie behind the crystallization of interests and outlooks in the professional stratum. Analyzing these three dimensions is therefore essential both for understanding professionals as a social and economic stratum and for understanding the political interests that divide the contemporary professional class.[1]

SPHERES OF SOCIAL PURPOSE

As a social force, formal knowledge is neither unified by a central developmental trend like the rise of an information economy, nor infinitely plastic and differentiated. Instead, formal knowledge clusters around five major spheres of social purpose pursued by sets of interrelated occupations and organizations. Taken as a whole, these constitute a societal-level answer to the questions "knowledge about what?" and "knowledge for what?" I will call these spheres of related purpose (1) the business services sphere; (2) the applied science sphere; (3) the culture and communications sphere; (4) the civic regulation sphere; and (5) the human services sphere.

A sixth sphere, the sphere of culture creation, helps to shape and renew professional practice in the other five. It is made up of the researchers, writers, and teachers who are the main link between the universe of formal knowledge and the organization of professional practice. To avoid confusion from discussing too many categories, I will treat this knowledge elite in connection with the sphere of culture and communications. Nevertheless, in their primary activities, they are clearly a distinct element, serving as a cognitive center for each of the other spheres.

Spheres of social purpose are not constituted exclusively by occupations. Although occupations are the best single indicator of the sphere of social purpose to which a professional person belongs, occupations can, at times, be a deceptive indicator taken alone. Lawyers, for example, are variously involved in activities serving the needs of business corporations and in activities related to civic regulation and human services. Consideration of the "audiences" for whom work is produced and the organizational and institutional frames within which work is produced is therefore a necessary part of the discussion.

Anatomizing the Purposes of Formal Knowledge

To provide criteria for marking boundaries between spheres of formal knowledge, one can ask two questions: first, are the forces driving growth and development of a set of related activities different from those driving development in other spheres? And, second, is the fundamental purpose of the set of activities different from those in other spheres?[2]

My anatomization is based on answers to these two questions. The business services sphere is driven by the developing production needs and capacities of the advanced sectors of the economy. The applied science sphere is driven by the application of scientific knowledge to technological development and the needs of production. The culture and communications sphere is driven, principally, by the interests consumers have in information, recreational entertainment, and the social status that comes from information and arts participation. The civic regulation sphere is driven by the need to maintain and regulate political society through administrative and political decision making. The human services sphere is united by a common focus on maintaining (and, where possible, improving) the social and economic situation of individuals so that they can meet accepted minimal standards as functioning members of society.

In this typology, the first two spheres of professional activity (business services and applied science) are primarily producer services. The third (culture and communications) is primarily a consumer services sphere (though, to be sure, it responds to some aggregate political interests as well). The fourth (civic regulation) is a mix mainly involving producer services and aggregate political interests, and the fifth (human services) is another mixed sphere mainly involving consumer services and aggregate political interests.

The spheres vary greatly in size. If we use a conventional calculation based on all census professionals with four or more years of college, human services dominate numerically. During the last decade, over half of baccalaureate-level professionals were members of the human services group. Professionals in applied science and business service were also numerically important, accounting for one out of five and one out of seven of all baccalaureate-level professionals, respectively. The sphere of civic regulation (nine percent) and the sphere of culture and communications (six percent) were substantially smaller.[3] Raising the criterion to six or more years of higher education increases the relative size of the applied science and cultural professions by nearly 5 percent each, while it reduces the relative size of the human services to just over 40 percent.

The spheres also vary in economic dynamism. Here the patterns reflect control over important resources and levels of consumer demand for services. One of the smaller spheres—business services—has been highly dynamic over the last quarter-century. Medical services, a part of the human services group, has been the most dynamic of all in recent decades.

Business Services. In retrospect, it seems clear that the old distinction between "public-minded" professionals and "self-interested" business people has long been something of a myth advanced by partisans of the nonbusiness professions. One of the ways it managed to be convincing was by ruling out of the ranks of the professional class the rather large segment of people whose formal knowledge is directly related to improving and protecting the performance of business enterprise.

Business service professionals include financial analysts and business economists, accountants and auditors, corporate attorneys, advertising and corporate public relations specialists, personnel and labor relations specialists, computer scientists working in management information systems, and management consultants.[4] At the higher levels, these people audit the corporate books, offer tax and strategic advice, defend corporations against lawsuits, polish corporate images, improve communications among management, and subcontract to solve problems that management can't or doesn't wish to solve for itself.

It is precisely their shared concern with maintaining the health of business corporations in their relations with internal constituencies and with the outside world that unites the business services group. These people are paid to monitor, protect, and improve organizational performance for those who manage corporations, and to attend to the public responsibilities (like independent audits, SEC reports, tax payments, and environmental protection assessments) that are required of corporations by the state. New work generally develops out of new organizational resources or new demands for organizational response. When a large oil company forms a subsidiary, it brings new accountants and lawyers on board. When one of its tankers has a serious spill, it brings in public relations people, lawyers, and sometimes, management consultants. When a strike is threatened, a similar panoply of experts is deployed to protect management's sense of the organization's interests.

From the mid-1970s through the mid-1980s, some business service industries (notably, advertising, computer services, and management consulting) grew at twice the rate of GNP, and none were less than 60 percent higher.[5] In the wake of this sustained expansion, business services are now among the leading export industries in the American economy. They are also among the most international in scope. Foreign operations for the largest accounting, management consulting, and advertising firms account for nearly as much revenue as their U.S. operations.[6]

Organizationally, the business service sphere is divided between a largely unsung segment of professionals who are employed directly by business firms and a more powerful independent segment that works in (or directs) professional firms.[7] For the most part, business service professionals employed in corporations are involved in less financially weighty and more routine matters than are their colleagues in professional firm practices: monitoring the standard accounts of the firm, settling consumer or contractual complaints, drawing up new contracts, developing systems to generate desired reports for management. For more specialized and more momentous activities, independent professional firms are usually called in.

The entrepreneurial outlook of many business service professionals is based organizationally on the frequency of professional firm-based practice. Architects, consultants, and corporate lawyers are overwhelmingly employed in professional firms, as are certified public accountants.[7] Professional firms themselves tend to mirror in organization and ethos the kinds of clients they serve.[8] Smaller firms tend to work for small businesses and moderately affluent individuals.[9] The largest firms work for the largest businesses and the most affluent individuals. As one goes up the size and wealth scale, the proportion of work for organizations increases and the proportion of work for individuals decreases.[10]

Most business service professionals are decidedly middle or upper-middle class in income. Yet the sheer size and scope of the largest business service firms, and the wealth of the partners who own them, no doubt comes as a shock to those who hold too exclusively to the view of professionals as a middle- and upper-middle-class stratum.[11] In the mid-1980s, the five largest accounting firms had worldwide fees of over a billion dollars and staffs of 20,000.[12] Worldwide revenues in the hundreds of millions of dollars were also found among the leading management consulting firms and the leading advertising firms.[13] The largest law firms have legal staffs of up to 1,000 lawyers and do enough business that some senior partners earn more than $1 million per year.[14]

Applied Science. In turning to the sphere of applied science, I will be surveying more familiar professional terrain. These are people who apply scientific knowledge to practical problems of production. The sphere includes nearly all engineers, physicists, chemists, geoscientists, biotechnology and product-related medical scientists, production-centered computer scientists, mathematicians, statisticians, and economists and organizational psychologists working on practical problems of production.

If business service professionals can be thought of as the "reproductive arm" of private capital, applied science professionals are the "production arm." Collectively, these people are responsible for designing much of the technology and creating the consumer goods that make contemporary American life a marvel of ingenuity and convenience for those who can afford its pleasures.

The group is, by any estimate, a sizable proportion of the professional stratum. Engineers are the third largest of all census professional occupations, numbering nearly one and a half million. There are, in addition, nearly half a million computer scientists, some 200,000 physical scientists, over 150,000 life scientists, as well as tens of thousands of mathematicians, statisticians, and economists working on practical problems of production.[15]

Professionals in applied science are almost exclusively employees; self-employment is of negligible importance. Indeed, most applied science professionals work not just in the private sector but in large enterprises. Recent estimates suggest that 60 percent or more of engineers work in corporations employing more than 5,000 people.[16] Nonacademic scientists also tend to work in large corporations, though a somewhat higher percentage overall work in smaller specialized firms and in firms attempting to exploit new scientific developments.

Corporate life consequently provides an essential context for understanding the work of most applied science professionals. Their projects tend to involve large teams of people working in concert in a highly bureaucratized context. These conditions alone help to explain the intense concern with coordination and teamwork that is found among applied science professionals. It is also true that however useful they may be, the products scientists and engineers design will not be produced unless they can be profitably marketed. In a capitalistic economy, scientific know-how, without entrepreneurial will and muscle, is little more than a cipher. Even the patents scientists generate are legally the property of the corporations for which they work.

Nevertheless, the applied science group is not quite as centrally involved with corporate premises and corporate contexts as are the business service professions. This is principally because they apply *science*, not the normative frames regulating business. However much profit considerations may influence their activities, the applied science professions are directly concerned with the production of things, not with management problems or organizational representation per se.

In addition, a significant share of applied research and production work is done in the public sector—particularly in the area of infrastructure development, in the defense industry, and in housing and urban development. A

measure of the public/nonprofit versus private split can be gained by comparing sectoral employments, excluding academics. These comparisons suggest
that approximately a third of all physicists, more than one-fifth of chemists,
nearly one-fifth of geoscientists, and at least one-tenth of engineers work
outside of private industry.[17] These figures must be interpreted with care; they
are based on imperfect surveys. Nevertheless, applied science clearly includes
a sizable number of people working outside of the private economy, and these
numbers may in fact underestimate the influence of the public sector. A substantially larger proportion of scientists and engineers work for government
indirectly through contractual relations between their employers and public
agencies.[18]

Culture and Communications. Formal knowledge can clearly also be applied
to the production and transmission of culture. The people in this sphere create and maintain the symbolic environment in so far as it is relevant to
the universe of scholarship, literary and artistic expression, and other spheres
of formal knowledge. The culture and communications sphere is composed,
at a minimum, of professors at research universities and the leading liberal
arts colleges; curators and research staff at museums, special collections,
and archives; writers and editors for intellectual and specialist periodicals;
most editors at scholarly presses and also some editors at the major trade
publishers; many journalists and editors working for the national news
media; perhaps a majority of artists and writers working in "high culture"
organizations, such as symphonies and repertory theater companies; some
writers, artists, designers, and directors working in television and motion
pictures; and an unknown number of freelance writers and performing
artists.

   One essential basis for the growth and influence of the culture and communications group is the expansion of higher education and of the professional
middle and upper middle class itself. These changes have helped to give rise to
more specialized needs for information and research, and to expand the
audience for "high culture" activities. Another important factor has been the
moderate population-wide increases in discretionary income over time. In the
wealthier market economies, strong consumer markets exist not only for
educational credentials, but for information and analysis, for clashing view-
points, and for edification, amusement, and aesthetic pleasures. Professionals
who specialize in the production and transmission of these cultural goods are
at the center of the organizations that service these markets.

   Higher education is the largest of the culture industries. In the postwar
period, it too has been among the more dynamic industries in the country. The
number of professors alone has increased more than fivefold since the beginning of World War II and the number of undergraduate students more than
eight times.[19] Its enormous expansion can be traced to the importance of
educational credentials as a mode of access to higher-level positions, the
preferences of employers for an educated labor force, and the sheer demo-

graphic push of the large postwar birth cohorts who came of age in the 1960s and 1970s.

Other "high culture" activities have also flourished. Nearly four times as many new books appeared annually in the late 1980s as appeared in 1950.[20] Both opera and symphony attendance showed steady growth from the 1950s on.[21] Theater attendance, both a popular and a "high culture" indicator, showed a similar pattern of steady growth.[22] A further sense of the strength of consumer demand for cultural services involving arts and edification can be conveyed by looking at the financial picture of the more intellectually oriented cultural industries over time. Industry receipts in book publishing increased nearly three times in constant dollars between 1950 and 1988,[23] newspaper publishing receipts increased 2.5 times,[24] and magazine publishing receipts increased by more than 50 percent.[25] Receipts in most of the performing arts also grew.[26]

The research universities, the scholarly presses, the world of museums and archives, and the design-oriented architectural firms are the most highly professionalized environments in the culture and communications sphere.[27] Journalists and editors do not work in markets controlled by the credential system, but journalists working in the national media and in the world of publications directed at highly educated audiences (e.g., business and professional periodicals and periodicals of intellectual opinion) do tend to work in professionalized environments. Post-graduate study, sometimes with required subject-matter expertise, is the norm, and a good many journalists and editors combine real learning with an unusual nimbleness of mind.[28]

The arts are divided organizationally by the audiences to which producers are oriented and the institutional contexts in which they produce their work. The literate and classical high culture forms are mainly directed toward educated elites and are organized almost exclusively in the nonprofit sector. These are often professionalized environments. High levels of formal training are typical. Peer recognition tends to be highly valued and popular success to be treated with some skepticism.[29] A second major setting can be found in the visual arts and the more explicitly market-oriented architectural and design firms. Because visual artists produce work with financial and status value to investors, they are oriented at least as much toward monied elites as they are to educated elites, and they also operate in an extremely competitive market setting. This context encourages a high level of entrepreneurialism and, at least in the contemporary period, a comparatively low average level of interest in literate culture.[30] A third major setting is the popular culture industry, where the application of formal knowledge is necessarily joined to strongly commercial interests. Although some very learned people work in the visual arts and popular culture industries, neither setting encourages active identifications with the world of formal knowledge.

Civic Regulation. Expert knowledge can be directed also toward the regulation of social relations in organized political jurisdictions. The sphere of civic regulation can be defined as encompassing those people who are most actively involved in the maintenance and enhancement of the quality of civic life and government operated systems (such as public works and mass transit), the maintenance of civil relations (including the resolution of conflicts), decisions about the allocation of government services, policy-related research, and planning for the future. The sphere of civic regulation is a kind of "brain center" or "advanced functions" center, similar to the complexes of corporate headquarters in the private sector, but its object of concern is the broader political and social environment. Unlike the corporate sphere, it is based on legally constituted jurisdictions, and it is also far more pluralistically organized.

The sphere of civic regulation includes professionals who are both directly employed by, and those who are indirectly connected to, governmental institutions. Those directly employed by government include prosecutors and judges; administrative, budgetary, and planning officials working in government agencies, and their staffs. Professionals indirectly connected to government include researchers in public policy think tanks and institutes; professors in universities who study particular public policy issues; consultants hired to provide advice to government panels; foundation staffs concerned with social welfare and civic regulation issues; experts and lawyers attached to interest groups seeking to influence government policy; and the liaison people from large organizations, who consult with government on matters that affect their organizations.

In the twentieth century, government administration, the largest part of the sphere of civic regulation, has tended to expand in Democratic and Republican administrations alike. Much of this expansion has been demographically driven. Governmental services necessarily expand when the population eligible for services expands. But a large part of the expansion also comes from aggregate political forces supporting the implementation of new services. Most government employment and expenditure takes place below the national level. Nearly two-thirds of all government is local; one-quarter is at the state level; and less than one-fifth is federal.[31]

The largest functions of government at the Federal level are those closer to the hearts of conservatives, and moderates than to liberals.[32] The military is the largest employer, and activities related to commerce and law enforcement employ approximately two-fifths of all federal employees. They are also substantial in terms of expenditures, accounting for approximately a third of the total.[33] Social welfare functions, by contrast, represent less employment but more expenditure (with a very large proportion of that amount in social security expenditures). At the state level, the largest functions are connected to the provision of higher education and medical services. At the local level, the major responsibility has been primary and secondary education.[34] Even at the state and local levels of government, commerce and public safety—related functions figure prominently, accounting for no less than one-fifth of employment.[35]

The extent to which government settings are professionalized environments naturally varies from place to place and even office to office. A good deal of government work is routine. The more professionalized environments tend to involve staff experts of relatively high rank. At all levels, professionals in government are typically appointed through civil service procedures; only the higher levels are appointed by political leaders. The political views of civil servants are, in theory, irrelevant to the performance of their prescribed duties; they are meant to be expert agents of policymakers. The situation is more complicated in practice.[36] Nevertheless, it is the views of the governing party, not the civil service bureaucracy, that is usually decisive in the policy arena.

Representatives of interest groups, who are active on a continuous or relatively continuous basis in the governmental process, are the other major participants in the sphere of civic regulation. The number of professionals involved in interest representation has grown greatly over time. At the national level, the greatest growth over the last quarter-century has been among business representatives and among representatives of advocacy groups connected to ethnic groups and the women's movement. During the same period, labor representation declined.[37]

Human Services. Human service professionals apply formal knowledge in the treatment of the problems that afflict individuals and in the service of the minimum standard the society deems necessary for a person to be able to live a normal and productive life. The society's "minimum standards" have mainly to do with the cultural literacy, skills, and values that are imparted through schooling, but they can also involve health services and economic and social support activities. Doctors, dentists, nurses, attorneys working on the legal problems of individuals (rather than for corporations or other organizations), schoolteachers, counselors, psychotherapists, social workers, and other professionals engaged in the treatment of personal problems are all, functionally, part of the human services sphere. Because of their active role in counseling and advising on personal problems, I include pastorally oriented clergy in this category as well.

Except in medicine and law, human services professionals are usually employed by government or in nonprofit organizations, but there is nevertheless a clear distinction between them and those professionals who are centrally involved in the sphere of civic regulation. Professionals working in the civic sphere are directly involved in the creation and implementation of broad conceptions of public order, while human service provision involves a more focused concern with the current situation and future prospects of *individual* patients, clients, and consumers.

The human service professions have grown tenfold in numbers since the 1930s, the fastest rates of growth of any professional sphere over the half-century. Behind this enormous expansion are several quite distinct forces. On the one hand, there is the public push for "social citizenship rights." Although the term "entitlement" has developed a pejorative connotation, it nevertheless remains true, as Daniel Bell has written, that "from Bismarck and Disraeli through Franklin Roosevelt and Dwight Eisenhower, the very idea of 'one nation,' rather than 'two,' has dictated the acceptance of the idea of a welfare state, and with it the principle of entitlement."[38] A second important force has been independent consumer demand for health and educational services. With increases in disposable income, consumers have shown a distinct propensity to invest in the personal services market in an effort to improve their quality of life. New or much larger markets have consequently arisen in the areas of psychological counseling, marriage counseling, health and nutrition advising, and educational preparation.

In several of the human services areas, a third important force—perhaps as important as the other two—has been the effective demand of producers for a healthy and well-educated labor force to deal with the requirements of modern organization and technology. Expansion of education, health, and social services is, as the economists note, "very much a reflection" of the state's emphasis on investment in human capital.[39] Indeed, because of the importance attached to shaping up the work force by employers and state officials who support human services, it is nearly as accurate to describe this sphere as "human capital services."

Schoolteaching is the largest occupation classified by the census bureau as among the "professional specialty" occupations, with more than 2.5 million practitioners, and nursing is next largest, with over 1.6 million. Doctors (over 500,000), clergy (nearly 500,000), social workers (200,000), dentists (over 150,000), and psychologists (over 10,000) are other large occupational groups in the human services sphere. The equivalent of 300,000 lawyers (as measured by percentage of attorney effort) might be counted in this sphere as well, as a proxy for the percentage of attorneys' time spent on services to individuals rather than businesses.[40]

The economic fortunes of human services workers have varied enormously by industry. The human services sphere is fundamentally divided between the enormously successful medical services industries and all other activities. Most medical services in the United States are provided by independent entrepreneurs,[41] supported by third-party health insurance payments.[42] In the U.S. economy, medical services now contribute over 12 percent to the GNP, and the exceptional growth over time as yet shows few signs of slowing down. This growth has been driven by the third-party payment system, by the aging of the population, and most emphatically, by the exceptional importance attached to health in contemporary American society.[43]

The nonmedical human services have, by contrast, tended to grow slowly, if at all, largely because of resource restrictions in the public sector. Grants-in-aid to states and localities were cut dramatically in the early 1980s, but many of the affected programs were replaced through increased taxes at the state level.[44] Overall, programs tended to be "stabilized as they had evolved by 1980."[45] Nevertheless, some patterned variation in response is evident: the programs suffering the largest cutbacks were those aimed at the poorest populations, the populations with the weakest economic and political support. Welfare, job training, and public housing programs were cut back, while social services benefitting politically organized and middle class groups fared better.[46] Program areas that were central to the partisan struggle of the era—programs for the elderly, for farmers, and some "safety net" programs for the poor—also tended to survive "with surprising resilience."[47]

Social Purposes, Ethos, and Politics

Societal purposes and professional politics are connected through the mediating influence of the dominant mentalities that exist in the five major spheres of professional activity. Three of the spheres—business services, applied science, and human services—can be characterized in terms of a "dominant ethos." By this, I mean the dominant mentality governing conceptions of purpose and the spirit in which work is pursued in light of those purposes. No dominant ethos exists in the smallest of the professional spheres—"culture and communications" and "civic regulation." In these spheres, the play of interests and ideologies is especially complex, and professionals working in them are greatly divided in both ethos and ideology.

The dominant ethos of the business service professionals combines a profit-centered focus—typified by the constant pressure in professional firm practice for increased billing hours—with a degree of entrepreneurial flair. In their organization and their activities, business service professionals are not easy to distinguish from the business people they serve. Under the circumstances, it would seem unreasonable to expect that the political interests and values of the people in these spheres will be extremely different either.

Such divisions as exist among business service professionals tend to follow the lines of division found generally in the business world. In an age of highly coordinated business political activity, professionals contribute no greater "systemwide rationality" to the analysis of political issues. Large professional firms are likely to worry about the same issues as corporate chief executives. In recent years, these have included escalating health-care costs and the federal deficit.[48] By contrast, principals and associates in the smaller professional firms are more likely to favor further reductions in government regulation and taxes, mirroring the "Main Street" businesses they serve.

Differences in style and taste also appear to mirror differences in the business world, though business service professionals often take the lead in setting fashion, since they are less encumbered by the inhibitions surrounding coordination in large bureaucracies. Among the younger business service professionals in the big cities, a culture of "quick-witted discourse" and sophisticated style is the reigning fashion, as perhaps it has been since at least the 1920s.[49]

The dominant ethos of applied science professionals is shaped by their interests in problem-solving, as these are influenced by the conceptual framework of the large organizations they work for. Because they are so intimately connected to the production process, professionals in applied science are typically highly integrated with management even when they are not themselves managers. Scientists and engineers are used to bringing cost-benefit calculations into their technical considerations. Indeed, for engineers, nearly as much as for accountants, this information constitutes an essential constraint, almost universally acknowledged as legitimate, within which professional knowledge is applied.[50] Engineers are also very much prone to think in terms of the values of teamwork and coordination, and to defer to the plans and decisions of higher management. This sense of connection with management is evident in all ethnographic and survey studies of corporate scientists and engineers. It is reinforced by, but not necessarily dependent on, the comparatively high levels of mobility of engineers and other applied science professionals into management.[51]

Disagreements, of course, sometimes exist between applied science professionals and their managers over such matters as safety versus cost considerations, speed in bringing products to market versus quality of design, and the other kinds of issues that Thorstein Veblen and his followers hoped would eventually split "efficiency-minded" and craft-conscious engineers from the "wasteful" capitalist context in which they worked.[52] Nevertheless, the commitment of scientists and engineers to pure craft values and pure "intellectualism" have been greatly overestimated in the Veblen tradition, while their commitment to the price system and the rationality of managerial authority have been greatly underestimated.

In fact, the applied science group is not necessarily any less conservative politically than the business services group—or, indeed, than business owners and executives. By a whisker at least, the opposite may be true. Because they work with data and things more than with people, and because they are often convinced that there are singular right answers to problems, scientists and engineers can be more inflexible and more conservative on principle than their bosses, and they can also be prone to adopt less participative decision styles. By contrast, managers and executives must interact with and understand real human beings, which can encourage a sense of empathy.

Culture and communications is a sphere of extraordinary diversity, reaching out to every corner of the larger society. Indeed, virtually all of the concerns a society can have are represented among culture and communications professionals. This fragmented character of specialization almost guarantees a high level of diversity within the sphere of cultural production. Among professionals in the culture and communications sphere, means-ends orientations also differ greatly in relation to this great variety of objects of interest. The major goals underlying practice may be to instruct, to entertain, to compile valid facts, to search for "fundamental truths," to express understandings, perceptions, or emotions, or some combination of these goals.

In spite of these obvious elements of diversity, many social scientists have argued that the cultural sphere attracts a disproportionate number of people whose politics are left-of-center.[53] There is some evidence suggesting that this observation is true in a very modest way.[54] A mixture of iconoclasm and comportment is prevalent among successful people in this sphere, and it is not surprising that young people with middle-class aspirations and an unconventional turn of mind feel more comfortable in a sphere where emphases on conformity are not as pervasive. "High culture" institutions, in addition, operate on a significantly different principle of authority from the principles underlying markets and hierarchies, and this difference, too, can encourage criticism of social authority. In the high culture sphere, status rewards are based, to a significant degree, not on satisfying consumer wants or organizational superiors, but on satisfying peers who judge performance in terms of contributions to a body of knowledge or preexisting cultural expression. This pattern of evaluation leads to a good deal of concern with the truth value of statements, with the aesthetics of expression, and with the quality of insights—value criteria that do not necessarily conflict with, but also do not exactly parallel, the value criteria that are dominant in the economy and polity. There is, as a consequence, a marked sense among elite culture producers of a "higher court" of cultural meaning.

At the same time, many culture producers are strongly influenced by forces that lead in the direction of satisfaction with the established order, rather than dissatisfaction. Where upper-class-status cultures dominate in the high culture sphere, the political climate will often tend to be associated with social and political orthodoxy, rather than with any sort of heterodoxy. Even when strongly intellectual concerns predominate, as is true perhaps in the majority of "high culture" arenas, many artists and intellectuals find, on rational grounds, that the established institutions and freedoms of bourgeois democratic societies represent the best supports for "high culture" activity and the other values they defend. They may, on these grounds, be very much on the side of established authority. The national media, with their unusual power, have simultaneously the resources and social contacts that encourage greater sympathy with the interests of elites and also the power and autonomy to engage in regular criticism of elites. However, in the news media, the injunction to throw an "accurate mirror" up to society encourages many to conform, almost as a matter of professional ethics, to the prevailing fashions and powers. If this is not sufficient, the desire to remain on good terms with newsmakers often is enough to encourage a deferential attitude to the powerful.

It is often assumed that professionals connected to the sphere of civic regulation are also comparatively liberal, because of their greater distance from business, and because they are directly concerned with aggregate political interests. With some asperity, conservative writers have suggested that Democrats and liberals are drawn to the civic arena as a way to put their ideals into practice at public expense, while Republicans and conservatives are relatively indifferent because they are too busy making money in business.[55]

Identifications with the Democratic party do predominate in the civic sphere. During a recent fifteen-year period, for example, Democrats outnumbered the combined category of Republicans and Independents by nearly three to two—proportions that were almost exactly reversed in the business services and applied technology spheres.[56] However, the decisive voices in the civic sphere are not mid-level professionals. On the national level, the decisive leadership is provided by political appointees, who come from the president's party. Over the last quarter-century, this has meant that they have been members of the conservative party more than 75 percent of the time. Democrats have tended to hold only a slight edge in the control of statehouses over the last 50 years. Much of town government operates on an independent, nonpartisan model. Only in the big cities do Democrats consistently control the machinery of government.[57]

Some of the most important functional areas in government at all levels are the least involved with liberal social goals. Capital investment is vitally important to state economies, and economic development offices, in particular, are highly deferential to the needs of business. Indeed, this is increasingly true as many states and municipalities veer close to the edge of bankruptcy. Where the competition between states and localities was once over finding the most attractive tax breaks and government infrastructural aid for business,[58] the trend recently has been toward outright payments to corporations for promises to locate.[59] Nor are these the only functional areas in which conservatives are found in significant proportions. Defense and law enforcement are arenas of social control in which conservatives have long been numerous, if not wholly dominant. The foreign policy establishment, while not without serious concerns about domestic cohesion, is closely associated with the investment banking community, a center of liberal Republicanism. By contrast, the planning and administration of social programs, public utilities, transportation, and basic services are very often Democratic domains.

The professional staffs of interest groups, like the interest groups themselves, are ideologically heterogeneous. The only safe generalization is that the ideology of the staff tends to mirror the ideology of the association they work for, in so far as those associations have a definable ideology. Given the changes in representation over time, this means a somewhat greater voice for business and trade associations, and also for ethnic and women's groups. Domestic policy interest groups described as "public interest" and "civic" organizations usually offer a comparatively liberal agenda. In the fashion of the Progressive Era, these terms have come to connote a sense of the larger collective interest, over and above the private interests of employers. Recently, conservatives have attempted to reappropriate the "public interest" label—with some success.[60]

Most professionals working in human services have little directly to do with commercial and financial life. Moreover, the dominant ethos in this sphere has to do with improving the quality of life and the opportunities of the individual human beings served. It is not surprising, under these circumstances, that concentrations of welfare state sentiment, egalitarianism, and sympathy for the poor will be more frequent in this occupational sphere than in the others.

The human service professions are, however, only moderately liberal in profile, and they include many conservatives. One basis for heterogeneity comes from the bureaucratic and social control context in which so much human services work is conducted. Social control is as much an issue in human services as is social reform. Students, patients, and clients have to be managed, frequently against their will, as well as "helped." Often, case loads are much higher in human service bureaucracies than can reasonably be served effectively, even by the more talented and committed of practitioners. Under the circumstances, it is not surprising that many teachers, nurses, and social workers are highly authoritarian and oriented far more to social control than to active engagement with the lives of their clients. Even those who are sincerely interested in the welfare of their clients are only rarely zealous partisans. These people, after all, are close to the "front lines" in the social problems arena. Their sense of obligation to help is very often mixed with disapproval of the manner of living they find among their clients, patients, and students. The pressures of working with needy people lead many human service providers to disengage emotionally and, sometimes, to worry more about following authorized procedures than about solving problems. In short, this is a moderately reformist sphere, by and large, but its reformism is thoroughly mixed with "realism"—a sense of the severity of problems faced by those who are most in need of services, the limited effectiveness of many remedies, and the unreachableness of many who are afflicted by the problems of poverty and dependence.[61]

Although nominally part of the human services sphere, doctors and personal services attorneys are, in many ways, separate cases. They are far more affluent, in general, than other human services workers, and their training and self-image are also different. Most doctors think of themselves as applied scientists (in particular, as clinicians), rather than as members of a "helping profession."[62] Training in medicine is scientific, and doctors are taught to objectify their patients to a much greater degree than are other "human services" professionals. This training encourages an attitude that is not too different from that of applied scientists working on inanimate materials.[63] Social influences are also at work in the shaping of medical orientations. The objective, impersonal style of medicine has affinities with cultural orientations common among many high-income, predominantly male occupations from business executive to engineer.[64] Medical and legal professionals in human services work, do however, have some work-related attitudes that are consistent with the functional situation they share with other human service professionals. At every income level, they are somewhat more liberal politically than are comparable professionals from the more conservative business service and applied science spheres, and they are also somewhat more likely to talk at length about the problems of clients.[65]

ORGANIZATIONAL SECTORS

Sectoral location is the second great dimension in the organization of the contemporary professional stratum. The key analytical question in relation to sectoral development is why some forms of expertise are joined to profit-making activities and others are not. My analysis will be based on an application of theories about "collective goods" that are generally familiar to economists. To these economic theories, I will add, primarily, a somewhat stronger emphasis on the political forces influencing sectoral development. In this section, I will concentrate on showing why many professional activities are organized outside of the market economy, and how this fact influences the political and cultural divisions found among professionals.

Consumer and Collective Goods in the American Economy

In all of the advanced societies, the market is the economic tool and the private sector is the employer of first resort. All production that can be individually consumed, without involving extreme consequences due to information imbalances or large external effects, tends to develop as for-profit activity. This includes both the production of commodities that professionals work on, such as the engineering of airplane design or electronics components, and services that they provide, such as architectural design. In general, professions involved in the spheres of business services and applied technology are organized as private sector activities.

In theory, the state takes over only those activities where the market cannot be trusted to generate meaningful prices or adequate levels of provision. These include activities that cannot be parcelled out in discrete units to individual consumers (e.g., defense and public health regulation), that are necessary to control economic externalities (e.g., environmental regulation), and in other instances where the interests of the entire society are involved (e.g., historically, the provision of free public education through adolescence). Consequently, professions primarily involved in the provision of large-scale collective goods, such as legal administration, civic planning, mass transportation, utilities, education, social welfare, and national security are organized primarily as public sector activities.[66]

The American economy also includes a relatively large third sector (representing over 5 percent of the national income and more than 9 percent of total paid and volunteer employment).[67] This nonprofit sector is enormously heterogeneous. It includes everything from the National Geographic Society to the YWCA and the Sierra Club to the American Heart Association. It also includes labor unions, country clubs, charitable organizations, foundations, and scientific research laboratories. The organizations in the nonprofit economy cannot distribute profits to members or shareholders and are eligible for a variety of tax advantages and public subsidies, ranging from exclusion from income tax obligations, reduced postage rates, free public service advertising on radio and television, and, in many places, exemption from local property and sales taxes. Those who support nonprofits are able to deduct their donations from their own income taxes.

The nonprofit sector is composed of a crazy quilt of financing and operating forms. There are federally supported and privately operated research and development firms, particularly in the atomic energy field. There are privately organized institutions, like private universities, that rely on large levels of federal funding in scholarship and research support. There are nonprofits that spin-off profit-making activities, and for-profits that seek to protect some of their activities in nonprofit forms.

In theory, nonprofits are expected to respond to "the diversity of demands for public goods." Government provides collective goods for the majority, and nonprofits for "the undersatisfied." They provide collective commodities —education, charitable aid and comfort, research, culture, valued training, or membership benefits—either for a minority of the population, or above the minimum provided by government.[68] Nonprofit status turns on making a persuasive argument that market provision is dangerous or unsatisfactory to the society. Sometimes, as in the case of health care, the argument has emphasized that too many will be excluded if organization is primarily on the market. In other instances, the case relies on the argument that, regardless of the size of the interested group, some "socially beneficial" activity will not be provided adequately if provision is left to the private market.[69] This is the argument that provides nonprofit protection for many high culture and basic scientific research activities. Those organizations, like the Sierra Club and the Heart Fund, whose presumed benefits extend beyond its membership, usually gain the full range of benefits from nonprofit organization, while those, like labor unions and country clubs, whose benefits are limited to a particular membership, enjoy less extensive advantages and protections.

Economic theory provides a good general guide to the nature of the distribution of activities across sectors. This distribution, however, also reflects the imprint of political and legal decisions that might well have taken a different course. Many countries, for example, have publicly operated health systems, a course rejected in America for reasons having a good deal to do with the political power of the medical profession, the insurance industry, and other industries with a strong financial stake in the existing structure of health services.[70] Certain industries, like the railroads, energy companies, and the telephone service, have moved in and out of public ownership and regulating statuses, depending on their levels of profitability and the power of their allies in Congress and the courts.[71]

Recently, the theory of public goods itself has been subject to revisionist criticism. In the 1980s, advocates of privatization[72] argued for the greater efficiency of private vendors in many areas of service traditionally provided by government.[73] The combination of hard-pressed state resources and a conservative turn in ideology encouraged many new experiments with privatization and even a clear sectoral transformation in a few areas.[74] Two-thirds of American cities subcontracted garbage collection, and many states and localities also began to rely on private contractors to provide such "public goods" as day care, government office cleaning, water treatment plants, mass transit, and public-housing management. Other notable efforts to privatize in the 1980s included the selling of a major railroad system, the movement toward private management of corrections facilities, and experiments with public-private school choice programs. Recently, the federal government issued an executive order making it easier for state and local officials to sell public assets like airports, roads, bridges, and sewage treatment plants to private businesses.[75] For the time being, however, the experiments with privatization represent marginal changes involving a relatively small transfer of the public economy into private hands.[76]

The Sectoral Distribution of Professionals

Some professions have a very distinct profile based in the private sector. Engineers work overwhelmingly in business and industry (more than 80 percent are employed in the private sector), as do accountants, computer scientists, chemists, advertising and public relations people, journalists, and editors. Only about one in seven active lawyers works outside of private practice or other business employments.[77] Other professions are distributed rather evenly across sectors. Nondoctoral physicists are found mainly in industry, but government and educational institutions are also important employers.[78] Even among doctoral physicists, who are mainly academics, nearly one-quarter work in industry and more than one in five in government (including the national labs).[79] Foresters work both for the timber industry and for the national parks. Geologists are found in the largest numbers in the petroleum and mining industries, but over a third work in nonprofits or government.[80]

Yet one of the striking aspects of the division of expert labor is the extent to which professionals are employed in the public and nonprofit sectors. Indeed, the center of gravity for the stratum as a whole is in the nonprofit and public sector. This is true for no other major socioeconomic group. More than 85 percent of schoolteachers and social workers are employed in the public or nonprofit sectors,[81] as are nearly three-quarters of planners.[82] Judges, of course, are exclusively public officials. Among social scientists, private sector employment is also uncommon. Only economists and psychologists are employed in the private sector as much as 10 percent of the time.[83] Even among natural scientists, private sector employment is the norm only at the bachelor's and master's levels.

The extent of the public and nonprofit tilt in the distribution of the professional stratum depends quite a bit on the educational requirements that are used in the definition of the group. In so far as postbaccalaureate training becomes the norm for professional standing, the sectoral distribution of professionals increasingly runs in the opposite direction of that of the population at large. According to my calculations from General Social Survey and U.S. Census Department data, some 48 percent of all census professionals with bachelor's or higher-level degrees work in the public or nonprofit sector. When the educational criterion is raised to master's level or more, the proportion employed in the public or nonprofit sector increases to 55 percent. It reaches 60 percent when only people with doctorates or highest-level professional degrees, such as the M.D. or LL.B., are counted.[84]

The sectoral distribution of professionals is remarkable relative to the other major strata in the society. Less than one-third of blue-collar and clerical workers are employed in the public and nonprofit sectors, and scarcely 20 percent of executives, managers, and administrators are employed outside of the private economy. Organizationally, professionals alone among the major strata contribute to the production of "collective goods and services" more than they contribute to the production of "individual consumer goods and services." And the higher the educational criterion used for defining the professional group, the more likely they are to work outside of the private economy.

Sector, Ethos, and Politics

Many people continue to think of professionals as a kind of functional aristocracy in the Tocquevillian sense, that at their best professionals provide a kind of protection for desirable social values that a market society might otherwise threaten. But much of the "public spiritedness" of professionals is more accurately thought of as reflecting the ethos of the public and nonprofit sectors in which a disproportionate number of professional people work.

Several studies have established that public sector workers tend to be more public spirited and more liberal on matters of economic distribution. In the 1960s, sociologists established that a "professional service orientation," as opposed to an "organizational career orientation," was more common among public and nonprofit sector professionals, and particularly among human services workers.[85] More recently, the sociologist Michael Macy has shown that professionals' sectoral location is substantially associated with attitudes related to egalitarianism, concerns about the less advantaged, and opposition to the increased power of business.[86]

In part, these sectoral differences are due to differences in recruitment. People who feel a strong ideal interest in social reform are likely to find the public and nonprofit sectors comparatively congenial settings, and the private sector relatively less congenial. One study of law students found, for example, that, among equally able students, those attracted to public interest law were willing to trade off high incomes for the "nonpecuniary rewards" of activity they considered to be in the public good.[87] It is natural, under these circumstances, to find more criticism of the soullessness of the marketplace from outside of the marketplace, just as it is natural to find more criticism of the ham-handedness of government from outside of governmental organizations.

The internal organization of for-profits and nonprofits can reinforce these sorts of differences in the value profile of new recruits through a kind of motivational climate control. Frequently, implicit norms are built into the structure of organizations. Some years ago, the organizational sociologist Charles Perrow pointed out that cooperative organizations tend, among other things, to be those where continuing interactions are minimized, where the measurement of individual effort or contribution is discouraged, where interdependent effort through design of work flow and equipment is minimized, and where flat hierarchies are favored.[88]

In a similar fashion, public and nonprofit organizations may inadvertently reinforce egalitarian attitudes and concerns with equity issues through the way they structure ranks and rewards, as compared to the private sector. The variation in incomes across ranks tends, for example, to be notably lower in public and nonprofit organizations than in the corporate world.[89] This condition of low-income variance may be conducive to a greater degree of egalitarian sentiment (at least with regard to income) than would be typical if income differences were greater. Nor is it surprising to see more concern with broad social issues involving participation and community in environments where equity issues tend to figure more prominently in the structure of rewards.

These are, at most, contributing factors. It is the broad intersection of the social history of professional status and the political economy of sectoral development that is most important. Both the economic interests and mundane activities of the public and nonprofit sectors lend themselves to the projection of "public-spirited" ideologies. This connection flows directly out of the characteristic legitimations and characteristic activities surrounding the two sectors. It is, after all, explicitly the responsibility of the public and nonprofit sectors to provide collective goods. It follows that the tendency of professionals to uphold public interest ideologies owes more to their unusual sectoral distribution than to any more broad-based responsibility for the public good or to any latent "class conflict" with business elites.[90] Class conflicts certainly exist, but, to paraphrase Karl Marx, modern history may be more nearly a history of struggle between rival principles of cultural authority and organization than it is a history of struggles between classes as such.

Although both are comparatively liberal sectors, the public and nonprofit sectors have rather different political profiles. In the public sector, labor relations, consumer protection, and social spending agencies tend to be centers of what remains of welfare state liberalism in the United States. Other agencies are most often moderately Democratic in profile. Yet highly educated people with broadly progressive political views are attracted to the nonprofit sector to a greater degree than they are to the hard-pressed and singularly tax-dependent public sector, where constraints on imagination and the capacity to create and realize projects are greater—and where the problems of the disadvantaged are so manifestly pressing. While the public sector displays the more traditionally Democratic and liberal profile, the nonprofit sector consequently represents the major site for the joining of expertise to the broad goals of political progressivism.

The funding and recruitment patterns in the two sectors may well be connected, at least as a contributing factor, to the changing conceptions of "progressive" politics in the United States. The market-oriented "neoliberalism" and "neoconservatism" found so often in the third sector owes less to the New Deal and Great Society and more to the mixed reform and efficiency-mindedness of the Progressive movement.[91] Many of the ideas for "reinventing government" through entrepreneurial incentives originated in the nonprofits, including school vouchers, enterprise zones, and privatization.[92]

Professions in the Political Economy II: Markets

THE RELATIVE market value of different forms of expertise is the third—and in many ways the most important—dimension in the organization of expert labor in the American political economy. In this chapter, which continues the analysis of the political economy of professions begun in chapter 3, I will discuss the sources of market advantage and disadvantage among professional occupations, and I will also discuss the connections between market position and political outlooks.

The issue of market position is important because professional people, far from constituting an economically homogeneous stratum, are exceedingly diverse in the market situations they encounter. Near the summit of the professional world are the enormous and sprawling medical complexes, spanning primary care hospitals, university teaching hospitals, research institutes, physician offices, specialized medical businesses, and the various commercial enterprises that grow up around these complexes. Near its quite humble base are the comparatively spartan facilities of so many municipal welfare offices.

The people working in these settings are not typically part of the same income class. Doctors enjoy earnings that all but guarantee them upper-middle-class status or higher by mid-career. Social workers and other less well paid professionals may find themselves living from paycheck to paycheck—middle class in education, but not in income. Within the range marked by these extremes fall the remaining markets for expert services.

SOURCES OF MARKET ADVANTAGE

The claim to "formal knowledge" or "expertise" is one thing; being rewarded in relation to those claims is quite another. The collective claim to expertise is fruitless without people or organizations willing to pay for the expertise. But what makes people and organizations willing to compensate professionals at different levels for different kinds of expertise?

This is a more complex matter than it might seem at first. It is not simply a matter of how vital the service is. What could be more vital—in a literal sense—than the expertise of military officers, who are rather moderately paid as servants of the state? Nor is it simply a matter of certifiable effectiveness. In the years before the bacteriological revolution, physicians were unable to cure many diseases and often had the effect of making matters worse than they already were. Today, psychoanalysts, the leading therapeutic group, have not been able to establish conclusively that they are more effective in general than other forms of therapy, whatever benefits they may be shown to provide for particular individuals.[1] Nor is the market value of professional knowledge simply a matter of rigor and complexity. Physicists and mathematicians, whose knowledge is among the most complex in the professional world, are paid less, on average, than optometrists. These exceptions suggest the degree of complexity involved in understanding the market situation of people whose economic prospects nominally derive from their "specialized cultures" but actually derive, to a greater degree, from a complex mix of market, organizational, legal, and compositional factors.

Individual-level sources of market value among professionals are comparatively well understood as compared to sources of market value at the *occupational level*. As in the labor force generally, the high-income professional labor force is composed disproportionately of older white males with many years of seniority and experience and with advanced degrees. The lower income layers are composed more often of younger nonwhites and women with less experience and lower-level degrees.[2]

Since the income differences at the occupational level are much less completely understood,[3] I will concentrate on this level.[4] A good many of the sources of difference between the professional occupations have to do with features of the organizational environment in which professions are situated; private practice and organizational centrality are major influences. "Upper professionals" are precisely those people who have not only highly valued intellectual resources, but who also work for resource-rich organizations. It is the combination, not the one or the other, that is important. A few other influences are also important. My analysis will concentrate on five sources of market advantage among professions. These are, in approximate order of importance: (1) the capacity of professions to organize in private or group practice; (2) for salaried professionals only, the industrial location in which members of the profession are predominantly employed; (3) again, for salaried professionals, location in the "industrial-corporate core" (or "technostructure") within organizations; (4) legal and other sources of valuable task area monopolies; and (5) the gender composition of the occupation.[5]

Advantageous Forms of Practice

Private and group practice settings are, in general, the most advantageous setting for professionals, at least for those who are entitled to share the profits of practice. When professionals work for others—whether these others are private corporations, universities, or government—their earnings tend to be lower than they are when they are organized to share directly in the revenues produced by practice. At the same time, the market situation of private practitioners is clearly related not just to the situation of self-employment per se, but also to the social status of clients and to the complexity of the work those clients require. Because of the low status of many of their clients and the routine nature of much of their work, solo practitioners are at the bottom of the economic hierarchy in law, while, for opposite reasons, firm-based practitioners with largely corporate clients are at the top.[6]

Nevertheless, in the typical case, the capacity to organize autonomously is of the utmost importance, because it gives a few favored professions leverage over potential state and corporate employers, who are inclined to limit compensation to professional employees at least in relation to higher-level managerial employees. It also provides a high level of leverage over individual consumers, who are unorganized and, as such, are largely dependent on the good counsel of practitioners.[7]

Comparative Income Data. The advantages of private practice are evident in the comparative income data on professional occupations. Those occupations where private practice is the norm are the most highly remunerated on average, although they also have high standard deviations around the mean income level.[8] In the professional world, the highest average net incomes (after expenses, and before taxes) are made by doctors (over $130,000 in 1989),[9] psychiatrists—who, of course, are also doctors—(over $100,000 in 1989),[10] lawyers (approximately $80–$85,000 in 1989),[11] dentists ($75,000 in 1988),[12] and optometrists (approximately $71,000 in 1989).[13] All of these are predominantly private-practice professions.

These average income levels contrast sharply with those of more decidedly middle-income professional occupations like college professor. The average optometrist, performing the comparatively humble task of evaluating eyesight and prescribing corrections, earns nearly twice the income of the average liberal arts professor. The average dentist earns approximately twice as much; the average lawyer in private practice two and one-half times as much; and the average doctor more than three times as much.[14]

The existence of a realistic private-practice option also has an indirect effect on salaries; it tends to raise the salaries of professional people in the same occupation who are not in private practice, provided that the option is viable (that is, a large proportion work in private practice) and provided that the customary differences in earnings between sectors are large.[15] Thus, according to the most recent survey, medical professors earned in university salary alone more than twice as much as the average full professors earned.[16] Where the private-practice option is less significant and where the differences in earnings between sectors are less pronounced, the effects of the private practice option on earnings outside of private practice are relatively weak.

In business service occupations, the traditional economic advantages of private practice are even more profound but limited almost exclusively to the partners of the firms and their senior associates.[17] In architecture, for example, the size of the firm is the most important influence on whether building is done mainly for organizations or for individuals, and also on the size of the incomes of partners and senior associates.[18] It is not, however, an important influence on the size of the incomes of lower-level architects. The same highly stratified pattern, with substantial advantages to partners but only weak income advantages to lower-level associates, holds also in the larger law, accounting, and management consulting firms.[19]

Sources of the Private Practice Option. High incomes in the private practice professions can be regarded as a return to the risk of failing in entrepreneurial activity, and as compensation for the capital outlays involved in setting up a practice, which are substantial and include equipment, insurance, and business development activities. It is true that the standard deviation of incomes for those in private practice is much greater than for those who are salaried.[20] However, outright failures and other substantial risks are apparently not common in most fields where private practice is the norm.[21]

Even if failures were relatively common, a challenging question would remain: why are these risks—and the very substantial rewards—of private practice available to some professions and not to others? This question involves two separate answers: one for personal-service occupations and another for business-service occupations.

Client vulnerability is the original source of advantage in the personal-service professions. People quite naturally like to feel a special confidence in those who are in the position to save or ruin them in gravely important, event-focused situations. Most would prefer to work with a personally trusted individual, and also with one whose skill and performance level is known to be well-tested and guaranteed at the highest levels, rather than, say, with the hired hands of an impersonal organization, who are more easily perceived as "just doing their job."

From the beginning, the "gentlemanly" status of practitioners backed up their implicit claims to trustworthiness, and frequently substituted for more direct evidence of this trustworthiness. It is also true that a number of institutional elements quickly came into play in protecting the position of the most favored professional occupations. Legal entitlements to monopolization of key practices—pleading in court and diagnosing disease—supported, indeed cemented, the favorable position of the "classical" professions. Once these legal entitlements entered into regulating professional life, doctors, who had been powerful because they were trusted in existentially important circumstances, became powerful, in large part because they were the only ones with the legal right to diagnose and prescribe and, therefore, intervene directly in these kinds of situations.

Over time, other institutional factors have further reinforced the favored situation of some of the established private-practice professions. For example, the medical insurance system, while often attempting to contain health costs, actually helped to guarantee the ability of doctors to sustain autonomous professional organization by guaranteeing demand for services and assuring steady flows of income among those protected by health insurance.[22]

Business services are organized autonomously for reasons having to do with the episodic demand for these services. Business services are generally required by clients for a one-time-only purpose (or, at most, involve highly discontinuous demands). This sort of one-time-only or episodic work is precisely the kind that organizations characteristically subcontract, because it is not economically rational to keep a staff of specialists on the payroll who will work infrequently at most.[23] The same discontinuous demand situation underlies private practice among management consultants, advertisers, and CPAs.

It follows that the greater the costliness of discontinuous projects and the more they require specialized teams of professionals to accomplish, the more likely that work will be organized through autonomous professional firms rather than through the employment of professional staffs by corporations or government. These factors make the cost of keeping professionals on staff much too great for any given organization to handle. Large-scale building projects, large-scale publicity projects, and large-scale interventions into management organization are handled more or less exclusively by autonomously organized professional firms. By contrast, most corporations (and all of the largest corporations) have their own legal and accounting staffs to handle relatively routine, ongoing legal and financial work and seek outside professional services only for highly consequential or highly specialized projects.[24]

Advantageous Industry Locations

The private sector is where the largest share of wealth exists, and, from a purely economic point of view, it is highly advantageous for professions to be located predominantly in the private sector. Of the forces related to industrial organization, sectoral location has the most general effects on professional salaries. However, some important specific advantages also exist for professionals working in particular industries and markets.

Sectoral Differences. The major reason for the difference in professional salaries between sectors is plain. In a mixed economy, people are more willing to pay for goods and services they can individually consume than for goods and services that are collectively consumed. For collective goods, consumers will be inclined to "let the other fellow pay" and ride along for free, enjoying benefits and little cost. To overcome this problem, the state must impose obligations for payment, but can do so only at a rate that neither fuels resentment about "confiscatory" tax rates nor harms the capital accumulation process. The public sector is always comparatively poor, more or less so depending on the moods of taxpayers, the state of the economy, and the nature of the prevailing fiscal conditions.

The situation in the nonprofit sector is far more varied because of the many different funding patterns that can be found in this sector. Nevertheless, except in a very few instances, each of the conditions leads to a financial situation more like the public than the private sector. Many nonprofits (such as labor unions and environmental groups) rely mainly on contributions and donations. These nonprofits face the same difficulties as public sector organizations. Some nonprofits (such as opera companies) sell their services on the market but have high costs and limited audiences, which keeps the surplus that can be distributed to the professional staff low. Even where a market rate could theoretically be established at a profitable level (as in the case of Ivy League colleges), publicly subsidized nonprofits accept an obligation to keep prices below the potential market rate so as to respond to social and not simply to economic goals.

Comparative Income Data. The comparative evidence confirms that employment sector has a substantial independent influence on incomes. Where the support of an organization is from taxes, dues, or contributions, the average salaries of professional staff are lower than when the organization runs on profits from the sale of commodities or services. Differences in median salaries across sectors are on the order of $10,000 annually between business and government salaries and more than that between business and academic salaries.

The professions that are mainly located in business and industry are able to bring up the incomes of those in the profession who are working outside of the private sector. In Table 4.1, this effect is particularly notable in occupations like engineering and chemistry where the great majority works in the private sector. Similarly, geoscientists and computer scientists, two groups for whom private sector employment is typical, show a relatively tight clustering of industry, government, and academic salary levels. Foresters, who are located more often in the public sector, show, by contrast, greater income gaps across sectors.[25] The private sector option quite naturally provides less pressure on salaries in occupations like physics, mathematics, and psychology, where the majority work outside of the business world.

Specific Industry and Market Effects. In the United States, a handful of industries are uncommonly profitable, and the professionals employed in them benefit proportionately. These industries either tend to monopolize the provision of a critical resource, like petroleum or health diagnosis, or have benefitted from high barriers to entry in relation to a product (like military hardware, prescription pharmaceuticals, consumer electronics, and broadcast and film entertainment) that has been rather insatiably demanded by government or private consumers.[26]

In a few professional occupations, the size of the market served also makes a difference on incomes. This is particularly true in journalism. Senior reporters and editors in the national media earn more than twice as much as their counterparts in the small regional markets.[27] In television, salaries are very closely aligned to the size of the market in which the professional personnel are working. The larger the market, the higher the price of the advertising

72 · CHAPTER 4 ·

TABLE 4.1
Median Base Salaries across Sectors for Selected Professions (in dollars)

Occupation	Business and Industry	Government	Academe
Ph.D. Physicists (1989)	69,000	56,900	51,300
Ph.D. Chemists (1988)	64,600	55,600	50,000
M.S. Chemists (1988)	48,000	42,000	35,500
M.S. and Ph.D. Engineers[a] (1989)	52,600	45,900	48,000
New Ph.D. Mathematicians (1989)	49,500	37,800	36,500
Midcareer Ph.D. Psychologists (1989)[b]	67,000	47,000	49,900
Midcareer Ph.D. Economists (1988–89)[c]	65,000	>49,000	>53,000

Sources: American Mathematics Association, *Annual AMS-MAA Survey,* 1224–26; American Institute of Chemists, *The Chemist* 66 (May 1989); American Institute of Physics, *1989 Salaries: Society Membership Survey* (New York: AIP, 1990), 9; American Geological Institute, *North American Survey of Geoscientists* (Alexandria, Va.: AGI, 1988), 35; Commission on Professionals in Science and Technology, *Salaries of Scientists, Engineers and Technicians* (Washington, D.C.: CPST, 1990), 121, 175, 177; American Psychological Association, *1989 Salaries in Psychology* (Washington, D.C.: APA, 1989); National Association of Business Economists, *NABE Salary Survey 1988* (Cleveland: NABE, 1989); U.S. Department of Commerce, Bureau of Labor Statistics, *Occupational Outlook Handbook, 1990–91 edition* (Washington, D.C.: Government Printing Office, 1990). Bulletin 2350; College and University Personnel Association, *1989 Faculty Survey* (Washington, D.C.: CUPA, 1989).

[a] The salary data for engineers combines data from three surveys: the National Society of Professional Engineers survey (for industry and government) and the two College and University Personnel surveys (for faculty). The business and industry figure is based on engineers employed by manufacturers and extractive industries. The government figure is based on a weighted average of the median salaries of engineers employed by federal (including military), state, and local governments.

[b] Incomes of Ph.D. psychologists are approximate. These data, based on survey of members of the American Psychological Association, were available only by years of experience. The median figures provided are estimated for psychologists with 10–14 years experience. The business and industry figure is based on psychologists in applied industrial and organizational psychology and managers in applied industrial and organizational psychology. The government figure is based on psychologists' work in public mental health hospitals, VA hospitals, community mental health centers, and administrators in these settings.

[c] Academic figure for economists is for 1989. It is based on an average from separate surveys of public and private universities by the College and University Personnel Association. Business and government figures are for 1988 and estimated from National Association of Business Economist data, combined with data from the federal government on nonbusiness-related functional areas.

minute, and, consequently, the higher the salaries of the professional people who help to attract potential consumers to the medium.

In some markets, the character of competition for talent also matters. Computing and electronics engineering talent, for example, has tended to cluster around Silicon Valley in California, Route 128 in the Boston area, and a few other locales with numerous high technology employers, who are willing to pay premium salaries for top-flight talent. Where the concentrations of talent are great, and the number of potential employers numerous, salaries tend to be high, because professionals can play one potential employer off another.

Advantageous Positions within Organizations

Another important source of market advantage derives, to use John Kenneth Galbraith's phrase, from work in the "technostructure"[28] —or, to put it another way, in the "industrial-corporate core" occupations. These techno-structure occupations can be described as combining three specific sources of advantage: (1) high value-added organizational applications, (2) rigorous and demanding technical cultures, and (3) high levels of integration with management. By the term "high value-added applications," I mean work that is closely related to profit potentials, critical environmental uncertainties, or managerial effectiveness.

The occupations in the industrial-corporate core include engineers and scientists, mathematicians and statisticians, lawyers, economists, marketing experts, and applied psychologists (whose work mainly involves counseling and motivating men and women for organizational purposes). They also include the higher levels of accountants, financial analysts, computer specialists, and other information specialists.

Comparative Income Data. Comparative income data clearly demonstrates the importance of location in the "industrial-corporate core." The highest median salaries among professional people employed in private industry are earned by lawyers, engineers, mathematicians, physical and chemical scientists, and economists. Each of these occupational groups has a reputation for combining high "value added" applications to production and management, a highly rigorous technical culture, and high average levels of integration with management. (See Table 4.2.)

High value-added applications are the most important of the three sources of value in the "technostructure." For employed professionals, the critical question is: "What do organizations value in their specialists?" The answer is that organizations are disposed to value expertise that is translatable into profit, prestige, control of major environmental uncertainties, and/or improved managerial effectiveness. Engineers who design the products that are brought to market have high applied knowledge value for organizations. So do the computer scientists who simplify or augment management information systems. And so do the marketing experts who help to identify or broaden product markets.

Significant areas of variation in earnings by specialty area also follow the principle that "value added" applications are most important. In the engineering field, the more advanced and the more expensive the technology, the higher the average salary.[29] In law, corporate and tax lawyers earn more than

TABLE 4.2
Median Base Salaries of Selected Professional Groups
by Employment Characteristics (in dollars)

	Beginning Salaries for New Baccalaureate Graduates (1989–90)	Nonsupervisory Professionals with Master's or First Professional Degree (1989)	Doctoral Salaries in Business and Industry (1987)
Industrial-Corporate Core Occupations			
Engineers	32,000	52,300	60,300
Physicists	28,800	53,200	57,200
Mathematicians	25,000	52,100	58,000
Computer scientists	31,400	48,100	57,500
Chemists	26,000	47,600	55,200
Lawyers		>60,000[a]	
Business Economists[b]	>30,000	50,600	65,000
Other Occupations			
Life Scientists	20,700[c]	39,900	48,000
Accountants	27,000	>34,000[a]	
Nurses	27,400	>34,000[a]	
Social Scientists (other than Economists and Psychologists)	21,300		>49,000[a]
School Teachers	20,700	29,500	
Journalists	18,300	>34,000[a]	

Sources: (1) Recent college graduates: Michigan State University, Career Development and Placement Service, *Recruiting Trends, 1989–90* (East Lansing: Michigan State University, 1989); U.S. Department of Labor, *Occupational Outlook Handbook, 1988–89 edition* (Washington, D.C.: Government Printing Office, 1989); National Association of Business Economists, *Salary Characteristics 1988* (Cleveland: NABE, 1988). (2) Nonsupervisory personnel with Master's or First Professional Degrees: The Hay Group, *National Compensation Survey of Research and Development Scientists and Engineers* (Washington, D.C.: The Hay Group, 1989); U.S. Department of Labor, *National Survey of Professional, Administrative, Technical and Clerical Pay: Private Nonservice Industries* (Washington, D.C.: Government Printing Office, 1988); Abbott, Langer, and Associates, *Compensation in the Accounting/Financial Field, 1989* (Crete, Ill.: Abbott Langer Associates, 1989); American Nursing Association, *Nursing and the American Nursing Association* (Kansas City, Mo.: ANA, 1991); National Education Association, *Data-Search, 1990* (Washington, D.C.: NEA, 1990); National Association of Business Economists, *Salary Characteristics 1988*. (3) Doctoral Salaries: National Science Foundation, *Characteristics of Doctoral Scientists and Engineers in the United States, 1987* (Washington, D.C.: NSF, 1989); Commission on Professionals in Science and Technology, *Salaries of Scientists, Engineers, and Technicians* (Washington, D.C.: CPST, 1990); National Association of Business Economists, *NABE Salary Survey, 1988.*

[a] Where data was not consistent, an estimate is given, within a $5,000 range. Thus, nonsupervisory accountants, nurses, and journalists with professional degrees had average salaries

(continued)

those concerned with labor, consumer complaints, and general litigation. This follows from the hierarchy of upper management concerns.[30]

If organizational applications are significant enough, professional incomes will be comparatively high even if the occupational culture is not technical and, indeed, even if it is not especially deferential to business norms. This is clear in "talent professions" like screenwriting, acting, and athletics. But it is also clear in occupations that are more clearly part of the expert services group. Thus, for example, star reporters in the newspaper industry, graphic designers in the advertising industry, and marketing specialists virtually everywhere all fare relatively well, in spite of relying on rather weakly developed technical cultures. Conversely, even if the culture is rigorous, complex, and scientifically based, the occupation will not have high average incomes if, as in the case of lower-level computer and accounting work, the work performed is perceived by managers as relatively routine.

Technical culture is important as an independent factor, if only because it is taken by organizations to signal the ability of professional personnel to think, coordinate, and contribute. Technical training in highly demanding fields is taken by personnel officers to be a good guarantee that new recruits have organizationally relevant reasoning ability. The fields that contain the most students who score high on standardized tests are, in virtually every case, those where starting salaries are also highest—and indeed, in general, the higher the average test scores the higher the starting salaries.

Successful completion of work in these demanding fields may also be taken as an indicator of desirable work orientations (from the point of view of corporate management), in addition to sheer reasoning ability. These desirable work orientations include the capacity to concentrate on problems developed by others, to exercise "sound judgment" in relation to assigned problems, to turn in a respectable performance of assigned tasks, to present a businesslike appearance and demeanor, and to interact in a nonantagonistic way with organizational superiors.[31] The particular influence of technical culture on beginning salaries is one indicator that technical culture serves as an important market signal. (See Table 4.2, column 1.)

Advantageous Forms of Closure and Task Area Monopoly

It has often been argued that the chief advantages of professions lie in their ability to close off market opportunities from potential competitors, partic-

---

between $29,000 and $34,000 per year in 1988, but I am unable to be more specific given conflicts between or gaps in the available data.

[b] Figures are for 1988. More than one-quarter of business economists reported additional primary income above the base salary. The median amount of the additional primary income was $8,000. The beginning salaries are estimated from grouped data (0–4 years experience). Ninety percent of business economists had education beyond the baccalaureate.

[c] This figure is unavailable for 1989–90 and is estimated from the growth rate in average salaries from 1988–89 data.

ularly through legal protections and educational barriers to entry.[32] I am only partly in agreement with these emphases in so far as they are meant to explain the relative incomes of professional occupations. While some forms of "closure" are clearly beneficial to the providers of expert services, in other instances, closure efforts are a sign of weakness rather than strength. In particular, important differences exist between legal and educational forms of closure.[33]

Legal versus Educational Closure. The legal form of closure is nearly always economically beneficial. Legal mandates to exclusive practice are particularly important for the creation of exploitable market shelters in several of the private practice occupations. As the sole valid officers of the court, lawyers are in the position to add hundreds and thousands of unnecessary dollars to the processing of wills and real estate documents. Those with medical certifications can play on their unique rights to prescribe drugs to charge higher rates for services exactly equivalent to those offered elsewhere. Psychiatrists bill at twice the rate of social workers,[34] without providing verifiably superior treatment apart from the effects of the drugs they prescribe.[35] Sometimes, the benefits of legal guarantees are indirect. By creating a guaranteed market in one sphere, these legal rights of practice can also encourage privileged access to new markets for services in related spheres. This occurred, for example, in the development of management-consulting services out of the audit function of certified public accounting firms.[36]

In contrast to legally protected access, educational requirements often promise more than they can deliver. In particular, efforts to control supply and improve market power through increasing education and licensing standards are useless if the services provided are not in demand. Acupuncturists, for example, are carefully trained and tested, but most are barely able to scratch out an existence.[37] When a demand does not exist, as in the case of acupuncture, the numbers of practitioners are naturally limited; no matter how rigorous the training and licensing procedures, opportunities will be scarce. For the least advantaged professions, elaborate credentialing procedures represent a largely futile effort to improve a hardly improvable market situation.

By contrast, in the most advantaged professions, such as medicine, increasing the supply of credentialed professionals often has little effect on salaries. Far from following the laws of supply and demand, it appears that the great majority of doctors are able to set a target income, based on a (high) normative standard, and then work to the point that that target is met or surpassed. If necessary, the fees needed to meet targets can be generated through such mechanisms as increasing the number of procedures required for diagnosis or by accepting marginal and nuisance cases that would otherwise be avoided.

In many of the applied science and business service professions, the mechanisms for creating educational barriers to entry swirl like sticks in the wind of strong corporate demand for skilled personnel. Many academic programs in accounting, business administration, computer science, and even architecture (where certification requirements are otherwise stiff) are not accredited, and whether a program is accredited or not appears to have little effect on student enrollments.[38] Nor does it appear that graduation from accredited programs has a decisive effect on students' labor market opportunities in many of these fields. Engineering is an exception to the rule of indifference to accreditation in "industrial-corporate core" occupations. In 1991, some 90 percent of undergraduate engineering students (and 70 percent of master's students) graduated from accredited programs. One benefit of accreditation in engineering is that, in some states, graduation from an accredited program allows students to bypass licensing requirements.[39]

Certification tests also fail to attract support. The efforts of professional associations to develop certification examinations in fields such as engineering and computing fail to entice a majority and sometimes attract no more than a few.[40] Because of the frequent lack of demonstrable producer (or consumer) protection provided by such tests, the interests of the certifying agencies themselves often appear to be more in the area of making money than raising standards.[41]

It may be that in heteronomously controlled and highly hierarchical organizations, equal competence creates problems rather than advantages. Consequently, a simple rule may be that where organizational control over the conditions of professional life is great and opportunities for employment relatively abundant, the mechanisms of restrictive educational closure are often deemphasized by professionals and their employers alike. The truly incompetent are weeded out in the educational selection process itself.

Other Sources of Task Area Monopoly. Closure mechanisms are not the only way to strengthen task area monopolies. Professions can also improve or fortify their situation by outdoing competitors in controlling new technologies and organizational resources, providing more generalizable or efficacious solutions to problems, and by positioning themselves adroitly in relation to price and quality niches in the market for services.[42]

Is this competitive struggle for jurisdictions a key to understanding the relative market power of the various professions? Again, the effects of successful competition for task area jurisdictions are variable. Certainly, it is highly advantageous for an occupation to monopolize a high-demand task area. Whether this is due to legal guarantees or competitive success, the result is the same. To the extent that economists can gain a monopoly on giving advice in the area of public policy, for example, they are in a stronger position than would otherwise be the case. If construction engineers were somehow able to establish a monopoly in the area of building design, they would obviously be in a demonstrably stronger position than they currently are in their competition with architects for design and construction markets.

However, struggles for control over low-demand or low-price jurisdictions will have relatively negligible economic consequences. There is little advantage in successfully holding the exclusive right to treat the personal problems of the indigent if that jurisdiction is socially constituted as a very low-paying jurisdiction. Similarly, if the philologists succumb to the literary critics and social historians in the scholarly field of classical studies, the latter scholars nevertheless remain situated in a relatively weak market.

Because organizational managers are generally responsible for assigning work, it is not just the competitive situation between professions, but also the perceived organizational applications of the occupational competence that counts in who gets economically valuable work. Thus, it appears that the oil companies prefer petroleum engineers, who are comparatively singleminded in their interests, to geologists in assigning their geoscientific work.[43] Similarly, it was the leaders of the entertainment industry, influenced by the tastes of the consumer market, who decided that television news must have entertainment value as well as news value, thereby creating that hybrid occupation, the journalist-entertainer.

Precisely because organizations and markets are so consequential in the forming and fuzzing of jurisdictions, there are reasons to believe that task area monopolization is often less important than diffuse legitimacy. Organizations are primarily interested in accomplishing tasks in an effective way. They do not necessarily care very much that any particular occupation does the desired work. What many of the more successful professional occupations want is to gain recognition for the inculcation of high-level and highly efficacious skills. Some occupations—those in the "industrial-corporate" core, in particular— have succeeded to a considerable degree in this effort to gain diffuse legitimacy, while other occupations have tended to fail.

Advantageous Gender Composition

The effects of occupational sex segregation are apparent throughout the occupational structure; professional occupations are not unique in reflecting this pattern.[44] However, there are indications that professional occupations are affected more decisively than lower-status occupations by their gender composition.[45]

The traditionally female professions of schoolteaching, nursing, social work, and librarianship are among the least well paid professional occupations. In recent years, practitioners in these four occupations have attained average incomes only a little higher than that of the average American worker and far lower than was typical among the predominantly male professions. The earnings of employed, mid-level attorneys, engineers, chemists, and professors have remained, for example, between one and one-half and two times higher than the salary of mid-level schoolteachers in recent years.[46]

Observers have disagreed about whether the jobs are poorly paid because they are held mainly by women or whether poor pay has to do with characteristics of the jobs themselves. Certainly, the jobs share some characteristics that lead to low pay generally: location mainly in the public and nonprofit sectors; lower average educational qualifications and poorer average test performance; and, with the exception of nurses, a less certain and less demanding system of formal knowledge. The comparatively weak economic situation of the feminine professions is clearly overdetermined.

Comparative Income Data. The only reasonable conclusion is that gender composition is in all likelihood a separate source of low pay in these occupations. Nurses, for example, are paid at approximately the same rate as drafters and electronics technicians, two predominantly male occupations that require less education and much less independent judgment.[47] Nurses can also be compared with pharmacists, some three-quarters of whom are men and all of whom also work in the health field. Pharmacists, who after all mainly fill prescriptions, earn approximately 1.2 times the salary of nurses with comparable degrees.[48] A similarly illuminating comparison can be made between the predominantly male public sector occupation of planner and the predominantly female public sector occupations of teacher and social worker. Much planning work is quite routine, involving the processing of applications for zoning waivers, reviewing development plans, and routine monitoring of city services. Yet within comparable education groups, planners earn approximately 1.2 to 1.3 times more annually than the two predominantly female occupations.[49]

The Declining Significance of Gender? High female concentration may depress incomes directly and also indirectly, by encouraging less autonomy in relation to associated occupations than would otherwise exist. However, the market situation of the female professions can be improved by the same forces that improve the market situation of predominantly male professions.

For this reason, the prospects for at least two of the traditionally female professions may be more promising in the future, because of the work they do and the industries in which they work. Nurses already have made some advances. Starting salaries for nurses are comparable to starting salaries in most of the predominantly male occupations (see Table 4.2), and nurse-practitioners, the elite of the profession, now can expect to earn about as much as a middle-class group like professors. Nurses have succeeded, to a degree, in raising standards and expanding responsibilities, and, most importantly, they have caught hold of a small share in the fallout from the great medical boom of the 1980s and 1990s. Librarians continue to lag in earnings,[50] but it is at least possible to envision an upward trajectory in which a more assertive profession took advantage of its strategic location in the "information economy" by becoming more complete experts in the conception, management, and design of qualitative information resources.[57] In France, female librarians have led the movement into these new jurisdictions, and feminization has gone hand in hand with a rise in status.[52]

MARKET POSITION AND POLITICAL OUTLOOK

The political outlooks of professionals are associated in important ways with their situation in the labor and commodity markets. Indeed, income is one of the strongest predictors of political and social views in the population at large, and the relationship is no less strong among professionals.

Those who earn high incomes quite naturally tend to see the virtues in the system that has rewarded them so generously. They tend to associate with people who have strong economic stakes in the established patterns of authority and resource distribution, and, even when they are not business people themselves, they very often think like business people. They may feel some sympathy for the difficulties of the poor; they are unlikely to feel any livelier identification. By contrast, those who earn lower incomes, especially if they are intelligent and hard-working, are less likely to see the virtues of the established authorities so clearly.[53]

Professionals who fall lower on the ladder of economic success are more often the carriers of the "public service" ethic. These are people who have distinguished themselves from the masses by virtue of their educational attainment—and often also by virtue of their sense of themselves as "specialists"—but they have not greatly distinguished themselves in terms of economic class situation. They may even feel a certain amount of resentment toward the wealthy and powerful, who, for all their material success, may seem to lack moral virtue, that inexhaustible point of distinction among intelligent but relatively powerless people.[54] This is still more true of those who find themselves at the margins of the professional world—particularly in the sphere of "proletarianized" academic, artistic, and social service work. Here nominally professional workers are often in self-conception critical intellectuals, and may consider themselves not simply the protectors of the less advantaged, but also their uncompromising advocates.[55]

High income nevertheless has contrasting effects across issues. On the one side, affluence is associated with conservative attitudes on virtually all economic issues. At the same time, high income also encourages a sense of psychic security that can lead to greater tolerance on some social issues. More affluent professional people are less directly threatened by the aspirations of women and minorities, for example—many barriers and selection points exist between themselves and less advantaged people. They may, therefore, find it easier to express liberal views about improving the situation of the less advantaged. By contrast, ethnic and religious conflict has persistently influenced the high levels of social conservatism found among America's far less insulated white lower-middle-income classes.[56]

Income divisions are far from the only important influence on political views in the professional stratum, but they are of great importance. Indeed, as I will show later in the book, income differences among professionals are more important in America than they are in some of the other industrial democracies. Behind much of this unusual influence is an important national difference: traditional status characteristics related to higher educational training have more binding force in Europe, while sheer economic divisions are of greater consequence in the "born bourgeois" United States.[57] It follows that, in so far as income divisions grow between professional people, so too do the potential political divisions that separate them.

Culture and Politics

THE ANALYSIS of the last three chapters provides the foundations for a new way of thinking about the culture and politics of the professional middle class. It suggests reasons why professionals may have some cultural values in common and yet differ very substantially in their political views. In this chapter, I will analyze what the empirical evidence says about the culture and politics of the professional middle class, using survey data to test the implications of the theoretical work of the previous three chapters.

Most professionals, I have argued, share a distinctive matrix of experience by simultaneously occupying the situation of high-ranking organizational employee, merchant of marketable "cultural capital," and specialist in a body of complex learning. At the same time, professionals are not the same *kinds* of organizational staff officers, skill merchants, and occupational practitioners. The organizations they work for have different interests; their credentials and training provide different levels of privilege in the labor and commodity markets; and their occupations are based on substantively different kinds of knowledge bases. What is similar in the outlook of professional workers, as compared to other groups, is largely traceable to qualities arising from the particular matrix of conditions they share. The differences among them develop, in similar manner, along the lines of the most significant organizational, market, and occupational cleavages.

THE CULTURE OF PROFESSIONALISM

The most provocative views of the culture and politics of professionals emphasize differences between highly educated professionals and other middle and upper-middle-class groups, particularly between professionals and business people. Those who think of professionals as a "new class" in embryo note oppositional elements in the culture of professionalism. Two characteristics have been mentioned with some frequency as central to this alternative "class consciousness": an emphasis on *critical rationality* and an emphasis on *moral commitments*. Professionals, it is said, operate in a "culture of critical discourse" and project a high-minded moral idealism that stands in sharp contrast to the utilitarianism of business elites.[1]

The available evidence is not, however, kind to these ideas that emphasize oppositional qualities in professional culture. *Analytical rationality* is common among professionals, but critical rationality is not. *Critical rationality* requires examination of domain assumptions and standard understandings of problems; analytical rationality does not. Analytical rationality takes the framework in which it works as given. Strongly expressed commitments to analytical rationality are certainly common among professionals, but they are equally common among managers and executives. The major difference is in the ends to which analytic rationality is directed. In the corporations, these have ultimately to do with profitability. In the professions, they frequently have more to do with other ends, or toward profit in the market for reputations.[2] (It is worth noting that even analytical rationality may not strongly influence the actual practices of professional life. Most professional work is based on implicit knowledge, and follows a grid of standard procedures, routines, and uninspected understandings of situations that are tacitly supported by others.[3] Status-based deference patterns and political maneuvering for advantage also bulk large in the actual practice both of professionals and managers.)[4]

If moral commitment is measured as a concern with the social ideals served by the profession, the available evidence suggests that it is not a characteristic central to the major professional occupations, or even very common within them. Most professionals now justify their work on the basis of its technical complexity, not its social contribution. Professionals are becoming less likely to emphasize selfless service to clients than to emphasize the market demand for expert services. Great emphasis on the ideals surrounding professional activity is prevalent only among the "helping professions" and other professions that have a less secure cognitive authority. It is also relatively common among professionals who are sheltered from the market in activities of the nonprofit sector, and among professional elites who represent the professions and the professional associations to the broader public.[5]

Once we get past these provocative but false conceptions, the issue of common culture remains. It goes without saying that there are innumerable cultural differences among professionals. In the midst of this diversity, do any real points of cultural contact exist? The available evidence does suggest that professionals are distinctive in a few respects. It is possible to talk about these as characteristics of a kind of "class culture," but it is a class culture different only in degree—often rather small—from that of highly educated managers and executives.

Elements of the Contemporary Culture of Professionalism

Since traditional legitimations of social trustee professionalism no longer have great force, it is not surprising that discussions of professional culture are on stronger ground when they begin to concentrate on relations between cultural values and the special status and position of expert labor in the political economy. Because of their special situation of employment, professionals are inclined to show particularly strong support for education and academic meritocracy, to feel a strong affinity for the values of autonomy and self-direction, and to look sympathetically on ideas that attempt to synthesize or balance competing value commitments. In addition, the contemporary culture of professionalism is stamped by the expectations of others about the character and conduct of professional life. These expectations are virtually unchanged from the late nineteenth century. Today, as before, they focus on the combination of rationalistic outlook, matter-of-fact competence, and middle-class respectability.

Education and Academic Meritocracy. For professionals, higher education provides the credentials, skills, and training that allows for opportunities on the labor market and authority within organizations. Since no other group in the society is as dependent on education, it is not surprising that no other group values it as highly.

A number of empirical indicators suggest that professionals have a distinctively high level of commitment to education. These include their very high levels of support for spending on the educational system,[6] their children's rates of participation at the higher levels of the educational system,[7] their much higher volume of book buying and book reading,[8] and the singularly high value they place on "good schools" as a reason for family locational decisions.[9] High levels of support for policies designating education as a solution to social problems are popular among virtually all population groups in American society, but they tend to be at least slightly more popular among professionals than among others.[10]

Academic meritocracy is the practice of distributing scarce rewards principally on the basis of intellectual tests and academic qualifications at each succeeding level. Commitment to academic meritocracy is strong in all groups.[11] Yet the principles of academic meritocracy provide some disproportionate advantages early in the life cycle to the professional middle class and particularly to upper-middle-class professionals. High levels of parental education (until recently a feature mainly of professional life) have had a strong positive connection to test scores, which have, in turn, strongly influenced high levels of educational attainment and admission to selective colleges and universities.[12] In particular, the sons and daughters of professors (and, to a lesser extent, other teachers), engineers, scientists, doctors, and lawyers appear to be most clearly advantaged by the operation of test and grade-based status attainment processes.[13] The sons and daughters of owners, managers, and business executives also do well, but not as well as those from the major professions.[14]

Autonomy. The characteristic emphasis of professionals on autonomy also reflects underlying similarities in employment. Professional workers usually have a certain freedom of social movement, because of their skills and training, and they have been taught to expect to make independent "professional" judgments about proper courses of action in their spheres of occupational expertise.[15] They are relatively free and independent agents in this way, very much in the manner of the "old middle class" of small entrepreneurs. At the same time, they are confronted daily with the real or potential constraints of organizational power structures. Sociological realism suggests that an emphasis on autonomy is in the social interest of a relatively advantaged stratum that is nevertheless subordinate to other groups whose limits it understandably strives to reduce.

In survey studies, the autonomy concerns of professionals are evident in the very high value they place in their child-rearing practices on qualities encouraging independence[16] and in their concern for meaningful and self-directed work.[17] The importance of autonomy to professionals can translate, politically, into a relatively strong preference for keeping close scrutiny on the powerful. The powerful, after all, potentially threaten the conditions for the autonomy of others. Matters involving skepticism about the powerful, for example, are among the few issues on which professionals in general are substantially closer to their most politically liberal wing (i.e., specialists in fields of culture and social life) than to business owners and executives.[18]

Balancing and Synthesizing Ideas. The evidence is not good enough to say with certainty, but there may be one other distinctive tendency that unites professionals: a preference for balancing and synthesizing views on matters of public import. Certainly, statements of intellectuals close to the professional stratum often recapitulate the American Progressives efforts to join efficiency, order, and community through a synthesis of "pragmatic" and "idealistic" concerns. In the postwar era, the theme echoes memorably in John Gardner's famous Kennedy-era question: "Can we be excellent and equal, too?"—a theme that continues in work by many economists such as Arthur Okun and Lester Thurow on the difficult trade-offs between efficiency and equality— even, somewhat further to the right, in Irving Kristol's "two cheers for capitalism."[19] Some examples from recent years include efforts to unite useful principles found in both "business" and "civic" cultures; efforts to balance the obligations of individualism and community; efforts to balance cultural pluralism and universalistic standards; and efforts to unite the enjoyments of material plenty with the strictures of morality in a new "consumption ethic."[20] These synthesizing formulations, not more specifically liberal or conservative themes, appear to resonate quite widely in the professional stratum, though they may be of the greatest interest in the more liberal quarters.[21]

The frequent preference of professionals for synthesizing ideas may reflect the role professionals play in contributing to the "balancing mechanisms" of society. These preferences also resonate with underlying pressures and contradictions in the typical employment situation of professionals. As merchants of their own relatively marketable human capital, the typical professional worker experiences a strong stimulus to accept market-oriented theories. At the same time, as representatives of prestigious forms of knowledge, there are pressures also to identify with larger occupational ideals. The contradictory pulls of this situation may be resolved for many in their sympathy to efforts to synthesize conservative, market-oriented ideals and liberal, community-oriented ideals.

Continuities. The culture of contemporary professionalism shows substantial continuities with the culture of professionalism that developed among the professional middle classes of late nineteenth- and early twentieth-century America. The idea of work as a comprehensive representation of character may have diminished somewhat,[22] and fears of falling in status may in a realistic way be somewhat greater now,[23] but many continuities nevertheless remain. The culture of middle-class professionalism continues to combine analytic rationalism, an expectation of autonomy, and a balance of utilitarian and nonutilitarian concerns with the traditional ambitions of middle-class striving and respectability. The professional world is, in its public face, a picture of reserved competence and equanimity, semipermeable spaces of specialized knowledge, and the time-keeping pace of career advancement. (This dominant cultural model has rivals in the more intellectual quarters of the professional stratum—in the arts and sciences and in the colleges and universities—where creativity, contrariness, and nonconformity still figure a little more prominently.)

The survey evidence suggests that the dominant culture of professional middle-class America differs only in small degree from that of highly educated managers, and, indeed, form the values of Americans in general. The value elements I have discussed are most frequent among professionals, but they are also common in other classes. (They are also less mixed with the organizational frames and leadership concerns of managers.) The cultural values of the professional middle class take on an "oppositional" character only when they are compared to positions that give priority to "practical," vocationally oriented education over academic education, obedience to established authority over autonomy, and utilitarianism to the exclusion of other social values.

THE POLITICS OF PROFESSIONALS

If professionals expressed the politics of a "new class"—even in a partial way—we would expect at least the more liberal segment of professionals to take political stands decidedly to the left of business people. We would perhaps also expect professionals in general to be somewhat more concerned than business people about the condition of labor and the poor, perhaps more critical of business practices, and more accepting of many activities of government. We might also expect a higher proportion of liberal and Democratic self-identifications.

The available survey evidence, however, suggests that the liberal professional sphere is not decidedly left-of-center and that professionals in general are in fact moderately conservative on issues having to do with business, labor, and the welfare state. At the same time, professionals are relatively skeptical about moral certainties and tolerant of diversity. They are more liberal on these matters than are other strata in American society. They are, in short, a class in the middle on economic issues, and more liberal than other groups on social relations issues.

The survey evidence indicates further that important lines of cleavage exist among professionals around these modal views. These cleavage patterns do not follow any single formula—whether it be public-sector versus private-sector professionals, or "peripheral" versus "core" professions. Instead, they are the result of the multiple lines of cleavage in the political economy that I have discussed, plus some other lines of cleavage related to demographic divisions. The divisions are so great that it is difficult to describe the professional middle class as a politically coherent stratum.

The Political Profile of American Professionals

In so far as norms are defining, the distinctive political interest of college-graduate professionals appears to lie in support of the role of markets against government *and* in support of the role of diversity and personal freedoms against traditional authority. Because professionals in the aggregate tend to be moderate to conservative on economic issues and liberal only on social issues, they look most like liberal Republicans or "neoliberal" Democrats, the political groups in American society that most consistently combine generally conservative views on economic issues with relatively liberal views on social issues.

On economic issues, professionals are more conservative than blue-collar workers in their support for domestic social programs, in their willingness to help the poor, in their support for reducing income inequalities, and in their level of confidence in business. (They are also decidedly conservative, like all groups in American society, on issues related to crime control.) No more than 40 percent strongly favor current or higher levels of spending on government social-reform programs, and no more than 20 percent indicate significant interest in reducing income inequalities between rich and poor. They trust business far more than labor, and government is often considered more a problem than a solution to the problems facing the country. To speak of liberal and conservative zones on economic issues is to speak of liberal and conservative deviations from clearly conservative norms.

The profile of professional attitudes is quite different on most social issues. Professionals are more liberal than either business people or blue-collar workers on issues involving the protection of civil liberties and personal choices in regard to sexual mores, and they are also more liberal on issues involving the greater social acceptance of minorities and women. Although they are tough on crime and generally favorable toward the military, they are slightly more concerned about potential abuses of power by political authorities like the police and the military than are people in the other major social strata.

Professionals are, at the same time, greatly divided in their political views. Specialists in the civic sphere, in social relations, and culture—academics, artists, journalists, policy specialists, social scientists—are a relatively liberal segment of the professional stratum. Even this liberal segment, however, shows a conservative profile on issues involving labor, welfare, the reduction of income inequalities, and crime control. On most other issues shown in Table 5.1, they are 10 to 15 percent more liberal than the norm among professionals.

The internal divisions among professionals can be shown in a still sharper way by comparing two groups formed through a partitioning on five bases of division. The liberal group in this comparison consists of younger, non-religious, lower- and middle-income, government and nonprofit sector, social and cultural specialists. The conservative group consists of older, Protestant, high-income, private sector, applied science and business service professionals. Differences of *45 to 50 percent* have separated these two groups in recent years on matters involving support for domestic spending programs, reduction of income inequalities, women's advancement, environmental spending, and skepticism about business leaders. Still larger differences of *60 percent or more* have separated them on matters of party identification, support for the military and defense spending, and support for nonrestrictive attitudes on sexual behavior. The divisions within the professional stratum are far wider than the 10–15 percent differences that separate professionals and high-income business people on most issues.

Divisions among Professionals on Economic Issues

It is possible to provide a more specific analysis of the bases of division among professionals. However, since the bases of division on economic and social issues differ, it is necessary to discuss the two sets of issues separately. I will discuss the reason for division on economic issues first, and then, using data from the General Social Survey, discuss the relative importance of the various bases of division as predictors of liberal and conservative attitudes. For this analysis (and for the subsequent analysis of attitudes on social issues), I wanted to encompass the largest possible group of nominally professional people in order to understand patterns of political identification that extend beyond the major professions to the lower-level professional groups. I also wanted to compare professionals to business owners, executives, and managers. I therefore conducted the analyses on a sample of all census "professional specialty" and "executive, managerial, and kindred" occupations.

Employment-Related Divisions. Statistically significant divisions among professionals on issues related to economic distribution follow from their

88

TABLE 5.1
Political Attitudes in Three Socioeconomic Strata, 1974–1988

	Highly Educated Professionals (%)	High Income Business People (%)	Blue-Collar Workers (%)
Economic Issues			
Favors More Environmental Spending	66 (1578)	55 (815)	58 (6798)
Only Some Confidence in Business Leaders	58 (1401)	44 (714)	63 (6458)
At Least Some Support for Reducing Income Inequalities between Rich and Poor	39 (801)	25 (476)	56 (3377)
Low Confidence in Labor Leaders	39 (1374)	53 (702)	30 (6243)
Favors Government Programs to Help Blacks	37 (1622)	25 (844)	26 (7409)
Strong Support for Domestic Social Programs	31 (1635)	22 (848)	23 (7460)
Strongly Believes Government Should Help the Poor	18 (1514)	11 (790)	27 (6921)
Strongly Favors Reducing Income Inequalities between Rich and Poor	19 (801)	12 (476)	38 (3377)
Low Confidence in Business Leaders	5 (1401)	2 (714)	8 (6458)
Social Issues			
Strong Support for Civil Liberties	71 (1110)	62 (558)	29 (7236)
Strongly Favors More Complete Racial Integration in American Society	58 (1620)	44 (849)	31 (7236)
Supports Greater Female Equality in American Society	56 (1098)	50 (538)	31 (5087)
Tolerant on Individual Choice in Sexual Mores	44 (1745)	38 (850)	24 (7487)
Favors Reducing the Role of the Military	43 (1638)	31 (849)	23 (7411)
Rights of the Accused Definitely Take Precedence over Stopping Crime	19 (1626)	8 (847)	11 (7413)

(continued)

TABLE 5.1   (Continued)

	Highly Educated Professionals (%)	High Income Business People (%)	Blue-Collar Workers (%)
Party Identification			
Democratic Party Identification	50 (1620)	37 (839)	59 (7398)
Republican Party Identification	40 (1620)	53 (839)	30 (7398)

Source: Cumulative General Social Survey, 1974–88.

Note: "Highly educated professionals" refers to all census professionals with baccalaureate and higher-level degrees. "High-income business people" refers to managers, owners, and executives with family incomes in the top eighth of all American families. "Blue-collar workers" refers to all nonself-employed blue-collar workers.

organizational attachments, market situation, and occupational specialties. The primary source of political differences in each case comes from the extent to which professional workers are close to the institutions and norms of the business world. Professional people who are in close association with business managers and executives are likely to take on their outlooks, either because they were initially attracted to those outlooks—the typical case—or because they have learned to appreciate them.

In organizational life, the most important division is between those who work in the for-profit or nonprofit sectors. Persons working in the for-profit sector are naturally more closely tied to the core values of the business world than those working outside. (It is true, in addition, that liberals are more often found in private firms that place a special emphasis on the public trust—pharmaceuticals and insurance as opposed to industrial technology and manufacturing, for example.)[24] Within the nonprofit sector, professionals in organizations that are closely connected with economic development typically show a more conservative political profile than those in organizations that are more closely connected with social welfare.[25]

In professional labor markets, the key division is between professionals who earn higher and lower incomes. Professional people earning higher incomes are more likely to socialize in milieus in which business values predominate, while those earning lower incomes rarely do. (Even those earning lower incomes, if their resources allow them to anticipate an upward trajectory, often assume the values and politics of business-dominated spheres.) Those with higher incomes are also more likely to have the resources to invest directly in real estate and financial instruments. Because of these differences in interaction and opportunity, higher-income professionals are more likely to be conservative on economic distribution issues, while lower-income professionals are more likely to be liberal.

Among the professional occupational specialties, the key divisions are based on two factors: (1) the extent to which the actual knowledge base of the occupation incorporates business principles, *and* (2) the extent to which practitioners are likely to be in contact with business people. The knowledge base of the business professions of corporate law, accounting, personnel relations, advertising, and management consulting are thoroughly integrated with the principles of business practice, and many other professions like engineering and architecture incorporate principles of least cost and marketability in design decisions.[26] Business service professionals are prominent in the conservative zones of the professional stratum—indeed, many of these people are so close to the world of corporate business that it is more than a little formalistic to consider them as in any way separate from that world. Engineers and natural scientists are also comparatively likely to be in regular contact with business people. The liberal professional occupations include what I have called the "social and cultural" professions[27]—professions that span the worlds of social research and policy planning, the arts, media, and academe—and the "human service" professions—those that include social work, teaching, nursing, and psychotherapy.

In addition to level of integration with business, one other important source of employment-related division exists among professionals. The line of cleavage is between professionals who are employed in command-oriented settings and those employed in consultation-oriented settings. Professionals directly concerned with security (e.g., military officers and defense analysts) tend to be conservative, ultimately, I believe, because of their responsibilities in protecting the social order—forcibly, if necessary.[28] This institutional setting recruits and rewards an aggressive, command-oriented style, which is associated with political conservatism. Jobs that involve dialogue rather than authoritative action tend, by contrast, to attract a greater number of liberals, even when they are located in the private sector and/or provide high incomes. Thus, people working in professional specialties that are more consultative—internists as compared to surgeons, for example—tend to be more often liberal.[29]

Demographic Divisions. As the professional stratum has grown, new population groups have become more common in the stratum. What makes this demographic transformation important politically is that the new groups are more liberal than the groups previously occupying a larger proportion of professional statuses.

On economic issues, the association between liberal political views and liberal population groups has mainly to do with the group's socioeconomic history and current economic prospects. Blacks are more liberal than other groups, largely because their economic conditions as a group are less comfortable. They feel the pinch of inequality. For similar reasons, single working women tend to be relatively liberal on economic issues. In a society where "experience counts," younger people are more likely than older people to be liberal on economic issues because they are less well established than older people and more likely to associate with lower-income people. For similar reasons, less-educated people are likely to be more liberal than people with advanced degrees.

Relative economic condition is not the only source of liberal politics among demographic groups, however. Those who see a large number of social problems every day are more likely to think that these issues need to be addressed. This is the situation of people living in cities as compared to suburbanites and town dwellers. And, thirdly, the traditionalist's respect for established authority can extend to established economic authorities as well as to established political and moral authorities. Because of this, people with orthodox religious beliefs are often more likely to adopt conservative views on economic issues than less religious people or those from less orthodox denominations.

Survey Evidence. To examine these ideas about internal divisions empirically, I have taken the General Social Survey cumulated over a recent fourteen-year period (1974–88) and looked at the attitudes of professionals and managers on a wide range of economic issues.

The dependent variables in the analysis include: sympathy for the idea of reducing income inequalities between rich and poor (labeled EQUALIZE in Table 5.2), the degree of confidence in business leaders (BUSCONF in Table 5.2), an index measuring support for spending on domestic social problems (DOMESTIC), an item measuring support for increased spending on the environment (ENVIRON), an index measuring philosophical support for the idea of a welfare state (WELFARE), and identification with the Democratic Party (DEMOC ID).[30] These are dispositional measures rather than measures of concrete policy preferences or, on the other hand, measures of ideology. They are a strategic level to examine since support for concrete policies can be strongly influenced by situational factors, and since most people, including most highly educated people, do not identify with any strongly crystallized ideological outlooks.

To explain the economic attitudes, I used measures of organizational attachment; income levels; and occupational group.[31] The analysis also included the relevant demographic variables measuring age, education, religion, religiosity, urban/nonurban residence, gender, and race.[32] I also included a time period variable, so as not to mask the effects of political climate changes during particular periods. The time period variable was categorized by political eras, so that the earlier and, in some respects, more liberal period (1974–77) is divided off from a somewhat longer (1978–83) period of conservative strength. These two were separated from the slightly more "moderate" recent period (1984–88).

The analysis is based on multiple regression.[33] For reference categories on the nominal level measurements (designated by an "R"), I have chosen groups that tend to be either of less interest or those generally falling between the extremes. The best way to examine tables like these is to look for consistency and strength of relationships. In the highly imperfect world of statistical analysis of public opinion, these are our best guides to finding something of importance. A sense of the relative importance of the variables included in the analysis can be gained by looking at the size of the standardized regression coefficients ("betas") for each of the explanatory variables. Certainly, the coefficients should not be read too literally. There are error terms and confidence ranges attached to each of the coefficients reported in Tables 5.2 and 5.3. Indeed, approximately one out of twenty times a coefficient reported as statistically significant in a sample will actually be insignificant in the population from which the sample is drawn.

To facilitate interpretation, I have included in the tables only coefficients significant at a probability level of .05 or less. Dashes refer to variables that were not statistically significant at the .05 level of probability. On each of the variables, positive coefficients indicate more liberal views and negative coefficients more conservative views. The model is additive; the explanation is based on adding together the independent effects of each of the statistically significant predicting variables, and does not specify interactions between any of the independent variables in the analysis.[34] The adjusted "R^2" statistic at the bottom of the tables is a measure of how well the variables used in the analysis account for the total amount of variation on the index or item under consideration.

The analysis reported in Table 5.2 indicates that attitudes on economic issues were generally conservative—and, moreover, that these tended to be consensus issues. There is one exception to this rule, however: by and large, professionals and managers in the 1970s and 1980s were environmentally conscious. Otherwise, they were business- and market-oriented and not very supportive of "big government." They were notably lacking in confidence in labor unions, and not very interested in reducing income inequalities. The standard deviations around these means were low, indicating relatively high levels of consensus.

Not surprisingly, the variables in the analysis explained relatively little of this variance. Indeed, on two of the issues—confidence in business leaders and support for environmental spending—having information about all of the variables in the model helped improve the proportion of correct predictions over the mean response only 10 percent of the time or less. In these cases, the mean response was not only by far the most common response, but also a response held by large numbers of people in many different professional categories.

Within the context of relatively weak levels of prediction, the projected liberal employment sectors did tend to show a significant association with liberal views. The demographic categories also tended to show the expected patterns. In the professional middle class, liberals worked disproportionately in the public and nonprofit sectors, and they were clustered at the lower end of the income spectrum. They were also somewhat more likely to be salaried than self-employed. Social and cultural specialists were consistently liberal.

TABLE 5.2

Variables Predicting Liberal Views on Selected Economic Distribution and Party Identification Items[a] among American Professionals and Managers, 1974–1988

	EQUALIZE	BUSCONF	DOMESTIC	ENVIRON	WELFARE	DEMOC ID
Employment Variables						
Govt Sector	.07	.08	—	.04	.05	.08
NonProf Sector	—	.12	.04	.08	.07	.08
BusServ Sector[b]	R	R	R	R	R	R
MfgTrde Sector	—	—	-.05	—	—	—
Lower Income	.19	.05	—	.04	.11	.06
Self-Employed	-.04	.05	-.03	-.04	—	—
SocCult Prof	—	.04	.08	.04	.06	—
HumServ Prof	.05	—	—	—	.06	—
ApplTech Prof	—	—	—	—	—	—
Manager[b]	R	R	R	R	R	R
High Supervisor	—	-.05	—	—	—	—
Low Supervisor	—	-.05	—	—	—	—
Demographic Variables						
Younger	—	.14	.07	.13	.07	.05
Less than BA[?]	R	R	R	R	R	R
BA/BS Degree	-.07	.07	.08	—	-.05	-.05
Adv. Degree	—	.04	.12	—	—	—
Female	.10	—	.04	.04	—	.05
Black	.13	.08	.25	—	.19	.20

TABLE 5.2 (Continued)

	EQUALIZE	BUSCONF	DOMESTIC	ENVIRON	WELFARE	DEMOC ID
Urban	—	—	—	.06	.04	.04
Small City[b]	R	R	R	R	R	R
Suburb	—	—	-.05	.03	—	—
Town/Rural	—	—	-.09	—	-.05	.05
Protestant	-.10	-.07	-.07	-.04	-.10	-.16
Catholic[b]	R	R	R	R	R	R
Jewish	—	—	.06	—	.03	.08
No religion	—	.05	.07	—	—	—
Low Religiosity	—	.08	—	.03	.06	.04
Time Period						
1974–77	—	—	-.07	.03	-.07	.04
1978–83	-.08	—	-.16	-.03	-.12	.03
1984–88[b]	R	R	R	R	R	R
R^2/(S.E.)	.11	.07	.19	.06	.13	.11
	(1.80)	(.50)	(.37)	(.70)	(.38)	(.47)

Source: Cumulative General Social Survey, 1974–88.

[a] Mnemonics refer to the following items and/or indices: EQUALIZE = item on reducing income inequalities between rich and poor (+ = lib); BUSCONF = index on confidence in business leaders (+ = lib); DOMESTIC = index on support for domestic spending programs (+ = lib); ENVIRON = item on federal spending for environmental protection (+ = lib); WELFARE = index on philosophical support for the welfare state and government help for the poor (+ = lib); DEMOC ID = item on Democratic Party identification (+ = Democrat).

[b] R in this row indicates reference category.

Human service professionals were somewhat less often liberal, though they did show the expected higher levels of liberalism on the best measures of left-of-center attitudes—the questions that asked about welfare and equalizing income distribution. By contrast, the applied science professionals were no more liberal than business managers and executives.

The most consistent and substantial effects on the demographic variables were connected to age, race, and religion. Younger people were more liberal than older people, and blacks were much more liberal than whites. Protestants showed decidedly conservative views compared to Catholics, Jews, and the nonreligious. People with advanced degrees were more skeptical of business leaders and more likely to support domestic social programs. These findings on education may seem to provide support for the "new class" theory, but the support cannot be considered very strong. On four of the six issues, the most highly educated people in the sample showed no statistically significant pattern of liberalism.

The New Centers of "Progressive" Politics. The conservative zones in the professional stratum are unquestionably more important in the economic life of the country than the liberal zones. Engineering is the largest of the occupations whose professional status is undisputed, and engineers have been overwhelmingly conservative on issues of economic distribution, taxes, government, defense, and crime. The fastest growing professional occupations are in the business and medical service areas, two other relatively conservative sectors.[35] Even within occupations, the distribution of power greatly favors the more conservative spheres. Lawyers, for example, are primarily engaged in working for corporations and wealthy individuals. Fewer than 15 percent of lawyers are employed by government, and less than 1 percent are engaged in defending the rights of minorities and the poor.[36] Economic importance, moreover, often leads to political advantages. Throughout the postwar era, over 90 percent of federal grants to universities, for example, have gone to the more conservative spheres of professional activity—to natural scientists, engineers, medical researchers—and less than 10 percent to the social sciences and humanities, the branches of learning that are more often associated with political liberalism and dissent.[37]

Although the conservative segment of professionals is larger and closer to the centers of economic power in American society, the liberal segment has been of greater interest to social scientists because of its apparently anomalous character as a high-status group favoring left-of-center politics. Without doubt, the expansion of the social and cultural professions and of the public and nonprofit sectors represent an important development in the history of American progressive politics. For the first time, liberal professionals are large enough and have a strong enough organizational base to play a more or less autonomous role as seedbed of liberal politics in the United States. Moreover, the character of liberal politics in America has certainly been influenced in important ways by the increasing importance of these liberal zones of the professional stratum and the declining significance of organized labor. Both the rise of "social issues liberalism" and the declining interest in equality as a social ideal are, I believe, connected to the new social base of left-of-center opposition in the United States.

Some commentators have attributed the affinity between the social and cultural professions and liberal politics to the "intellectualism" of these more liberal professional spheres. The idea of intellectualism suggests diverse strands of nonconformity: "expressive values," unconventional patterns of consumption and personal display, a taste for "serious and unsettling" literature and art, and left-of-center politics. The available evidence suggests that there is virtually nothing useful in this characterization as an explanation for liberal politics among professionals. Neither expressive values[38] nor nonconformist patterns of consumption and personal display[39] nor avid participation in the arts[40] provides a unifying thread with which to understand the liberalism of professionals. The actual sources of liberal politics are varied. At least three important sources of liberalism exist in the major spheres of progressive politics: *people-centered motivations* (found most often in human services), *idea-centered motivations* (found most often in academic and public-policy circles), and *expression-centered motivations* (found most often in the arts).[41]

The designation of liberal professionals as a "high-status group"—a conventional label in the "new class" theory—is itself largely misfocused. With a few exceptions—Hollywood, the liberal arts colleges, and some foundations—centers of liberalism are found primarily in the least advantaged and most vulnerable quarters of the professional stratum—among people who are younger, have little income, and are located in the tax- and contribution-dependent sectors of the economy.

In assessing the connection between professionals and "progressive" politics, it is important to keep in mind that individuals and the institutions they work for frequently think differently. Organizational and market forces often shape the political meaning of professional activity in ways that run counter to the expressed views of professional staff themselves. Writers and producers in the entertainment industry offer a good example. They are not, strictly speaking, professionals, but they often work in professionalized environments. They are well known for their political liberalism and even for a high level of expressed alienation from American society.[42] They are at the same time enmeshed in a business controlled by large conglomerates and dedicated to the art and commerce of producing popular hits. To some degree, organizational forces encourage distinctive sorts of conservative biases. These organizational forces include the interests of sponsors in attracting "economically active" populations, and the interest of large mass-market organizations in reducing risks and relying on proven formulas.[43] Since the industry is dedicated to pleasing consumers, the preferences and prejudices of the audiences themselves are obviously important sources of constraint.[44] Audience preferences lead to the production of an enormous number of bright and violent adventure stories and sentimental romantic comedies, some mildly satirical comedies, a few films that take on controversial topics in an uplifting way, and relatively little else. Even controversial films that are meant to unsettle generally conform in significant ways—through the use of lavish sets, recognizable stars, bright colors, stereotyped roles, obvious struggles between good and evil, diversionary sex and violence, or through other appeals to popular taste.

The same sort of analysis can be made of another politically liberal institutional sphere, academe. Although professors are among the most avowedly liberal group in American society, their institutions reinforce the social order in many ways. Universities carry out research for government and private industry that, for the most part, has little to do directly with the needs of the less-advantaged groups in the society; they perform a crucial sorting function, judging those fit and unfit to assume high-ranking positions in the society; and, in doing so, they transform, under the aegis of meritocracy, privileges that are, to a considerable degree, based on preexisting family-related advantages into the "properly earned" rewards of intellectual ability and effort.[45]

Clearly, a two-sided view is required. Through their expressed opinions and their activities, people signal their willingness to support particular kinds of causes, to vote for particular kinds of candidates, and, at times, to devote time and money to extending the influence of their beliefs. The institutions staffed by liberal professionals may have one sort of political import, while the people who make them up, in their activity as private citizens, may have quite another.

Divisions among Professionals on Social Issues

Let me turn now to social issues. Significant divisions also exist among professionals on social issues, and again both employment and demographic forces are associated with these divisions. However, the patterns of division are quite different. In particular, demographic variables take on a larger importance. Just as a correspondence exists between the employment situation of professionals and their views on economic matters, another correspondence exists between the culture of different demographic groups and attitudes about personal freedoms, social relations, and traditional authority.

Demographic Divisions. Because demographic divisions are more important on social issues, I will discuss them first. On economic issues, the liberalism of demographic groups is connected primarily to experiences of relative deprivation. On social issues, by contrast, liberalism comes primarily from a degree of detachment from mainstream conservative values, while conservatism comes from an anchorage in those values. There are two major ways of becoming detached from conservative values: (1) either experiences can encourage distance from established authorities and established principles of self-denial, or (2) alternatively, experiences can lead to an appreciation of diversity by making the world appear more complex and diverse. (The latter encourages liberalism only in so far as the world does not simultaneously appear more threatening.)

These two sources of detachment can be seen to influence the views of younger people, more highly educated people, less religious people, urbanites, blacks and, to some degree, also women. Younger people have fewer stable responsibilities and more opportunity to experience the adventures of life. In a liberal society, it is natural that the young will feel distant from authorities who restrain their freedom of experience. Higher education encourages an appreciation of diversity. The highly educated are nowadays explicitly schooled in the culture of tolerance and pluralism, and they may also tend, on rational grounds, to be concerned about the potentially repressive power of authorities. The less religious are also likely to be skeptical of the power of moral authorities. The experience of diversity influences professional people who come from heterogeneous communities (urbanites) and ethnic and other nonmainstream backgrounds (Catholics, Jews, and blacks) in the direction of social liberalism. These demographic groups are likely to feel somewhat distant from traditional kinds of middle-class authority and to favor, as an alternative, broader social freedoms and more fluid kinds of societal community organization.

Employment-Related Divisions. Where conservatives on economic issues resemble corporate executives in their economic situation, conservatives on social issues are better described in terms of their degree of closeness to the characteristic "conservative middle-class morality" of hard work, religious belief, distrust of the culturally different, and conformity to social and political authorities. Under the circumstances, it is not surprising that only a few employment situations that are associated with liberal views on economic issues are also associated with liberal views on social issues.

Which are the spheres of employment most detached from "conservative middle-class morality"? The more intellectual spheres—those in the social and cultural professions—would seem to qualify, but other economically liberal spheres, like the human service professions and government employment, may not. And the situation of the income classes is very much reversed. It is often said that those who must work hard to make an adequate living are the most likely subscribers to conventional middle-class morality. These people have frequently lived and succeeded by following a highly disciplined moral code, rather than any grander (or more high-powered) codes. Again the metaphor of fixed anchors suggests that lower-income professionals are better candidates for social conservatism than professionals with higher incomes.

Survey Evidence. As before, it is possible to investigate these relationships using the General Social Survey. In the analysis, the data are again drawn from the cumulative General Social Survey from the years 1974–88.

To examine patterns of division on social issues, I included the following dependent variables: an index measuring tolerance of unconventional political and religious groups (labeled CIVLIB in Table 5.3), an index measuring attitudes about greater opportunities for women (FEMINISM), an index measuring attitudes about racial integration and increasing opportunities for blacks (RACIAL), an index measuring attitudes about the acceptability of tolerant views on sexual mores, among others (MORALS), an index measuring attitudes about defense issues (DEFENSE), and an index measuring attitudes on crime control (CRIME).[46]

As in the analysis of economic issues, I used multiple regression to evaluate the model of divisions on social issues. Again, I report only coefficients significant at a probability level of .05 or lower. To underscore the importance of conservative anchorages in the determination of attitudes on social issues, I have included some demographic variables that do not show up as significant on economic issues: family status and region. Marriage and child rearing encourage traditional moral anchorage, and the South is a region noted for the strength of its emphasis on traditional morality and traditional authority.

Professionals were conservative on the crime index and relatively conservative on the defense index. On the other issues, they were considerably more liberal than other groups, including managers. Americans have had a rather clear set of views about the proper relationships between business and government and the priority of business, but they are in significant disagreement about the proper grounding of social and moral community. Because of this, standard deviations on most of the social issue variables were large. There was more variation to explain on social issues—again, excluding crime and defense—and the variables in the analysis did a better job of explaining this variation than they did on the economic issues. This indicates that disagreements not only exist, but are patterned socially to a large degree. The experience of marginality or centrality, heterogeneity or homogeneity, unconventional experience or deference to authority—all of these have a strong effect on attitudes in the social issues domain.

Within this context, the data indicate that a good explanation of social issue divisions among professionals can be built around the concepts of detachment from and adherence to the anchors of conservative middle-class morality. The most consistent predictors of social conservatism were advanced age, lower levels of education, high levels of religiosity, and residence in the South. Other anchoring variables—residence in small towns and suburbs, marriage and child rearing, membership in the dominant gender and racial groups—all showed the expected associations with conservative views. Of the employment-related variables, lower incomes, human services occupations, and location in the manufacturing and trade sectors were associated with conservative views, while the more intellectual social and cultural professions were associated with greater liberalism. Salaried people, who must cooperate with others, were more liberal on many of these issues than were the self-employed, who must master the challenge of the market in a self-disciplined way on their own.

Although the translation of demographic change into political change is far

TABLE 5.3
Variables Predicting Liberal Views on Selected Civil Liberties and Social Authority Issues[a]
among American Professionals and Managers, 1974–1988

	CIVLIB	FEMINSM	RACIAL	MORALS	DEFENSE	CRIME
Employment Variables						
Govt Sector	—	—	—	—	.03	.05
NonProf Sector	—	—	—	—	—	—
BusServ Sector[b]	R	R	R	R	R	R
MfgTrde Sector	-.07	—	-.06	—	-.07	-.04
High Income	.12	.13	.07	.10	—	-.04
Self-Employed	-.05	-.04	-.04	—	—	.03
SocCult Prof	.04	.04	.08	.06	.05	.06
HumServ Prof	-.04	-.06	—	-.05	—	.04
ApplTech Prof	—	-.05	—	—	—	—
Manager[b]	R	R	R	R	R	R
High Supervisor	.05	—	—	.04	—	—
Low Supervisor	.04	—	.07	—	—	—
Demographic Variables						
Younger	.20	.28	.21	.17	.10	.07
Less than BA[b]	R	R	R	R	R	R
BA/BS Degree	.17	.11	.12	.07	.11	.05
Adv Degree	.20	.15	.15	.12	.13	.12
Female	—	.11	.04	-.03	—	-.05
Black	-.05	—	.13	.03	.05	.13
Protestant	—	-.04	-.07	-.04	-.06	—

	R	R	R	R	R	R
Catholic[b]	R	R	R	R	R	R
Jewish	—	.04	.03	.09	.06	—
No religion	—	—	.04	.07	.09	.12
Low Religiosity	.14	.11	—	.36	.08	—
Urban	—	.06	—	.07	—	—
Small City[b]	R	R	R	R	R	R
Suburb	—	-.08	—	.04	-.04	-.05
Town/Rural	-.06	-.07	-.04	—	-.04	—
Married	—	—	—	-.09	—	-.05
Children	—	.05	—	-.04	—	-.04
East	—	—	—	—	—	—
Midwest[b]	R	R	R	R	R	R
South	-.09	-.08	-.16	-.03	-.08	-.04
West	—	—	.05	—	—	—
Time Period						
1974–77	—	-.14	-.10	.07	—	.08
1978–83	.04	-.04	-.07	.03	-.08	—
1984–88[b]	R	R	R	R	R	R
R^2/(S.E.)	.22	.20	.22	.37	.12	.09
	(.36)	(.35)	(.33)	(.36)	(.45)	(.59)

Source: Cumulative General Social Survey, 1974–88.

[a] Mnemonics refer to the following indices: CIVLIB = index on civil liberties for nonconformists and radicals (+ = lib); FEMINSM = index on support for greater opportunities for women (+ = lib); RACIAL = index on policies encouraging greater racial integration and minority opportunities (+ = lib); MORALS = index on moral regulation issues (+ = lib); DEFENSE = index on defense issues (+ = lib); CRIME = index on crime control issues (+ = lib).

[b] R in this row indicates reference category.

from automatic, the analysis suggests that the liberalism of the professional stratum in recent years has almost certainly been conditioned by the changing composition of the stratum. As compared to other classes and strata in the society, professional people are more likely to be relatively young, highly educated, urban, and nonreligious. The professions have also been relatively open to women and minorities in recent years—more so, certainly, than the upper reaches of business. In the context of supportive cultural changes in American society, the cumulative effect of this compositional change has been toward improving the climate for liberalism on social issues.[47]

How Important Are Social Issues?   One question, of course, is whether social issues are really as significant as economic issues. For many sociologists, only the latter are easily recognizable as battlegrounds of consequential social conflict. Indeed, it is entirely reasonable to argue, as some critically minded social scientists do, that society is based fundamentally on an institutionalized structure of inequality, which provides great benefits to a few and marginal existences to a great many. Unlike the redistributive sentiments tapped by economic issues, sentiments about social freedoms do not necessarily seek any fundamental change in these patterns of economic inequality.

   Indeed, liberal attitudes on social issues represent a Lockean vision of social community: freedom-loving and skeptical of authority, but a community nonetheless in so far as it is inclusive and protective of the rights of the weak. In this respect, social liberalism can be interpreted as a complement in community and social relations to the market-based freedoms supported by economic conservatives.[48] Often, in fact, social-issue liberals seek only the perfection of a market-oriented society through the extension of principles of liberty, individualism, and opportunity to nonmarket institutions.

   Because of this, it is not difficult for the comfortable to endorse liberal views on social issues, provided these views do not come at the expense of personal security. The great variety of consumer goods, after all, which are the cornucopia of the market system, allow many middle-class people to implement their taste for self-expression and freedom from constraint. By contrast, it is relatively difficult for the comfortable to endorse redistributive and welfarist sentiments; they require a notion of equity that in some way competes with their allegiance to the equity of the market.

   Yet it is also true that social issues can have an explosive potential in a society where liberty is a fundamental principle, because they are so much rooted in the constitutive values of the society. Liberals on these issues accuse the society of not being freedom-loving enough—which is to say, not tolerant enough, not open enough to talent wherever it is found, and not committed enough to noncoercive ways of solving problems. The recent history of the United States provides many ready illustrations of the explosive potential of social issues. In the United States, during the civil rights and Vietnam eras, social issues were of great importance and so, by extension, was the force of professional and middle-class liberalism. The same applies for the more recent debates about abortion, homosexuality, and the rights of protestors.

Professionals have, since the mid-1960s, become more like the rest of the country in their voting, while managers have remained predictably more conservative. Some recent research argues that the Democratic voting trend among professionals can be largely explained by the importance of liberal views on social issues to voters in the professional middle class. The evidence for this argument is based thus far on only a small number of perhaps atypical elections.[49] My own evidence suggests that a large part of the reason why professionals now vote more like the rest of the country is because they *are* (demographically and economically) more like the rest of the country.

It is beyond dispute, however, that in their quite widespread opposition to educational training oriented to deference and conformity, in their sensitivity to civil liberties issues, and in their relatively strong support for the rights of protestors, professional people show that they are nonauthoritarian, open to the possibility of legitimate grievance, and susceptible to arguments about social justice. In these ways, the characteristic forms of middle-class liberalism, even if they are not at all overtly egalitarian in orientation, do provide an opening to arguments about the distribution of power in society. This is obvious in the case of attitudes warranting the full economic and social participation of women and blacks.

What can be lost in the shift of professionals to liberal views on social issues is a sense of real engagement with others rather than mere tolerance of diversity. Preaching is anathema to social-issue liberals, and this is an outlook admirably open to democratic discussion. The appreciation of difference avoids the suffocating moralism that mars so much conservative thought about community. But, at an extreme, social-issues liberalism accepts diversity to the impoverishment of civil society and public discussion. It counsels that people should be left alone to develop their own institutional and personal solutions, unhampered by state or religious authorities, to be sure, but also unchallenged by the social involvement and reasoned arguments of others. Voucher programs, watered-down school curricula, toleration of segregated communities, a too-easy acceptance of the equal value of nearly all "nontraditional" family arrangements—these positions embrace principles of diversity without a corresponding commitment to social strength or high cultural standards for all.

This is an ironic reversal of the older forms of professionalism, since these older forms were founded so explicitly on a connection between community and authority. "Principled indifference" indicates the extent to which the laissez-faire ethos of the market, rather than the ethos of social trusteeship, now shapes the politics of professionals.

The Rhythms of Political Change

SOME INTRIGUING anomalies challenge the picture I have presented of a business-oriented, but socially liberal professional middle class. One anomaly is that during periods of reform professionals often appear to be closely connected to the forces of change. Arguments about the connection of professionals and reform have been made by respectable historians for each of the American reform periods of this century: the Progressive Era, the New Deal period, and the New Frontier–Great Society period.[1] During the most recent reform period in the 1960s and early 1970s, educated professionals seemed at times to form a mass "conscience constituency" in opposition to the war and in support of protest aimed at ending the war and changing the society.[2]

This sense of episodic wellings of reform sentiment among professionals has led to the argument that the real interests of professional people can only be known during periods of particularly intense societal conflict, because these are periods when professionals reveal their true underlying interests. In this vein, some writers have interpreted twentieth-century American politics as showing periodic flash points of "class consciousness" among professionals. In these interpretations, the claims of professionals to moral and technical superiority can be seen most clearly during periods of reform, which are, simultaneously, periods of professional assertion in the political realm. In one such account, the "new class" emerged during Woodrow Wilson's administration, showing its dissatisfaction with Gilded Age business leadership by supporting Progressive movements. It developed a new sense of mission during the Great Depression and the McCarthy era. Subsequently, it was able to place its own candidates, including Adlai Stevenson and George McGovern, into nomination for the presidency as representatives of the liberal wing of the Democratic Party.[3] These interpretations suggest that, as liberalism has waned, the prototypical "new class" candidates of recent years have become lawyers of meritocratic background, public service careers, and moderate views.[4]

A second anomaly is that, even during periods of conservative politics, persistent gaps exist between the more liberal attitudes of professionals and the more conservative attitudes of business people.[5] In the 1940s, it was often difficult to find more than a sliver of difference between business and professional people.[6] Today, differences of 10 to 15 percent separate highly educated professionals and high-income business people on a wide variety of issues. Since the mid-1960s, professionals have also been significantly more likely than managers to vote Democratic.

Thus, two connections in the historical record between professionals and dissent would seem to require explanation: (1) the episodic surges of reformist energy that appear to affect middle-class professionals to a greater degree than other classes; and (2) the attitude gap that now exists between highly educated professionals and high-income business people during periods of reform and periods of conservative ascendancy alike. These are interesting puzzles in the trajectory of professional politics, and in this chapter I will try to provide answers to them.

While polling data is available going back to the 1930s, not very much of the data before the 1960s can be recoded to allow for analysis of trends over time among the specific segments of the population in which we are interested. Therefore, I will concentrate in this chapter on the contemporary period—the most recent half-cycle of American politics, moving from liberal to conservative activism between the years 1960 and 1985—and now returning to something of a reform agenda. When I discuss the data on "professionals," I will again be referring to professionals with baccalaureate and higher-level degrees. When I discuss the data on "business people," I will be referring to managers, owners, and executives whose family incomes are at least in the top quarter of the income distribution.

Class conflict interpretations of the period between 1960 and 1990 seem to me problematic. Highly specific demographic forces and historical circumstances are more important than class conflict for the understanding of middle-class politics during the most recent era of reform. The demographic forces include a compositional change in the professional stratum that greatly augmented the numbers of people sympathetic to liberalism. The historical circumstances include the rotation of the political axis to issues like war and protest on which highly educated professional people and high-income business people are most likely to disagree. At the same time, I agree with the "new class" theorists on one point: periods of swelling discontent do provide fertile ground for social movements and political entrepreneurs, who can draw on traditional legitimations of professional and intellectual culture for purposes of mobilizing value-oriented dissent in the professional middle class.

PROFESSIONALS AND THE LAST AGE OF REFORM

The most important contextual fact about the last American era of reform (1960–72) is that all groups in the society were supportive of at least some features of governmental activism. Trends favoring increased government activity in providing social services and social protection were, in fact, evident beginning in the 1940s, as were gradually increasing levels of support for racial integration, women's rights, and civil liberties protections. The period from World War II through the early 1970s is best described as a period of increasing liberalism among Americans.[7] On most issues involving social liberalization, professionals were in the vanguard of these trends, and on most issues involving government spending, they were closer to the rear but nevertheless moving in a liberal direction.

The Democratic mandate of 1964 greatly reinforced these commitments to the welfare state and social equality. It also helped to convert professionals, a lagging group in many respects, to the cause of governmental activism. The survey data from the period between 1964 and the first years of the following decade shows a clear movement among all groups in the society toward greater support for social spending on education, health, housing, improving the conditions of minorities, and many other features of the Great Society program.[8] Professionals also became increasingly supportive of the Democratic party for the first time, breaking a long-standing preference for the Republican party.[9]

The reputation of professionals for particularly high levels of support for liberalism during the Great Society era is only partially deserved. A majority of professionals was not liberal on many issues, including some of those most closely associated with the Great Society. They were, for example, by the end of the decade, only moderately supportive of government efforts to improve the condition of minorities, and substantially less than half indicated warm feelings about liberals as an ideological group. In these respects, they were very much like other classes and strata at the time.

Only a rather small minority of professionals were what came to be known as "New Politics" liberals—people who favored the mix of social spending to improve the conditions of the less advantaged, the advancement of individual rights against restrictive social and political norms, and opposition to the war in Southeast Asia. The proportion of "New Politics" liberals did not exceed 15–20 percent of the college-educated professional stratum even at the high point of liberalism in the later 1960s and early 1970s.[10] Among highly educated professionals, there were, moreover, at least as many "consistent conservatives" with the opposite views on these matters.[11]

The Changing Issues Axis

What is true is that professionals were comparatively liberal on some issues that were particularly salient at the time. The most salient issues of the late 1960s and early 1970s had to do with public order and the war in Southeast Asia. In the years between 1967 and 1972, at least 70 percent of Americans considered one of these two issues to be the "most important problem" facing the country.[12]

Their level of support for student and black protest during the period was never high in an absolute sense; less than one quarter of college-educated professionals felt at all warmly toward protestors.[13] Nevertheless, this was a significantly higher level of support than other Americans expressed. Similarly, professionals were relatively respectful of rights to protest and the need to protect the civil liberties of protestors. They were also on occasion significantly more likely than other groups to criticize the police for using too much force on demonstrators.[14] College-educated professionals also tended to be most numerous (along with students) among the groups protesting the war in Vietnam on moral grounds.[15] Because issues of war and protest were the most important issues dividing liberals and conservatives during the period, professionals were somewhat less likely than other groups to eschew the otherwise quite unpopular descriptive label "liberal."[16]

Thus, one source of the reputation professionals gained for liberalism during the late 1960s and early 1970s has to do with the nature of the issues that were salient at the time. During this era of civil rights and Vietnam war protest, the agenda of American politics briefly rotated from the substantially class based New Deal "economic issues" axis separating conservative business and professional people, on one side, from liberal workers, on the other, to a new "social issues" and "foreign policy" axis that separated relatively liberal professional people (usually joined by blacks and other minorities) from conservative business people and white workers. While middle-class professionals were still comparatively conservative on many issues of the day, they were relatively liberal on the *salient* issues of the day: protest and war.

The characteristic pattern of division is evident in graphs from the American National Election studies on issues related to the military, public order, and ameliorative social policies to restore public order.[17] The "new divisions" of social and foreign policy liberalism are evident in the years at the beginning of the series (1968–74). The graphs do not show that professionals are liberal—only that they are a little more liberal than business people and workers. In the social policy area, divisions soon closed for reasons that I will discuss.

Liberalism and Demographic Change

Demographic influences also contributed to the liberalism among professionals in the late 1960s and early 1970s. Two of these demographic influences involved the effects of political socialization on groups disproportionately represented in the professions (or preparing for the professions): the young and the highly educated.

The political attitudes of young people are shaped by secular trends affecting each succeeding cohort,[18] and also by the climate prevailing when a cohort of young people comes of political age.[19] Young people, far from being intrinsically liberal, tend to adapt to the political climate during their late secondary school and early college years. In the 1960s and 1970s, the socialization influences were almost entirely on the liberal side: the government was liberal for most of the period; throughout the period, the dominant, activist political stance was liberal or further to the left; and the popular culture also encouraged an attitude of rebellion. Just as students in the 1930s, growing up in the Depression, were more liberal than the cohorts preceding and succeeding them, the students of the 1960s and early 1970s were also more liberal than the cohorts preceding and succeeding them.[20]

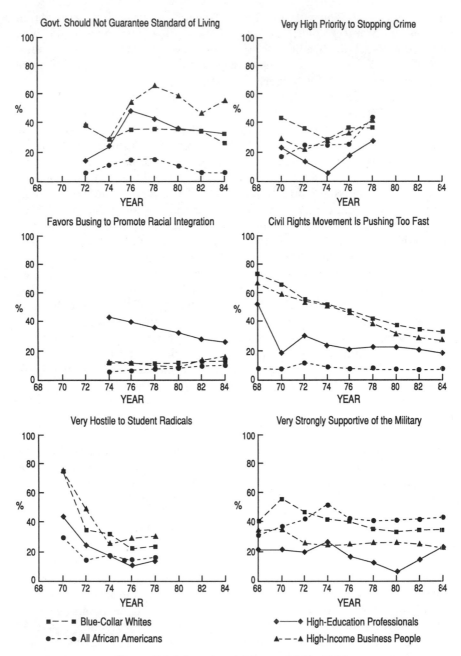

Figure 6.1 Selected social issues, 1968–1984.

These environmental influences led to a tremendous increase in liberal views (and, to a much more limited degree, radical views) among college students and young people generally. Where college students in the 1950s and early 1960s only infrequently considered themselves "liberals," this became the mode in the early 1970s. In 1970–71, nearly 40 percent of college freshmen thought of themselves as either "liberals," "left-liberals" or "radicals."[21] Because older students were already acclimated to the liberal climate of the universities, it is highly likely that liberals and those further to the left represented a clear majority of college students at the time.[22]

College students preparing for professional careers were becoming more liberal and even radical at precisely the time that the professions were growing most rapidly and, therefore, in need of a large number of new recruits. A comparatively large proportion of the new professional stratum of the 1960s and 1970s was composed of these new more liberal cohorts of college graduates. Whereas in the 1980s, only 25 percent of college graduate professionals were under age thirty, in the 1970s, nearly one-third were. The younger professionals brought with them a radical edge on issues ranging from egalitarian sentiments to liberal sexual morality. If reports from the period are accurate, they made the professions temporarily more attentive to issues involving the moral bases of professional practice.[23] The views of most of these people changed as they aged and as the political climate changed, but, for a brief time, they were an important part of what appeared to be a "march through institutions" of an increasingly liberal professional "class."[24]

Political socialization also had an impact on a group that was still more consequential to the professional stratum: the highly educated of all ages. Although they were not interested, by and large, in fundamental social change, the highly educated did become strong supporters of ameliorative social spending[25] and improved opportunities for disadvantaged groups; they also became more favorable than most groups in society to the protest movements of the day and were more likely than most groups to identify with the "New Politics" movement.[26]

Why were highly educated people liberal in so many domains during this period? Since good data has been available, higher education has been associated with some forms of "tolerance" for unconventional behavior and less advantaged groups, and it has also been reliably correlated with support for civil liberties. People with higher education tend to be more open-minded and less insular than those with lower levels of education. But, in other respects, higher education does not necessarily contribute to the molding of "enlightened" reformers, much less "oppositional intellectuals." Rather, the experience of higher education primarily encourages responsiveness to whatever stands as the prevailing climate of opinion among political elites. When political elites are mainly Democratic and progressive on matters of public policy, the highly educated will also be more likely to endorse Democratic and progressive views. When popular political elites are mainly Republican and conservative, the opposite will be true.

The responsiveness of the educated to the prevailing climate of opinion enhanced the reputation of professionals for liberalism to an even greater degree than did the analogous processes that affected the young during this period. Higher education and high-level intellectual skills are the most important constitutive properties of the professions as a status category, and very high levels of education are still far more common in the professions than they are in any other occupational category. As the professions grew in the 1960s, higher levels of education in the professions also became more common. Whereas just over two-thirds of census professionals had four or more years of higher education in 1960, nearly three-quarters had reached this level by 1970.[27] Thus, the professions were becoming more highly educated at precisely the same time that educated people were becoming more liberal.

Liberalism and the Changing Occupational Structure

The liberal occupational and sectoral categories in the professional stratum also grew faster than other categories during the 1960s and early 1970s. College teachers, nonacademic social scientists, social workers, counselors, personnel and labor relations specialists, educational administrators, and health administrators—all relatively liberal in orientation—were, along with computer specialists, among the ten fastest-growing professional occupations in the 1960s.[28] Quite a bit of the growth was due directly or indirectly to a more activist government. Social services grew, education grew, labor relations became more important (and more highly regulated), and the nonprofit sector, in general, found a supportive legal and political environment.

Compositional changes like these do not translate automatically into changes in the political profile of professionals.[29] However, in the context of a supportive political climate, the growth of liberal employment spheres did contribute to the enthusiasm for reform among professionals. Much of this support is simply due to the ideological salience of these spheres during periods of reform.

It is possible that numerical growth itself can also make a difference. If, for example, the social and cultural professions grow from one to two million at the same time that support for reform is growing, there may be a real surge of reform sentiment in these quarters, based on the larger size of the group, augmented by the tendency of people in liberal spheres to adapt to a liberal political climate more completely than other groups do.[30] By encouraging the growth of more liberal categories during periods of reform, liberal governments inadvertently gain a surge of political allies, just as conservative governments are abetted by encouraging the growth of conservative categories during periods in which they are ascendant.

Sources of Polarization in the Mid-1970s

Declining governmental legitimacy was the final important factor in the politics of the period. The continuing crisis of the war and protest was joined in the 1970s by two new sets of salient problems· the economic problems of inflation and slowed growth that had been brewing since the mid-1960s, and the moral crisis of Watergate.

The economic trends from the postwar period show an economy moving at a continually slowing pace beginning in the mid-1960s and beset by continually increasing problems.[31] The initial problems of inflation can be laid mainly at the doorstep of the Johnson administration, which imprudently sought to fight a full-scale war against domestic poverty without raising taxes. The Nixon administration at first fought inflation successfully using conventional monetary and fiscal tools. However, in order to improve the president's electoral prospects, the White House imposed wage and price controls while abandoning the fiscal and monetary constraints. This insured a new bout of inflation as soon as the controls were lifted. The OPEC-organized oil embargo of 1973–74, which led to a quadrupling of producers' price of oil, had an enormously intensifying effect on an already inflationary climate. In its wake, inflation reached a new high of 11 percent in 1974.[32]

During this period, Americans, in general, were clearly angry about the economy and losing confidence in the capacity of business and government to solve economic problems. For most Americans, including most professionals, business was a part of the problem of a failing economy. Many felt that the oil companies were trying to take advantage of the oil crisis to reap windfall profits, and they also blamed business for failing to exercise restraint on prices. Others felt that business had failed to meet its social responsibilities. Though confidence in business tended to be higher than confidence in government or labor unions, 56 percent of Americans in 1975 said that business profits were a major cause of inflation.[33] Professionals retained a comparatively high level of faith in government and the capacity of the political system to solve problems.[34]

By contrast, most business people felt unfairly blamed for problems that were beyond their control. What business people saw was that economic conditions were changing, and that government had not responded appropriately to the changes.[35] For business people, the economic problems of the era were often perceived as involving too much unproductive government spending, too much government willingness to support labor unions and their wage demand pressures on prices, and not enough support for capital accumulation and investment, the vital engine of wealth production in the society.[36] Instead of responding to help business under the new circumstances it faced, by controlling spending (and, even better, by cutting taxes), government had responded with a lack of clarity and piecemeal policies that had made a bad situation worse. In short, business people tended to see government—and, in particular, the excesses of the welfare state—as the great impediment to economic improvement.[37]

On top of the economic problems of the era, the Watergate scandal erupted in 1973, greatly damaging the credibility of the Republican president and his party. The percentage of Republican identifiers dropped into the low twenties in 1974, a historic low. Evaluations of Watergate also differed among profes-

112   • *CHAPTER 6* •

sionals and business people. For many professionals, as for many other Americans, Watergate was a symbol of the corruption of the Republican party and its business benefactors. For many business people, economic problems far exceeded Watergate in importance. In light of the pressing economic concerns, the Watergate issue, while unpleasant, was considered by many top business leaders to be of comparatively little consequence. They tended to think of Watergate as an unpleasant episode of political skullduggery, but insignificant in relation to the real problems of the day.[38] And, in view of the Democrats' flawed approach to fiscal management and regulation, the Republican party continued to be perceived by most business people as the best hope for economic improvement.[39]

These different patterns of response led to a temporary widening of attitude differences between professionals and business people in the early and mid-1970s on issues having to do with business, political parties, and political ideologies—but not, it should be emphasized, on most issues having to do with the effectiveness of government or the desire to press for further social reforms. Whereas professionals were inclined to become more cynical in the Watergate era about the power of business and "big interests," business people were much more likely to blame liberals, labor, and Democrats. (See Figure 6.2.)

These patterns would seem to support class-oriented interpretations of business-professional conflict in the 1970s. Nevertheless, class conflict interpretations are not without problems. The views of professionals on economic issues tend at all times to be conservative and market-oriented, and, as economic problems worsened in succeeding years, an increasing number adopted the emerging business consensus on the problems of the welfare state and capital accumulation. Business was only beginning to mobilize during this period of the early and mid-1970s, and leading business groups had not yet communicated a coherent program. Without the complicating factor of Watergate, it seems to me unlikely that professionals would have had as strong a reaction against either business or the Republican party as they did during the period. It is in large measure because of Watergate and its connection with powerful interests and the Republican party that attitudes remained in a liberal and Democratic direction for as long as they did. Watergate helped to delegitimate the Republicans at precisely the time that larger numbers of professionals might well have been receptive to business thinking on the economy. The structural problems of the American economy during this period are no accident. Yet the unpredictable historical contingency of Watergate is just as essential to the temporary polarization of business and professionals in the mid-1970s as it is peripheral to the issue of economic interests and class oppositions that the class conflict interpretation highlights.

Social Movements and Discontent

Whether the surge of liberalism in the late 1960s and early 1970s was due to the cumulative force of several distinct and separable trends, as I have argued,

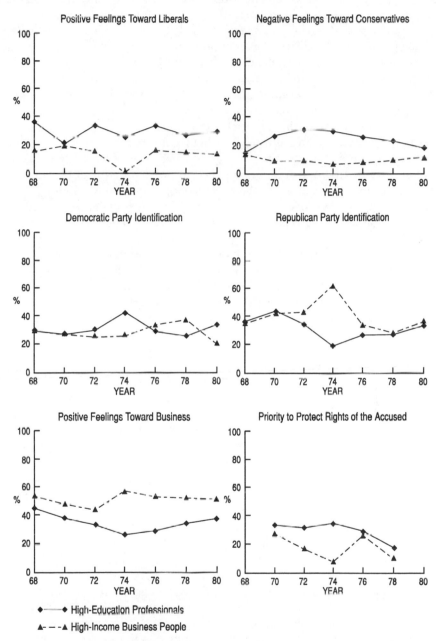

Figure 6.2 Selected mid-1970s indicators of business-professional conflict.

or to a flashing of class antagonism, there was, to be sure, a singular result: a swelling of progressive sentiment and even radicalism among the educated middle class people who were employed in or preparing for the professions. During this period, social movements of the left were working on unusually fertile ground for the creation of an oppositional class consciousness among professionals and college students preparing for the professions.

Many organized groups and activist intellectuals worked to create an independent (and, in some instances, also clearly oppositional) consciousness out of the set of liberalizing forces that came together in the late 1960s and early 1970s. To some extent, though briefly, they were clearly successful in their efforts. These years stand as a modern high watermark in the birth, public prominence, and, perhaps also, the success level of professionally led consumer groups, environmental groups, liberal public-interest organizations, antiwar groups, and radicals-in-the-professions groups.[40] It was also a period in which rebellion was occasionally encouraged in the popular culture and in which the urge to challenge traditional authority reached broadly into the middle classes.

The movements of the period built on elements of professional ideology, on the rights–based vocabulary of liberal jurisprudence, and on the antinomian culture of bohemia. From the traditional legitimations of social trustee professionalism came an emphasis on the public interest, on the integrity of communities, on the protection of the vulnerable, on the responsibilities of intellect.[41] The specifically professional inspiration behind the rhetoric of reform can be seen most clearly in the consumer and environmental movements—and, of course, in the public interest movement. As in social trustee professionalism, all three reflexively projected a larger social interest as an ultimate and absolute court of appeal. Most of the individual leaders of reform during the period also borrowed from the worldview of social trustee professionalism. A strong resonance is there, for example, in the Port Huron Statement, whose authors assert that "Money, instead of dignity of character, remains a pivotal American value, and Profitability, instead of social use, a pivotal standard in determining priorities." It is there also in Martin Luther King's warning that American society, for all its "glittering technology" lacks the "moral purpose" to "raise man to new heights."[42]

Had these oppositional trends continued and congealed into a more stable and less internally divided political force, it would be possible to write retrospectively about the era's importance in the development of a distinctive "class consciousness" of professionals. However, as economic conditions worsened and liberals fell out of favor, the more aggressive voices of "new class" liberalism and dissent receded in importance and, by the end of the decade, remained influential only at the margins of political life. At most, the politics of the period suggest that if economic conditions deteriorate in a serious way, while at the same time conservatives lose legitimacy as economic stewards, the possibility exists for significant class conflict between business leaders and professionals close to the culture of the universities, the government, and the nonprofits.

PROFESSIONALS AND THE CONSERVATIVE ASCENDANCE

The brief season of liberalism and dissent in the professional middle class ended after 1974—ironically, at about the time the "new class" idea gained something of a popular vogue.

The subsequent period is poorly understood. In the population at large, the trend toward conservatism, beginning in the mid-1970s, was neither as comprehensive nor as headlong as is often assumed. Attitudes about civil liberties, racial integration, women's rights, and sexual freedoms either remained stable or moved in a liberal direction.[43] More liberal attitudes about abortion were also in evidence for a good part of the 1970s and 1980s. Americans never rejected the welfare state during this period, nor did they reject many concrete programs of the welfare state.[44] Some forms of governmental social spending, for example on education and the environment, continued to gain overwhelming support throughout the period, if at slightly reduced levels. Nor, in spite of the popularity of Ronald Reagan, did identification with the Republican party show a sustained climb throughout the period.[45]

At the same time, some attitudes did tend to move in a conservative direction beginning around 1973–74. The most important of the conservative trends of the mid-1970s had to do with social spending, taxation, defense, and crime.[46] The sociologist James A. Davis measured conservatism on spending items in the General Social Survey by adding the change in the proportion saying "too little" was being spent in a particular policy domain to the proportion saying "too much" was being spent on it. Using this measure, Davis calculated that shifts of 15 to 20 percent in a conservative direction occurred in the years between 1973 and 1978 on most issues related to social welfare spending. Conservative shifts on military spending were even more profound.[47] Strong feelings about the waste of tax dollars by inefficient government were evident in American public opinion as early as the late 1960s, but only in the mid-to-late 1970s did trust that the government would not waste taxpayers' money drop to perilously low levels. In 1976 and 1978, more than three-quarters of voting age Americans said that government "wastes most tax money."[48] These kinds of sentiments fueled the tax revolt movements of the late 1970s.[49]

In the 1970s and 1980s, professionals moved very much in concert with the general trends in public opinion. They continued to be liberal, and sometimes increasingly liberal, on many social issues, while moving in a more conservative direction on issues involving government spending, taxes, defense (for most of the period), and crime. The trends in voting and ideological self-assessments also tended to move in a conservative direction. Like the rest of the country, professionals voted three to two for the Republican candidates in each of the presidential elections of the 1980s. By the later 1970s, laissez-faire conservatives outnumbered pro-government liberals three-to-two in the professional stratum, where in the years just after Watergate they had held no numerical bulge and had perhaps been slightly less numerous than liberals.[50]

Not surprisingly, the term "liberal" all but disappeared from political discourse as a positive label, and the conservative label grew increasingly popular.

A New Rotation in the Issues Axis

During this period, the axis of politics turned decisively away from the kinds of social and foreign policy issues that tend to bring out the liberalism of professionals and in the direction of the kinds of economic issues that tend to bring out their conservatism. From the mid-1970s through the 1980s, economic issues dominated polls on "the most important problems" facing the country. By adding together the rates of inflation and unemployment during the period, the sociologist Seymour Martin Lipset devised a simple but powerfully predictive "misery index." Feelings of confidence with the major institutions of the society were strongly associated with changes in the "misery index," as were levels of optimism and pessimism about the overall situation of the country.[51]

Statistical analyses of voting and popularity trends during the period indicate that incumbent parties were consistently punished by defections and low popularity ratings for their failures to bring inflation and unemployment under control, and for their failures to encourage sustained growth.[52] In this context, the bad economic conditions of the mid and late 1970s had the same impact on professionals as on others; they encouraged defections from leaders under whom the economy performed poorly, while rewarding the Republican leader under whom the economy performed well.

Liberals favoring activist government were most adversely affected by the bad economic news of the 1970s. Committed to macroeconomic management that no longer seemed to work as promised and to social provision that was often blamed for inflation, liberals appeared to many to be floundering in counterproductive policy commitments. As early as 1968, Republicans were beginning to make political gains by accusing liberals of taxing the majority for the benefit of small minorities and by arguing for the negative consequences of too much social generosity and too much humanitarian concern. Following the 1972 election, these ideas about the unintended consequences of reform were taken up by the spokesmen for the conservative wing of the Democratic party, and they continued to stand as a powerful rebuke to liberals throughout the 1970s and 1980s.[53] In a period of economic distress, without a clear vision, or a clearly working set of policy tools, liberals ceased to encourage much confidence.

Again, the conditions of the age created fertile grounds for social movements—but this time for movements of the right. Spurred by the efforts of the American Council on Capital Formation and the Business Roundtable, both flourishing as early as 1972, business people began to promote a pro-growth policy of reduced government spending, reduced tax rates on corporations and the rich, decreased government regulation of industry, and new government services aimed at improving the competitive situation of business through more clearly focused human capital development and incentives for new investment. The mobilizing efforts of business leaders to build a philosophical and policy consensus for market-oriented economic renewal included the formation of political action committees to finance the candidacies of pro-growth politicians, the founding of conservative "think tanks" to help fight the war of ideas, the funding of conservative publications and policy research for similar purposes, and the use of advocacy advertising to publicize the new thinking and to attack opponents.[54]

The end of the war and protest movement and the worsening economic conditions encouraged reconciliation of business and professional people around this pro-growth economic agenda.[55] Indeed, Americans in general moved toward approving the new priorities of the capital development agenda. The success of these efforts clearly built on public attitudes that were increasingly cool to "big government" and Democratic leadership, if not to specific social programs.

Cumulative Trends—in Reverse

In this context, many of the processes that promoted liberal views among professionals in the 1960s and early 1970s worked in precisely the reverse fashion in the later 1970s and 1980s. Essentially the same forces were at work, but the cumulative force now gathered in the direction of increasing conservatism.

As the governing climate shifted in a conservative direction, political socialization and political adaptation influences on the young and highly educated began to work in a conservative, rather than a liberal, direction. The 1980s cohorts of professional workers came of political age during a period of conservative revival and apparent conservative success in the wake of Democratic "failures," and they were the first cohort in modern memory to adopt positions that were more Republican than the cohorts preceding them. The proportion of self-identified "liberals" fell from a high of 38 percent in 1971 to 22 percent by 1980.[56] Of all age categories, 18–29 years olds were the least Democratic by the end of the Reagan era.[57]

The shift to the right on issues of economic distribution and social regulation was hardly limited to the youngest professional cohorts. Frequently, new family responsibilities paved the way toward rapprochement with the center and the right among professional people approaching mid-career. Many began to look more sympathetically on the religions of their youth and toward more voluntarist visions of community.[58]

Indeed, polling data suggests that an even more interesting change occurred in relation to the highly educated than in relation to the young. In the 1970s, higher education was associated with liberalism in both economic and social issue domains. However, in the 1980s, higher education ceased to be associated with liberal views on issues of economic distribution, military power, or crime control.[59] These trends provide further evidence that higher education mainly encourages people to be more sensitive to the prevailing views among political elites and to the related expectations of their peers.

As conservatives gained power, they encouraged the growth of the more conservative occupational categories, while cutting back on some of the more liberal categories. The declining tax revenues for social services supported a decisive shift of resources to the wealthier provinces of the private sector. Some business service sectors grew at twice the rate of GNP, and none were less than 60 percent higher.[60] In the wake of this boom, business services became one of the leading export industries in the American economy—one of relatively few rays of economic light during a period in which American industries were largely overshadowed by foreign competitors. By contrast, the strategists connected to the human services wrote mainly about ways to forestall further layoffs and cutbacks by federal, state, and local governments that have been thrown into chronic and debilitating deficits. As early as the Carter administration, the old liberal coalition was "fighting largely futile budgetary battles under the limp rallying cry, 'Cut less!'"[61]

The Motivated Use of Public Policy

These patterns of occupational and sectoral decline were explicitly encouraged by national policy. In 1986 dollars, the Reagan administration oversaw an annual $70 billion transfer from domestic programs (other than social security and medicine) to the military alone.[62] Many Reagan administration officials, including budget director David Stockman acknowledged that "defunding the left" was an explicit goal.[63]

Just as spending priorities reinforced sectoral divisions among professionals, tax policies greatly reinforced income divisions. The tax cuts of 1981, in particular, helped to bring higher-income professionals (and higher-income voters generally) into the Reagan coalition, by reducing their federal income tax burden by some 29 percent at the highest levels. The Administration plan also indexed the new reduced rates for wealthier Americans to changes in the inflation rate, which had the effect of locking in a rate structure that disproportionately benefitted the rich and the upper-middle class. The administration successfully encouraged a sharp reduction in corporate tax rates as well, by replacing the existing rules on depreciation with rules allowing businesses to write off the value of an asset at an accelerated rate.[64]

The evidence suggests that these benefits carried over into electoral preferences. Data on partisanship by income class show how marked a change occurred. Increasingly, politics became a contest between the top and bottom of the income distribution.[65] Not surprisingly, professionals in private practice and in the industrial-corporate core were drawn to conservative politics, while professionals outside the core remained among the stalwarts of "progressive" politics.

Many middle and upper-income suburban voters who once saw themselves as beneficiaries of government programs now identified themselves as "tax-

TABLE 6.1
Party Allegiance by Income, 1956 and 1984

Income Group	Democratic Advantage (+) or Disadvantage (−)	
	1956	1984
The Affluent (91%–100%)	−22	−33
The Upper Middle Class (61%–90%)	+13	0
The Middle Class (31%–60%)	+17	+6
The Working and Lower-Middle Class (11%–30%)	+22	+29
The Very Poor (the bottom 10%)	+18	+36

Source: Martin Wattenberg, "The Hollow Realignment: Partisan Change in a Candidate-Centered Era" (Paper presented at the annual meeting of the American Political Science Association, New Orleans, 1985). Data from the University of Michigan's National Election Studies.

payers, individuals whose chief concern is the cost of federal programs."[66] By encouraging an unprecedented budget deficit, the Reagan policies also had the effect (perhaps at first unintended) of greatly reducing the revenues available for reforms at the national level. The deficit created during the Reagan years has made it virtually impossible for Democrats to talk about major new domestic spending programs unless they also raise the unpopular subject of taxes. In this sense, it was not just the strength of the Republican party that changed, but the entire institutional structure of government.

The use of public policy to drive a wedge between private- and public-sector workers, and between rich and poor, tended to reinforce long-standing divisions in the professional stratum, rather than to create new divisions. At most, it may portend a new professional politics on economic issues, in which sector and income level are of singular importance in the structuring of political outlooks, while other factors that have had a discernible impact in the past, such as occupation and cultural outlook, recede in importance.

New Areas of Discord

While economic issues became an area of relative consensus between business people and professionals, an interesting countermovement occurred on some social issues. Here increasing gaps became evident. Table 6.2 below contrasts

TABLE 6.2
Political Attitudes over Time in Four Strata, 1974–1976 and 1974–1988

Issue	Soc/Cult Profs	High-Educ Profs	High-Inc Business	Blue Collar	All Adults
I. Public Opinion Moving to the Right					
Constant Gaps between Professionals and Business People (%)					
Republican Identifier	35/37	36/40	51/53	23/27	30/34
Democratic Identifier	56/54	54/50	40/37	62/59	57/54
Great Confidence in Business	25/38	31/42	49/56	24/37	25/37
Increasing Similarities between Professionals and Business People					
Hardly Any Confidence in Labor	41/42	33/39	51/53	27/30	31/35
Liberal on Sexual Mores	79/66	52/44	44/38	25/24	29/27
Liberal on Crime	39/23	23/15	15/ 8	13/11	14/11
Liberal on Welfare Programs	35/25	23/18	13/11	28/27	24/23
II. Public Opinion Stable/Moving Left					
Constant Gaps between Professionals and Business People					
Liberal on Civil Liberties	98/85	70/71	61/62	27/29	40/39
Liberal on Spending for Middle Class Programs	38/41	34/33	23/22	20/21	23/24
Liberal on Environmental Spending	73/73	68/66	58/54	57/58	59/58
Liberal on Domestic Spending	43/47	33/31	26/22	21/23	22/24
Increasing Gaps between Professionals and Business People					
Cut Defense Spending	68/55	46/53	38/31	22/23	27/27
Liberal on Racial Attitudes	76/72	61/58	51/44	30/31	37/38
Liberal on Gender Issues	67/68	59/56	60/50	30/31	37/37

Source: Cumulative General Social Survey, 1974–1988.

issues on which public opinion has taken a more conservative cast over time, and those on which it has taken a more liberal cast. In every instance, the first percentage figure is for the 1974–76 period, and the second is for the total 1974–88 period.

As public opinion moved to the right, professionals and business people became much more alike in their attitudes about business, labor, and crime. At the same time, as public opinion has moved to the left, professionals and business people became less alike on issues involving race and gender. For the most part, this is because business people moved in a conservative direction—against the grain of public opinion—while professionals did not, or did only marginally. The new battlegrounds were increasingly over social issues, and here professionals sometimes have held the upper hand.

THE ATTITUDE GAP

As the data in Table 6.2 indicates, an attitude gap exists on a wide range of issues between highly educated professionals and high-income business people during periods of reform and periods of conservatism alike. Indeed, opinion surveys suggest gaps of 10 to 15 percent on virtually every political attitude item on which a time series is available.[67] Among the few exceptions to this rule are the most liberal positions on the causes of crime and the reduction of economic inequality. These positions are rejected overwhelmingly by both groups, and such differences as exist are minimal.

Some writers have taken the continuing gaps as evidence of a difference in the emerging class interests of business people and professionals. This explanation is perhaps plausible, but it is not the most convincing explanation, in my opinion. At a minimum, growing compositional differences between the business and professional strata suggest an alternative to a class interpretation of the attitude gap.

Compositional Trends and the Attitude Gap

The comparisons below focus on high-income managers and highly educated professionals, excluding human services. These comparisons isolate the core of the economically advantaged business class and the credentially advantaged professional class. They indicate that, over time, compositional changes have created a new kind of professional stratum composed of more people working in employment spheres (and representing demographic groups) that are comparatively receptive to liberal politics.

The comparisons show that about 5 percent of high-income managers were age thirty or less in 1980, as compared to nearly 30 percent of professionals. Some 25 percent of high-income managers had advanced degrees in 1980, compared to nearly 60 percent of professionals. Less than 4 percent of high-income managers were nonwhite in 1980, compared to more than 7 percent of professionals. And less than 5 percent of high income managers were women, but well over one-quarter of professionals. In each case, the more liberal employment and demographic categories were far more common in the professional world than in the business world.

The changes over time have also tended, in many cases, to widen the divergence between business and professional demographic profiles. The differ-

TABLE 6.3
Selected Demographic Characteristics of Highly Educated Professionals[a]
and High-Income Managers, 1940–1980

	1940	1960	1980	% Change 1940–80
Highly educated Professionals (except human services)				
% of Labor Force	2.2	2.6	3.9	+1.7
% Expanded Public Sector	66.3	58.0	39.6	−26.7[b]
% Self-Employed	36.5	23.2	22.2	−14.3
% Soc/Cultural	23.5	20.2	31.8	+8.3
% Top Income Fifth	44.5	51.2	60.3	+16.0
% 30 or younger	23.4	24.8	27.8	+4.4
% Advanced Training[c]	41.0	44.8	58.3	+17.3
% Nonwhite	3.0	3.3	7.3	+4.3
% Women	17.2	16.2	17.9	+.7
Upper-Income Managers and Executives[d]				
% of Labor Force	3.9	3.5	2.7	−1.2
% Expanded Public Sector	11.8	10.0	8.7	−3.1
% Self-Employed	27.1	37.8	30.7	−3.6
% Top Income Fifth	100.0	100.0	100.0	0.0
% 30 or younger	12.4	7.1	5.4	−7.0
% Advanced Training	2.3	5.1	25.8	+23.5
% Nonwhite	1.1	1.2	3.0	+1.9
% Women	10.1	13.9	4.8	−5.3

Sources: Public-use microdata .001 percent sample of population from U.S. Census of 1940; Public-use microdata .0015 percent sample of population from U.S. Census of 1960; Public-Use mirodata .001 percent sample of population from U.S. Census of 1980.

[a] Salaried, highly educated professionals are Census 1980 professional specialty occupations (excluding athletes and public relations personnel) who have at least four full years of college.

[b] The large percentage change in the expanded public sector is difficult to understand. Analysis errors are not to blame, however.

[c] Advanced training refers to at least five full years of college training.

[d] High income managers and executives are all persons in the 1980 census executive and management occupations category whose family incomes are in the top quarter for the managerial category.

ences in composition between professionals and managers increased over time in terms of the proportion self-employed, the proportion under thirty, the proportion urban, the proportion nonwhite, and the proportion women. Professionals also grew as a proportion of the labor force, while upper-income managers declined. Differences narrowed a little, but remained large in absolute terms on the proportion earning high incomes, the proportion with advanced training, and the proportion employed in the public sector. Thus, the portrait is of two strata becoming increasingly different demographically and becoming only a little more alike in terms of employment situations.

This analysis does not necessarily indicate that a class-based interpretation of the attitude gap is wrong, but it does suggest that it might be misspecified. The gap may not be the result of class tensions arising in a more or less natural way from differences between the holders of "economic capital resources" and the holders of "knowledge resources." Rather, the gap is more likely based on the kinds of groups and institutions in which socially validated "knowledge resources" are embedded.

The most likely contributors to the attitude gap are the larger employment settings in which very different proportions of professionals and business people are located, and in which attitudes are distinctively more liberal than those in the relevant contrasting setting. For example, because public and private sector workers tend to have rather different attitudes, and because there is a large representational difference between the mainly private sector managers and the mainly public sector professionals, sectoral differences should be one of the more important compositional influences behind the attitude gap. This logic suggests that the most likely contributors to the attitude gap on economic issues are the three employment variables—sector, income, and occupation (particularly in relation to differences between human-services professionals and business people). On social issues, the most likely contributors are the education, age, and gender differences between professionals and business people.[68] These compositional differences are an underlying source of the attitude gap between professional people and business people, and they provide the cultural ambiance out of which sharper tensions sometimes flare.

The Erosion of Autonomy

It is important to emphasize that compositional differences do not automatically lead to political divisions. For differences to develop and persist, supports are necessary to guard the distinctiveness of the categories in question. Thus, for example, if public sector workers begin to feel their dependence on the private sector in a more profound way than they feel their connection to "public service," the public sector would cease to be a reservoir of progressive sentiment, even if it were to grow appreciably as the location of most professional work. Many large-scale political and cultural conversions of important demographic groups are documented in the historical record,[69] and modern professional groups are by no means exempt from forces that lead to the weakening of autonomy and ideological differences.

In fact, there have been a great many pressures leading toward the erosion of professional distinctiveness in our era and toward an increasing sense of dependence on corporate organization and consumer markets. This is, of course, not entirely a bad thing; we look to professionals to provide services where they are in demand. A responsiveness to new sources of demand is entirely in keeping with the market constitution of the original fee-for-service professions. At the same time, a market orientation, when it becomes overly-absorbing, can be destructive of institutional protections guarding professional life, leaving professionals as organizational staff and skill merchants only and relatively impoverished of the essential intellectual cultures and occupational values of their work.

In retrospect, it seems clear that the period of the rise of occupational professionalism was an age of many partial shelters against the influence of markets and employers on the practices of professionals. The mixed goals of the welfare state and the nonprofit sector were clearly two of the more important of these partial shelters, and these helped to guarantee that services would be provided to a broader segment of the population than would otherwise have occurred. The standards and traditions of academe, the institutions of elite culture, and even the inspirations of a progressive political culture provided other kinds of partial shelters—more cultural than economic— against the singular influence of markets and employers. The succeeding age of expertise has been, by contrast, an age of relatively less restrained consumer markets and corporate power.[70] Where it is allowed to do so, this countermovement against the elitism, high standards, and broader purposes of the sheltered professions has shucked off the old barriers and restraints like a constricting skin.

The most important causes of the countermovement are political in the broadest sense of the term. Real financial pressures exist that influence the actions of political and corporate leaders,[71] but very often these pressures have been interpreted in a highly selective way against the education of consumer and citizen preferences and in the direction of the rationalization of expertise in a more utilitarian, market-oriented direction. The prevailing ideologies of both politicians and leaders of American private corporations and public institutions have come to reflect an often panicky obsession with competition and efficiency.

Another major cause of this countermovement is demographic. Where the number of people in expert occupations increases faster than the traditional markets for their services, competitive pressures encourage one or more of several possible responses: where services are greatly in demand (as in many medical specialties), some practitioners will be able to maintain their position through adding auxiliary services that might have been considered unnecessary in the past. Where demand in traditional client populations is less elastic, professionals (and the organizations that employ them) will search for new previously unserviced or underserviced markets, sometimes encroaching on the work of other professional groups. Some professions will attempt to use government to legitimate or underwrite professionals activities (as is true of many legal specialties and psychotherapies). And, finally, pressures may exist for innovations in the understandings or paradigms governing practice to allow for more fluidity in the selection of new incumbents for existing positions. Each of these responses can reduce the social control of autonomous professional gatekeepers, and each tends to increase the role of markets (and governments) in the control of professional practice.

Signs of the erosion of autonomy are evident at the elite level in some professions that have great importance in intellectual life and public culture. According to surveys, university scientists and researchers say they are now less likely to pursue high-risk basic scientific inquiries and prefer instead to stick "to research in which an end product is assured, or [to work] in fields they feel are favored by funding agency officials."[72] In the view of a recent president of the American Association for the Advancement of Science, this tendency to pursue assured applications and externally created priorities "raises serious questions about the very future of science in the United States."[73] The issue of market applications also has influenced some social science fields. In psychology, for example, there has been a sharp decline in traditional academic research areas, as the field becomes "increasingly focused on health service provision" through counseling and therapy. Leaders in the profession worry about "the possible erosion of psychology's overall ranking in the national scientific community."[74]

The arts, for their part, have become increasingly connected to the entertainment industry. During the last age of reform, a dominant impulse in the arts community, under the leadership of men such as Claes Oldenburg, Jasper Johns, and Andy Warhol, was to forge a connection with popular culture. Studies of artists suggest that major sources of inspiration are found in the popular culture rather than in the humanities.[75] "[P]op artists . . . attempt[ed] to bring the aesthetic tradition into contact with visual imagery from commercial art and popular culture. With the Neo-Expressionists [of the early 1980s], the conception that the artists's insights were superior to those of other image-makers in American society disappeared. These artists saw themselves as entertainers, using visual imagery to amuse and provoke the public, rather than as aesthetic innovators contributing to an artistic tradition."[76] To a greater degree than previously, the visual arts community has become an appendage of the popular culture and communications industry, and the connection of the visual arts to traditional high culture has progressively weakened.[77]

Journalism has also followed a course of closer connection with the world of entertainment, even at the more professionalized national level. One indicator is the extent to which the reporting of news has become interlaced with the subjective opinions of journalists, opinions sometimes founded on superficial impressions of the moment. In the view of a former president of CBS News, the news media have become a "tremendous advocacy group": "Look at [the major newsweeklies]. The subjectivity that . . . runs through them [is] absolutely stunning."[78] Some leading reporters contribute in an unabashed way to the merging of personal perception and news by appearing on television talk shows and entertainment programs where they express personal points of view on public affairs. As in the arts, the decline of impersonal occupational authority and the rise of consumerism have been great contributors to these changes. In the view of the curator of the Nieman Foundation at Harvard University, "The proliferation . . . of outlets for news and information . . . has simply magnified" every tendency of the press to treat public affairs as sport, gossip, and entertainment.[79] According to public opinion research, readers and viewers say they don't approve of the subjectivity and slant of modern journalism, but consumption patterns suggest that their disapproval has had little effect on what they buy, read, and watch.[80]

It is possible that trends toward the commercialization of the professions and questions about the validity of "public purposes" will continue. If so, the remaining differences between professional life and business life as spheres of cultural orientation are likely to diminish further, whatever compositional differences exist between the two strata.

PART TWO

Experts, Intellectuals, and Professionals

The Influence of Policy Experts

THUS FAR, I have focused on the development of the professional stratum and its forms of consciousness over time. Most professional people are not, of course, directly active in politics. Instead, they form a reservoir of attitudes and opinions that can encourage politicians and interest groups who represent their interests and ideals more directly. In the next two chapters, I will turn my attention to two groups that are more directly active in public life. I have chosen to write about policy experts and intellectuals because they seem to me to represent in the clearest way the two sides of professionalism—technical skills and moral standards, respectively—that are potentially relevant to public life. I wanted to see what the fate of these sides of the traditional status culture of professionalism have been in modern public life, as they are represented by people who are actively involved in public life.

Although the focus is different, in many ways the analysis of these two chapters parallels the analysis of the earlier chapters. As before, I will focus on the influence of organizations, markets, and occupational cultures. The most frequent characterizations of policy experts and intellectuals are connected to images of "advancing technocracy," on one side, and an "adversary culture" of intellectuals, on the other. I will take these two characterizations as the starting point for my analysis of the influence and outlooks of policy experts and intellectuals. Rather than reinforcing views about an "advancing technocracy" or the "adversary culture," I will show that the organizational context in which experts and intellectuals work effectively narrows their role in public life. This narrow role is also encouraged by the occupational cultures of the two groups—by the "unfinished rationality" of policy experts and by the "culture of particularizing refinement" that dominates discourse in the leading periodicals of intellectual opinion.

ADVANCING TECHNOCRACY?

In the social sciences, the central debate about policy experts concerns their influence on the decisions of governments. Those who see experts as influential take the view that—whether for good or ill—experts have become an increasingly important power behind the scenes.

Certainly, no government in the developed world finds itself able to do without the armies of experts who conduct research on matters of consequence to public policy, consult and advise decision makers, and develop policy options for the future. These people have gained enough respect for their effective works and cool judgments that even the most powerful of democratic politicians sometimes mimic their style, while others—in the United States, mainly politicians of a more populist stripe—have made careers out of ridiculing the expert cadre as dangerously out of touch with the values and aspirations of ordinary people.

The major conclusion shared by writers who endorse the idea of advancing technocracy is that the power of technical experts is increasing, while the power of traditional kinds of politicians is declining.[1] The argument is often based on a sense that, as public policy issues become more complex, the public (including the politicians who represent the public) become less and less able to make informed decisions. Because of this, the responsibility for making decisions tends to become located in the hands of experts who understand the technical issues involved in the creation of policies.

One piece of evidence often cited in support of a trend toward technocratic decision making is the sheer number of experts now working in and around government. Until the postwar era, both congressional and executive branch staffs were rather small. "Most congressional committees did not have permanent professional staffs, personal staffs [of Congressmen] were miniscule, and support staffs were not much larger."[2] Between 1947 and 1980, the size of professional legislative staffs—those working primarily on legislation rather than correspondence and constituency service—increased at least six-fold.[3] These legislative staffs are now the size of a moderately sized town of 15,000.[4]

The professional staffs in the executive branch have also grown swiftly in the postwar era, without regard to the party in power. Between the beginning of Franklin Roosevelt's first term and the end of the 1980s, the size of the White House staff increased from thirty-seven to 900, with thousands more employed in "satellite operations" that also serve the president, the fastest-growing of which has been the Office of Management and Budget.[5] Most of these professional staff people in the executive branch are either young lawyers or academics. The emphasis on hiring staff with very high levels of education began, in particular, under John Kennedy and increased again under Richard Nixon.[6] While their educations have become more impressive, the political experience of these staff experts has decreased over time, helping to fuel the complaints of populists.[7]

A second type of evidence, also frequently cited, is the proliferation of policy-related research conducted for and by government. In *The Coming of Post-Industrial Society*, the sociologist Daniel Bell argued that "[t]he major intellectual and sociological problems of the post-industrial society are . . . those of 'organized complexity'—the management of large-scale systems, with large numbers of interacting variables, which have to be coordinated to achieve specific goals. . . . Since 1940, there has been a remarkable efflorescence of new fields whose results apply to problems of organized complexity: information theory, cybernetics, decision theory, game theory, utility theory, stochastic processes."[8] Bell went on to provide illustrations of how these intellectual technologies have been applied to a range of problems, such as the realignment of strategic and tactical programs in the Department of Defense, the development of indices of the necessary scale of funding of science, and the best means of directing monies into the revitalization of urban centers.[9] Clearly, an enormous amount of policy-related research, some of it sophisticated in design and execution, is now conducted each year.

Case studies can also be found that lend credibility to the idea that experts have gained power in American government at the expense of popularly elected decision makers. In his study of American foreign policy making from the late 1960s, Henry Kissinger emphasized the tendency for busy and preoccupied decision makers to be captured, for particular purposes, by their staffs.[10] More recent studies have sometimes come to quite similar conclusions. According to the political scientist Michael Malbin, in the "new Washington" of the postwar era, where the issues are complex, the interests many, and the politicians overburdened, "we [increasingly] see members relying on staff technocrats . . . whose knowledge of the world is limited to what they learned in school or from other participants in the specialized Washington issue networks [to which they belong]."[11] Pockets of staff power of this sort have been well documented in Congress and the White House alike. In his book about Washington during the Reagan era, Hedrick Smith, the Washington bureau chief for the *New York Times,* describes the prominence of staff as a virtual revolution in the workings of power in Washington. One powerful staff member in Congress is described as "using technical expertise, hard work, and tenacity" to build a base "as powerful as a [congressional] subcommittee chairman."[12] Another is described as the intellectual force behind tax reform. And a third is singled out for his success in using his role in the processing of policy materials to the president to provide a personal stamp on the intellectual substance of the administration's domestic policy.[13]

Experts and the Organization of American Pluralism

To evaluate these arguments about the growing influence of policy experts, it is necessary as a preliminary matter to agree upon who is an expert and who is not. It is not difficult to distinguish experts from lay people. Experts participate in the political process *as experts* only by virtue of an assertion of "knowledge-based" authority. This is obviously not true of lay people. Since politicians and other elites may be—and indeed are increasingly—professionally trained, the more difficult contrast is between elites and experts. It seems to me that a distinction is necessary since the responsibilities and patterns of association of elites and experts are quite different. I will define elites as those people occupying the "command posts" at the top of the central institutional domains in the society. These central institutional domains are the corporate economy; the three branches of government; and the military. I will define experts as highly trained professional staff working in these central institutional domains, either on a salaried or contractual basis, and including also professionals in the surrounding institutional arenas of scientific research, cultural and communication services, social service, medical, legal, and educational organizations. When highly trained experts assume positions that qualify them as elites, they cease, in this definition, to be experts—even if they continue to use professional knowledge as a basis or justification for decisions. Experts must also be differentiated from representatives of interest groups. This is an important distinction, because highly educated people very often act as agents of interest groups, rather than as agents of professional knowledge. In these cases, it is a mistake, I think, to talk about "policy experts." The activities of experts in these circumstances are much more clearly described as a kind of service to organized interests.

The most useful way to evaluate the idea of advancing technocracy is to begin by specifying the political and organizational context in which experts operate in the United States. When this context is properly drawn the notion of advancing technocracy largely collapses on its own weight due to a lack of fit between the implications of the theory and the actual workings of the political system. The equally sweeping notion of expert subordination to formal power holders and influential lobbies also finds little support. What emerges in their place is a picture of a political system that allows some room for independent—and occasionally rather important—activity by professional experts, but which, for the most part, effectively limits their influence.

The American political order can be described as a system of stratified and segmented pluralism. This is a wordy formulation, but all the words are necessary. The American system is pluralistic in the sense that it is relatively open to the influence of pressure groups of many different types. As the political sociologist Theda Skocpol observes: "Such basic features of the U.S. [political] structure as federalism, the importance of geographic units of representation, nonprogrammatic political parties, fragmented realms of administrative bureaucracy, and the importance of Congress and its specialized committees within the national government . . . all encourage a proliferation of competing, narrowly specialized, and weakly disciplined interest groups."[14]

At the same time, it is clearly the case that some of these interests are more equal than others. In this sense, the structure of policy making is stratified; both formal and informal authority is concentrated in the hands of a relative few. In the executive branch, the president and his leading advisers are preeminent, followed by the cabinet secretaries in rank prestige order. In Congress, too, a structure of stratification exits. Formal and informal authority is concentrated among the senior members, the formal leadership groups, and the committee chairs, in a descending order of the prestige of their committees, with the economic and foreign affairs committees as central in Congress as the corresponding departments are in the executive branch.[15] To some degree, members may also gain influence informally through recognition by their peers of their knowledge and seriousness of purpose.[16]

The powers of interest organizations are also steeply stratified—by resources, political connections, and reputation. Only the wealthiest and most well staffed organizations are central players in policy making networks. This stratification structure leads to a model of influence that can best be described as structured around concentric bands of organizations surrounding the principal government authorities in a policy domain.[17] The larger organizations mediate between the central authorities and the more peripheral specialist organizations that also have an interest in policy. "In explaining most [policy] decisions, the peripheral organizations may be ignored."[18]

This political structure is also segmented. It is segmented, in the first place, by organizational policy fields. The principal actors in the health field are, for the most part, not the same as the principal actors in the energy field, and the actors in tax matters are not the same as the actors in labor affairs. If we look at the amount of time top government officials spend on issues in different policy fields, it appears that the polity can be divided, at the most basic level, into two major parts. One polity—the polity of large organizations—is a relatively tightly integrated set of policy fields associated with the interests of large organizations in economic and national defense areas. It includes tax policy, foreign trade, the domestic economy, and national defense. The second—the polity of citizens and human beings—is a less tightly integrated set of fields involving the economic and citizen rights of individuals. It includes education, welfare, and labor affairs.[19] According to the organizational sociologists Edward Laumann and David Knoke, within the two polities, at least twenty different policy domains exist,[20] and these in turn can be broken down into smaller and more specific issue networks.

Crosscutting this structure of organizational segmentation is a separate structure of issue segmentation. Perhaps the best way of thinking about this issue structure is by looking at the degree to which the costs being imposed by a policy and the benefits being conferred are widely distributed or narrowly concentrated.[21] In James Q. Wilson's framework, a policy proposal that would lead to an increase in the income tax rate, to general price increases, or to a higher crime rate is considered to have widely distributed costs; one producing cleaner air or higher social security benefits, on the other hand, is said to have distributed benefits. A policy imposing a costly regulation on a particular industry (say a requirement that a particular kind of agricultural producer change the pesticides they use) entails narrowly concentrated costs; while subsidies paid to particular industries or occupations, such as licenses granted for the operation of television or radio stations, confer concentrated benefits. Different types of issues encourage a different pattern of political activity and response—from a war of narrowly constituted interests groups (in the case of concentrated costs and concentrated benefits) to the momentous public issues of "majoritarian politics" (in the case of distributed costs and distributed benefits).

Policy making is a complex, many-staged process. In many cases, it is virtually impossible to identify the particular group or individual who has had the decisive say in the development of the policy. A typical policy might be studied and discussed first by experts, drafted in legislative form by the president's staff, argued for and against by the representatives of different interest groups, reviewed and perhaps reworked by White House staff experts on the basis of these arguments, changed slightly by higher-level staff on the basis of their perception of national and political interests, discussed with key congressmen before being submitted to Congress, reviewed and redrafted by congressional staff, supported and attacked again in its revised state by interest group representatives, modified by congressmen on the committee to which the bill has been submitted, amended on the floor of the House or Senate, and put in a final form by a joint committee of Congress, before it is submitted back to the White House to be studied by staff and signed or vetoed by the president.[22]

While recognizing the complexity of the process, my presumption is that, in most instances of politicized policy making, the decisive impact is made by political elites, who, after all, have the final power to adopt, amend, or reject. It is proper to talk about the decisive influence of policy experts only when their recommendations are adopted without significant changes by political leaders, or in cases where experts are either explicitly delegated power in a particular area, or assume and maintain it in a *de facto* way.

The Structurally Induced Illusion of Expert Influence

Looking at the situation from an organizational perspective helps, among other things, to show how some distinctive features of the American political structure can encourage the appearance of more expert influence than actually exists. In the American system, power is shared by legislative and executive offices and at several different levels of government.[23] In this structure, organized interests have multiple access points in their efforts to gain influence. This degree of openness—some have called it, with an eye to the more centrally organized European systems, "structural fragmentation"—tends to disperse power to a wider array of actors, and it also increases the interdependence of bureaucrats and politicians, both of whom tend to be in constant contact with parties interested in a particular piece of legislation or a particular policy.[24]

As the authors of a leading comparative study note, the American situation leads to staff experts embracing a more political role and politicians a more technical role than is found elsewhere. "Uncertain lines of authority encourage American bureaucrats to play political roles—to cut deals with congressmen who can protect their agencies from central executive control, to pursue interests of clienteles who can help to protect their programs and to act as advocates for interests inadequately represented through politics. . . . The bread-and-butter of congressional politicians and high-level bureaucrats [alike] is earned by their responsiveness to . . . relevant local constituencies, whether these are composed of electorates or local interest groups or bureaucratic clients."[25] The situation contrasts very markedly with some of the European systems, particularly the British, where "traditions of collective cabinet responsibility, cohesive and disciplined parties, a relatively integrated executive . . . and especially a party-centered Parliament, reduce the propensity for bureaucrats to develop intense contacts outside the administrative system."[26]

Thus, in the American system, bureaucrats and politicians are more similar to one another than they are in many other less fragmented and less open systems.[27] Both need to gain political support for favored policies, and therefore both feel the incentive to act as policy entrepreneurs. Indeed, it is not uncommon in the American system for high-level bureaucrats to recruit politicians and representatives of interest groups to support policies.[28] This is, of course, very much the opposite of the usual picture of lobbying.

It is this structurally induced activism that underlies some part of the widespread sense that technocracy in America is particularly powerful and dynamic. But it is structural fragmentation, not technocratic power, that is behind this buzz of activity. The sheer activity level of professional staffs and technical experts should not be mistaken for an unusual level of expert power or influence.

EXPERT INFLUENCE: THE EMPIRICAL EVIDENCE

To investigate the question of how much real policy influence experts have in the American system—and on what kinds of issues, if any, their influence tends to be great—I have examined case study materials on policy making. I have by no means attempted a comprehensive study of the existing case materials—a formidable task, to say the least—but I have drawn from a wide range of case studies some seventy-five separate studies drawn variously from the areas of health, education, welfare, defense, and the economy. In this section, I will provide a summary of the results of this inquiry.

The Norm: Limited Mandates, Limited Influence

Experts, for the most part, have limited mandates and limited influence—except on issues of narrowly technical interest. It is important, of course, to know what constitutes a policy of comparatively broad public import and what constitutes a policy that is of only narrowly technical interest. Wilson's framework of concentrated versus distributed costs and benefits is helpful in making the distinction, but it is possible to specify more clearly the range of distributed costs and benefits. I will define as substantively more significant those policies that (1) create a new class of resources (including weapons), ban a class of resources, or alter the locus or means of their control; (2) significantly alter institutional arrangements or the relative power of existing institutions; (3) significantly alter the distribution of group benefits; (4) expand or contract individual or group rights; and (5) alter the recognition of categories of the population through the means of official classificatory frameworks.

The empirical evidence is not kind to the stronger forms of the argument for technocracy. The evidence confirms that experts working within government are typically functionaries with quite limited powers. Perhaps the most systematic study of the role of experts within government is John Padgett's work on budget making in the Department of Housing and Urban Development.[30] Padgett concluded that the broad parameters within which budget decisions must be made are determined by cabinet-level officials in the executive branch, with the president's macroeconomic and geopolitical goals uppermost in mind. At the department level, officials have the role of implementing these guidelines. They do so by taking into account the legal status of programs (whether cuts can legally be made) and by trying to save especially effective or visible programs from across-the-board cuts. Other studies of staff experts working within government have also emphasized their generally circumscribed powers.

As advisers to government, experts tend to have limited policy-making influence except on narrowly technical matters. Technical matters would include, for example, the setting of produce and personnel standards in pre-set categories, the minor refinement of statistics of social and economic measurement, and the determination of whether particular drugs are safe enough to be released on the market. On matters like these, experts often have a near monopoly of influence.[31] The same high level of influence is found in many instances of improvement in transportation safety and communications capacities, as in the recent case of the introduction of microburst detectors designed to improve air-transport safety.

On matters of larger public interest, politicians are in a position to claim higher priorities and more binding responsibilities, priorities and responsibilities that override the mere conviction of expert knowledge. Thus, no existing studies have shown that the influence of experts is typically great on committees concerned with issues of broad public import, such as "whether or not to finance a supersonic transport, to build anti-missile defenses in space, to ban the use of a carcinogenic chemical, or to extend high levels of additional aid to debt-ridden nations."[32] Nor have experts played a decisive role on issues like the nuclear arms race, the depletion of natural resources, or race relations.[33] These issues are clearly complex and have significant technical content, but experts have no special mandate on those grounds alone. Indeed, several researchers have found that when the findings of scientific studies do not fit the purposes of top political officials, they are very often suppressed, distorted, or simply ignored,[34] and even purely technical considerations may take a back seat to political considerations in the allocation of benefits or the distribution of costs.[35]

Similarly, historical studies have documented the failure of movements of leading scientists to stop the use of atomic forces against Japan in 1945, to stop the use of force against the Vietnamese in the 1960s, or to prevent the further development of nuclear forces in later years.[36] Scientists have repeatedly lost out to military men for the control of government organizations in defense-relevant areas.[37] In nonmilitary areas, even united scientific opinion does not easily prevail when it is faced with popular opposition, as the occasionally heated debates on the teaching of creationism in the public schools attest.[38]

The case materials suggest that the policy influence of experts must be examined in relation to the norm of policy management by government political elites and the daily contention of rival interest organizations. Within the American political structure, experts are, for the most part, relatively minor players. They support competing elites or competing interest groups with data, information, and proposals, or they analyze and champion policy in a framework set by others. It seems reasonable to conclude in a general way with the political scientist Sanford Lakoff, "Professionals lack political resources to exercise determining influence whenever the issue turns on political choices rather than on technical considerations alone. . . . In no actual society is scientific or technological knowledge considered to be a sufficient source of moral or legal authority."[39]

Lakoff's conclusion does not, however, do full justice to the matter of expert influence. The conclusion is correct as a general characterization, but the extent of expert influence does vary. Policy making by experts on substantively important matters is not common, but it does occur. In particular, two sources of opportunity can lead to high levels of expert influence: either the volume of demands on the time of politicians, or the failure of experts' policy-making actions to become politicized. When either form of opportunity exists, experts can have a high level of influence even on public policies that are not at all narrowly technical in scope or import.

Expert Influence and the Volume of Demands on Politicians

The volume of demands on politicians' time tends to encourage devolution of policy-making influence to professional staff.[40] As the political scientist Michael Malbin has put it, "[I]nstead of freeing the members to concentrate, the staffs contribute to the frenetic pace of congressional life that pulls members in different directions, reduces the time available for joint deliberation, and makes concentration all but impossible. . . . The situation feeds on itself. The members need staff because they have so little time to concentrate, but the new work created by the staff takes even more of the members' time, indirectly elevating the power of the Washington issue networks in which the staffs play so prominent a role."[41]

The writing of legislation has also changed because of the many demands on the time of politicians. Legislation is increasingly written in vague terms that can leave a considerable amount of interpretation up to experts in the executive branch. The political scientist Steven Kelman, for example, notes that during the days when legislator's had less to do, legislation was often drafted to be as specific as possible. The Smoot-Hawley Tariff Act of 1930 ran 170 pages and included detailed provisions about the treatment of specific commodities. Now, as Kelman observes, "statutes that establish programs typically set only vague standards for the specific content of political choices."[42] Legislative language like this leaves a good deal of final authority to staff experts to make what amount to political choices.

In some instances, substantial levels of expert influence reflect the purely personal triumphs of talented individuals working to make the most out of the opportunities for influence that exist. Within the context of formal subordination to higher-level officials, staff people do sometimes gain substantial power informally. For the most part, these cases of expert influence appear to be a matter of unusual talent wedded to unusual opportunity—which is to say, either very weak or extremely busy superiors.[43]

Expert Influence and Nonpoliticized Issues

The influence of experts is also sometimes extensive and consequential when policy making is undertaken in the absence of public controversy or outside formal decision-making settings.[44] These situations maximize the potential influence of experts because they complement the tendency of professional organization to convey a sense of nonpartisanship and removal from the politics of passion and interest. In instances of overt conflict, experts give up the singular asset that they enjoy as policy makers: the appearance of nonpartisan and noncontroversial technical knowledge.[45]

Instances of extensive and significant expert power outside of formal settings can occur in one of two ways: (1) when power that belongs ultimately to the state has been successfully assumed in a de facto way by professionals in the absence of state activity and is, at some later date, legitimated by law; and (2) in cases where the state itself delegates power to professional experts and then legitimates the resulting policies in law or administrative regulations.

Unlike the gradual accretion of power by staff people in government, which is usually due to a fortuitous mix of unusual talent and unusual opportunity, the conditions under which experts exercise influence outside of formal decision-making settings can be specified rather clearly, since only a small number of conditions are important. These conditions have to do with the political environment, the framing of issues, and the relative centrality of the different professional occupations. Greater expert influence is associated with opportunities in the political environment, the successful framing of issues as purely technical or as involving consensus values, and with issues that fall into the province of professions that are central in social regulation—notably, law, economics, medicine, and higher education.

The Political Environment. Features of the political environment may provide opportunities for the informal assumption of power by experts or incentives for the delegation of power to experts. The informed assumption of power occurs when policy fields are unorganized and when resources are relatively abundant, while delegation occurs primarily when resources are tight and the government is overburdened.

The de facto capture of policy domains can by definition occur only before a particular policy domain has come under the control of government. Thus, the situation that is most congenial to expert influence is at the time of the discovery of problems, the founding of institutions, or the inauguration of regulatory proposals. As policy domains become better defined and more subject to state regulation, there is a general tendency for expert influence to be channeled through governmental offices, on the one hand, and through the larger and more important interest group organizations, on the other.

Research on the creation of two-year colleges in the early twentieth century provides a good example of how professionals can move into unorganized policy fields and construct solutions that are later legitimated by law. The idea for community colleges (or, as they were then called, junior colleges) developed among late nineteenth-century educators, who sponsored the new organizations in several parts of the country during the first decades of the twentieth century. From early on, these educational reformers found funding predominantly through state governments, but even so, the community colleges were by no means creatures of the state. Indeed, in terms of curriculum and organization, the colleges continued to be directed by educators through their own professional association/interest group, the American Association of Junior and Community Colleges. Once the colleges were well-established, political leaders moved quickly to embrace them and attempted at times to use them for their own purposes, but this occurred some seventy years after the founding of the first colleges.[46]

This principle of professionals moving first into unorganized policy fields largely explains why the Progressive Era is so widely considered an era of exceptional professional influence,[47] and why independent professional influence has appeared to most observers to be weaker in succeeding years, in spite of the rapidly increasing number of experts. In the Progressive Era, rather weak governmental authorities were confronted by a large number of new challenges, arising from industrialism, mass immigration, urbanism, and a very dynamic phase of unregulated capitalist enterprise. Professional people, constituted as knowledge-based authorities, and typically acting through professional associations or expert-dominated "blue ribbon" commissions, were in a position to substitute for weak-state authorities as potential problem solvers. The case study materials indicate that a great many policies associated with extensive professional influence are the products of professional reform projects of the Progressive Era.

It is easier to fund professionally sponsored projects when resources are perceived to be comparatively abundant, and, on that basis, government is active. State sponsorship of public colleges, public art, and antipoverty programs, to name but three examples, would not have been as easy to adopt usually favorable conditions for the advancement of professional policy influence. Fiscal stress provides a much less congenial environment for the opening of new domains, since it tends to increase scrutiny of existing policies and resistance to new ones.

If professional usurpation is favored when potential policy fields are unorganized and when the public fisc is sound and government active, delegation is typically based on the technical incapacity of state elites to decide, or on the incentives that overburdened resources create for governmental elites to encourage others to decide.

The most important example of technical incapacity in a consequential realm has to do with economic policy making. The fate of governments rests, to a very considerable extent, on the performance of the economy, but top political officials themselves are usually technically incompetent to make decisions on economic policy making. Since the rise of Keynesianism, economic policy has been a domain very significantly under the control of experts. Naturally enough, politicians have tried to influence policy in relation to the electoral cycle. They have also sometimes held prejudices in favor of particular economic ideas. But these influences do not diminish the evidence that this is an area significantly controlled by experts.

Delegation occurs, not just when top officials are incompetent to decide, but also when the state is overburdened. One strategy of overburdened states is to delegate areas of decision making to groups with the capacity to improve the functioning of particular policy domains. Indeed, power delegated by the state is the typical mode of professional influence in well-established policy domains. In recent years, overburdened states have occasionally subcontracted out to communities of experts such policy-relevant matters as the standardization of tax codes[48] and the organization of schools, prisons, and public health care.[49] A good example of the delegation of state authority to professional experts comes from the sociologist and legal scholar Terence Halliday's study of "rationalization" of the Illinois tax and commercial codes by the state's bar association. Here an overburdened state government asked the bar association to create order out of the previously existing jumble of regulations. The new code was adopted by the state, but it was developed exclusively by professional experts. The codes were, in the end, made more comprehensible and consistent, but this process of "technical improvement" also built into the codes substantial tax benefits to particular commercial interests.[50]

In general, pluralistic conflict discourages expert influence, since interest groups tend to jealously guard their areas of influence from the encroachments of experts.[51] There are, however, some conditions under which pluralistic conflict may encourage expert influence. When passions about a policy run very high, or when interest groups are equally balanced and in a position to stalemate one another, politicians may decide to appoint independent commissions of experts to make nonpartisan policy recommendations.[52] In some cases, the recommendations of these expert panels are followed, as occurred recently in the case of decision making about military base closings.

The Framing of Issues. Expert influence also depends on how issues are framed. Expert influence tends to be maximized when experts successfully define matters of substance as narrowly technical issues, or when they successfully define responses to issues as based on the protection of a central cultural value.

"Rationalization projects" are the archetypal frame within which very substantive policy choices may be advanced (often inadvertently) by experts as narrowly technical issues. By rationalization, I mean the creation of standardized systems of impersonal rules. These standardized systems typically replace practices that are either unstandardized, or at least much less completely standardized. Very important substantive effects sometimes creep into rationalization projects under the guise of purely technical improvements. The case tax code rationalization discussed by Terence Halliday is such an example of benefits to particular commercial interests resulting from what was depicted as a purely technical improvement.[53] Efforts to rationalize educational systems can be interpreted in much the same way. The rationalization of untidy systems, as in the path-setting case of the California Master Plan for higher education of 1960, can establish a distinctive distribution of opportunities in the population, which might well be challenged if the policies were considered to have substantive content. Intelligence and aptitude tests, widely used as instruments of social sorting, are based on a particular theory of intelligence—that it is distributed on a normal curve in a single dimension. This theory has a distinct set of implications for social stratification. All successful theories of intelligence are rationalizations in the sense that they bring a standard ordering process into social life, but one test may represent a quite different form of rationalization from that represented by some other test, based on a different underlying theory of the distribution of talent.[54]

The case of "no-fault" divorce is another well-known case of very important substantive impacts arising from questions framed as essentially technical. The advocates of no-fault laws argued that their efforts either involved the codification of laws that already existed in scattered statutes or appellate decisions, or that they consisted of bringing their state's law into conformity with practices elsewhere. In either case, the reformers could claim that their initiatives were compatible with existing law rather than constituting radical innovations. The policies, however, were in fact innovations, and had the unintended consequence of leaving a large number of women subject to economic hardship.[55]

Experts can also exercise substantial influence through the successful framing of issues in relation to a central cultural value. Nineteenth-century abortion policy represents a clear case of de facto capture of policy making on a consequential issue through the successful assertion of a central cultural value. The sociologist Kristin Luker has shown that, as part of their effort to establish authority for the still scientifically weak medical professions, nineteenth-century doctors rallied around the central value of life over, for example, the potentially conflicting value of "freedom of choice." The doctors, aided by their social prestige, had their policies ratified in virtually every state until the organized feminist movement began to challenge them in the 1960s.[56]

At times, expert influence has been gained through the uncontested assertion of policies to protect personal liberties against the possible abuses of the powerful. Instances of expert policy influence in relation to this value include the successful advocacy of freedom of information bills in the 1960s by a coalition of journalists, public interest lawyers, legal scholars, and social scientists,[57] and the extension of civil rights and protections to new populations, such as the disabled, in the 1970s.[58] Another example is the important role played by the organized bar in opposing McCarthyism because of the potential it showed for violating individual rights. (Of course, in this case the legal profession did not act alone.)[59]

In institution-building efforts, the assertion of hierarchical values has often been successful. One example is the success of late nineteenth and early twentieth century educators in developing meritocratic policies in public higher education in the face of long-standing popular ideals about democratic access.[60] In behavioral matters, on the other hand, nonhierarchical values are often more successful. Here, for example, one can find many expert-sponsored policies encouraging a shift toward "individual self-expression" and "emotional adjustment" in public schools and therapeutic facilities and away from ideals of strict behavior conformity.[61] And one can also see, as a final example, the success of professional artists and humanist scholars in developing requirements for the placement of modern art in and around public buildings, where the values of "aesthetic beauty" and "modern expression" were successfully asserted.[62]

Occupational Centrality. Not all professional occupations are in a position to take advantage of opportunities for the informal capture of power, or to be likely beneficiaries of delegated power. Very little of the variation has to do with the accepted technical competence of the occupation per se. Rather, it is primarily those professional occupations that are central in social regulation that are likely to have the necessary standing among elites to substitute as surrogate powers to the state.[63]

In American society (like all modern liberal democracies), the professional occupations that are central in social regulation include lawyers, economists, doctors, and higher education authorities. Each has jurisdiction over a primary sphere of normative regulation. Law provides the primary normative framework for the conduct of social relations. It is virtually synonymous with the legitimated basis of social control. Economics is central because it is the body of knowledge that regulates the major institutional frame of the society—the market system and the profit-making organizations. Medicine is central because it provides primary regulation in relation to physical and emotional well-being. Higher education is central because it provides primary regulation of personnel categories and what counts as legitimate knowledge. In liberal societies, occupations that are central to social regulation must compromise to some degree with the forces of economic and political power, but cannot appear to compromise too much, or, on the other side, to be too aloof and superior.[64]

As I have indicated, the independent policy influence of lawyers has developed primarily through the efforts of legal reformers to protect and extend rights and to "rationalize" statutes. Of the other significant occupational groups, the policy influence of educators is most like that of lawyers. It too is based, in large part, on efforts to expand widely valued goods—in this case opportunities, rather than rights per se—and to rationalize systems. Social historians have documented the late nineteenth- and early twentieth-century creation of standardized schooling systems by an "educational trust" of top professional educators.[65] This "one best system"—and its later extensions—has had important implications for the classification of personnel and the distribution of group benefits, because the systems come to provide a major mode of access to the better jobs in the economy. The same sort of significance can certainly be found in the rise of IQ and aptitude testing. The influence of educators can also be based on their control over what constitutes legitimate knowledge. This influence may be great, even where public disagreement exists. Recent studies, for example, have shown the decisive influence of educational experts in setting the accepted criteria used for textbook selection in the states, even in cases of highly politicized controversies.[66]

In the medical area, a primary process appears to be the gradual movement of medical authority into previously unmedicalized areas of social life. Social historians, for example, have documented the medicalization of behavior once treated as unusually religious, eccentric, or bizarre, but within normal tolerance levels.[67] Indeed, doctors have continued to assume authority in moral as well as medical matters, due to the easier validation of physical as opposed to moral well-being. In recent years, medical authority has been extended to child care and welfare cases previously left under the jurisdiction of family, neighborhood, or parish.[68]

Economists probably represent the best example of a politically influential knowledge-based elite. Some people consider economic policy to be mainly technical, based on the use of well-understood tools to stimulate economic growth while maintaining price stability. This is far from true. Consensual goals about growth and price stability provide a frame within which economists work, but the policies that economists pursue are usually far from minor in their sociological implications. Economic policies may or may not build in incentives for saving versus consumption, for example, and they may or may not encourage high levels of foreign investments.[69] Economic policies may also tend to redistribute income to investors or to wage earners, or to redistribute it to particular strata or sectors in the economy. The economist Robert

Gordon, for example, has shown that the use of escalator clauses based on the Consumer Price Index created a "two-class society" in the 1970s, separating those who were protected against inflation by the escalator clauses and those who were not.[70]

THE SOCIAL CONSEQUENCES OF EXPERT INFLUENCE

Because of the increasing numbers of experts in our midst and the mixed results of the policies they advocate, the idea of advancing technocracy has generated both more fear and more applause than is warranted. At most, the case materials provide a sound basis for including experts with elites, interest groups, and electorates as potentially significant actors in the politics of pluralist democracies. They suggest that analyses of political influence will gain something by including experts. But to realize this gain, analysts must be willing to look, not only at formal decision making, but also outside of formal decision-making settings. It is here that experts tend to play a somewhat more consequential role.

Answers to the "Who governs?" question do not, of course, fully satisfy our curiosity about the policy influence of experts. We still wish to know the answer to the question: "Governing for what purpose?" Or, as Robert and Helen Lynd once memorably put it: "Knowledge for what?" Does expert influence entail any distinctive political implications? Is there greater "rationality" when experts are the decisive influence behind public policy? Is there any greater progressivism than would be the case if elites or interest groups were more exclusively in command? Or conversely, is there any more significant boost to the existing power centers due to the application of a system-wide rationality that might otherwise be lacking?

The issue of the substantive rationality of experts has been confused almost from the beginning because of the awe-inspiring—but, in this instance, somewhat misleading—work of Max Weber. For Weber, the great drama of human history was the progressive "rationalization" of the world—the absorption of ever-increasing spheres of human activity and human fancy into a predictable, calculable, organizing stream of categorizations and rational actions. Weber had little regard for experts and bureaucrats, who appeared to him as spirit-sapping technicians. What hope Weber held out for the future laid with politicians and other leaders whose visions, he felt, might allow for new truths and new forms of social organization to break through the "mechanical petrification" of modern life.

Yet politicians are often poorly cast as the Romantic creators of meaning of Weberian myth, and experts are similarly too quickly assigned to the bleak background of dronelike rationalizing activity.[71] What we do know is that politicians are very much prone to serve the interests that are visible and salient to them and do not tend to be very interested in unorganized and/or nonvoting citizens. Experts, by contrast, have an interest in spheres of activities, rather than in spheres of salient and mobilized organization, and, there-fore, may at times serve the broader citizenry better than politicians.[72] Since most politicians are trained in law, their sensitivity to the style of rational argumentation is often rather high. However, their time is scarce and their tendency is often to look for the popular and powerful causes, or those that reward in an emotional way their sense of justice.

Unlike legislators, experts make their way in the world primarily on the basis of good arguments rather than resources, risk taking, and association with visible, popular issues. Consequently, as compared to elected officials, experts tend to be more resistant to the appeals of groups with popular and visible issues.[73] In the cultural traditions of the West, expertise and bureau-cracy are closely connected, and many of the values of experts parallel the values of bureaucracy: rational argumentation, clear means and ends, univer-sal standards of treatment, nonpartisan approaches to the distribution of costs and benefits, and technical soundness in line with the available re-search.[74] It is because of their relative disinterestedness that nonpartisan "expert administrations" have long benefited from comparisons to party and patronage-based administration as a guard against political corruption and the misuse of public funds.[75]

The Unfinished Rationality of Experts

Not all of the effects of expert influence are as unexceptional as these, however. The application of expertise to public policy has also gained some negative connotations, and for good reason. There are, to be sure, characteristic biases in the values and goals of experts. It is possible to gain some perspective on these characteristic biases by looking at the character of the policies that experts propose, and not just at those that are realized.

A large part of the reputation of experts for narrowness and purely instru-mental interests comes from experts' characteristic weakness in appreciating the broader social and historical context in which they work. The expert on alcoholism, for example, may know all of the demographic, psychological, and biological correlates of alcoholism, but have no appreciation whatsoever of the extent to which alcoholism as a social problem was itself constructed by an ironic twist of early industrialism, which simultaneously introduced new demands for greater regularity among workers and increasing supplies of spirits to reduce that regularity.[76] Experts, who are not also broadly knowl-edgeable, are the leading contemporary example of "bounded rationality" at work.

Experts are sometimes naive about   even uninterested in—the political uses of their ideas. They may find political applause a sign of the rationality of their ideas rather than of the political utility of their ideas. This too is a kind of narrowness that gives rise to criticisms of the unfinished rationality of experts.

It is also true that the social values of experts, in keeping with the main thrust of the rationalizing process, tend to favor centralized control and hierarchy, since these are associated with the virtues of predictability. They tend, in addition, to favor increasing levels of expert authority, since this is associated with the virtues of competent analysis and decision making. For the most part, these preferences encourage a dismissive view of policy alternatives involving decentralization, dehierarchization, and democratized participation.

Perhaps major limitation of experts as policy makers, however, comes from their tendency to rely overly on logic and not enough on understanding what makes human beings tick. An illuminating story is told in this regard by James Q. Wilson about Robert McNamara and Melvin Laird, two former secretaries of defense. Although McNamara raised the defense budget more than any peacetime secretary had ever done, he left office one of the least popular secretaries ever among his associates in the military. Laird, by contrast, cut the defense budget significantly at a time when the military was already much disliked, but left with the high esteem of his associates in the services. According to Wilson, the reasons have to do with the different sensitivities of the two men to social relationships. McNamara and his staff imposed their well-researched rationalizing plans without regard to the personal feelings and territorial loyalties of the people in their command. Laird, on the other hand, consulted almost obsessively and spent a good deal of time learning about the attachments and antipathies of the people with whom he worked. McNamara may have been a logical planner, but he was not an adept hands-on politician.[77]

This story gets to the heart of what goes wrong with expert decision making when it does go wrong, and why the best-laid plans of experts often have unintended, negative consequences. If the strength of social problem solving by scientific means is its logic and fairness, its weakness is a tendency to ignore the feelings and sentiments of real people. This includes both the more noble and the baser sentiments of humankind: the courage people will show when they have the desire to fight for something important to them, and also the opportunism they will often exhibit so as to take advantage and avoid costs where they can. Mistakes about the depth of loyalties help to explain why "the experts" (and the politicians who depended on their judgment) were wrong about the costs of fighting the war in Vietnam and about the costs of instituting busing in the cities. Mistakes about opportunism help to explain why policy experts were wrong about "no-fault" divorce, about some forms of industry deregulation, and, in relation to "white flight," in a second way about busing.[78] Similarly, experts who urged wider access to public housing only belatedly realized that gangs could become more of a threat if screening requirements were loosened.[79]

Unintended consequences are often poorly monitored by experts. The deregulation of the savings and loan industry was a mistake made on rational grounds, but one that could easily have been more quickly rectified if the unintended consequences of deregulation had been monitored more completely. Very often, the creative efforts of experts go into developing policies—

this is where the bulk of the political and media attention resides—while monitoring and evaluation is relatively perfunctory.

It is also true that not every social or political problem is best approached through the lens of professional inquiry and expertise. Some alternatives to the scientific style of social problem solving include the application of ordinary, nonscientific knowledge and values, the learning of new behaviors by groups connected to a problem, and mutual adjustment through discussion or bargaining.[80] These modes of social problem solving are sometimes more in keeping with democratic values and are also more effective.

The future prospects of experts will depend, to a considerable degree, on their ability to develop a more finished rationality.[81] It is not so much the abstract goals or values that are at issue in many instances, or the technical calculations about how to reach those goals. Instead, it is the *contextual rationality* and the *contextual pragmatics* of policy making that are most in need of attention. These issues involve experts' frequently faulty sense of the political uses of ideas, of the diverse human interests that are given encouragement by new policies; of the organizational systems that can create impediments to successful adoption of even the most logical policies; of unintended consequences that emerge in the wake of purposeful action; and of alternative modes of social problem solving. These contextual issues ought to be a central part of the rationality of experts, but they usually are not.[82]

The Two Polities

These remarks do not as yet address the matter of the social interests represented by experts. Unfortunately, questions about the interests served by experts are impossible to answer in any general way. In this chapter, I have reported some important expert-developed policies that had an inegalitarian thrust (e.g., IQ testing); some that were intended to increase opportunities or fairness, but had unintended inequitable consequences (e.g., divorce law); and some that were intended to increase opportunities and did (e.g., freedom of information laws, civil rights for the handicapped). I have reported policies that reinforced the existing structure of the economic order, and some that were intended to change it in the public interest.

The most that may be possible to do is to point out some of the organizational factors influencing the content of the policies advocated by experts. Here it is helpful to reintroduce the conception of national policy domains as divided between a polity concerned primarily with the needs of large organizations and a polity concerned primarily with the needs of citizens and human beings. The social meaning of the work of experts tends to differ somewhat in the two polities. Some of these differences have to do with the internal organization of the two polities. The activities of policy experts in the second polity appear to foster a view of the field of relevant organizations as largely cooperative rather than competitive. This leads to more interaction between the organizations and more information for management to use in decision making. It can also lead to the development of new "master" agencies and a sense of systemic goals.[83] Though the implication is as yet not well tested, it follows that expert activity encourages fewer of these "coordinative bureaucratic environments" in the first polity, where the organizations are individually more powerful and where more of them are competitive, profit-making enterprises.

In terms of the values served, expert influence in the first polity, like the influence of all other important actors, is principally oriented to serving the needs of the larger organizations in the country. Experts often serve these needs in a somewhat more standardized and, in that sense, equitable way than would be the case if policies were solely determined by interest organizations or politicians. Before tax experts in the Senate reviewed the 1986 tax reform act, for example, it was composed of a welter of special exemptions and provisions for businesses. After the bill was worked over by committee experts, the structure was simplified and virtually all the loopholes closed. The wealthy still benefited, to be sure, but they benefited in a relatively standard way, with fewer exceptions and special advantages for special categories.

Experts in the first polity, then, can be described primarily as a rationalizing force working within the logic of business development and national economic and security goals. They work to develop standardized policies that create, within the opportunities and constraints provided by this structure, more efficient and fairer outcomes. What is regarded as more efficient and fairer, of course, changes from time to time, but these purposes remain constant.

It is tempting to assume that the second polity is a more clearly progressive sphere of professional activity. Certainly the expressed attitudes of professionals working in that sphere are, as I have shown in chapters 3 and 5, somewhat more egalitarian. It is also true that the policies experts have developed in the second polity are often reformist in spirit. These include, for example, policies extending rights to the handicapped and opening up previously restricted information files. Experts in this sphere can be described as involved in the creation of a set of social citizenship rights that enhance the quality of life for the majority of people at the minimum, and for some people, through educational opportunities, up to a high level.

Yet experts working in the second polity are also clearly influenced by the needs of the more powerful and better-organized first polity, and consequently their activities very often reflect a dual purpose.[84] The reformist side of expert activity in the second polity is evident in the efforts of experts to win new rights for disadvantaged groups, to improve opportunities, and to reduce waste of resources. The hierarchical, organization-serving side is equally evident, however. It is evident particularly in the tendency of policy makers in the second polity to align their policy thinking in relation to their sense of the needs and interests of business leaders. Because the second polity is, in many respects, structurally subordinate to the first, experts and other policy makers tend to make these alignments whether or not business is actively involved in pursuing its interests politically.[85]

Very often the egalitarian and the organization-serving sides of expertise are evident in the same policies. In the educational field, both IQ testing and educational master planning, for example, show the imprint of these two distinct pressures. IQ testing simultaneously extends opportunities to many people previously unrecognized and supports a new kind of hierarchy of qualified personnel. Master planning extends opportunities by opening the gates of higher education and strictly orders opportunities through the organization of highly differentiated tiers. Similarly, urban renewal projects have usually represented (in this case a rather one-sided) compromise between the desire of business to renovate for profit and the desire of reformers to renovate for the safety and benefit of the residents of poor neighborhoods.[86]

This tension between progressive impulses and a social structure dominated by powerful organizational hierarchies is one of the more significant features of the environment faced by experts working in the second polity.

The Moral Imagination of Intellectuals

WHERE POLICY experts represent the technical side of professionalism as it is connected to public purposes, intellectuals are the group that comes closest, in my view, to representing the moral aspirations of professionalism as a force in public life. For many sociologists, they are, as Lewis Coser once put it, "the guardians of standards often ignored in the marketplace and the houses of power."[1] The critical questions about intellectuals concern their level of integration with the larger social structure and the specific character of the moral imagination they represent. Do they tend to represent oppositional currents of thought, or are they largely conformist? Are the moral standards they represent in fact different from those of "the marketplace and houses of power"?

As I will use the term, intellectuals are people associated with the world of thought who, at least on occasion, address a broad educated public on matters of political and cultural interest. There are, without question, many learned people engaged in "intellectual work" whose orientation is entirely or almost entirely disciplinary. These people may contribute to the fundamental rethinking of problems arising within the various academic disciplines. They do not, however, fit the definition of the publicly oriented intellectual that is at the heart of all discussions of the political and moral influence of intellectuals.

In this chapter, I will show that dissent is far from the major orientation among intellectuals, and particularly not among those intellectuals who are most likely to have influence on patterns of thought in America. One important reason for this is the organizational and market context in which intellectual writing is produced. Periodicals of ideas, politics, and culture are market-based organizations, and the interests of the audience for opinion and commentary therefore have a great effect on the content of the ideas expressed. This audience is much less interested in the consumption of worldviews than it is in the consumption of authoritative evaluations of literary and scholarly work and articles that provide a refined and sophisticated view of personalities and events.

AN ADVERSARY CULTURE?

The idea that intellectual life begets stances that are critical of established authority is a venerable theme in social thought, beginning in the modern era with Edmund Burke's critique of the utopianism of the writers of the French Enlightenment as an influence on the leaders of the French Revolution.[2] Since Burke, the idea has been used and developed by a long series of important thinkers, including Alexis de Tocqueville, Max Weber, Joseph Schumpeter, and Raymond Aron.[3]

The contemporary American form of the idea is associated with the phrase "the adversary culture." In a preface to a collection of his essays, the literary critic Lionel Trilling wrote: "Any historian of the literature of the modern age will take virtually for granted the adversary intention, the actually subversive intention, that characterizes modern writing—he will perceive its clear purpose of detaching the reader from the habits of thought and feeling that the larger culture imposes, of giving him a ground and a vantage point from which to judge and condemn, and perhaps revise, the culture that produced him."[4]

In the hands of Trilling's followers, this rather modest and self-limiting concept hardened and expanded into a sweeping indictment. Criticisms of intellectuals reached a crescendo in the 1970s, during a time when the liberal consensus in America was unraveling under the pressure of divergent reactions to the war in Vietnam and social protest movements at home. Trilling's followers on the conservative wing of liberalism claimed that the "adversarial culture" had directed an "assault against the spiritual and cultural power of business . . . in the most strident tones,"[5] had developed a "virulent hatred of . . . middle-class society,"[6] and "had become increasingly apocalyptic, hedonistic, and nihilistic."[7] The existence of an "adversary culture" of intellectuals became an "insight" appreciated by nearly all well-read moderates and conservatives.[8]

Empirical Evidence

Little in the way of empirical foundation exists for this "insight." In fact, the moderation and antiradicalism of American intellectuals has been pronounced even during periods of heightened social protest. Three studies from the last era of reform in the United States—two of college professors, the other of the "American intellectual elite"—all showed intellectuals to be a moderately liberal group, actively hostile to radical and utopian views.

The professoriat obviously includes a great many people who are not intellectuals in the sense in which I have used the term. Nevertheless, the professoriat forms a major seedbed and audience for intellectuals, and its politics are of some interest in this regard. Surveys of several thousand American professors in 1969 and 1975 by Everett Ladd and Seymour Martin Lipset showed the professoriat to be liberal, by and large, but not radical. Professors opposed the war, favored the civil rights movement, supported busing to integrate the schools, and tended to vote for Democrats. At the same time, a decided majority disapproved of student radicalism, affirmative action policies that included "relaxing" academic criteria, and countercultural preoccupations, such as the legalization of marijuana and the relaxation of sexual mores. One in twenty thought of themselves as "leftists."[9] On the basis of their findings, Ladd and Lipset concluded: "American academics constitute the most politically liberal occupational group in the United States but [are] far from being a hotbed of radicalism. . . . They manifest values, expectations, orientations to government, moods, and concerns that broadly reflect those of the American public."[10]

Active dissent was also rare in Charles Kadushin's study of the American intellectual elite from the same period. In 1970, less than half of 110 leading intellectuals interviewed by Kadushin wanted the United States to withdraw from Vietnam immediately, and their opposition to the war was mainly pragmatic (i.e., it wasn't working) rather than ideological or moralistic. Although they were concerned about racial injustices, most of Kadushin's intellectual elite were strongly opposed to the more militant black groups, and the great majority were "passionately hostile" to the New Left and the counterculture.[11] Far from representing an antinomian tendency in American life, they were more concerned about restoring cultural norms than either the general public or other elite groups.[12] The elite intellectuals were also relatively unlikely to engage in the more dramatic forms of protest, such as marching in demonstrations or participating in civil disobedience. They were much more likely to engage in conventional forms of politics—signing petitions, working on campaigns, donating money, and the like.[13] If adversarial means what it probably should—a clearly critical attitude, opposed to the basic structure of existing institutions and distributions of power—the number of adversarial intellectuals in America, even during this period of intense social conflict, was extremely small indeed.

It is true, of course, that a radical intelligentsia also existed at this time, stimulated by antiwar and civil rights protest and by the bohemianism of the student "counterculture." This intelligentsia was centered in college communities, among left-wing students and faculty, and among young white-collar workers and "hangers-on" who found the combination of book reading, intellectual friendships, and radical politics appealing. This intelligentsia was, for a time, numerically substantial. By the end of 1968, the leading radical student organization had as many as 60,000 dues-paying members.[14] The intelligentsia also had a significant influence for a brief period. It helped to stimulate wide-ranging and often boisterous criticism of American society and culture, and it contributed greatly to the climate of antiwar protest that involved hundreds of thousands of students at over 500 colleges and universities in the years before the end of the war.[15] The intelligentsia was not, however, supported by most leading intellectuals or by most academic professionals.[16]

The Sociology of Intellectuals

Ironically, at the time Trilling wrote his influential but misleading preface, social scientists were in the midst of a particularly productive period of serious thinking about the politics of intellectuals and the relations between people of ideas and people of power.[17] Here the degree of affinity between intellectuals and powerful people was rightly considered a variable, rather than a constant. The characteristic statement was that of Edward Shils: "Moderates and partisans in civil politics, quiet apolitical concentration on specialized intellectual tasks, cynical antipolitical passivity, and faithful acceptance [of] and service [to] the existing order are all to be found in substantial proportion among modern intellectuals, as among intellectuals in antiquity."[18] For every member of the "avant garde," one would likely find, in Shils' view, a member of the "clerisy"—indeed, usually many more than one. Radical intellectuals were a segment, usually a rather small segment, albeit one that was on rare occasions particularly influential.

At the same time, some bases for tension between intellectuals and "men of power" were noted by the mid-century writers. Some argued, along the lines of Joseph Schumpeter, that the very critical qualities of mind that make people intellectuals also dispose them to be dissatisfied with uncritical acceptance of "mere" custom, utility, and accepted norms.[19] Shils argued that the oppositional traditions of Western intellectual life—romanticism, populism, scientism, and millenarianism—encouraged episodes of dissent, acting as functional equivalents, so to speak, to the "union consciousness" of discontented workers.[20]

However, for the mid-century writers, the long-term trend among politically engaged intellectuals was toward greater moderation and "pragmatism," not toward greater alienation. This was the so-called "end of ideology" thesis, which perhaps might better have been called the "end of radical ideology" thesis.[21] The evidence marshaled in favor of the argument included statements indicating notable levels of consensus among left, right, and center intellectuals about the desirability of democratic freedoms in a mixed economic framework with a dominant private sector, and the increasing sense, even among socialists, of socialism as a "utopian myth . . . often remote from the realities of day-to-day politics."[22] As one proponent of the thesis put it: "The ideological issues dividing left and right [have] been reduced to a little more or a little less government ownership and economic planning."[23]

The mid-century social scientists also examined the range of relations that could be found between people of ideas and people of power in contemporary Western societies. Of those intellectuals who were in some fashion politically active, there were four typical situations, according to a typology developed by Lewis Coser. (1) Intellectuals sometimes, though rarely, hold power themselves, generally following periods of revolutionary change, as was true of the American Founding Fathers, the Jacobins, and the Bolsheviks. (2) They more often work with greater or less success as powers "behind the throne," as has been true of such recognizable groups as the Fabian socialists, the Swedish Social Democrats of the Myrdal generation, the Brain Trusters during the New Deal, and the so-called "wise men" of American Cold War foreign policy, as well as countless individuals throughout the modern era. (3) They may, in what is surely one of the more common situations, work to legitimate (or undermine) power with their visions of the proper order of society and

154   • *CHAPTER 8* •

their evaluations of the fidelity of the current ruling elites to that proper order. (4) They may provide many-sided treatments of an important contemporary issue that influences the climate of educated opinion.[24] Typically, the scope of these academic intellectual experts (my term, not Coser's) is narrower than that of the ideologists, and yet less directly involved with the nuts and bolts of government than that of the policy intellectuals.

Intellectuals in Transition

The late 1960s and early 1970s represent a recent high watermark of intellectual dissent in the United States. The combination of weak government legitimacy due to the unpopular war in Southeast Asia, high levels of social conflict, and the still-expanding role of the university encouraged a relatively high level of criticism among American academics and intellectuals.

Since that time, an intelligentsia has continued to exist in and around college campuses, but one that is quite different in interest and composition than its predecessors. As broader movements for social change have declined, the intelligentsia has become increasingly inwardly focused on matters of more strictly academic interest. Rather than focusing on structures of power and inequality, texts and images have become favored topics of analysis and the more radical forms of literary theory the great inspiration. Both schools of feminism and schools of ethnic particularism have become more prominent, reflecting in part the larger role of women and minorities as members of the intelligentsia.[25]

The more talented members of this intelligentsia have begun to assume significant positions in the larger world of intellectual discourse. These are people from left-wing backgrounds outside the cultural establishment who are now becoming part of it. It is a position that makes the new black and feminist intellectuals sociologically similar to the upwardly mobile Jews ("the New York Intellectuals") of interwar and postwar New York.

Outside of this new intelligentsia, the intellectual strata have followed a generally conservative course, very much like the country at large. Far from becoming filled with "tenured radicals,"[26] the professoriat has included an increasing number of self-described conservatives in the 1980s and a declining proportion of liberals. Liberal self-identifications were down seven percent between 1969 and 1984, and conservative self-identifications were up six percent.[27] Some notable examples of "political correctness" certainly existed on the campuses, and also some notable examples of administrative failures to protect the standards of free and frank exchange. Yet for all of the talk of increasing political correctness, studies showed an overall decrease in political correctness, at least in so far as this can be determined by responses to questions about affirmative action.[28] Even English and literature departments, the supposed centers of the new academic left in the 1980s, continued, by and large, to assign the same classic texts as before, though they did frequently study the canonical texts in new ways.[29]

The shifts toward more conservative views occurred across virtually the full range of disciplines,[30] with the high-quality research universities leading the way toward more conservative views. As of the mid-1980s, it was no longer the case that the most productive and highest prestige faculty were the most liberal politically. That position now belonged to faculty in liberal arts colleges.[31] Nor were the veterans of the "alienated" 1960s generation the most liberal. Instead, they showed the greatest trends toward more conservative identifications.[32]

INTELLECTUAL DISCOURSE IN THE LEADING PERIODICALS

No recent study exists of American intellectuals that is comparable to Kadushin's study of the American intellectual elite in the early 1970s. To fill in this gap, I have conducted my own study. Where Kadushin's study was based on face-to-face interviews, my study is based on content analysis. I have tried to combine something of the depth of memoirs and histories with the greater generalizability of survey analysis by analyzing the content of several hundred articles and reviews written over a recent three-year period for the leading American periodicals of ideas, politics, and culture.

I chose the periodicals to be sampled on the basis of responses to a mail survey of eighty-five American writers, thinkers, and editors, selected from all points on the political continuum and virtually all points on the cultural compass. Those surveyed ranged from William F. Buckley, the conservative editor of the *National Review,* to Edward Said, the radical literary theorist at Columbia University. The surveys were sent to such people as the novelists Toni Morrison and John Updike, the historian C. Vann Woodward, the sociologist Daniel Bell, the philosopher Richard Rorty, the paleontologist Stephen Jay Gould, the critics John Hollander and Henry Louis Gates, Jr., and the essayist Susan Sontag. Nine percent of the panel were African Americans, and 20 percent were women. Some leading journalists were included on the panel, as were a number of intellectual historians.[33]

The survey asked members of this expert panel to mark intellectual periodicals that they read themselves and also to mark those they considered "influential," a term I defined as referring to periodicals whose contents were "widely discussed in academic, government, and/or media circles." The response rate to the survey was 72 percent. The results are given in Table 8.1.

I calculated a "prominence score" for each periodical by adding together the number of panelists who said they read the periodical and the number who said they considered the periodical "influential." On the basis of these scores, I selected the following nine periodicals from which to draw a sample of articles and reviews: the *New York Review of Books,* the *New York Times Book Review,* and the *New Republic,* which were regarded as the most influential; and also *The Atlantic Monthly, Commentary, Foreign Affairs,* the *Nation,* the *New Yorker,* and the *Public Interest.* These nine periodicals can

Table 8.1

Influential Intellectual Periodicals as Determined by 61 American Intellectuals

Periodical	Read Regularly	Consider Influential
The American Prospect	15	9
The American Spectator	5	2
The Atlantic	20	32
Commentary	13	35
Daedalus	17	16
Dissent[a]	12	4
Foreign Affairs	15	37
Harper's	14	16
The Nation	20	18
National Review	5	18
The New Criterion	14	10
The New Republic	43	47
The New York Review of Books	53	50
The New York Times Book Review	53	39
The New Yorker	34	31
Partisan Review	14	3
The Public Interest	13	30
Salmagundi	16	4
Science	6	15
The Washington Monthly	10	6
Others Mentioned but Not Included on Initial Survey[b]		
Critical Inquiry	2	3
The Economist	3	4
Scientific American	3	3
Times Literary Supplement	6	6

[a] Due to a compositional error, *Dissent* did not appear on the first surveys sent out. Because the subsequent addition of *Dissent* to the typed list of periodicals did not appear to influence the frequency with which *Dissent* was mentioned by respondents, I concluded that the compositional error had little bearing on the results of the survey.

[b] Those listed include only periodicals mentioned more than once in each category.

be considered the mainstream periodicals of intellectual opinion in the United States.

To allow for a somewhat richer political analysis, I supplemented the analysis of this representative sample with an analysis of articles from periodicals of the right and left. For this purposive sample, I formed the conservative group out of the three highest-ranking conservative periodicals, the two conservative periodicals (*Commentary* and the *Public Interest*) from the main sample and the *New Criterion*. I formed the liberal-left group of periodicals from the two highest-ranking liberal-left periodicals, the *Nation* and *Salmagundi*. In addition, I added a small number of more general articles from the mainly academic journal *Critical Inquiry,* so as to provide some representation for the younger "cultural left," a group often singled out as representative of new theoretical trends in the discourse of intellectuals and intelligentsia.

I excluded reviews of one page or less, short and unsigned editorials, short stories and poems, and novelty features from the sample universe. The sampling procedure corrected for the differing publication schedules of the periodicals[34] while, at the same time, keying the probability of selection to the relative importance of the periodical, as determined by the panel of expert raters. From this initial sample of over 2,000 articles and reviews written in the years 1987–89, I drew a smaller subsample using a random number selection procedure. The final sample for the mainstream periodicals was 296 articles and reviews, which formed the main data base for the study.

The same procedure was adopted for selecting the purposive sample of periodicals with more clear-cut political profiles. I continued to weight the number of articles by the prominence of the periodicals as determined by the expert panel. More articles in the conservative sample come from the *Public Interest* and *Commentary* than from the *New Criterion,* and more in the liberal-left sample came from the *Nation* than from *Salmagundi* or *Critical Inquiry.* Altogether, forty-seven articles came from the three periodicals of the liberal-left, and sixty articles came from the three conservative periodicals.

With the help of a team of graduate students,[35] I analyzed these articles and reviews using a codebook covering over 100 variables. Some of the questions in the codebook concerned the demographic characteristics of authors: their sex, occupations, and institutional affiliations. They also included questions on topics covered and how those topics were treated; on positive and negative mentions of groups in society (such as business, labor, government, professors, women, and minorities); on positive and negative mentions of ideologies and intellectual approaches; and on the major opponents noted. The articles were also coded for social criticisms, if any were included. These coded questions were supplemented by a qualitative coding sheet, where the articles' main themes, rhetorical strategies, and key words of value and opprobrium were noted.[36]

Political Outlooks

I provide some indicators of the concerns and sympathies of American intellectuals during the later 1980s in Tables 8.2 and 8.3. I created group-mention indices in Table 8.2 by subtracting the total number of negative mentions of particular groups as a percentage of all 296 articles from the total number of positive mentions of the group as a percentage of all articles. The numbers in parentheses refer to the absolute number of positive and negative mentions, respectively. The ideology indices were created similarly.

When political references were made in the articles and reviews, they tended to tilt slightly to the left. Business was criticized more often than it was

TABLE 8.2
Positive and Negative Mentions of Groups and Ideologies in Leading Periodicals of American Intellectual Opinion, 1987–1989

	Nine Mainstream Periodicals[a] (N = 296)	Center-Liberal Periodicals[a] (N = 189)	Foreign Policy Periodical[a] (N = 33)	Conservative Periodicals[a] (N = 69)	Left-Liberal Periodicals[a] (N = 47)
Index of Business Mentions	−2.1 (22/28)	−5.9 (13/22)	+6.1 (3/1)	+7.2 (8/3)	−10.7 (1/6)
Index of Labor Mentions	+5.7 (16/5)	+3.7 (10/3)	+3.1 (2/1)	0.0 (1/1)	+6.4 (3/0)
Index of African American Mentions	+1.4 (12/8)	+2.7 (9/4)	0.0 (0/0)	−4.3 (2/5)	+6.4 (3/0)
Index of Other Minority Mentions	+2.0 (13/7)	+2.2 (8.4)	0.0 (0.0)	+4.3 (5.2)	+2.2 (2.1)
Index of Mentions of Women	+5.4 (19/3)	+6.8 (15/2)	0.0 (0/0)	0.0 (2/2)	+17.0 (8/0)
Index of Mentions of Liberal Intellectual	−7.1 (7/28)	−2.7 (5/10)	+3.0 (1/0)	−35.0 (0/24)	−4.2 (4/6)
Index of Mentions of Conservative Intellectual	−5.4 (4/20)	−4.8 (1/10)	+3.0 (1/0)	−4.3 (3/7)	−14.9 (1/8)

Index of Mentions of American People	+4.3 (25/12)	+2.6 (16/11)	+15.1 (5/0)	+4.3 (4/1)	+4.3 (2/0)
Index of Democratic Party Mentions	−5.1 (11/26)	−3.7 (9/16)	−6.1 (0/2)	−5.3 (2/6)	−8.5 (0/4)
Index of Republican Party Mentions	−2.0 (16/22)	−3.7 (9/16)	−3.0 (0/1)	+8.7 (7/1)	−8.5 (0/4)
Index of "Liberal/Left" Ideology Mentions[b]	+7.5	+19.8	−5.1	−28.8	+41.1
Index of "Conservative" Ideology Mentions[c]	−7.6	−19.4	−1.9	+18.9	−23.3

Source: American Public Intellectuals Study data.

[a] Purposive sample. Center-liberal periodicals: *The Atlantic, The New Republic, The New York Review of Books, The New York Times Book Review,* and *The New Yorker.* Foreign Policy periodical: *Foreign Affairs.* Conservative periodicals: *Commentary, The New Criterion,* and *The Public Interest.* Left-liberal Periodicals: *Critical Inquiry, The Nation, Salmagundi.*

[b] Liberal/Left ideologies include the following: welfare-state liberalism, neoliberalism, socialism, social democracy, left populism, progressivism, egalitarianism, feminism, new cultural left in academe, and postmodernism, but do not include any forms of Marxism-Leninism. The index is based on relative proportions. To avoid confusion, absolute number of mentions are not given.

[c] Conservative ideologies include the following: classical liberalism, conservatism, neoconservatism, right populism, Christian right, Social Darwinism, new cultural conservatism in academe, conservatism elitism, and anticommunism, but do not include any forms of authoritarianism or right totalitarianism. The index is based on relative proportions. To avoid confusion, absolute number of mentions are not given.

TABLE 8.3
Frequency of Social Criticisms Advanced in Leading Periodicals of American
Intellectual Opinion, 1987–1989 (N = 315)[a]

Relatively Frequent Social Criticisms (7 or more)	Percent (N)	Infrequent Social Criticisms (5 or fewer)	Percent (N)
Politicians' Timidity, Self-Interest and/or Incoherent Goals	14.0 (44)	Increasing Inequality	1.7 (5)
		Executive Branch Too Strong	1.3 (4)
Intellectuals' Hypocrisy, Utopianism or Other Failings	8.3 (26)	Materalism of American Life	1.3 (4)
Business Power, Ethics	5.1 (16)	Treatment of Women	1.3 (4)
Problems with Associational Life or Relations in Civil Society	4.4 (14)	Taxes Too Low	1.3 (4)
U.S. Competitive Situation, Decline	3.8 (12)	Public Withdrawal from Politics	1.0 (3)
Media Power, Bias	3.8 (12)	Too Much Government Meddling in Social Issues	1.0 (3)
Conservatives' Power	3.5 (11)	Too Much Violence in Country	1.0 (3)
Liberals' Power	3.2 (10)	Too Little Business Power	1.0 (3)
Environmental Problems	2.9 (9)	Weak Welfare State	1.0 (3)
		Treatment of Workers	1.0 (3)
Elites "Out of Touch"	2.5 (8)	Cities Decaying	.6 (2)
Too Much Government Meddling in the Economy	2.2 (7)	Lagged Technological Development	.6 (2)
Education Failing	2.2 (7)	Oil Dependence	.3 (1)
		Health System Failing	.3 (1)

Source: American Public Intellectuals Study data.

[a] In each article, three separate social criticisms were coded. Some articles contained fewer than three social criticisms, and some may have included more than three criticisms. N for this table is based on the 349 total number of criticisms coded, minus the "other" category for the second and third coded criticisms. From the qualitative coding sheets, we were able to track down the first criticism coded "other" but were unable to track down the "other" references for criticisms two and three.

praised, and labor was praised more often than it was criticized. The articles also expressed more favorable than critical views of women and minorities, and they were more likely to mention liberal ideologies favorably and conservative ideologies unfavorably. The political profile was not left of center in every respect, however. Authors in the mainstream periodicals were more likely to find fault with liberals and the left than they were to find fault with conservatives and the right. The mainstream periodicals were also more likely to criticize the Democratic party than the Republican party, and they were almost twice as likely to mention favorably that one-time bogeyman of the left, the capitalist economic system, than they were to mention it unfavorably (thirteen and seven times, respectively).

The major finding, however, is that explicitly political comments were rare. Even authors in periodicals of the left scarcely mentioned labor, the poor, or provision for basic social welfare. None of the groups shown in Table 8.2 were referenced, positively or negatively, in more than 10 percent of the articles, and most were referenced in fewer than 5 percent. The four ideologies most frequently mentioned in a positive way were democracy, liberal democracy (i.e., freedom-oriented democracy), capitalism, and pluralism. These four choices represented 43 percent of all positive mentions of ideologies in the sample. Table 8.3 indicates that the social criticisms raised in the articles had to do far more with the self-interest, timidity, and "incoherent goals" of politicians than with the advocacy of social values or political stances. Concerns about the character or goals of politicians were raised forty-four times (14 percent of the total number of social criticisms mentioned). Concerns about intellectual utopianism, hypocrisy, or activism were also raised quite often, twenty-six times (8 percent of the social criticisms). By contrast, in the 296 articles and reviews, issues related to race relations were raised in eleven, and issues related to inequality were raised explicitly in just five. Concerns about levels of taxation and social provision were raised seven times altogether, and concerns about the treatment of women and wage workers, four and three times, respectively.

Only writers for the foreign policy periodical, *Foreign Affairs*, were consistently concerned with the major issues of the day. If *Foreign Affairs* articles are subtracted from the sample, the level of concern with the major issues of the day is relatively weak. Of the following issues—economic competition, relations with Japan, the end of the Cold War, the prospect of European integration, racial tensions, multiculturalism, the budget deficit—none were a significant focus of more than 5 percent of the articles in the set of periodicals excluding *Foreign Affairs*. All but economic competition were the subject of fewer than 3 percent of the articles. Interest in the affairs of other countries was also limited. Less than 7 percent of the articles had to do with the domestic or foreign policy affairs of other countries.

Sampling variation alone could account for some of the more surprising omissions and some of the low frequencies in counts of the social criticisms contained in the articles. Some of the articles perhaps contained important subtextual meanings that were not captured by my coding procedures.[37] Nevertheless, the overall pattern of moderation and disengagement is difficult to ignore.

Two Cognitive Frames

The data lead me to propose the existence of two distinctive cognitive frames that different kinds of readers find challenging and "interesting." One frame, found most frequently in both the liberal-left and the conservative periodicals, is a more highly crystallized and contentious political-sociological frame. I will call this the *stance-taking* frame. The other frame, found primarily in the center-liberal periodicals, is a relatively weakly crystallized, accepting, and refined literary-historical frame. I will call this the frame of *particularizing refinement*.

The stance-taking frame assumes a pugnacious attitude; it intends to take a position. It tends more often to rely on highly crystallized verbal weapons— the naming of opponents, the appeal to ideology, and the appeal to distinctive methods and theories. It very often shows a level of alienation from dominant points of view, by proposing better alternatives or by developing criticism that is meant to condemn rather than to correct actions of which it disapproves. The intention of the refined frame, by contrast, is to educate sensibilities, and its work is done through indirection. It discusses positions but does not take them directly. It refuses to work with highly crystallized verbal tools, and it shows little alienation from dominant points of view, very often hoping to correct bad actions rather than to condemn them.

Stance taking is an orientation and a style, and it can frame discussions of a full range of topics from concert criticism to the most abstract discussions of philosophy. I will concentrate on evidence about stance taking in relation to public affairs and cultural movements. The content of stance taking tends to reflect the influence of three forces: (1) traditional or at least long-standing opposition to perceived sources of threatening power (e.g., business power for the liberal-left; liberal intellectuals for the right); (2) support for ideologically compatible, politically mobilized groups in society (e.g., feminist women for the left); and (3) emerging issues in the political culture (e.g., failure of political leadership, perceived declines in associational life and civil society).

Political stance taking cannot accurately be depicted as a mechanical reflection of ideological predispositions, however. In the first place, values of coherence, complexity, and scholarship come into play at times. Thus, radical trends in academic literary theory such as deconstruction were roundly rejected on both the left and the right. Secondly, the existing *rapport de force* is also an important influence on stance taking. During this period of conservatism, even the liberal-left periodicals show, for example, high levels of self-criticism and even significant appreciation for conservative intellectuals.

Although I found a certain amount of stance taking in all periodicals, the frame of particularizing refinement was the dominant form of intellectual discourse in the United States during the late 1980s. It was found most frequently in the periodicals with the highest prestige. The world of leading periodicals during this period can consequently be characterized as less *engagé* than donnish. This cognitive frame and cognitive style requires close observation and analysis of particulars, without use of standard guides (like traditional ideological categories or even preferred analytical approaches), which tend, perhaps it is thought, ineluctably toward over-generalization.

The data in Table 8.4 suggest that there may be a connection between the frame of particularizing refinement and closeness to centers of power and influence. The writers in the center-liberal periodicals were not only less prone to adopt highly crystallized or generalizing views; they were also closer to established centers of power and influence. The proportion of writers from Ivy League settings was comparatively high, and articles that self-consciously position themselves as going "against the grain" of established intellectual opinion were comparatively rare. The writers were also somewhat more likely (though not by a statistically significant margin) to take an insider's stance, hoping to correct bad actions rather than simply condemning them.

Most of the articles and reviews were based on highly refined analyses of highly particular phenomena. The predominant style is based on synthesis, elegant writing, and an "unusual" or "interesting" perspective. Close observation, fullness, and breadth are prized characteristics. One sees this combination very clearly in many of the articles in the sample. One article, for example, praises a new biography of Dickens, for, unlike previous biographies, this one "gives us a Dickens who demands all-around attention rather than presenting a single elemental clue to the source of genius."[38] Another article, on a political and social topic, offers an exhaustive description of how sugar cane cutting is done, details of the working conditions, what precautions are taken to protect workers, histories of individual workers, and other economic, political, and social aspects of the sugar cane industry.[39] This approach is consistent with the history and literature backgrounds of the majority of writers in the mainstream center-liberal periodicals. It contrasts sharply with the usual form of social scientific thinking, which is to explore a single hypothesis or set of hypotheses in relation to a range of cases.

Within the dominant frame of "particularizing refinement," it is safe to say that it is more important to "say something worthwhile and interesting"—to educate the sensibilities—than it is to take a stance as the "guardian of values," no matter whether these values are threatened, ignored, or widely acclaimed. *The dominant form of intellectual discourse can be seen as another kind of professional culture. From this perspective, intellectuals are specialists in situating and dissecting arguments, and they have at their disposal both their judgment and their acquired tools of commentary and interpretation.* Consequently, one key to understanding the moral imagination of intellectuals is to understand the tools of commentary and interpretation that intellectuals use to educate.

TABLE 8.4
Cognitive Frame Indicators in Leading Periodicals of American Intellectual Opinion, 1987–1989

	Nine Mainstream Periodicals[a] (N = 296)	Center-Liberal Periodicals[a] (N = 189)	Foreign Policy Periodical[a] (N = 33)	Conservative Periodicals[a] (N = 69)	Left-Liberal Periodicals[a] (N = 47)
Background Measures					
Ivy League (Professors only)	39% (75)	47% (53)	—	22% (18)	18% (22)
Historical Discipline (Professors only)	26% (80)	31% (58)	—	14% (21)	11% (19)
Crystallization Measures					
Any Ideology Positively Mentioned	44% (296)	36% (189)	58% (33)	58% (69)	57% (47)
Any Ideology Negatively Mentioned	51% (296)	40% (189)	64% (33)	65% (69)	77% (47)
Any Intellectual Approach Positively Mentioned	30% (296)	29% (189)	18% (33)	46% (69)	39% (47)
Any Intellectual Approach Negatively Mentioned	22% (296)	19% (189)	9% (33)	48% (69)	26% (47)

Main Opponent Is Named	23% (296)	20% (189)	9% (33)	35% (69)	43% (47)
Main Opponent Is Any School of Thought[b]	18% (230)	14% (127)	7% (15)	27% (79)	22% (51)
Alienation Measures					
Utopian Stance Evident	2% (200)	1% (181)	5% (33)	4% (69)	11% (46)
Stance of Opposition to Intellectual Opinion	15% (295)	7% (188)	9% (33)	42% (69)	36% (47)
Stance of Opposition to Public Opinion	11% (295)	8% (188)	3% (33)	23% (69)	6% (47)
Goal of Criticism is to Correct, Not Condemn[c]	33% (101)	33% (48)	42% (12)	23% (35)	14% (21)

Source: American Public Intellectuals Study data.

— = fewer than 10 cases.

[a] Purposive sample. Center-liberal periodicals: *The Atlantic, The New Republic, The New York Review of Books, The New York Times Book Review,* and *The New Yorker.* Foreign Policy periodical: *Foreign Affairs.* Conservative periodicals: *Commentary, The New Criterion,* and *The Public Interest.* Left-liberal Periodicals: *Critical Inquiry, The Nation, Salmagundi.*

[b] Coding allows for two main opponents to be named. Percentage is only for articles where a main opponent is named.

[c] "Goal of Criticism" refers to critical mentions of groups in society. N is less than total since not all articles contained critical mention of groups.

Educating the Sensibilities

Few of the articles and reviews followed such traditionally humanistic paths as the investigation of manmade or natural curiosities for their larger import,[40] or the deep examination of the effects of character on events.[41] There were also very few instances of close critical reading of a text for the keys to structural relations and a symbolic meanings.[42] For the most part, the articles addressed a different set of interests and followed a different set of rhetorical conventions. The rhetorical strength of the articles was based largely on the development or questioning of analogies; the offering of new interpretations; the debunking of standard approaches to a problem or personality; the highlighting of the perils of reification and rigidity; and the contemplation of ironies of history. Because these patterns of rhetoric are important for understanding the moral imagination of intellectuals, I will provide examples from the study of each of these means of educating sensibilities.

Analogy-based thinking in the articles either aimed to disconnect the previously connected or to connect the previously unconnected. Disconnecting arguments revolved around the development of analytical distinctions, and the exposure of false analogies or mislabeling. Thus, divorced and never-married single parents were distinguished from one another for purposes of understanding welfare behavior;[43] and communist societies with elaborate planning bureaucracies were distinguished from those without such bureaucracies for purposes of understanding processes of reform.[44] The prohibition era was regarded as an improper model for plans to decriminalize drugs because of the greater social costs of drug legalization,[45] and "talk shows" were regarded as mislabeled because "real talk" involves exchange, whereas talk shows involve mainly the release of aggression and the sensations of voyeurism.[46] Connecting arguments included the exposure of hidden connections and the extension of existing principles to new territory. Thus, one review attempted to show how Vietnam and Watergate were of a piece in so far as they both represented executive branch arrogance combined with public apathy,[47] and another article suggested that people who expose fraud and deception may be sensitive to fraud and deception because of their own damaged characters.[48] In another instance, the language of political rights was extended to the heretofore virgin territory of "nature's rights."[49]

Interpretation-based methods of saying something worthwhile and interesting were based on new readings or new perspectives, or the suggestion of ambiguities that had previously been missed. Thus, one article discussed Winston Churchill's life, not in the usual biographical terms, but as a last magnificent effort of defiance in the face of British decline.[50] Another cast doubt on philanthropy, using the now-unfamiliar viewpoint that philanthropy reduces the incentive of the poor to fight poverty themselves because it undermines the principle that poverty is repulsive to them.[51] Some articles and reviews highlighted ambiguities as a way to rethink interpretations. One review, for example, asked whether a particular painting was "sentimental" or an "ironic commentary on the cult of youth."[52]

Debunking is perhaps the most venerable way that intellectuals (and also journalists) have of challenging the minds of their readers. Certainly it was common in the articles and reviews I studied. Thus, in the articles, workfare is shown to be popular, but unproven;[53] the Framers' intentions for the Constitution, far from implying "original intent," are shown not to be fixed, but various and open to interpretation;[54] the real problem the economy faces is shown not to be the deficit, but the misallocation of the national output;[55] and education is shown to be a popular way of fighting drug use, but almost completely ineffective.[56] One version of debunking is to argue that conventional ways of thinking miss the true underlying problem. Thus, the homeless are not mainly homeless, they are poor;[57] the problem is not abuse of the elderly, but neglect;[58] and misdeeds during the Iran-Contra affair were not those of executive branch adventurism, but rather of embezzlement.[59] Some of these arguments, of course, are plausible, and some are strained.

The articles in the sample also frequently highlighted the *perils of reification and rigidity*. Statistically driven policies, for example, were criticized in one article for "treating unlike groups alike."[60] Journalistic ethics were discussed in another as generally obligatory, but not in instances where "catastrophes" might be averted through their violation.[61] Another article emphasized that policy makers should avoid imposing a free-market model of the world on countries that follow such a model only very partially, and another summed up the lessons of the Cuban Missile Crisis as proving that rational models and rigid worldviews are often less helpful in managing crises than keeping channels of communication open, exercising prudence, and monitoring every step of interaction.[62] Another article argued that even optimism, so often helpful in breaking down rigidity, can itself become rigid and counterproductive.[63] Similarly, because of their concern about rigidity, American intellectuals, who would never proclaim themselves pro-kitsch or pro-communist, can be anti-anti-kitsch[64] or anti-anti-Communist.[65] Rigidity causes problems not only in its own right, but because it can obscure equally important elements that do not conform to conventional ways of thinking. Thus, one article observed that Casanova's reputation as a lover has "obscured his greatness as a social historian."[66]

There were also a number of articles relying on an appeal to *the ironies of history* as a way of educating the sensibilities. For the most part, these involved tracing the downward trajectory of ideas in the hands of epigones, or the tendency of laudable programs and sensitivities to become counterproductive in the face of new circumstances. Thus, Keynes was not wrong about the ability of government to correct the business cycle. Instead, his followers raised false expectations by introducing the concept of "fine-tuning."[67] Similarly, new southern writers were discussed as having taken on the same topics as William Faulkner, but as having failed to enrich these concerns with a Faulknerian quality.[68] Writers also noted on occasion the tendency for understandable reactions in one era to become blinders in a succeeding era. Thus, the Vietnam generation's "distrust of government power" comes to obscure its appreciation of the importance of confidential testing for AIDS.[69] For the most part, arguments about unintended consequences tended to become linked to conservative arguments against reform. Thus, rent control, initially intended to help the poor and struggling, becomes in time another resource of the rich,[70] and the well-intentioned desire to create business people with broad social vision produces, over time, people unfit to manage businesses.[71]

The dangers of ideological or otherwise highly crystallized thought are well known; the possible shortcomings of refined and particularizing thought are naturally less frequently examined.[72] There is good reason for this. In most instances, there is no question that the dominant frame of particularizing refinement encourages the testing of what Kenneth Burke called our "equipment for living" by sharpening capacities for critical thought and interpretive appreciation. At the same time, the dominant cognitive frame is clearly not a style of thought that is likely to encourage broad public projects of any type, or to focus collective aspirations for justice or improved life conditions.[73] Nor is it very often directed toward the kind of "deep and probing" considerations that intellectual work once suggested, almost by definition. Certainly, in the instances when it is at its most glib and formulaic, the culture of intellectual periodicals reflects the extent to which the world of entertainment has made inroads even among members of the intellectual elite.

The Organizational Context

At a minimum, the findings of my study reflect the principle that intellectuals—or at least those who publish in the leading periodicals— "manifest values, expectations, orientations to government, moods, and concerns that broadly reflect those of the American public." The later 1980s were a period of conservative ascendance both in electoral politics and in economic ideology, and the major audience for intellectuals, the educated middle classes, were, in many respects, more conservative than the population at large. The moderate views found in this sample may reflect, in part, a fear of "being out of step," understandable but hardly expressive of the disposition to defend unpopular values that intellectuals are so often credited with by their admirers and detractors alike. Indeed, the interests and sentiments of intellectuals as reflected in my sample of articles and reviews were, in some respects, significantly more disengaged than those expressed by the public at large. In the Gallup survey reports for 1987–89, most Americans, for example, cited economic problems (such as unemployment and competitive challenges), the budget deficit, poverty, and drug abuse as the most important problems facing the country. Intellectuals were, by contrast, far more concerned about the failings of national politicians and the failings of their brothers and sisters in the intellectual world.

If the prevailing political climate is one crucial factor bearing on the politics of intellectuals, another is the market and organizational context in which intellectual writing is produced. Intellectual writing is produced for the market of educated consumers of opinion and commentary. It is safe to assume that maintaining market share in the intellectually oriented periodicals means providing material that these consumers will find challenging (though perhaps not too challenging) and at the same time "interesting."[74] Cultural goods are, in this sense, very much like other kinds of goods. Producers do not go out of their way to insult the sensibilities of their likely consumers.

One important fact of intellectual production, then, is that it is production for a market. It is helpful in this regard to look at intellectuals as operating in different segments of the market for opinion and commentary. There are markets for "secular religious views" on the left and right that are relatively highly crystallized and that tend to activate convictions and feelings of indignation. In these markets, there is a greater willingness to talk in terms of highly crystallized categories and schools of thought. There is also a market (and a much larger one) for middle-of-the-road periodicals. A different cognitive frame tends to predominate here, one based on close analysis that is perhaps counterintuitive or otherwise interesting and that works against the grain of these highly crystallized perspectives. This is the culture of history and literature: skeptical, ultimately (but not easily) moral, aesthetic, and humanistic.

Many of the tendencies in the market for opinion and commentary can be understood in terms of the concerns and sensibilities of readers, as interpreted by editors and publishers of the periodicals. Some part of the findings almost certainly reflect the fact that a large proportion of the readers of the leading periodicals are academic and other professionals who are more interested in keeping abreast of developments in nearby fields than they are in the expression of particular points of view.[75] In addition, certain characteristics of intellectual writing can be understood at least partially in organizational terms. Both circulation size and frequency of publication are connected to the styles of expression found in the periodicals. As Table 8.5 indicates, the higher circulation publications tended less often to take explicitly provocative stands and they tended also to make fewer references to ideologies and intellectual approaches. Smaller circulation periodicals have the freedom to be undiplomatic, since their audience is presumably relatively homogeneous. Diplomacy, by contrast, is a feature more common among larger circulation periodicals, serving relatively heterogeneous audiences. Publication frequency also encourages a somewhat reduced tendency to "go against the grain," and a particularly acute desire to eschew explicit mention and use of ideologies and intellectual approaches. Presumably, typifications of this sort are regarded as dangerously "predictable" and/or demanding for publications that must excite reader interest so regularly.

A Time of Historic Change without Guides

It is already clear in retrospect that the period studied was one in which epoch-making changes were occurring. These changes included the mounting movement toward European integration; intensified economic competition be-

TABLE 8.5

Organizational Characteristics of Nine Mainstream Intellectual Periodicals
Correlated with Selected Style Variables (Spearman's Rank-Order Correlations)

Organization Variables	Cognitive Style Variables			
	Stance of Opposition to Public Opinion	Stance of Opposition to Intellectual Opinion	Any Ideology Positively Mentioned	Any Ideology Negatively Mentioned
Circulation Size[a]	−.11*	−.20**	−.07	−.08
Publication Frequency[b]	−.16**	−.21**	−.16**	−.15**

	Any Intellectual Approach Positively Mentioned	Any Intellectual Approach Negatively Mentioned	Any Intellectual Approach Used	Any Social Criticism Given	Any Major Opponent Named
Circulation Size[a]	−.16**	−.13**	−.08	−.14**	−.14**
Publication Frequency[b]	−.06	−.12**	−.34**	−.01	+.07

Source: American Public Intellectuals Study data.

[a] Circulation size is coded as an ordinal variable, with the periodicals coded in rank order by circulation. Data for circulations come from *Ulrich's International Periodicals Directory, 1991–92*, 30th ed. (New Providence, N.J.: R. R. Bowker, 1991).

[b] Weeklies were coded 1; biweeklies were coded 2; monthlies were coded 3; quarterlies were coded 4.

** $p < .05$
* $p < .10$

tween Japan, Europe, and the United States; the end of the Cold War and the collapse of state-socialist regimes in Eastern Europe; the beginnings of dissatisfaction with the outcomes of the Reagan revolution in this country; continuing racial and cultural discord on a wide variety of issues; and, perhaps particularly, a troubling sense of American limits. Leading intellectuals were not very much engaged in the discussion of these matters or other matters plausibly linked to issues of public culture.

It would be unwise to dismiss entirely the possibility of some sharp differences by historical period. The evidence of histories, memoirs, and biographies suggests a good deal of intellectual ferment on the left in the late 1950s and early 1960s. Similarly, considerable creative ferment is evident on the right in the early and mid-1970s. It is possible that systematic studies of intellectual production during these periods would uncover higher levels of stance taking.

At the same time, it may be that many of the features of the situation of public intellectuals in our own era have been evident for some time—the rare episodes of engagement masking the deeper underlying trend. Perhaps, in fact, we see in this data the latest chapter in the transformation of an intellectual class, dominated by the relatively disengaged and particularizing disciplines of history and literature, largely unwilling to take positions on public issues.

Given the weak representation of the bolder forms of intellectual stance taking in the leading periodicals, it is not surprising that some intellectual historians have begun to ask whether the specific characteristics that gave many European and some American intellectuals their distinctive cultural identity in times past—that extraordinary combination of good amateur (or, more rarely, professional) scholarship, seemingly penetrating tools of understanding, authoritative-sounding criticism, sophisticated sensibilities, and hope-renewing conviction—have not become monopolized, more or less completely, by the better institutionalized spheres of American life: serious scholarship in academe; conviction (where it exists at all) preeminently in science and politics; and many of the old tools of understanding in the archives of the history of ideas.[76]

THE POWERS AND THE INTELLECTUALS

A study of periodicals can, of course, go only so far in providing evidence about the moral imagination of intellectuals. Intellectuals participate in many other forums: they write books; they write articles for smaller, but perhaps influential, publics; they address conferences; they serve on committees. The study does, however, suggest what may be a common thread in the trajectory of intellectuals. It is more difficult now to make a case for the notion that the influence of intellectuals is based primarily on the intrinsic qualities of the intellectual community[77]—be these qualities of mind, or distinctive resources and traditions. Rather, the qualities of the situations in which intellectuals find themselves and the quality of their ties to other groups and organizations now seem more often decisive.

Since the 1970s, great events have transformed the intellectual community and its relation to powerful elites. Ideologically, these events include the waning of the "New Left" and social democracy, the rise of new conservative ideologies, and, perhaps most importantly, the crumbling of Marxism-Leninism and the state based forms of socialism in the Soviet Union and Eastern Europe. Great social changes have also occurred that bear on the relations between people of ideas and people of power. These include the ever-increasing capabilities of organized power centers, such as political parties, state bureaucracies, mass media organizations, and universities; the now very large number of highly educated professionals who pour out of our universities each year and into government or government-related activities; and the fiscal crises of universities.

In this context, a revaluation of the sociology of intellectuals leads to a somewhat greater sense of modesty about the influence of intellectuals. It takes some probing to see this, because surface impressions do not necessarily suggest that intellectuals have become less important politically. With the collapse of communism in Eastern Europe, intellectuals, after all, came to power, at least temporarily, in Czechoslovakia, Hungary, and Poland. There is, similarly, no escaping the sense that political ideology has become a formidable power, not only in the postcommunist world, where such a thing is to be expected, but also in the West where new conservative ideologies have provided an important resource and support for recent conservative administrations.

And yet if we evaluate the situation unsentimentally, we can see how much of the influence of ideological intellectuals depends on forces that have created repeated disruptions in the fiscal and political health of states. A crisis of the state is also a crisis of legitimation. This is perhaps obvious in the case of Eastern Europe, where the faltering fiscal and political health of the state created a legitimation crisis of obvious profundity. But it is also true in the West.

In the United States, the New Deal coalition, the fiscal rules of Keynesianism, and the distributive rules of an interest group—based pluralism provided the necessary foundation for the dominant liberal ideology among intellectuals. Though the elements were never exactly the same, similarly stable rules and conditions existed in many parts of Europe during the period and provided the same sort of foundations for the prevailing social democratic views among intellectuals. It is possible to see now that the association between intellectuals and the liberal-left in the postwar era was supported less by the so-called "adversary culture" of intellectuals than by effective fiscal and distributive practices of the state that held together coalitions supporting the growth of the public economy.[78]

These conditions no longer exist. Indeed, throughout the West, the dominant left-of-center, egalitarian ideology of intellectuals suffered a tremendous shock in the early 1970s when the logic of Keynesianism came unraveled and increases in government services started to be perceived—fairly or not—as greatly interfering with, rather than enhancing, economic development. Nor have the old governing rules been replaced, in many countries, by stable configurations of another sort. This enhances the importance of ideologists, and it also reduces the level of consensus that ought to be expected among intellectuals in their ideological beliefs. At the more elite levels, conservative ideologies have clearly flourished in recent years. Unless fiscal and political conditions stabilize, there is no certainty that this will continue.

Policy intellectuals are another group that does not appear to have experienced any obvious decline in prominence or influence, judging from the memoirs of those who have served in recent administrations in this and other western countries.[79] Yet confidence in the independence of policy intellectuals has faltered greatly since mid-century, precisely because of their dependence on political elites. It is difficult in the wake of events like the fabrications surrounding the war in Southeast Asia and the economic forecasting of the Reagan administration to feel much confidence in the ability of policy intellectuals to offer the large vision and purpose that many earlier writers so hopefully expected in the face of the bureaucratic pressures encouraging administrative loyalty. Instead, policy intellectuals appear increasingly to be creatures of the state—and perhaps also of rather self-contained policy communities closely tied to the state. The ties of policy intellectuals to the broader intellectual community are, frequently enough, very tenuous indeed. Under these circumstances, it is usually too much to expect that their primary affiliations will be other than to the political leaders who invite them into the councils of government.

In many respects, it is Coser's fourth group, the academic intellectual experts, who are now best able to occupy a responsible, relatively independent position. If one thinks, to choose a few recent American examples, about the extent to which arguments highlighting the "second shift" in women's work entered into discussions of the social condition of women,[80] or how critiques of "reverse discrimination" helped to mobilize reactions to affirmative action,[81] or how advocacy of "cultural literacy" helped to recast discussions of education in many areas of the country,[82] or how ideas about American decline stimulated new thinking about the global situation of the United States,[83] it seems clear that the leading figures among the academic intellectual experts constitute a rather important group.

Yet an important kind of dependence exists even in this relatively independent quarter of the intellectual stratum. The work of these issue-oriented intellectuals is conditioned by the changing moods of the educated classes. Indeed, a compelling case can be made that changing attitudes call forth intellectual responses at least as frequently as new intellectual conceptions influence educated opinion. Thinking about affirmative action provides one recent example. Significant changes in public opinion about affirmative action were occurring at precisely the time that intellectuals were beginning to rethink these policies.[84] An independent intellectual influence is apparent, but the influence is in relation to the framing of the issue, not in the initial raising of the issue or in the creation of a receptive climate of opinion. Framing, of course, can be important for energizing and channeling opinion, and even for converting the uncertain. In their ideas about "reverse discrimination" and the "culture of victimhood," conservative intellectuals in this case produced powerful and measurably effective dialectics based on the marriage of conservative thematics to the vocabulary of liberal moral concern.[85]

In most instances, academic intellectual experts stand in relation to a mix of changing facts and perceptions—whether these be of longer work weeks, race-sensitive policies, declining test scores, or new global challenges—the selective spotlighting of these facts and perceptions, and the development of public feelings of hope and discomfort in relation to them. Occasionally, they may offer new "truths." More often, they provide interpretive shape and rhetorical force to what audiences, at a much less articulate level, already "know."

Professionals and Politics in Postindustrial Societies

IT IS STILL controversial to use the term "professions" to discuss the organization of middle-class labor in Europe. This is because professions did not develop in the same way in Europe as they did in England and America.[1] The structural characteristics of contemporary professions—the organization of labor markets through the credential system and the status honor associated with applied formal training—clearly exist also in Europe, but these structures were carved out, for the most part, by states, rather than by occupational organizations working collectively to organize markets.[2] Smaller, more passive, and more decentralized, the state in England and the United States was less an organizer of the division of labor and more an object of the attentions of organizing occupations. On the continent, by contrast, the activity of the state in the creation and control of professions was much more comprehensive, and the history of professionalism is therefore, to a considerable degree, the history of universities developing training programs for expert personnel "needed by the state."[3]

Not surprisingly, middle-class groups on the continent looked more directly to the state and to their employers, rather than to their occupational associations, for security and status. As Joseph Ben-David put it, "Their status and security were gained by their attendance at state-controlled, elite institutions of higher education, which assured them elite positions in the civil service or other technical-managerial positions. Their economic protection lay in sinecures in bureaucratic organizations, not in privileged competitive position in the labor marketplace."[4]

These differences have had some important consequences. In countries like Germany and France, the professions had at first a much closer connection to the civil service as a normative ideal of expert status, rather than with the autonomous "free professions." Bureaucracy was, from the beginning, a larger part of professional identity.[5] In addition, because occupation was a less salient and class a more salient source of identity in Europe, it was common for the Europeans to think of the people we call "professionals" as part of a larger stratum in society defined by middle-class standards of living, education, and culture. In Germany, for example, the *burgertum* was a definable social stratum, particularly important in the early and mid-nineteenth century, and it was sometimes broken into two major segments, the *bildungsburgertum* (or "educated middle class") of mainly professional and civil service occupations, and the bourgeoisie of commerce and industry.[6] In

France, it has been common for professionals to identify themselves not by their occupational activities, but by their employment. "If they are in private practice, they tend to consider themselves part of the bourgeois entrepreneur class, and if they are salaried, they consider themselves officials of a certain rank, rather than chemists or engineers."[7]

In recent years, some signs point to possibilities of convergence between the Anglo-American model and the Continental model of professions. This convergence is based on a conception of experts working in markets for services organized in a mixed economy dominated by the larger corporations. Convergence around a model of marketable expertise has been encouraged by the waning of social trustee professionalism in the Anglo-American world and by the decline of the status distinction of state service in Europe.[8] The European Economic Community has fostered convergence by emphasizing the idea of "markets for expert services" along the lines that come naturally to American economists.[9]

Professional Politics and National Context

With these historical differences in mind, it is possible to compare the Europeans and the Americans for commonalities and differences in their social and political views. *My investigation of the comparative evidence suggests that the professional stratum is an important political force in all of the postindustrial democracies, but that national contexts are preeminently important in shaping the specific relation of professionals to the political order.*

In many European countries, professionals express a kind of reformist class politics built around support for the regulation of business, support for government spending programs benefiting the middle class, and support for civil and personal liberties. I will call this "regulatory liberalism" and contrast it with the "redistributive liberalism" of the working classes. Throughout Europe it is also true that students and members of the nonprofit social and cultural specialties have tended to replace blue-collar workers as the main source of political dissent and protest on the left. These are clearly developments of significant political importance and bear long-term watching.

At the same time, the professional middle class is not the same kind of political force in all countries. Where national political norms are social democratic, the differences within the professional class are not as large as when national norms are conservative and business-oriented. Moreover, the politics of the professional middle class cannot be separated from the larger political divisions that exist in a society. Where Protestants are sharply divided from Catholics, for example, they will also be sharply divided in the professional class.

National context is important also for understanding the other two topics that I will examine in this chapter, the role of experts in government and the connection of the middle class to protest politics. The few cases of structurally significant levels of expert influence in government (e.g., Sweden and France) are based on an institutionalized connection between scientifically oriented higher education and elite political offices. They also depend on the concentration of political power in the executive departments of the state rather than in its dispersal through other institutions, like Parliament or powerful interest groups. Even the rather general connections between a new middle class intelligentsia and the "new social movements" are conditioned by national differences in social structure and history. This is particularly true with regard to the frequency of actual expressions of protest through demonstrations, marches, and the like.

These patterns of national variation defeat all efforts to make generalizations on a grand scale. There is no common specter haunting the advanced world of a competition between "new class" professionals and "old class" business people. Nor is the political contest of the future necessarily a battle within the professional class, between conservative technocrats and dissenting intellectuals. The first of these images will make some sense to Swedes, and the second, at least historically, to many of the French. But both images would necessarily be regarded with something like incomprehension in the many countries, like Italy and Great Britain, where they do not begin to explain the main consequential patterns of division in political life.

Political Outlooks in Comparative Perspective

The International Social Science Program (ISSP) studies provide useful data for answering questions about the political attitudes of middle-class professionals in countries other than the United States. In these studies, the same set of questions have been asked to representative samples of respondents from several industrial democracies. The United States has also been included, so there is a good comparative benchmark for our purposes. The data that I will rely on primarily come from the 1985 study on attitudes about the role of government.[10] The surveys from this year were conducted in Australia, Austria, West Germany, Great Britain, Italy, and the United States, and explicitly addressed a very wide range of relevant political attitudes.[11] Many of the same questions were repeated in the 1990 study, and I will consequently also refer to that study. The data from 1990 are not quite as useful, since Austria was not included that year.

This evidence from Europe and Australia[12] enriches our understanding of the politics of American professionals by demonstrating the importance of national context. The evidence indicates that the model I advanced in chapter 5 of multiple bases of division within the professional stratum is wedded to a particular national context—that of an economically advanced, politically conservative society. It is less useful, although not irrelevant, in countries whose political norms are of the social democratic type. Moreover, as compared to other countries, the American pattern is strongly influenced by the conservative role of religious identifications, by the unusually strong role of income as an influence on political views, and also by an atypical regional pattern of core-periphery relations in which the wealthier areas are more liberal rather than more conservative.

The Political Profile of Professionals

The first analysis, presented in Table 9.1, looks at differences between workers, high-income managers, highly educated professionals, and a left-of-center wing of the professional stratum—the social and cultural specialists. It is based on a summary of the full range of opinion items included in the 1985 ISSP surveys. The data show that in all the countries surveyed, professionals were in the middle of political differences that turn on matters of distribution, welfare, and equality. As in the United States, they constitute a moderating force in the occasional discord of economic conflict. In no country were professionals more often on the left than blue-collar workers. The data also indicate that the same divisions found in the United States between a liberal social and cultural wing and a conservative technical and business-services wing also exist in most of the European countries and Australia. The applied technical wing was always closer to business than to blue-collar workers on economic issues, and the social and cultural specialists were always closer to workers. Indeed, the social and cultural specialists do rival blue-collar workers in their levels of expressed liberalism on economic issues—although they do not usually surpass them.

Neither blue-collar workers nor social and cultural specialists tended in any absolute sense to be supportive of political ideals of the left. Blue-collar workers were typically without strong egalitarian sentiments and, by and large, endorsed market principles and high levels of business influence in society. The same was true, to an even greater degree, among professionals in the social and cultural occupations. The 1990 data show similar patterns, though with somewhat stronger liberalism among professionals, particularly in Italy.

Regulatory vs. Welfare Liberalism. In the face of a good bit of negative evidence, the ISSP data do indicate at least one point of partial support for the theory of "professional class" liberalism. This has to do with the pattern of responses on issues involving middle-class spending programs and the regulation of business. In several of the countries represented in the ISSP data, the social and cultural professionals were the most liberal group in their attitudes about government control of banking, business influence, regulation of business, and, not surprisingly, in their support for spending on education and the arts. On these business regulation and middle-class spending issues, professionals as a whole tended to be somewhat closer to the social and cultural specialists than to the more conservative views of managers and executives.

The data suggest further that in countries outside of the Anglo-American sphere, a new kind of distinction may be developing on the left between

TABLE 9.1
Bivariate Comparisons of Managers, Professionals, and Blue Collar Workers
on 46 Political Attitudes[a] in Six Countries, 1985

	Australia	Austria	West Germany[b]	Great Britain	Italy	USA
10 Egalitarian and Basic System Commitment Items[c]: % of Items in Which Selected Groups Are Most Liberal						
Blue Collar	75	46	69	58	71	83
Highly Educated Social and Cultural Professionals	17	23	31	33	21	17
Highly Educated Professionals[d]	0	23	0	8	0	0
High-Income Business Owners and Managers	8	8	0	0	7	0
9 Welfare State Items[c]: % of Items in Which Selected Groups Are Most Liberal						
Blue Collar	78	73	100	73	54	89
Highly Educated Social and Cultural Professionals	22	17	0	17	15	11
Highly Educated Professionals[d]	0	9	0	9	0	0
High-Income Business Owners and Managers	0	0	0	0	31	0
10 Business Regulation and Middle Class Spending Items[f]: % of Items in Which Selected Groups Are Most Liberal						
Blue Collar	29	30	38	21	0	23
Highly Educated Social and Cultural Professionals	50	50	38	43	16	55
Highly Educated Professionals[d]	21	40	31	29	38	38
High-Income Business Owners and Managers	0	0	0	7	23	0
8 Civil Liberties and Civil Rights Items[g]: % of Items in Which Selected Groups Are Most Liberal						
Blue Collar	8	15	8	8	0	8

(*continued*)

TABLE 9.1 (Continued)

	Australia	Austria	West Germany[b]	Great Britain	Italy	USA
Highly Educated Social and Cultural Professionals	42	31	54	38	31	58
Highly Educated Professionals[d]	50	46	31	46	54	33
High-Income Business Owners and Managers	0	8	8	8	15	0

7 Social Control, Protest, and Defense Items[h]: % of Items in Which Selected Workers Are Most Liberal

Blue Collar	0	0	11	0	0	22
Highly Educated Social and Cultural Professionals	62	25	11	56	62	22
Highly Educated Professionals[d]	38	75	67	44	38	56
High-Income Business Owners and Managers	0	0	11	0	0	0

Source: ISSP 1985.

[a] When liberal responses from two occupational categories were not statistically different, both categories were credited as giving the most liberal answer. Thus, percentages reflect cases of double counting. In addition, they may not add to 100% because of rounding.

[b] Because the West German respondents were not coded for income, respondents in the high-income managerial category for the West German case only are older (36 and above) private-sector managers, the managerial group most likely to have high incomes.

[c] Egalitarian and Basic System Commitment Items include the following: (1) Is government responsible for reducing income inequality? (2) Should income inequalities be reduced? (3) Should the rich pay a higher proportion of their incomes in taxes? (4) Should government own the auto industry? (5) Should government own the steel industry? (6) Should government own the banking industry? (7) Does labor have too much power in society? (8) Do big corporations have too much power in society? (9) Is government responsible for keeping prices down? (10) Should prices be controlled?

[d] Includes Social and Cultural Professionals, plus Applied Technical and Business Service Professionals.

[e] Welfare State Items include the following: (1) Should government provide grants for low-income students? (2) Is government definitely for helping the unemployed? (3) Should government spend more on the unemployed? (4) Is government responsible for the elderly? (5) Should government spend more on the elderly? (6) Is government responsible for health? (7) Should government spend more on health? (8) Is government responsible for creating jobs for those who need them? (9) Does R strongly favor creating jobs for those who are unemployed?

[f] Business Regulation and Middle Class Spending items include the following: (1) Should

(continued)

working class–based preferences for *redistributive* forms of government action and professional class-based preferences for *regulative* forms of government action.[13] Higher proportions of workers want material improvements, including more services, while higher proportions of professionals want to maintain balance and control in the system by keeping business from gaining too much power. Blue collar workers were concerned about the traditional bases of social democratic politics; they were the most liberal group, in virtually every national context, on reducing income inequalities, government ownership of industry, control of prices, job creation, and on government spending for health, the elderly, and the unemployed.[14] Yet in Germany, Austria, and Italy, professionals were somewhat more concerned than blue-collar workers about the control of business power. In 1990, these patterns continued. A sociological explanation comes readily to mind for these patterns. The professional middle class is a relatively privileged stratum whose privileges do not arise directly from business activity, but rather from the skills they bring to the workplace. Their level of privilege make them less interested in welfare state activities, while the nature of their privileges make them at least relatively concerned about the power of business.

Social Issues. As in the United States, highly educated professionals in Europe and Australia *were* comparatively liberal on issues having to do with freedom of expression, tolerance, and the use of force. In most of the countries, the social and cultural specialists remained the most liberal group, but in West Germany and Austria, the applied technical professions were every bit as liberal on these issues as were the social and cultural specialists.[15] These issues have to do with the bases of solidarity in the society and the nature of preferred rules of political order. Professionals clearly prefer a liberal and tolerant form of societal solidarity, while other groups feel more conviction about common

---

educational opportunities be increased substantially? (2) Should the government spend more on education? (3) Should government spend more on the environment? (4) Should government spend more on the arts? (5) Is the tax on business too low? (6) Is R against less regulation of business? (7) Does R favor government helping business? (8) Is government responsible for helping industry? (9) Should government spending be cut? (10) Is government power in society too great? For question 10 only, a "yes" answer was coded as liberal under conservative governments; a "no" answer was coded as liberal under liberal governments.

g Civil Liberties and Civil Rights Items include the following: (1) Is computer surveillance a serious threat? (2) Is it a greater mistake to convict an innocent person or free a guilty person? (3) Should racists be allowed to meet? (4) Should racists be allowed to teach? (5) Should racists be allowed to publish? (6) Should revolutionists be allowed to meet? (7) Should revolutionists be allowed to teach? (8) Should revolutionists be allowed to publish?

h Social Control, Protest, and Defense Items include the following: (1) Should people always obey the law or sometimes follow their conscience? (2) Should the government spend more on law enforcement? (3) How essential is it that the schools teach discipline? (4) How essential is it that the schools teach respect for authority? (5) Should national labor strikes be allowed? (6) Should mass protest marches be allowed? (7) Should the government spend less on defense? Austrian respondents are missing on questions 1, 3, and 4.

TABLE 9.2

Percent Liberal on Selected Economic Issues[a] in Three Strata and Six Countries, 1985

	NATEDUC	REGULATE	NOBUSAID	NATHEAL	CREATJOB	TAXRICH	EQUALIZE
Australia							
HE Prof	68.0	18.7	4.9	52.0	8.7	11.7	13.7
S+C Prof	72.7	23.1	3.1	61.5	10.6	13.6	13.8
BI Collar	66.9	19.5	9.8	63.9	31.6	18.2	30.5
West Germany							
HE Prof	47.8	20.3	27.5	31.4	17.4	34.8	6.1
S+C Prof	42.9	22.9	34.3	33.3	22.9	45.7	6.1
BI Collar	41.2	25.0	28.6	59.1	34.1	39.6	33.2
Great Britain							
HE Prof	50.4	19.4	5.8	85.9	27.0	18.0	31.7
S+C Prof	87.6	20.4	9.4	87.6	24.5	18.0	38.5
BI Coll	75.5	11.5	8.4	89.7	43.6	30.8	57.3

USA

HE Prof	57.1	5.3	26.6	51.5	11.8	5.6	.9
S+C Prof	74.4	6.4	36.4	56.0	15.1	6.7	1.9
Bl Collar	64.1	23.4	30.3	67.5	33.4	22.5	22.8

Austria

HE Prof	60.3	22.9	21.3	43.7	30.2		24.2
S+C Prof	56.9	23.3	24.0	47.8	31.2		28.8
Bl Collar	44.1	20.4	32.2	60.6	30.0		42.4

Italy

HE Prof	57.4	34.3	27.2	59.3	43.5	18.4	39.2
S+C Prof	64.9	36.0	27.2	66.9	46.7	20.0	42.3
Bl Coll	60.9	18.0	22.7	85.1	61.3	37.0	51.2

Source: ISSP 1985.

Key: HE Prof = Highly Educated Professional. S−C Prof = Social and Cultural Professional. Bl Coll = Blue Collar Worker.

[a] Responses included are as follows: NATEDUC = Favors government spending more on education; REGULATE = Against less government regulation of business; NOBUSAID = Not in favor of government aid for business and industrial development; NATHEAL = Favors government spending more on health care; CREATJOB = Strongly favors government creation of jobs to help the unemployed; TAXRICH = Favors the rich paying a much higher percentage of their income in taxes; EQUALIZE = government definitely responsible for reducing income inequalities between rich and poor.

moral sentiments. Thus, as in the United States, professionals in Europe and Australia are a force promoting personal freedoms and pluralism in the cultural arena, while they remain at least a little aloof from the implications of the free-market forms that business people most actively promote in the economic arena. The patterns of support for regulatory liberalism found in Europe may reflect not just the class interests of professionals, but the residuum of historical differences between the European and the Anglo-American professions, particularly with respect to the importance of state service as a source of status honor in the European middle classes.

Three Patterns of Internal Division

In earlier chapters, I explained the patterns of liberal and conservative opinion found among American professionals by developing an argument based on the cumulative force of multiple bases of division. In this explanation, I also took into account compositional changes and short-term temporal shifts. This explanation might be referred to, in a shorthand way, as an argument based on "multiple cumulative trends." Analyses of the ISSP and other comparative data suggest that the argument does not hold as well for Continental Europe or for most of the industrialized East Asian countries. Rather, it appears to be one of three major patterns—the other two being fewer (but sometimes sharper) bases of division in relation to either left-of-center or right-of-center national norms.

To analyze the specific social bases of politics in the professional strata, I examined five indices related to economic issues,[16] five indices of social issues,[17] and also political party identifications.[18] The economic scales included attitudes about business regulation, labor, egalitarianism, social welfare spending, and government ownership of specific industries and services. The noneconomic scales included attitudes about protesters, civil liberties, the teaching of deference to authority in the schools, academic versus practical training, and support for government spending on "quality of life" programs.[19]

Women were more conservative in Europe than America,[20] but otherwise the main variables in the multiple cumulative trends model showed significant net associations with at least several of the dependent variables in the countries included in the 1985 ISSP survey. Moreover, of the 121 significant net associations for the main variables in the analysis, the signs of just four were the opposite of the expected direction. Thus, the model was wrong in this most obvious way only 3 percent of the time. However, the proportion of correct net associations to possible correct net associations was less impressive: only 32 percent. The model fit the noneconomic issues (38 percent correct net associations to possible correct net associations) better than it fit the economic issues (27 percent correct to possible correct associations).

The expected relationships were found frequently in Australia and the

United States, but they were found less frequently in Great Britain and Italy, and less frequently still in West Germany and Austria. (See Table 9.3.) Both the proportion of correct to possible correct predictions and the average adjusted R^2 are higher in the Australian and U.S. cases than elsewhere.[21]

These patterns can be explained by differentiating between national norms that are "social democratic" versus those that are "classically liberal." The four Western European countries have "social democratic" political cultures in which most middle-class segments tend to hold welfare-oriented and egalitarian views. In this context, few groups stand out as distinctively more left-of-center than the population generally. It is possible that the historic connection of professions to the state and the civil service as a normative ideal help to reinforce this relatively statist pattern. At the same time, the very success of the state has apparently fostered the growth of a few distinctively leftist segments: the young (who have perhaps taken its assumptions most seriously), the public sector workers, and the social and cultural specialists, in particular.

This is a very different pattern than that found in the United States and Australia, where the many distinct bases of liberalism and conservatism can be aggregated together to form quite divided segments within the professional class, but where no single group constitutes the same embedded and distinctive base of liberal and left-of-center views that public-sector social and cultural specialists do in much of Europe. It is the classically liberal antistatism of the American and Australian political culture, not the nature of professional life per se, that creates the many bases of liberal politics among professionals in those countries. The pattern of many bases of liberalism emerges out of conservative norms in a way that appears not to happen if norms are anchored a little to the left, rather than substantially to the right. Like figures on a carpet, the lighter shapes stand out only when the carpet itself is very dark.

Examination of other comparative evidence suggests that a third pattern may be characteristic of most of the industrial countries of East Asia; few bases of division exist in the context of strong nation-building ideologies. This pattern may indeed be typical of all countries during dynamic phases of economic or nation-building development. No examples of this pattern exist in the ISSP data, but reports from Hong Kong, Singapore, South Korea, and Taiwan suggest that professionals and managers of all types in those city-states and countries represent a rather undifferentiated conservative front.[22] Because of its association with the most dynamic phases of capitalist development and nation building, this pattern is found not only among the emerging powers of Asia, but also in instances like nineteenth-century America,[23] and Israel during the nation-building period of the 1950s.[24] Some might expect Japan also to fit this third pattern, but, in so far as we can tell from the unsatisfactory data available, Japan is a much more complex case. There are clear divisions in the professional and managerial ranks in Japan—including rather left-leaning intellectuals and teachers—but, at the same time, the divisions appear, for the most part, to be somewhat more limited than in com-

TABLE 9.3
Social Characteristics Showing Net Significant Associations with Liberal Political
Views among Professionals and Managers in Six Countries, 1985

I. Six Economic Scales[a]

			Country			
	Australia	Austria	West Germany	Great Britain	Italy[b]	USA
Focal Variables						
Soc+Cult Prof (+)	4	2	0	1	1	2
Public Sector (+)	6	0	2	2		1
Lower Income (+)	6	3		2	2	5
Salaried (+)	0	0	1	0	1	1
Younger (+)	0	1	3	2	1	2
Female (+)	1R	2R	0	0	1	1R
Other Variables in Model						
Manager (−)	1R	3	0	0	0	0
High Educ (−)	0	1	0	0	0	1
Urban (+)	1	1R		2	0	0
Lib Region (+)	1	0		2	2	4
Con Region (−)	0	2		0	0	1
Protestant (−)	2	2	1	0		2
Catholic (−)	0	2	2	0		2
Religious (−)	0	0	0	2+1R		2

II. Five Noneconomic Scales[c]

			Country			
	Australia	Austria	West Germany	Great Britain	Italy[b]	USA
Focal Variables						
Younger (+)	3	3	3	3	4	1
High Educ (+)	3	0	3	3	2	3
Urban (+)	2	2		3	0	2
Protestant (−)	5	1	0	1		2
Catholic (−)	5	0	2	0		2
Religious (−)	0	1	1	0		2
Soc+Cult Prof (+)	2	1	0	1	1	0
Other Variables in Model						
Public Sector (+)	0	0	0	0	0	1
Manager (−)	2	0	0	1	1	0
High Income (+)	0	0		0	0	1

(*continued*)

TABLE 9.3   (*Continued*)

II. Five Noneconomic Scales[c]

	Country					
	Australia	Austria	West Germany	Great Britain	Italy[b]	USA
Salaried (+)	0	1	0	0	0	0
Female (−)[e]	0	0	0	0	0	1
Lib Region (+)	0	0		0	0	2
Con Region (−)	0	0		1	0	0

Source: ISSP 1985.

Note: R indicates reversal of expected direction.

[a]The six economic scales measure attitudes about the regulation of business; egalitarian attitudes; attitudes about government ownership of industries; attitudes about labor and labor unions; attitudes about welfare state programs; and political party identification. For information about the variables that make up these scales, see notes 16 and 18, chapter 9.

[b]Left party identification missing for Italy.

[c]The five noneconomic scales measure attitudes about the following: civil liberties; training for independence in the schools; the importance of humanist culture; protest; and spending on the arts, education, and other programs appealing to the middle class. For information about the variables that make up these scales, see note 17, chapter 9.

[d]Independence Training and Humanistic Culture scales missing for Austria.

[e]Women expected to be more conservative on all noneconomic scales except liberal culture and spending on "quality of life" programs, where they are expected to be more liberal due to their traditional role in cultural reproduction.

$^*p < .05$.

tries like the United States.[25] Democracy has encouraged some patterns of cleavage, while successful nation-building ideologies have limited the extent of division.

The Importance of National Context

A final analysis of the ISSP 1985 data, which introduces country explicitly as a variable into the regression models, shows that national differences are at least as important as social characteristics in accounting for liberal and conservative views in the six ISSP countries.[26] Indeed, on the economic questions— questions about government regulation of industry, the role of labor, the social welfare responsibilities of government, and the desirable level of equality—the country variables generally showed up as more important than the social bases of political division.

Just as in the zero-order correlations, the United States and Australia stood out as particularly conservative countries in these analyses, while Italy stood out as comparatively egalitarian. The West Germans showed a high level of commitment to guaranteeing civil liberties and sensitivity to the threat of too much training for deference and were relatively liberal on the economic scales. The English were the mirror opposite of the West Germans on the civil liberties and deference scales but were supportive of the welfare state. The Austrian profile was somewhat more centrist, except on the government ownership scale where relatively positive experiences have led to rather widespread acceptance of a strong government role.[27]

Some of the country differences reflect short-term temporal influences. The sensitivity of the West Germans to civil liberties issues appears, for example, to be a part of the *zeitgeist* of the time—a time when Germans were trying to put the ghosts of World War II behind them and before the anti-immigrant movements of the early 1990s.[28]

Other national differences have deeper structural and cultural roots. The United States and Australia were "born bourgeois" and remain that way, while the European countries have experienced a long history of statism and working-class rebellion that has left its mark on the national norms of political culture. Italian egalitarianism has deep cultural roots in, among other things, the common antipathy to cultural and political authorities. It is one of the hidden balance wheels that allows the country to survive and prosper even in the face of constant government crises and divisive regional and subcultural cleavages.[29]

Much of the intraclass conflict in Great Britain and Italy is based on divisions between people living in economically developed and less developed areas. To a much greater degree than in the more evenly developed countries, political interests in unevenly developed Italy and Britain are filtered through the economic interests of regions and (in the case of Britain) also of cities. Region also plays an important role in the United States, but the pattern of effects is the opposite of the typical industrial pattern pitting conservative core against liberal periphery. In the United States, it is the economically dominant core regions of the northeastern and mid-Atlantic states that are most liberal and the economic periphery that is more conservative.

In the European countries, the politics of generational conflict are particularly intense. In Austria, West Germany, and Italy, this conflict no doubt has at least partly to do with the radically divergent experiences of the prefascist and postfascist generations. As other research has also shown, the younger cohorts in these countries show a markedly more liberal pattern, particularly on issues having to do with the protection of civil liberties and civil rights.[30]

In the two most conservative countries—Australia and the United States—religion (and particularly Protestantism) plays an important role in supporting conservative views. This is true not only in the cultural domain, where it is to be expected that religion will play an important role, but also in the economic arena, where it ought logically to have less bearing. Higher income also plays a comparatively greater role in the United States and Australia than in the other countries, further reinforcing our sense of these countries as more thoroughly market-oriented societies. Indeed, the data provide strong sup-

TABLE 9.4

Social and National Influences on Political Attitudes and Identifications in Six countries, 1985

I. Economic Issues Scales[a]

	BUSREG (+ = con)	EGALIT (+ = con)	GOVOWNER (- = con)	LABOR (+ = con)	SOCSPEND (+ = con)	RGTPARTY (+ = con)
Employment Variables[b]						
S–C Professional	-.14	-.14	-.06	-.15	-.12	—
Manager	—	—	—	—	—	—
High Income	.08	.22	.10	.20	.16	.14
Salaried	-.17	-.03	-.04	—	—	-.09
Demographic Variables[c]						
Younger	-.07	—	—	-.09	-.10	—
High Education	—	—	—	—	.07	—
Female	—	—	—	—	.08	—
Urban	—	—	—	—	—	-.08
Protestant	.08	.06	.08	.09	—	.16
Catholic	—	—	—	—	—	.13
National Variables						
Australia	.14	.26	—	.20	—	—
Austria	.15	—	-.10	—	—	—
West Germany	Ref.	Ref.	Ref.	Ref.	Ref.	Ref.
Great Britain	.24	.08	—	—	-.31	.09
Italy	—	-.15	-.31	-.13	-.25	—
USA	—	.27	.11	.23	—	—
R²/(SE):	.10	.23	.17	.22	.20	.08
	(.34)	(.35)	(.50)	(.32)	(.31)	(.48)

(continued)

TABLE 9.4 (Continued)

II. Noneconomic Issue Scales[d]

	CIVLIB	INDEP	HUMCULT	PROTEST	MCSPEND
	(+ = con)	(+ = con)	(+ = con)	(+ = con)	(+ = con)
Employment Variables[b]					
S+C Professional	—	—	-.11	-.10	-.13
Manager	—	.07	—	—	—
High Income	-.08	—	—	—	—
Salaried	—	—	—	—	—
Demographic Variables[c]					
Younger	-.14	-.20	—	-.26	-.12
High Education	-.16	-.10	-.12	-.16	-.10
Female	.07	.10	-.10	.09	—
Urban	-.08	-.06	-.07	-.11	-.09
Protestant	.14	.09	—	.20	.09
Catholic	.13	.15	—	.13	.10
National Variables					
Australia	.14	.40	-.12	.08	.49
Austria	.07	—	—	—	—

West Germany	Ref.	Ref.	Ref.	Ref.	Ref.
Great Britain	.19	.42	—	.12	.40
Italy	.15	.15	-.18	—	—
USA	—	.27	-.12	—	.26
R^2/(SE):	.12	.17	.09	.12	.25
	(.50)	(.54)	(.44)	(.33)	(.30)

[a] The economic scales measure attitudes about the regulation of business (BUSREG), egalitarian attitudes (EGALIT), attitudes about government ownership of industries (GOVOWNER), attitudes about labor and labor unions (LABOR), attitudes about welfare state programs (SOCSPEND), and political party identification (RGTPARTY). For information about the variables that make up these scales, see notes 16 and 18, chapter 9.

[b] Sector was not coded for Italy. Five-nation regressions, excluding Italy, indicated that the public sector showed significant net negative associations with all of the economic scales, except attitudes about the regulation of business, and with none of the noneconomic scales.

[c] Frequency of church attendance was not coded for Italy. Five-nation regressions, excluding Italy, indicate that religiosity showed a significant net association, in this case positive, only on the scale measuring attitudes about government ownership of industry.

[d] The noneconomic scales measure attitudes about civil liberties (CIVLIB), attitudes about training for independence in the schools (INDEF), attitudes about the importance of humanist culture (HUMCULT), attitudes about protest (PROTEST), and attitudes about spending on the arts, education, and other programs appealing to the middle class (MCSPEND). For information about the variables that make up these scales, see note 17, chapter 9.

[*] $p < .05$.

port for the stereotypical image of Australia and the United States as dominated by an optimistic and utilitarian, if sometimes moralistic, middle-class ethos. They also provide support for the less familiar notion that religious identification provides an important undergirding for this ethos.

TECHNOCRACY IN COMPARATIVE PERSPECTIVE

The second issue that I will take up in this chapter is the rise of technocracy outside the United States. To examine patterns of technocratic strength in government, I have drawn on the handful of useful comparative studies that now exist. With a small number of cases and a large number of potential causes of variation, it is impossible to draw statistically valid conclusions about the sources of variation in expert influence that exist in the polities of the industrial democracies. Instead, judgments must be based on controlled comparisons and close study of individual cases.[31]

Technocracy in Europe

The coherence and influence of scientifically trained elites in government, while never absolute in the West, does vary from country to country. Those who wish to find Western societies that approximate the picture of a "new class"-dominated government can look with some confidence in the direction of the Scandinavian countries, particularly Sweden, Norway, and Denmark. With their glorification of the pragmatic and public-spirited policy expert, their very large public economies (over 50 percent of GDP in several cases) based largely on welfare expenditure, and their tendency to incorporate all spheres of society and economy in governmental planning, these countries are as close as we are likely to come to "new class" domination in the mixed economies of the West. Some Scandinavians are aware and worried about the applicability of the "new class" thesis to their societies. One American social scientist has described his adopted country as a "rationalized society in which many of the irrationalities of capitalist social and productive relations have been replaced or at least held in check by an efficient yet democratic state machine, dominated by intellectuals."[32] This observer, sociologist Ron Eyerman has gone so far as to argue that the first generation of social democratic intellectuals in Sweden—the generation of the Myrdals, Tage Erlander, and Ernst Wigforss—were "if not themselves members of the cast . . . at least stage hands, preparing the way for the arrival of the new class." Today, he says, the state is dominated "by the same sort of intellectuals, technocratic and pragmatic," but "lacking in the tempered utopianism" that gave their movement its dynamism.[33]

France is another country very often described as under the rule of "technocratic" experts. As Ezra Suleiman observes, "Most studies of the subject of technocracy dwell in some detail on the French case, which is generally regarded as exemplary."[34] Indeed, the first sustained development of the concept of "technocracy" came from the French theorists Jean Meynaud and Jacques Ellul in the early 1960s.[35] Many contemporary observers of French society remain convinced of the importance of this state-based expert elite. According to Alain Touraine, "the programmed society," of which France is a prime example, is dominated by "technocrats—administrative elites in the state and corporations tied to the state" who rule on the basis of their control of relevant "knowledge and information."[36] Sidney Tarrow argues that French mayors must "accept the technocratic values of the policy elite" to make gains for their communities.[37]

In the case of France, these experts are invariably described as conservative meliorists, much more concerned about showcase industries, state prerogatives, and their own corporate powers than about the social welfare of the average Frenchman. They are in this sense a mirror of their Swedish counterparts—a right-leaning, rather than left-leaning, "new class."[38] There is some evidence that Spain is developing along similar lines in the post-Franco era.[39]

Social Democratic Technocracy in Scandinavia. The conditions under which a left-leaning political-technical elite can emerge are obviously rare. Indeed, the more we look into these conditions, the more fragile and unlikely the combination of left-leaning ideology and technocratic ascendance would appear to be. In Scandinavia, there is first of all the unusual ability of intellectuals to rise to power in the social democratic parties. Industrialization occurred in Scandinavia during the heyday of socialism on the European continent. The labor parties quickly adopted a socialist identity, and, owing to their early incorporation in the polity, a socialist identity that was of a thoroughly reformist rather than revolutionary cast.[40] The unusual permeability of the labor parties to intellectuals appears to have most to do with the rapidity with which the Scandinavian countries industrialized—leaving a large but politically inexperienced class of labor and only a weakly developed workers' culture to support the parties—and the numerous complex problems facing the countries when the Social Democrats assumed power in the 1930s.[41]

Secondly, an expert culture at the top cannot grow without the experience of governing. The Social Democrats quickly established themselves as the leading party in Scandinavia. Their successful anti-Depression policies in the 1930s boosted their popularity, just as it did for the Democrats in the United States. In Sweden and Norway, this led to four decades of uninterrupted rule. The long-term popular appeal of the Social Democratic parties is unusual and must be explained by the economic conditions, institutions, and policies that support the parties. Many writers have argued that very high levels of export dependency in Scandinavia helped to create conditions favoring active state coordination of economy and society.[42] More obviously, the loyal support of an unusually well organized and centralized labor movement is no doubt an extremely important factor sustaining social democracy, if not the most important factor.[43] The rule of left-leaning experts could not have survived a decline of organized labor in the early years of the movement, and it is still dependent on it today. The strategies that the Social Democrats in power have used to divide the opposition, and to unite middle-class and working-class supporters, is another. These include—as one might expect in a system that is strongly influenced by "new class" experts—high levels of stabilizing and responsive reform and an institutionalized spirit of cool, rational appraisal.[44]

Perhaps most important of all, however, have been the mechanisms developed to encourage structured consultation and the corporate representation of the main interest groups in policy making.[45] One of the principal features of this "neocorporatist" organization has been the willingness of organized labor to trade off wage demands for increases in benefits through the welfare state.[46] In this way, the state has come to dominate more thoroughly than it otherwise could.

Finally, of course, a key to the success of the Scandinavian "new class" has been their skill in developing policies that have not divided elements in the electoral coalitions that keep them in power. As the sociologist Gösta Esping-Andersen has shown, the lesser skill of the Danish social democrats in creating "solidaristic" policies in areas like housing and incomes led to considerable partisan decomposition in their electoral coalition and their loss of power for long periods in the 1970s.[47]

The influence of the expert stratum is further encouraged by recruitment and organizational patterns in government. From early on, rigorous and stiff higher education requirements existed in Sweden for entry into the higher levels of the civil service. These requirements tended to create a distinctive classlike separation between employees at the different levels of government, including a high degree of homogeneity by background among the higher civil servants.[48] Although law rather than social or natural science was at first the dominant form of training among the higher civil servants, legal training was tailored to meet the needs of state service by requiring courses in economics and elementary statistics, and by allowing for optional courses as well in sociology and political science. Since the 1960s, the training patterns have shifted away from law and toward the social and natural sciences.[49] Swedish civil servants have an unusual level of influence in the development of policy. This partly reflects the scarce resources available to legislators and partly the historical effectiveness of the expert stratum. But it is perhaps primarily explained by organizational factors. Both the volume of reform efforts and the intricate and lengthy process of institutionalized consultation more or less require the assignment of responsibility for policy recommendations to particular officials in government.[50]

Conservative Technocracy in France. No such intricate chain of conditions and contingent events is necessary to explain the prominence of right-leaning experts in France. To be sure, the influence and activism of the French technocrats is unusual, but their ideology is less difficult to explain. It is of a type that is much more a "natural fit" under the business-oriented conditions of modern capitalist societies.

The French expert stratum owes its prominence to two legacies of the Napoleonic era. The first is the legacy of a highly centralized and activist state.[51] The second is the unique structure of higher education in France dominated by the specialized *grandes écoles*. The *grandes écoles* provide the personnel for the activist state, and the activist state allows the scope of action for these officials to exercise their specialized powers. Ezra Suleiman describes the *grandes écoles* as "practical endeavors on behalf of the state." "The state, more than ever, is responsible for the training, organization, and experience not only of the elites that directly serve it, but even of those who work in the nationalized and private sectors. [These schools] produce . . . elites whose task has always been and continue to be the training of those destined to serve the state."[52]

With the exception of the specialized teacher-training institution, the *Ecole Normale Superieur*, the *grandes écoles* are utilitarian institutions, organized to train civil engineers, financial analysts, administrators and other highly applied professionals. The graduates of these *grandes écoles* are pragmatic conservatives, owing in part to their trained contempt for theory and in part to their concrete contact with the power centers of French society. They are also strongly inclined toward centralized and elite-dominated structures, perhaps partly because their own positions are dependent on these sorts of structures.[53] By design, a direct channel runs between the *grandes écoles* (particularly the specialized technology and management schools) and the higher levels of French state administration. A sense of elite consciousness is developed among the graduates, not only because of the rigors of competition, but even more so by the many links that tie graduates to the positions at the pinnacles of French society.[54]

Even given a self-conscious and technically competent elite, we could not plausibly speak of expert dominance unless the French state also allowed significant play to the judgments and recommendations of the administrative elites. In most democratic systems, civil service elites are constrained by the power of interest groups, party leaders, politicians, and private sector influentials. But the French state empowers the administrative elite to an unusual degree. Part of the Napoleonic legacy is the high prestige of state officials.

Moreover, at the highest levels, the line between politics and administration in France is, in the words of Vincent Wright, "singularly blurred" because of a frequent pattern of holding several political and administrative posts simultaneously.[55] If they wish, higher civil servants can, in fact, devote themselves full-time and with full pay to politics. Frequently success at the national level as a civil servant leads to success at the local level as a politician. In the 1980s, between forty-five and fifty-five deputies in the French parliament were former (or current) civil servants—a figure far higher than elsewhere.[56]

The ideological cast of the French technocracy is perhaps most clearly colored by the virtual absence of organized labor as a political force. Although historically active in the Communist and Socialist parties, labor influence on government is as weak in France as it is strong in Sweden. French labor is not only highly decentralized but also poorly organized. Only about one-fifth of workers are members of unions—a figure not much higher than in the United States.[57] Instead of seeking wage restraint through greater incorporation in the state, the French government has relied on price controls to stiffen employers' resolve against wage demands and on periodic devaluations to neutralize the effect of sporadic wage increases on export prices.[58] The same indifference and opposition to business is not evident among French technocrats. Indeed, business people are consulted frequently by the government. In view of these patterns, Gerhard Lembruch has characterized France as an example of "neocorporatist" concertation without labor.[59]

Patterns of National Variation

In most Western democracies, neither the ethos nor the means exist to support the growth of a self-conscious and influential expert stratum. This is why the idea of technocratic ascendance tends to fall on deaf ears outside the United States, Scandinavia, and France (and, of course, Eastern Europe). Perhaps the two best examples in Europe of a weak expert stratum are Great Britain and Italy. In both countries, a few spheres of governmental activity are greatly influenced by technically trained experts of the modern political-bureaucratic type, but the dominant framework is hostile to the development of an expert ethos or expert power.

In Great Britain, the higher civil service—the natural home of the experts—has, until quite recently, been constituted as a humanist elite, hostile to the idea of "scientific policy making," insulated from political practice, and, consequently, thoroughly subordinate to the governmental ministers.[60] The dominant education of the higher British civil servants continues to be classics and history rather than social and natural science. Typically, these are people from "families of great diligence and little prosperity," who have taken good, but not the highest, degrees.[61] In the apt phrase of Richard Rose, they are "socialized, not trained."[62] They are apt also to be lifetime employees of the government, and to work very much in the background. Robert Putnam and his associates observed in the early 1980s that British civil servants were, of seven national groups, the least likely to have regular, direct contact with the ministries (for example, with members of parliaments or with representatives of interest groups) and the most likely to leave "the power to establish agendas in the hands of the cabinet."[63]

This subordination of the administrative elite to the politicians remained, the norm to an even greater degree under Margaret Thatcher. As Thatcher worked to replace traditional patriarchal Tory conservatism with a more modern market conservatism, she intervened actively in the civil service. Under Thatcher, the old mandarin civil-service class gradually gave way in many spheres.[64] However, in neither the old (pre-Thatcher) nor the new (post-Thatcher) English civil service does the image of an autonomous expert stratum fit. In both cases, the civil service has been too thoroughly subordinate to the political elite; and in neither case has its ethos been in any significant sense scientific.

In Italy, the idea of a ruling technocracy is, if anything, even less plausible. The higher civil service, still largely recruited from the uppermost ranks of Italian society, has been trained mainly in law rather than social or natural science. In many respects, it is the descendant of the old *classe dei colti,* which played such an important state and nation-building role in the years before Fascist rule. However, in the modern context, the descendants of the old professional elite often appear to be out of step. "The typical member of the Italian administrative elite," according to Robert Putnam, "appears as the very essence of the classical bureaucrat—legalist, illiberal, elitist, hostile to pluralist politics and fundamentally undemocratic."[65] The thoroughgoing subordination of the administrative elite complicates and deepens this sense of detachment and alienation. In the party- and patronage-dominated politics of postwar Italy, the civil service has become evermore dependent on politicians for career preferment. Moreover, the comparative evidence[66] suggests that a great many have also become alienated from the inefficiencies, corruption, and dealmaking that are so characteristic of Italian public life.[67] In this entrepreneurial and clientalistic environment, the idea of a powerful expert stratum—whether of the left or right—is a far-fetched notion indeed.

These contrasts lead to the conclusion that educational training and political organization are the essential sources of variation in the situation of Swedish and French technocrats, on the one side, and British and Italian bureaucrats, on the other. For a technocracy to exist, the training of higher civil servants must be predominantly scientific rather than humanistic or legal. For a degree of self-conscious status honor to exist as well, competition for admissions into training institutions must be stiff, or, at the very least, educational requirements for entry into service must be set at a high standard. The development of a technocracy is also closely connected to the scope of influence of the state. A centralized and powerful state organization is very nearly a prerequisite. Neither pluralist nor party-based interest representation is congenial to the development of technocracy. For a technocracy to flourish, the locus of power must be in the executive, rather than in interest groups or the relations of political parties. Features of state organization must also encourage the blurring of political and administrative roles. This can occur in a number of ways: through the volume of policy business and the massive requirements of consultation, as in the Swedish case; through the need to cultivate Congress and interest groups to sustain policy initiatives, as in the American case; or through the formal assignment or responsibilities that are both political and administrative, as in France. Well-traveled channels between government and administration encourages the merging of technical-administrative and political roles that is essential to the development of a powerful expert stratum.

Because these conditions are rare, powerful and self-conscious expert strata are also rare. It is possible, but by no means certain, that they will be less rare in the future. Certainly there are forces in the environment that would seem to encourage the more widespread creation of techno-political elites. The continuing growth of state power and of higher educational qualifications, the continued complexity of many policy issues, and the continued insufficiency of *purely* technical approaches to policy making all would seem to encourage greater movement in the French and Swedish direction in the future. However, political elites in many countries have done well without technocracy in the past, and institutions of government change only slowly.

Given the capitalist context in which all states in the advanced world operate, the French model of conservative technocracy must be considered the normal condition of any future development toward greater expert influence in government. For a left-of-center ideology to prevail among experts, it is necessary that the labor movement be strong and active and closely integrated into government. It is also necessary for the policies of the social democratic experts to be effective and sufficiently "solidaristic" to blunt tendencies toward decomposition in the electoral coalition that keeps them in power.

MIDDLE-CLASS PROTEST IN COMPARATIVE PERSPECTIVE

The final issue that I will take up has to do with the link between the middle class and protest in the advanced societies. Many social scientists have suggested that an intelligentsia growing out of the nonbusiness segments of the professional stratum has increasingly replaced the radicalized working class as the major source of protest in the industrial democracies. The comparative evidence suggests that these images, while sometimes overstated, do contain a sizable element of truth. At the same time, the extent of protest and levels of support for protest vary considerably in crossnational comparisons, and once again it is essential to understand national context in order to explain these patterns.

Middle-class protest movements are concerned with gender relations, environmental protection, human rights, and peace. Throughout the West, the rise of these "new social movements" is closely connected to higher living standards and the declines of the socialist ideal since the 1970s.[68] All European countries, even those governed by socialist parties, have tended to move toward market-based solutions to social problems, divestiture of state-owned businesses, and sharp restrictions on the extension of the public economy.[69] Although socialism remains relevant as a moral aspiration for many Europeans—particularly in Catholic Southern Europe[70]—its influence on practical political economy has become increasingly marginal. In this context, active protest has largely shifted from concerns about inequality and the organization of the industrial economy to concerns about "quality of life" issues and the treatment of women, minorities, and nonconformity.

The Social Bases of Middle-Class Protest

The connection between intellectuals and radical politics has sometimes been strong in Europe. However, the continuing problems of the Western economies and the decline of communism as an ideal led to the decline of radicalism among the intellectual classes of Europe in the 1970s and 1980s. As in the United States, the main leaders and supporters of protest movements during the period were those in the orbit of intellectuals, not intellectuals themselves—at least not the leading intellectuals. Above all, this means students in the humanities and social sciences, younger people working in the creative and public welfare professions, and professors who covet a popular, rather than a strictly professional, influence. These teachers and intellectually oriented professionals have been the decisive stratum in all the newer forms of pacifist, "quality of life," and inclusionary protest activities—including anti-war movements, nationalist and other communal protection movements, environmental movements, and movements for improving the situation of women, ethnic minorities, and homosexuals.[71]

Data collected on social movement activists in several European countries indicate the importance of the social and cultural professions, relative youth, and lack of religious identification as social bases for protest. University students, teachers, and professors alone constituted 30 to 45 percent of activists in eight of ten movements studied by the sociologists Richard Hamilton and Maurice Pinard, and members of other creative and public welfare professions added another 10 to 15 percent in seven of these movements. For the most part, the activists were also young—typically in their twenties and thirties.[72] Similarly, the most complete single-nation study of left and liberal protest in Europe found support for five Dutch movements (including the peace movement, feminism, and ecology) to be associated with the social and cultural professions, the younger cohorts, higher levels of education, and lower levels of religiosity.[73]

Comparative study of the "Green" movements in Western Europe leads to very similar conclusions. Although the parties and movements were at one time marked by significant national differences in the social bases from which they recruited,[74] a considerable amount of similarity now exists. The members of these parties are primarily people whose educational levels are higher than their occupational attainments and on the social and cultural wing of the "new middle class." The conclusion of Wolfgang Ruedig's comprehensive review is indicative: "Peace and ecology movements have generally drawn most of their activists from an identical social base. They come disproportionately from the young and well-educated; their background is generally 'middle class,' but they are drawn only from a very particular part of the middle classes: a high share come from the 'non-productive service sector' . . . i.e., they are employed in education, arts, the health sector and social work, or they are still in full-time education."[75]

Patterns of National Variation

Patterns of national variation have an important bearing on the intensity and frequency of protest and the degree of support for protest in the middle class. Throughout most of the contemporary period, support for protest has been quite common in France and the Netherlands; somewhat common in the United States, Canada, West Germany, Great Britain, and Italy; and rather uncommon in Sweden, Norway, Switzerland, and Austria.[76]

Variations in political culture help to explain these patterns, particularly for those countries that have been most notable for protest in recent years. The spirit of the French Revolution and of 1848 still reign to a degree in France, which has historically been the spiritual home of radical protest. Dutch support for protest is one product of the prominence of Amsterdam as a center of the international youth culture in the 1960s. It is also related to the "depillarization" of Dutch society during the same period.[77]

Differences in political structure also influence protest politics in the middle class. Countries relying on neocorporatist structures of social concertation as a primary means of organizing interests have experienced relatively low levels of protest, while countries like the United States that rely on pluralist competition as a primary means of organizing interests have experienced relatively high levels of protest.[78] Pluralism provides a congenial ground for protest by encouraging mobilization outside of government. Neocorporatist and consociational structures, by contrast, constrain protest by centralizing interest representation and bringing interests directly into the policy-making process.

The activities of government are a final significant influence on the scope of middle-class protest. The middle-class left wants governments that do not abridge basic human rights or use force gratuitously. Governments that fail to satisfy these concerns can experience sharp deflations in legitimacy among the middle classes.[79] During these periods of legitimacy deflation, levels of protest increase—sometimes very rapidly. The most widespread periods of middle-class protest experienced by Western governments in the modern period occurred in the years 1968–69 and sporadically in the five years thereafter, when all governments were tarred by relatively privileged young people for their association with U.S. policy in Southeast Asia. During the period, incidents of violence among the radical intelligentsia were most frequent in the three countries—West Germany, Italy, and Japan—where state legitimacy still suffered from past associations with fascism.[80] Demographic forces fed into protest during this period, very much as in the United States. The greater the growth of higher education enrollments in the 1960s and 1970s, the greater the number of protest activities on average; countries with the high proportional increases in enrollments—notably, Italy, Germany, France, and the United States—also experienced high levels of protest.[81] Since the 1970s, protest movements have continued to mobilize in direct reaction to unpopular governmental actions. The passage of unpopular laws or the threat of unpopular court decisions have, for example, been the precipitating force behind surges in antiwar and abortion rights protest movements in many European countries.

Governments do, in addition, sometimes provide resources or symbolic support for middle-class protest. Often, this support is a by-product of governmental reform efforts or efforts to make amends for bad policies of the past. In West Germany, for example, socialist governments in the 1960s and 1970s underwrote protest by providing resource support for the German peace institutes. The neutralist and anti-NATO climate of opinion of the German peace movement (and, to a lesser degree, of German society) in the 1970s and 1980s was in all likelihood partly connected to this material support of intellectual dissent.[82]

In sum, the comparative evidence suggests that although impressive levels of similarity exist in the social bases of middle-class protest, some countries have strong and active protest traditions, while others have weak protest traditions. The sources of these national differences have less to do with norms of the political culture generally than with cultural traditions—largely socialist and Romantic in origin—supporting intellectual dissent and popular protest; with the political structures that exist for the expression of interests in society; and with the degree to which governments have been able to avoid losses of legitimacy on issues that are of greatest interest to the middle-class left.

Conclusion: The Transformation of the Professional Middle Class and the Future of Intellectuals

ONE HUNDRED years ago, the great French sociologist Emile Durkheim envisaged a society in which most traditional forms of social connection had been effaced by the force of an impersonal market economy and an ever more highly specialized division of labor. He thought that occupational associations might help the larger society to develop new forms of social solidarity through their propagation of values and through their devotion to occupational craft and high ethical principles in relation to their work.[1] Durkheim's vision also involved advocacy of occupational syndicalism as a representational device in government, but it is otherwise very much a standard late nineteenth–early twentieth-century idealization of professionalism as moral and technical guide to the "better society."[2]

Our sense of the implausibility of Durkheim's vision is a mark of how much our understanding of professions has changed over the last century, and particularly over the last thirty years. In many ways, to be sure, professions can still be considered social as well as economic institutions. Like other social institutions, they provide spheres of thought and action that are buffered from markets and states.[3] In particular, ties to a knowledge base, practical craft, and collective organization stand as protections against the overriding influence of markets and external hierarchies.

The professional pattern of organization has, moreover, many attractive features. As Eliot Freidson has emphasized, professions provide a level of security that encourages relatively strong levels of identification with work— very much the opposite of the alienated labor that Karl Marx, among others, foresaw as characteristic of capitalist employment. The credential system also protects consumers from incompetent practitioners, at least in an imperfect way, through admissions screening and by requiring a lengthy and self-denying period study. The knowledge base of professionals provides an alternative form of authority to managerial hierarchy, and in this respect the professions are important for preventing modern organizational life from becoming the kind of "iron cage" of strict bureaucratic control that Max Weber prophesied.[4]

Yet the many late nineteenth-century idealizations of the professions— Durkheim's included—were at least partly inadequate from the start. From the beginning of the modern era of occupational professionalization, professions represented efforts to organize and protect markets, as well as to propagate values in relation to important services, and they were embedded in the hierarchies of large organizations as much as they were organized along the lines of occupational solidarity. The positive characterizations of professions have always focused in a one-sided way on one set of the relevant embeddings of professions.

THE CHANGING PROFESSIONS

Markets and organizations have become still more important in recent years, as the fortunes of professionals have varied in the market, and as many of the institutional supports for old ideals have given way. In view of these changes, the contemporary professions show a pronounced dual movement: toward the rise of marketable expertise as a more or less exclusively important status element, and toward the splintering of professions in relation to their spheres of social purpose, their market situation, and their organizational attachments. The dual movement can be described as, first, a movement from "social trustee professionalism" to "expert professionalism," and, second, from professions as collective organizations in the division of labor to professions as collective organizations intersecting markets and organizations in the political economy of expert labor.

From Social Trustees to Experts

Expert professionalism has always been the dominant orientation among professionals in some scholarly fields and in most fields of applied science. The question is why other professions have moved from a conception of status based on the combination of technical knowledge, "disinterested" service to society, *and* high-minded ethical standards to a conception of status based more exclusively on expertise. I have traced this movement by looking at the internal contradictions of social trustee professionalism and by looking at the weakening of its supporting institutions.

The lower-status professional occupations—teachers, nurses, social workers, city planners, and others—have long experienced difficulties sustaining fully "professional" work conditions and fully "professional" levels of prestige. From the late 1960s on, these difficulties became a kind of status disqualification among many students of professions, who increasingly emphasized expertise and autonomy as the defining features of "true professions." It is possible that the new, more exclusive emphasis on expertise will in the end help to improve practice in occupations (such as secondary school teaching) where a clinical mentality is appropriate but only occasionally encountered.[5] For the time being, however, it has primarily helped further to reduce the status of several occupations that are of great value from the perspective of their social contribution.

At the other end of the professional stratum, great opportunities have existed for certified public accountants, corporate attorneys, corporate architects, management consultants, doctors, and a few other highly advantaged providers of expert services. Under the new institutional and cultural conditions of the last two decades, these opportunities had the effect of making some professionals think of themselves more exclusively as business people and of reducing the influence of the traditional ethical and cultural legitimations of professionalism. The tremendous growth of the professional stratum also undoubtedly played a role in some overcrowded occupations. The professions attracted large numbers of intellectually able people who were interested in the kind of security and community orientation that professionalism traditionally promised. Ironically, as the professional occupations grew, demographic pressures encouraged these new recruits to think more exclusively as enterpreneurs and less as members of an occupational collective with a stable set of community-minded ideals.

Most of the supports for social trustee professionalism have weakened. When the professional stratum reached its maximum size in terms of the core occupations considered professional, new status claimants were no longer available to reinforce the moral elements associated with the dynamic phase of white-collar professionalism. In their absence, the moral elements of this dynamic phase began rather quickly to recede in occupational spheres where they were becoming more of an impediment than an aid. Legal supports for the older forms of professionalism were also modified to give greater scope to markets. The professional occupations, when they were accepted as based primarily on formal knowledge, began to think of themselves as offering a service of economic value more or less like any other. In the universities, the professional schools—once an appendage of the liberal arts core—increasingly moved to the center of the university's mission, and they now begin to overshadow the liberal arts both in budget and prestige, thereby reducing the role of the liberal arts as a frame of reference. Welfare-state liberalism, a third sustaining force for the older forms of professionalism, experienced a sharp political and ideological decline throughout the West beginning in the 1970s, a decline from which it shows no immediate signs of recovering. In its place has arisen a political culture far more generally supportive of market mechanisms and of private sector concerns.

With the transformation of the professional stratum in the direction of an "expert stratum" whose main distinction lies in its ability to bring negotiable resources to the labor market in the form of credentials and technical knowledge, a greater emphasis on cognitive exclusion enters into the constitution of the stratum. This principle of exclusion tends, increasingly, to take precedence over the "collective morality" that once acted as a principle of inclusion among those claiming professional status. As professional knowledge comes to be seen more strictly as a marketable resource, it is also treated in a more purely commercial vein and regulated in a more rigorous fashion by external authorities. The public has always insisted on some external checks on the fee-for-service professions, usually in the form of governmental monitoring, to complement the internal checks promised by collegial control and internalized professional norms. These external checks have increasingly substituted for, rather than complemented, the old internal controls.

From Self-Regulation to the Political Economy of Expert Labor

What remains common to professions is a social structure that is the product of neither markets nor of government bureaucracies, but rather of a credentialled body of producers of "expert services" organized around a common body of formal knowledge and claiming authority on that basis. What is in the process of changing greatly is the homogenizing role of the "collective conscience" and, consequently, the blurred lines of stratification within and between the occupations formerly accepted as "professions."

In this context, the connections of professionals to markets and organizations have become at least as important as the similarities that remain among them. In this book, I have investigated patterns of division by the spheres of social purpose to which professions belong, their sectoral and industrial attachments, and the market value of the various professional services. I identified five major spheres of social purpose—business services, applied science, culture and communications, civic regulation, and human services—based on common functions and common societal sources of demand for services. Using a modified theory of collective goods, I discussed why some forms of professional knowledge develop more or less exclusively in the private economy, while others develop in the public economy. And I analyzed the sources of variation in market demand for professional services based primarily on the vulnerabilities and uncertainties of clients, and the value of professional knowledge bases in organizational applications.

It is my sense that future studies of professions will need to follow this lead and think rigorously not just about the relations between occupations in the division of labor, but also about the situation of professions in markets and organizations. A recent study of hospital social workers attached to neonatal intensive care units provides a good example of this multidimensional perspective. These workers are described as providing the "social prepping"—transforming emotional parents into manageable patients—that accompanies the medical prepping in the operating room. Their services are now required because hospital-based doctors have increasingly subcontracted work in social relations for the more purely technical involvements of the consultation and operating rooms. The activities of the social workers are shaped not only by their relations to medical personnel, but also by organizational procedures and the market situation of the hospitals in which they work. More time and attention, for example, is often given to the people who need it least, because of the implicit requirement that hospitals in the more affluent markets provide stronger demonstrations of service.[6]

Enough good studies have been done that some generalizations are already emerging. A common denominator in these studies is the picture they give of the channeling of interests in relation to market opportunities and centers of institutional and organizational power. In the more entrepreneurial environments of business and medical services, we see a movement toward "multiservice oligopolies."[7] We also see many new specializations in relation to specific parts of natural or human systems, as in the proliferation of medical specialties[8]—virtually one for every body part—and the development of "boutique firms" serving highly specific client needs in law.[9] And we see energetic searches for new sources of making reputations and sales, as in the forging of new links in the art world between artists, business corporations, and regional nonprofits.[10] In professions that become embedded in the public sector, we see, by contrast, a movement toward standardized cultures and highly coordinated organizational fields.[11]

In these new fields of force, the very term "professional" may become increasingly misleading. It is already possible to talk sensibly about professionals as divided between two relatively new classes and three quite ancient classes. The two new classes are a "for-profit expert class" and a "nonprofit expert class." These are distinct because of the quite different market situations they occupy and the quite different political and cultural interests they typically represent. The three older classes are large employers (e.g., partners in the major accounting and corporate law firms—if one likes, the "haute expertoisie"), small business people (i.e., partners in small professional firms and sole practitioners), and the educated, but economically insecure "lesser specialists" in technical support, education, and human services. Below this stratum is an "apprentice class" of graduate students, research assistants, interns, and the like—a good many of whom remain in economically tenuous circumstances only temporarily. It is not impossible to envision a time when the term "professional" might come to be reserved as an honorific to describe those people whose role orientations emulate the older ideal forms of professionalism: a close connection to the cultural aspirations and public issues involved in occupational activities, in addition to high levels of competence in the performance of an intellectually demanding activity.

From Community Authorities to Classical Liberals

The great forces that are transforming the professional stratum have made an imprint also on the politics of professional people. In the United States, professionals as a whole have been a moderate-to-conservative stratum politically on all issues involving resource distribution, attitudes about business and labor, and in their party preferences. This moderation largely reflects the relatively privileged position of professionals in the structure of social stratification. To the extent that professionals are more liberal than business people on these issues, their liberalism has much to do with the compositional differences between the two strata, particularly the more frequent public sector employments of professionals and the greater tendency of the professional occupations to be composed of women, minorities, and younger people.

The liberalism of professionals on social issues, which is distinctive compared to other key strata in American society, reflects the attitudes of an educated and relatively cosmopolitan group connected to the modern liberal tradition inspired by John Stuart Mill. This tradition is rooted in concerns about the power of potentially repressive authorities, toleration of differences, and support for the full liberties, rights, and societal integration of citizens. Yet the movement toward expert professionalism also leaves its mark in this sphere of political thinking. In particular, the tendency toward principled consumerism among professionals on issues of cultural and moral choice, their frequent sympathy for new movements of ethnic particularism and their withdrawal from the problems of developing social strength in unstable communities suggests a movement past liberalism toward laissez-faire in social relations.

The political profile of professionals equally bears the imprint of the splintering of the professional stratum in the political economy. Where highly valued professional skills intersect with resource-rich organizations, professionals are very much prone to adopt the norms prevailing in the corporations and the highest levels of the Republican party. Politically, these people are worlds apart from lower-income, nonprofit-sector social and cultural professionals, who are stalwarts of the Democratic party and "progressive" movements. Not surprisingly, the moral earnestness that Durkheim associated with the professions generally is more often evident at the middle and lower levels of the professional stratum. People like to display qualities that bring them credit. For those without the means to make an effective display of wealth and social connections, social credit can be gained by a conspicuous display of moral earnestness.[12] In the private sector "new class," this moral earnestness takes a generally conservative form on issues involving the amelioration of inequalities. The emphasis is consistent with moral individualism, the commandment of personal responsibility for difficult circumstances. In the public sector "new class" and among the lesser specialists, this is less often true; A greater degree of public-minded morality exists in these spheres.

I have emphasized that other kinds of compositional factors also come into play in the patterns of political division among professionals. Older white males have tended to become a security-conscious and business-oriented group, while, in many places, high-achieving nonwhites and women have taken on the lion's share of such "social justice"-oriented activism as continues to be found among professionals.[13]

The Middle Class and Eras of Reform. For all of their moderation and conservatism as a group, it is certainly true that educated middle-class people have provided an important source of support for reform leaders and reform movements during periods of American history. There is no necessary contradiction here. In times of reform, the traditional ideals of social trustee professionalism can be reinhabited by those who feel the need for moral renewal— feelings that are more generously supported during these periods.

The historical ideals of social trustee professionalism certainly tend to be different from, if not in contradiction with, those that are most common in the business world. Already by the mid- and late-nineteenth century, professionals had largely inherited the old patrician ideals of public service and concern about the commonweal. They considered themselves experts in human problems as well as the efficient and effective solutions to those problems. The values professed differed from occupation to occupation, but they were structurally similar in so far as they were all considered "higher" values. *If economism is an insistence on the priority of trade-offs, the older type of professionalism reflected an insistence on the ordering of action by priorities.* The latent humanism and concerns about public well-being of social trustee professionalism frequently expanded even to take in broader questions of social relations.

The great period of middle-class reform in this country occurred during the Progressive Era, when the state was poorly equipped to take care of the many social and political problems facing the country, and when, consequently, middle-class professional people took the lead in creating organizational and intellectual solutions to public problems. In reform periods since the Progressive Era, professionals closely linked or employed directly by the state have been the principal actors (along with social movement activists). Consequently, it often makes more sense now to talk about the influence of state experts during reform periods than the influence of the professional stratum at large. The professional stratum, particularly the liberal quarters of the professional stratum, provides a reservoir of support for reform—and also benefits from reform—but as a reform-oriented group it is now in the orbit of the state rather than vice versa.

Old Issues and New. The political analysis in this book is conditioned by the historical circumstances of the Cold War era. It reflects a period during which major conflicts existed over the reach of the welfare state and its entitlement programs, over race and gender relations, over military actions in foreign countries and the proper level of military spending, and over issues involving personal freedoms in relation to traditional religious proscriptions. Issues involving race and gender, religion, and nonconformity will presumably continue to provoke political passions for years to come. Other issues have begun to pass out of public debate. With the collapse of the Soviet Union, a new consensus has emerged about the desirability of a somewhat decreased military presence. With the intensification of international economic competition, interests in a Great Economy have come to supersede considerably interests in a Great Society.

As some of the old issues fade, new political issues are emerging, and these may well define the major lines of political division in the years to come. Will professionals feel more inclined than the hard-strapped working class to aid the economic development of Eastern Europe and the republics of the old Soviet Union? Will they feel less threatened than manufacturers by trade problems with Japan or other new economic powers? How will they react to further pressures to increase the productivity and decrease the costs of labor? Will they champion new conceptions of pluralism in the controversies surrounding educational curricula, or will they express renewed support for the study of the existing Western traditions? How will they react to plans to restructure education, involving "choice" or other reform projects? Will they be as interested in privatizing governmental services as are some executives and managers in the private sector? And what efforts will they make to build stronger social structures in communities with the highest levels of segregation and concentrated poverty?

On the basis of the existing evidence, it seems likely that the professional middle class will be only slightly less hostile to the protectionism of economic competitors than business leaders, and that they will also be only slightly less concerned about the condition of labor in relation to any new plans to increase labor productivity or reduce labor costs. They may, however, be notably less enthusiastic about plans to privatize governmental functions, and, in general, less confident about market-based solutions to social problems. Some emerging social issues, such as the new conceptions of pluralism associated with multiculturalism in education, do not cut across the usual liberal and conservative lines, but rather are likely to pit professional elites against the professional periphery, and to become particularly a test of the persistence of ethnic and gender identifications within status groups based fundamentally on other criteria.

THE FUTURE OF INTELLECTUALS

While the professions, transformed by the culture of expertise and increasingly divided in the political economy, decline as a source of collective moral force in public life, intellectuals remain, however tentatively, as a potential source of social and moral vision. Several traditions of intellectual thought—notably socialism, romanticism, progressivism, and humanism (including the religious forms of humanism)—contain themes of proven efficacy in activating visions of a "good society."[14] Moreover, as higher education has expanded, a larger potential constituency group for intellectuals now exists.

Two Scenarios for the Future

Some have seen enough possibilities in this situation to suggest that intellectuals—more properly the intelligentsia—may yet play an important role in the social conflicts of the future. There is no reason to think that such a scenario is impossible. Yet a good deal mitigates against it. The anxieties and pleasure of the middle class are such that it is difficult to imagine that alternative visions of society will soon become anything but peripheral to the utilitarian norms and rigorous competitive practices that resonate so strongly in the core of the economy. Ideas about the role of intellectuals are still less credible when they suggest images of classes locked in a struggle leading to fundamental social change. The intelligentsia has sometimes distinguished itself as a "constituency of conscience," but it has never successfully shown that it can augment national standards of living while at the same time pursuing the various other ends—such as social justice, bonds of community, and enlarged sensibilities—that it has on occasion so eloquently championed.

Indeed, it is far easier to imagine a future in which the audience for broad social, cultural, and moral argumentation will in effect gradually disappear. This second possibility suggests a future in which intellectuals, far from contesting for status and power in society, are no longer moved by any sort of meaningful social ideals. And it is a future in which the members of the professional middle class have rather completely cut off their connection to the traditions of dissent that have grown out of intellectual culture.

There will, of course, always be intellectuals as long as there are needs for scholarship and learning, but there may not always be great debates about the proper organization of state, society, and economy. One needs only reflect on the number of constants that are seemingly set for the immediate future. With the decline of socialism as practice and ideal, capitalism is now essentially unchallenged in the economic domain. Mixed economies are accepted, with debate focusing on comparatively minor adjustments in public versus private responsibilities. Democracy in the sense of competition for office has also triumphed with apparent finality against its long-time rivals in the more developed societies. The social concerns of the majority are framed by commitments to family, job, entertainment, and consumption.[15] It is not surprising, under the circumstances, that the old ideas about the "end of ideology" seem increasingly plausible again and have even been recast, with greater ambition, as the "end of history."[16]

Perhaps partly as a reflection of these conditions, the conservative mood in intellectual life remains strong. A long line of anti-left polemics descend from the conservative "new class" theories and the attacks on the "adversary culture" of the 1970s, many of them the products of self-proclaimed liberals. These include attacks on feminism in the name of family stability and children's welfare, and, from another direction, in the name of sexual freedoms; attacks on peace movements as "neo-isolationism"; attacks on "entitlement liberalism" in the name of "civic liberalism"; attacks on the secular orientation of liberal thought as a "culture of disbelief"; and a veritable battery of attacks on the student left as enforcers of "political correctness." It has become customary in the leading periodicals to salute the courage of authors of these anti-left polemics, as if they were the Davids and not the Goliaths of contemporary intellectual opinion.

Political and Literary Liberalism

For the most part, however, intellectuals appear to have withdrawn from public life. The study of the contents of leading American periodicals reported in chapter 8 suggests that intellectuals write as people who are responsible for educating sensibilities, not for taking principled positions on matters of public interest. Indeed, it would appear that political liberalism is now but a weak interest, if it is an interest at all, for many intellectuals who would be considered liberals. Many of these people—people as diverse as James Clifford, Robert Coles, Joan Didion, and Helen Vendler—find their major inspiration in the literary form of liberalism. Liberalism in this sense is a way of seeing and evaluating character, society, and human life through the aesthetic and moral lenses of literature. It is based on the ability to understand and hold in balance many perspectives, identification with the predicament of many types of human beings, a sense of the existential issues bearing on men and women, an appreciation of the importance and fatefulness of judgment, insights into the dark recesses and unexpected generosities of human hearts, and a willingness to consult conscience as a guide, as well as sheer logic.[17] As Helen Vendler has written, the literary imagination honors "depth of feeling, struggle with internal contradiction, seductive musicality, and intelligence of heart."[18]

The appeal of literary liberalism is not difficult to appreciate. The thirst for human understanding builds not just on the progressive widening of scientific knowledge and instrumental rationality, but also (and not secondarily) on ethical sensibilities cultivated by the culture of the humanities. Alone among the moral possibilities of the modern world, the culture of literature is a culture of empathy in opposition to dogma. Overly neat and precise scientific or theoretical formulations are as much a threat, in this regard, as are the facile stories and instant analyses of the mass media. At its best, intellectual work exemplifies qualities of mind and feeling that are always in too short supply.

There are nevertheless limits to what sort of comfort the continued influence of literary liberalism, in the absence of an accompanying political impulse, can be said to provide. Lionel Trilling, for one, saw an intimate and inevitable association between literary and political liberalism.[19] But historically the connection is much less intimate than Trilling suggested. The "liberal imagination" in Trilling's sense is as remarkable historically for its self-limiting quality as for its fine sensibilities. It is perhaps by its very nature a "mandarin" sensibility, and it has, in any event, very often been content to work within the constraints of whatever social order has existed around it. It persists, it probes, it criticizes, it evaluates, it sets an excellent, thoughtful tone, but it does not disrupt and it does not very often make impolite demands on behalf of its human interests. This is why the continuation of political liberalism is important.

Intellectuals and the Revival of Political Liberalism

Contemporary political liberalism is feeble, however, primarily because of its dependence on the welfare state and the labor and civil rights movements, all of which are themselves weak and not likely to become strong very soon. Any revival of political liberalism will inevitably find energies channeled away from the state and toward the voluntary sector. There are reasons to believe that this is often a good idea on normative, as well as pragmatic, grounds.[20]

However weak the traditional institutional vehicles of political liberalism have become, the underlying social and cultural impulses contain some vital truths, and these are difficult to ignore completely in the long run. The first is existential—one might even say religious—in origin: that human existence is something separate from market, state, and organization; that it is all too short and full of suffering and ignorance and ought to be privileged for these reasons. A second, which is an equally humanistic impulse, is that something better is almost certainly possible for the weaker members of the society— and for us all. A third is that stratification and inequality have far-reaching and frequently corrosive effects on the social order—and certainly on the lives of the least advantaged. A fourth is that the powerful are prone to take unfair advantage of their situation and need to be closely monitored. A fifth is that obligations, affection, traditions, and a sense of the social whole are often important both for effective collective action and for personal well-being. A sixth is that cultural formulas and stereotypes frequently lead to unjust and self-serving simplifications. The Enlightenment tradition of which modern liberalism is a part also involves such elemental matters as faith in the importance of democracy, the insistence that human beings be emancipated from benighted conditions, and the expectation that freedom will in the end lead to a substantially greater development of human powers and human capacities, both those that are economically relevant and those that are not.

Liberal political views may be strongly associated with specific social milieus in the professional stratum. For many, they may be connected, below the surface, to experiences of marginality and even to feelings of social resentment. Yet liberalism as a political impulse persists, not because of these predisposing factors, but because of the social truths it contains and the resonance it strikes with long-standing Western cultural themes. To the extent that our society hopes to be a fully decent society as well as a successful one, some group or groups must serve effectively as social and cultural conscience, preserver, advocate, and activator.

The question, then, is not whether liberal political impulses will survive, but rather how they can be made effective in a world in which working-class community life, labor organizations, and welfare states all appear to be continuously diminishing forces in relation to markets, consumerism, and business organizations. It does not appear to me that the professions, as they move in the direction of legitimation through expertise, stand as a likely vehicle for this revival. However, some of the earlier community-minded forms of professional idealism remain relevant to it, and the institutions promoting the autonomy and social responsibilities of professional knowledge are certainly relevant to it as well.

CHAPTER ONE

1. The structural differences between professionals and managers are analyzed in Eliot Freidson, "Professions and the Occupational Principle," in Freidson, ed., *Professions and Their Prospects* (Beverly Hills, Calif.: Sage, 1973), 19–39; and Eliot Freidson, *Professional Powers* (Chicago: University of Chicago Press, 1986), chap. 7.

2. See, e.g., Daniel Bell, *The Coming of Post-Industrial Society* (New York: Basic Books, 1973).

3. See, e.g., Laurence Veysey, "The Plural Organized Worlds of the Humanities," in Alexandra Oleson and John Voss, eds., *The Organization of Knowledge in Modern America* (Baltimore: Johns Hopkins University Press, 1979), 51–106.

4. Barbara Ehrenreich, *Fear of Falling: The Inner Life of the Middle Class* (New York: Pantheon, 1989), 4.

5. Michael Goldfield, *The Decline of Organized Labor in the United States* (Chicago: University of Chicago Press, 1987), chap. 1. See also Thomas Edsall, *The New Politics of Inequality* (New York: Norton, 1984), chap. 4.

6. Calculated from the General Social Survey, 1988–90. See National Opinion Research Center, *The General Social Survey, 1972–1990 Cumulative Codebook* (Chicago: NORC, 1990), 368. See also John D. McCarthy, "The Structure of Mobilization of Professional Occupational Groups" (Paper presented at the Thematic Session on International Social Organization, 1985 Annual Meeting of the Southern Sociological Society, Norfolk, Va., 1985), 3.

7. Kay Schlozman and John Tierney, *Organized Interests in American Democracy* (New York: Harper and Row, 1986), 77.

8. See, e.g., Dewey Anderson and Percy E. Davidson, *Ballots and the Democratic Class Struggle* (Stanford, Calif.: Stanford University Press), 1943. See also C. Wright Mills, *White Collar* (New York: Oxford University Press, 1951), 353–54.

9. Variations of the "new class" theory have been developed by Alvin W. Gouldner, *The Future of Intellectuals and the Rise of the New Class* (New York: Seabury Press, 1979); Irving Kristol, "About Equality," *Commentary* 54 (1972): 41–47, and "On Corporate Capitalism in America," *The Public Interest* 37 (Fall 1975): 124–41; Seymour Martin Lipset, *Political Man*, rev. ed. (Baltimore: Johns Hopkins University Press, 1981), 503–22; Robert Heilbroner, *The Limits of American Capitalism* (New York: Harper and Row, 1966); and Peter L. Berger, *The Capitalist Revolution: Fifty Propositions about Prosperity, Equality, and Liberty* (New York: Basic Books, 1985). A great many other political writers, including Barbara Ehrenreich, James Fallows, Michael Harrington, Kevin Phillips, and Norman Podhoretz, have, at one time or another, endorsed the idea. Among social thinkers and social scientists, commentary on the "new class" argument has been developed by Daniel Bell, Pierce Bourdieu, Everett Carll Ladd, Daniel Patrick Moynihan, and Ivan Szelenyi, among others. Among historians, David Brion Davis, Richard Hofstadter, Robert Wiebe, Burton Bledstein, Dorothy Ross, Sheldon Rothblatt, Harold Perkin, and Martin Weiner have been associated with one or another version of the idea.

10. This is the dominant view, for example, in Lipset, *Political Man*. See also Bell, *Coming of Post-Industrial Society*.

11. See, e.g., Charles K. Derber, William Schwartz, and Yale Magrass, *Power in the Highest Degree* (New York: Oxford University Press, 1990).

12. Harold L. Wilensky, "The Professionalization of Everyone?," *American Journal of Sociology* 70 (1964): 137–58; and Magali Sarfatti Larson, *The Rise of Professionalism* (Berkeley: University of California Press, 1979).

13. Freidson, "Professions and the Occupational Principle."

14. For a discussion of these cases, see Richard Hofstadter and Walter Metzger, *The Development of Academic Freedom in the United States* (New York: Columbia University Press, 1955).

15. Among the many definitional efforts are the following: T. H. Marshall, "The Recent History of Professionalism in Relation to Social Structure and Social Policy," in Marshall, *Citizenship and Social Class* (Cambridge: Cambridge University Press, 1951), 128–55; Talcott Parsons, "Professions and the Social Structure," *Social Forces* 17 (1939): 457–67; M. L. Cogan, "The Problem of Defining Profession," *Annals of the American Academy of Political and Social Science* 297 (1955): 105–11; Ernest Greenwood, "The Attributes of a Profession," *Social Work* 2 (1957): 45–55; Bernard Barber, "Some Problems in the Sociology of the Professions," in Kenneth S. Lynn and the editors of Daedalus, eds., *The Professions in America* (Boston: Houghton-Mifflin, 1965), 15–34; and William J. Goode, "Professions and 'Non-Professions,'" in H. M. Vollmer and D. L. Mills, eds., *Professionalization* (Englewood Cliffs, N.J.: Prentice-Hall, 1966), 34–43. For a compilation of definitional efforts in the United States and Great Britain through the early 1960s, see Geoffrey Millerson, *The Qualifying Association* (London: Routledge, Kegan Paul, 1964), table 1-1.

16. See the useful discussion of cultural authority in Paul Starr, *The Social Transformation of American Medicine* (New York: Basic Books, 1982), 13–17.

17. Cf. Gouldner, *Future of Intellectuals*, 19.

18. R. H. Tawney, *The Acquisitive Society* (New York: Harcourt, Brace and World, 1948), 94–95.

19. See, e.g., David Noble, *America by Design* (New York: Knopf, 1977).

20. On the cultural affinities between the old aristocracy and the professions in England, see Sheldon Rothblatt, *The Revolution of the Dons* (London: Faber, 1968); Harold J. Perkin, *The Origins of Modern English Society* (London: Routledge and Kegan Paul, 1969), 258–66, 408–54; and Martin Weiner, *English Culture and the Decline of the Industrial Spirit* (Cambridge: Cambridge University Press, 1981).

21. See, e.g., Robin M. Williams, *American Society* (New York: Knopf, 1970), 464–68.

22. Herman E. Kroos and Peter F. Drucker, "How We Got Here: Fifty Years of Structural Change in the Business System and the Business School," in Peter F. Drucker, ed., *Preparing Tomorrow's Business Leaders Today* (Englewood Cliffs, N.J.: Prentice-Hall, 1968), 1–23. The first professional training in business was offered before World War I at the Amos Tuck Graduate School of Business at Dartmouth and the Harvard Graduate School of Business.

23. See, e.g., Gary John Previts, *The Scope of CPA Services* (New York: Wiley, 1985); and Wallace E. Olson, *The Accounting Profession's Years of Trial, 1967–1980* (New York: American Institute of Certified Public Accountants, 1982).

24. John P. Heinz and Edward O. Laumann, *Chicago Lawyers* (New York: Russell Sage, 1982; Chicago: The American Bar Foundation, 1982).

25. See, e.g., Julius Roth, "Professionalism: The Sociologist's Decoy," *Sociology of Work and Occupations* 1 (1974): 6–23.

26. For a discussion of the close connection between middle-class respectability and professionalism during the latter half of the nineteenth and the first half of the twentieth century, see Burton Bledstein, *The Culture of Professionalism* (New York: W. W. Norton, 1976).

27. Lincoln Caplan, "The Lawyers Race to the Bottom," *New York Times,* August 6, 1993, A29.

28. Michael Abramowitz, "AMA Votes to Ease Curbs on Self-Referrals," *Washington Post,* June 24, 1992, A2.

29. See Martin Kenney, *Biotechnology: The University-Industrial Complex* (New Haven, Conn.: Yale University Press, 1986); and Bruce Wilshire, *The Moral Collapse of the University* (Albany: State University of New York Press, 1990).

30. Caplan, "Lawyers Race to the Bottom."

31. The data is reported in Charles K. Derber, *The Project on Professionals: Report to Responding Organizations* (Chestnut Hill, Mass.: Boston College, 1983). An ethic of service is strongly endorsed only by lower-status professionals, such as librarians, social workers, and teachers. See Richard H. Hall, "Professionalization and Bureaucratization," *American Sociological Review* 33 (1968): 92–104. For a complementary discussion of the relationship between social position and moral rhetoric, see Pierre Bourdieu, *Outline of a Theory of Practice* (Cambridge: Cambridge University Press, 1977), 30–71.

32. The conference is discussed in the May 1922 issue of *The Annals of the American Academy of Political and Social Science.*

33. Katharine S. Mangan, "More Colleges Resort to Faculty and Staff Layoffs in Response to Sluggish U.S. Economy," *Chronicle of Higher Education* (November 13, 1991), A37–38.

34. Gerhard Lenski, *Power and Privilege* (New York: McGraw-Hill, 1966), 243–66. The metaphor is drawn from Lenski's discussion of the three types of middle classes typical of agrarian societies.

35. Not all of the social thinkers of the classical period missed the importance of the professions. Tocqueville commended the legal profession for playing a role in American life functionally equivalent to the better sections of the aristocracy in prerevolutionary Europe—as guardians of resources and values in the face of the passions and interests of the moment. He also emphasized the role of religion and education in restraining many actions that the laws in a liberal, democratic society would otherwise allow. And the French sociologist Emile Durkheim looked forward to a civic-minded society regulated on quasi-syndicalist principles by occupational associations modeled along the lines of the professions.

36. See, e.g., Randall Collins, *The Credential Society* (New York: Academic Press, 1979), 137.

37. Kristin Luker, *Abortion and the Politics of Motherhood* (Berkeley: University of California Press, 1985).

38. Adam Yarmolinsky et al., *Race and Schooling in the City* (Cambridge, Mass.: Harvard University Press, 1981).

39. See, e.g., Robert Venturi, *Complexity and Contradiction in Architecture* (New York: Museum of Modern Art, 1966).

40. For a study of the dangers of expert professionalism under conditions of authoritarian control, see Konrad Jarausch, *The Unfree Professions: German Lawyers, Teachers, and Engineers, 1900–1950* (New York: Oxford University Press, 1990).

41. See, e.g., Gouldner, *Future of Intellectuals,* 93.

42. On these themes, see, especially, Thurman Arnold, *The Folklore of Capitalism* (New Haven, Conn.: Yale University Press, 1937); Irwin G. Wylie, *The Self-Made Man in America* (New Brunswick, N.J.: Rutgers University Press, 1954); Raymond Williams, *Culture and Society, 1780–1950* (New York: Columbia University Press, 1958); Richard Hofstadter, *Anti-Intellectualism in American Life* (New York: Knopf, 1962); Christopher Lasch, *The New Radicalism in America, 1889–1963* (New York: Random House, 1965); and Norman Podhoretz, "The Adversary Culture and the New Class," in B. Bruce-Briggs, ed., *The New Class?* (New Brunswick, N.J.: Transaction Press, 1979), 19–32.

CHAPTER TWO

1. Laurence R. Veysey, "Higher Education as a Profession: Changes and Discontinuities," in Nathan O. Hatch, ed., *Professions and American History* (South Bend, Ind.: Notre Dame University Press, 1988), 17.

2. For a discussion of the usages of the terms "profession" and "professional," see Freidson, *Professional Powers,* 35–36. See also Bruce A. Kimball, *The "True Professional Ideal" in America: A History* (Cambridge, Mass.: Blackwell, 1992).

3. My understanding of professions as a type of social organization has been greatly influenced by the work of Eliot Freidson. See, in particular, Freidson, "Occupational Autonomy and Labor Market Shelters," in Phyllis L. Stewart and Muriel G. Cantor, eds., *Varieties of Work* (Beverly Hills, Calif.: Sage Publications), 39–54; Freidson, "The Theory of Professions: State of the Art," in Robert Dingwall and Philip Lewis, eds., *The Sociology of Professions: Doctors, Lawyers, and Others* (London: Macmillan, 1983), 19–37; and Freidson, *Professional Powers,* chap. 4.

4. The state and the professional associations frequently play other important roles in support of the credentialing system. Professional standards of practice are set by the associations and are at times supported by state regulation, including laws that require practitioners to keep abreast of developments in the occupation's disciplinary base.

5. Freidson, *Professional Powers,* 77.

6. The work of Charles Derber and his associates has established that professionals have much less complete control over the projects they work on, the support staff with whom they work, and the hours and pace of work than they do over the technical means they use to accomplish their work. See Derber, *Report to Responding Organizations;* and Derber, Schwartz, and Magrass, *Power in the Highest Degree.*

7. Howard S. Becker and James Carper, "The Elements of Identification with an Occupation," *American Sociological Review* 21 (1956): 341–47.

8. See Terence Halliday, "Knowledge Mandates: Collective Influence by Scientific, Normative and Syncretic Professions," *British Journal of Sociology* 36 (1985): 421–47; and John McCarthy, "The Structure of Mobilization of Professional Occupational Groups," unpublished paper, Department of Sociology, Catholic University, 1985.

9. Andrew Abbott, *The System of Professions: An Essay on the Division of Expert Labor* (Chicago: University of Chicago Press, 1988), 81–85 and *passim.*

10. This section of chapter 2 is intended primarily for nonspecialists. Specialists will be familiar with much of the material that I present and may wish to skim the section, at least until the beginning of the discussion of consolidation.

11. The best guide to usage of the term "profession" and its cognates is Kimball, *"True Professional Ideal."*

12. The first usage of the term "profession" in English (pre-sixteenth century) is to

denote a declaration, avowal, or expression of intention or purpose. This usage was originally connected with taking consecrated vows and stemmed from the clerical foundation of the medieval university. In this usage, as Freidson notes, the term carries a positive connotation, implying religious or moral motives and involving dedication to good ends. Thus, some of the moral flavor of the original usage persists even in contemporary usage. See Freidson, *Professional Powers*, 21; and Kimball, *"True Professional Ideal,"* chap. 1.

13. Kimball, *"True Professional Ideal,"* 5–6. See also A. M. Carr-Saunders and P. A. Wilson, *The Professions* (Oxford: Clarendon Press, 1933), 291–92; Millerson, *Qualifying Associations*, 16; Larson, *Rise of Professionalism*, 2–4.

14. Millerson, *Qualifying Associations*, 16.

15. Ibid.

16. Ibid., 17.

17. For a brief period in the early fifteenth century, physicians and surgeons set up a joint faculty, but this soon broke up due to strong disagreements between the two groups. See ibid.

18. Carr-Saunders and Wilson, *Professions*, 292.

19. Kimball, *"True Professional Ideal,"* 100–102.

20. Everett C. Hughes, "The Study of Occupations," in Hughes, *The Sociological Eye: Selected Papers* (Chicago: Aldine, 1971), 283–97. The discussion of "guilty knowledge" is on 287–92.

21. Freidson, *Professional Powers*, 22. See also Larson, *Rise of Professionalism*, 2–4; W. J. Reader, *Professional Men: The Rise of the Professional Classes in Nineteenth Century England* (London: Weidenfeld and Nicolson, 1966), chap. 1; and Philip Elliot, *The Sociology of Professions* (London: Macmillan, 1972), 14, 32.

22. Reader, *Professional Men*, chap. 8.

23. Ibid., 9–10.

24. See William McNeill, *The Pursuit of Power* (Chicago: University of Chicago Press, 1975), 126–30.

25. See Arthur Vagts, *The History of Militarism*, rev. ed., (Greenwich, Conn.: Meridian Books, 1959), 43–54; Morris Janowitz, *The Professional Soldier* (Glencoe, Ill.: The Free Press, 1960); and McNeill, *Pursuit of Power*, chap. 4.

26. On the origins of architecture as a profession, see Carr-Saunders and Wilson, *Professions*, 176–77. Some of the first architects of the seventeenth and eighteenth centuries were scions and associates of aristocratic families and others were hardly distinguishable from craftsmen. Because of these social divisions, professional organization lagged until the end of the eighteenth century.

27. This is itself partly a result of the successes of science and humanistic study and partly a result of cultural fragmentation along nationalist lines, following the Reformation. See Emile Durkheim, *L'evolution pedagogique en France* (Paris: Presses Universitaires de France, 1969). (Originally delivered as lectures in 1904–5 at the University of Paris.)

28. Other learned societies organized during the early nineteenth century include the Geological Society (1807), the Royal Astronomical Society (1820), the Zoological Society (1824), the Royal Geographical Society (1830), the Royal Institute of Painters (1831), the Royal Entomological Society (1833), the Royal Statistical Society (1834), the Royal Botanic Society (1839), the Chemical Society (1841), and the Royal Anthropological Society (1843). See Millerson, *Qualifying Association*, 254–55.

29. See, e.g., Reader, *Professional Men*, 6, 140, 150–51.

30. See ibid., 118–19, 148–49; and Carr-Saunders and Wilson, *Professions*, 177.

31. Reader, *Professional Men*, 70–71. Passages are reordered to bring out the sense of Reader's observations more clearly.

32. The connection between aristocratic and professional culture, as transmitted through the English dons, is discussed in Rothblatt, *Revolution of the Dons*, 86–93. See also Perkin, *Origins of Modern English Society*, 252–70; Weiner, *English Culture*, 30–40; and Harold Perkin, *Professional Society: England since 1880* (London: Routledge and Kegan Paul, 1989), 121–22. Matthew Arnold's *Culture and Anarchy* is a classic depiction of the social role envisioned for professional men by the leading English dons. An apposite faith in the leadership of the legal profession in the new age of democracy can be found in Alexis de Tocqueville's *Democracy in America*, vol. 1, chap. 16, and in many of the writings of John Stuart Mill.

33. Reader, *Professional Men*, chap. 8.

34. See, e.g., Larson, *Rise of Professionalism*, 118–35; Starr, *Social Transformation of American Medicine*, book 1, chap. 1; and Samuel Haber, *The Quest for Authority and Honor in the American Professions, 1750–1900* (Chicago: University of Chicago Press, 1991).

35. Elliot, *Sociology of Professions*, 14, 32.

36. The term is Magali Larson's. See Larson, *Rise of Professionalism*, chap. 4.

37. Laurence R. Veysey, *The Emergence of the American University* (Chicago: University of Chicago Press, 1965), 21–56.

38. The lower branch of the legal profession in Britain, the solicitors, also sought to improve their status through similar sorts of reforms. They were less successful than the surgeons and general practitioners in medicine largely because of the successful resistance by the upper branch. Nevertheless, according to Larson, the failure was "more apparent that real." The Law Society, which was the solicitors' main organizational vehicle, successfully repulsed encroachments by the barristers and "established a division of labor on solid grounds." Moreover, the attorneys gradually became "more indispensable to the barristers as a referral system than the barristers were to them as pleaders" (Larson, *Rise of Professionalism*, 95–96).

39. It is also a tribute to the bitterness of party politics in Great Britain at the time. The Medical Act of 1858 was the seventeenth bill presented to Parliament since 1840. Reader comments that "all of its predecessors were wrecked on the various hazards of disagreement within the profession, the opposition of interests outside the profession, and the changes and chances of party politics" (Reader, *Professional Men*, 66).

40. "The physicians had long established themselves in the upper ranks of society, and when scientific inquiry lost its novelty, they joined in the ample life of the great houses where elegance and wit were pursued. . . . Social qualifications became the first requirement" (Carr-Saunders and Wilson, *Professions*, 71).

41. Larson, *Rise of Professionalism*, 87.

42. The status hierarchy separating the lower and upper branches of law and medicine existed in a virtually unbridgeable form in England before the mid-nineteenth century. General practitioners and surgeons were regarded as "tradesmen," partly because of their long-standing association with guild structures, but largely because of their lower social origins. They seldom, if ever, enjoyed a classical secondary education, and the surgeons further suffered from the bloody nature of their work and from their past association with the barbers' guild. See Reader, *Professional Men*, 32–43, 59–66; and Larson, *Rise of Professionalism*, 83–90.

43. Reader, *Professional Men*, 67.

44. As described, somewhat sardonically, by Reader: "By 1860 or thereabouts, the elements of professional standing were tolerably clear. You needed a professional association to focus opinion, work up a body of knowledge, and insist upon a decent standard of conduct. If possible, and as soon as possible, it should have a Royal Charter as a mark of recognition. The final step, if you could manage it . . . was to persuade Parliament to pass an Act conferring something like monopoly powers on duly qualified practitioners, which meant practitioners who had followed a recognized course of training and passed recognized examinations" (Reader, *Professional Men*, 71).

45. Wilensky, "The Professionalization of Everyone?," 142–46.

46. N. S. Davis, quoted in Burton J. Bledstein, *Culture of Professionalism*, 85.

47. See, e.g., Roy Lubove, *The Professional Altruist: The Emergence of Social Work as a Career* (Cambridge, Mass.: Harvard University Press, 1965); and David Tyack and Elizabeth Hansot, *Managers of Virtue* (New York: Harper, 1982), espec. chap. 10.

48. Veysey, *Emergence*, part 1; and Bledstein, *Culture of Professionalism*, 269–86.

49. Larson, *Rise of Professionalism*, 166–71; Michael Powell, *From Patrician to Professional Elite: The Transformation of the New York City Bar Association* (New York: Russell Sage Foundation, 1988), 9–11.

50. Licensure assumed a consistent pattern, pioneered first by the medical and legal professions. The most salient feature was the creation of an expert board usually appointed by the governor of the state and made up of experienced practitioners who had the support of—and were sometimes nominated by—the relevant professional association. Education, experience, and fitness qualifications were set by the licensing act, and the board was then given the authority to decide which specific programs satisfied the criteria. Unlicensed persons were statutorily prohibited from professional practice. The board was also given authority to promulgate rules and codes of conduct, which at one time included restrictions on advertising, solicitation, price competition, competitive bidding, and other restrictions on practice. Codes of conduct included disciplinary mechanisms, including powers of investigation, prosecution, adjudication, and punishment. See Stephen Rubin, "The Legal Web of Professional Regulation," in Roger D. Blair and Stephen Rubin, eds., *Regulating the Professions* (Lexington, Mass.: Lexington Books, 1980), 29–60.

51. In recent years, at least one state could claim the licensing of the following occupations: abstracters, boiler inspectors, private detectives, egg graders, electrologists, elevator inspectors, guide-dog trainers, hoisting engineers, homeopaths, horseshoers, manicurists, masseurs, milk certifiers, mine inspectors, motion picture operators, oculists, pest controllers, plumbers, certified shorthand reporters, tile layers, watchmakers, well drillers, and ship brokers. This list comes from Jethro K. Lieberman, *The Tyranny of the Experts* (New York: Walker Publishing, 1970), 16. Among the state-recognized qualifying associations in Great Britain are those regulating travel agents, butchers, cleansers, printers, caterers, and welders. See Millerson, *Qualifying Associations*, 248–54.

52. In England, by contrast, the connection between the universities and the new professions was forged much later, because of the continued social exclusiveness and classical orientation of the leading universities, Oxford and Cambridge. The leading British universities remained determinedly linked to humanist scholarship and the traditional classical professions. See, e.g., Joseph Ben-David, *Centers of Learning: Britain, France, Germany, the United States* (New York: McGraw-Hill, 1976), 52–59; and Arthur Engel, "The English Universities and Professional Education," in K. H.

Jarausch, ed., *The Transformation of Higher Learning, 1860–1930* (Stuttgart: Klett-Cotta, 1983), 293–305. Because of this, professional development occurs largely outside of the university system through the distinctively British institution of qualifying associations, which give qualifying examinations, make efforts to advance the knowledge base of the occupation through the sponsorship of formal study, and also adumbrate rules for the control of professional conduct. The range of occupations that can hope to claim a degree of "professional" status through the regulation of qualifying associations is significantly larger in Britain than it is in the United States. However, the standards and prestige of the associations vary widely, and the great majority do not by any means lead to the successful acquisition of professional status. See Millerson, *Qualifying Association,* 246–54.

53. Benjamin Coit Gilman, quoted in Bledstein, *Culture of Professionalism,* 293.

54. A complication is that by the end of the Progressive Era, the universities were themselves highly entrepreneurial and on the lookout for new training markets at the high end of the hierarchy of social wealth and prestige. Indeed, some evidence suggests that the buccaneering university presidents of the Progressive Era introduced businessmen to techniques of promotion and entrepreneurship unfamiliar in the corporate world at the time. See Bledstein, *Culture of Professionalism,* 289; and Hofstadter and Metzger, *The Development of Academic Freedom.*

55. In the conception of the reforming dean of the Harvard Law School, Christopher Langdell, the law was not a body of learning that could be taught through apprenticeship; it was a "science," and it therefore required academic professors who devoted their careers completely to analyzing, mastering, and teaching legal principles. Langdell, quoted in Bledstein, *Culture of Professionalism,* 282. The original statement can be found in Roscoe Pound, "The Law School, 1817–1929," in Samuel Eliot Morison, ed., *The Development of Harvard University* (Cambridge, Mass.: Harvard University Press, 1930), 492. The first founders of the professional schools of business also consistently stated their aspiration for "scientific management."

56. Ernest V. Hollis and Alice L. Taylor, *Social Work Education in the United States* (New York: Columbia University Press, 1951), 128.

57. Frederick Rudolph, *Curriculum* (San Francisco: Jossey-Bass, 1977), 61–63, 103–8.

58. See John M. Burgess, *Reminiscences of an American Scholar* (New York: Columbia University Press, 1934); and Barry D. Karl, *Charles E. Merriam and the Study of Politics* (Chicago: University of Chicago Press, 1974).

59. G. Stanley Hall, *Life and Confessions of a Psychologist* (1923; reprint, New York: Arno, 1977).

60. For sociology, see Anthony Oberschall, "The Institutionalization of American Sociology," in Anthony Oberschall, ed., *The Establishment of Empirical Sociology* (New York: Harper and Row, 1972), 187–251. For anthropology, see T. K. Penniman, *A Hundred Years of Anthropology* (1935; reprint, London: G. Duckworth, 1965); and Melville J. Herskovits, *Franz Boas: The Science of Man in the Making* (1953; reprint, Clifton, N.J.: Augustus M. Kelley, 1973).

61. At the time of the Declaration of Independence, only two professional schools existed in the United States (both medical schools). See Henry Taylor, *Professional Education in the United States* (Albany: University of the State of New York, 1900), 1: 6. By 1899, over 8,000 students were studying divinity in the nation's 165 professional schools of theology; nearly 12,000 were studying law in the nation's eighty-six professional schools of law; and over 24,000 were studying medicine in the nation's 156

schools of medicine. The figures for the allied health fields were as follows: dentistry, 7,600 students at fifty-six schools; pharmacy, 3,500 students at fifty-two schools; and veterinary medicine, 378 students at seventeen schools.

62. The patterns in teacher training are characteristic. The first university department of education was at the University of Iowa in 1855. Separate teacher's colleges and graduate schools began at Michigan in 1887, Chicago, Stanford, and Harvard in 1891, and Berkeley and Columbia in 1892. Yale offered courses in education in 1891, but had no department until 1910. As late as 1914, teacher education was described by Abraham Flexner, a leading advocate of professionalization, as "heterogeneous to the last degree" (Geraldine J. Clifford and James W. Guthrie, *Ed School: A Brief for Professional Education* [Chicago: University of Chicago Press, 1988], 104).

63. For a sample of some characteristic ways of thinking about the role of knowledge in society during the period, see Veysey, *Emergence of the American University;* Veysey, "Higher Education as a Profession"; Harold Stearns, *America and the Young Intellectual* (New York: George H. Doran, 1921); Lasch, *New Radicalism in America, 1889–1963;* Thomas L. Haskell, *The Emergence of Professional Social Science* (Urbana: University of Illinois Press, 1977); and Haber, *Quest for Authority,* part 3.

64. John F. Dillon, "The True Professional Ideal," *American Law Review* 28 (1895): 671.

65. Roscoe Pound, *The Lawyer from Antiquity to Modern Times* (St. Paul, Minn.: West Publishing, 1953), 5–8. For further bibliographic reference, see Kimball, *"True Professional Ideal,"* 301–25.

66. Indeed, the ideals of social trustee professionalism eventually became enshrined in dictionary definitions of professions. See, e.g., *Webster's Third International Dictionary,* vol. 2 (Springfield, Mass.: G. & C. Merriam, 1967), 1811.

67. In the United States, some writers and thinkers in the northern states—notably the abolitionists and transcendentalists—began to acquire a sense of being at odds with the materialism of the rest of their society as early as the 1830s and 1840s. Seymour Martin Lipset and Richard B. Dobson, "The Intellectual as Critic and Rebel," *Daedalus* 101 (1972): 137–98; and David Brion Davis, *Antebellum Reform* (New York: Harper and Row, 1967).

68. Veblen's major works are *The Theory of the Leisure Class* (1899; reprint, New York: Penguin, 1979); *The Engineers and the Price System* (1921; reprint, New York: Harcourt Brace, 1963); and *The Higher Learning in America* (1918; reprint, New York: Hill and Wang, 1957).

69. John Dewey, *Democracy and Education* (1916; reprint, New York: Free Press, 1966), 320.

70. The ideal of "expert professionalism" had a second, though less important, source: the effort of some late nineteenth-century social scientists to separate themselves on the basis of an appeal to the "objectivity" of science from the reform-oriented "service orientations" of many early leaders of the American Social Science Association. See Haskell, *Emergence of Professional Social Science.*

71. Haber, *Quest for Authority,* 302–9.

72. Ibid., 307. See also Monte A. Calvert, *The Mechanical Engineer in America, 1830–1910* (Baltimore: Johns Hopkins University Press, 1967), part 3; and Clark C. Spence, *Mining Engineers and the American West* (New Haven, Conn.: Yale University Press, 1970), 253–77.

73. Robert W. Hodge, Paul M. Siegel, and Peter H. Rossi, "Occupational Prestige in the United States, 1925–63," *American Journal of Sociology* 70 (1964): 282–302.

74. With one exception, the highest-ranking occupations at the time of the North-Hatt study of 1947 were either professions or high-ranking political offices such as governor and congressman. (The exception was bankers—another "pillar" of local community structure.) In descending order, the most prestigious professions included physicians; scientists and college professors; civil engineers and ministers; lawyers, architects, and dentists. See Hodge, Siegel, and Rossi, "Occupational Prestige."

75. Bledstein, *Culture of Professionalism,* 146.

76. Ibid., 92.

77. Many close observers of the professional world would not rush to embrace the notion that a new phase in the social history of the professions is upon us. According to the English social historian Harold Perkin, for example, professionalism, since it is based on human capital and specialized expertise, can become "as extensive as there [are] human beings capable of skilled and specialized service" (Perkin, *The Rise of Professional Society* [London: Routledge and Kegan Paul, 1990], xii–xiii). See also Abbott, *System of Professions,* 35, 318; and Larson, *Rise of Professionalism,* chap. 11 and 12.

78. Wilensky, "The Professionalization of Everyone?," 156–57.

79. See, in particular, the articles in Amitai Etzioni, ed., *The Semi-Professions* (New York: Free Press, 1969).

80. See Philip Kraft, *Programmers and Managers: The Routinization of Computer Programming in the United States* (New York: Springer-Verlag, 1977).

81. See, for example, the interesting analysis of prestige stratification in the law in Edward O. Laumann and John P. Heinz, "Specialization and Prestige in the Legal Profession: The Structure of Deference," *American Bar Foundation Research Journal* 1 (1977): 155–216. These findings are essentially consistent across disciplines. See Steven Brint, "Stratification in Six High-Status Occupations," unpublished manuscript, Huron Institute, 1981.

82. Eliot Freidson, *Profession of Medicine* (New York: Dodd, Mead, 1970). See also Barbara Ehrenreich and John Ehrenreich, *The American Health Empire: Power, Profits, and Politics* (New York: Random House, 1970); and Jeffrey Berlant, *Professions and Monopoly* (Berkeley: University of California Press, 1975).

83. See, e.g., Roth, "Professionalism: The Sociologist's Decoy"; Collins, *Credential Society,* chap. 6; and Douglas Klegon, "The Sociology of Professions," *Sociology of Work and Occupations* 5 (1978): 259–83.

84. Social trustee professionalism retained some strength even in areas, like business management schools, where it might be expected to have had little appeal. See Kenneth R. Andrews, "Toward Professionalism in Business Management," *Harvard Business Review* 47 (March–April 1969): 49–60.

85. Bell, *Coming of Post-Industrial Society,* 25.

86. Ibid., 29.

87. Michael Oakeshott, "Learning and Teaching," in R. S. Peters, ed., *The Concept of Education* (New York: The Humanities Press, 1967), 164.

88. Nathan Glazer, "The Schools of the Minor Professions," *Minerva* 12 (1974): 349.

89. Duncan's socioeconomic index, on which most modern measurement is based, is discussed in Otis Dudley Duncan, "A Socio-Economic Index for All Occupations," in Albert J. Reiss, ed., *Occupations and Social Status* (Glencoe, Ill.: The Free Press, 1961), 116–17.

90. "Overall, it appears that variations in income status account for almost two-

thirds of the variation in general social standing, and that schooling status and job status split the remainder about evenly. Income is of overwhelming importance in how Americans think about social standing" (Richard P. Coleman and Lee Rainwater, *Social Standing in America* [New York: Basic Books, 1978], 220).

91. Ibid., 68, 72.

92. Richard B. Freeman, *The Overeducated American* (New York: Academic Press, 1976), chap. 1. See also the Carnegie Commission, *College Graduates and Jobs: Adjusting to a New Labor Market* (New York: McGraw-Hill, 1973).

93. Michael Useem, *Liberal Education and the Corporation* (New York: Aldine de Gruyter, 1989), 6.

94. Alexander W. Astin, Kenneth C. Green, and William S. Korn, *The American Freshman: Twenty Year Trends* (Los Angeles: Higher Education Research Institute, University of California, Los Angeles, 1987).

95. Cf. Abbott, *System of Professions,* 81, 106. On trends toward specialization, see Rosemary Stevens, *American Medicine and the Public Interest* (New Haven, Conn.: Yale University Press, 1971); Heinz and Laumann, *Chicago Lawyers;* Richard Abel, *American Lawyers* (New York: Oxford University Press, 1989); Frances Oakley, *Community of Learning: The American College and the Liberal Arts Tradition* (New York: Oxford University Press, 1992), 158; and William G. Bowen and Neil L. Rudenstine, *In Pursuit of the Ph.D.* (Princeton, N.J.: Princeton University Press, 1992).

96. Unpublished data from the Project on Professionals, available on request.

97. In nine out of ten cases, doctors and lawyers in the sample considered professors and scientists to be in the same "social class" as themselves. In seven out of ten cases, they also accepted engineers. Moreover, although a majority of professionals saw themselves as occupying a social position below the highest levels, they were substantially more likely to indicate class identifications with business executives and federal agency heads than they were to consider members of such "minor professions" as nurse and computer programmer to share a common social class identity. See Steven Brint, "The Occupational Class Identifications of Professionals: Evidence from Cluster Analysis," *Research in Social Stratification and Mobility* 6 (1987): 35–57.

98. Eliot Freidson, "The Changing Nature of Professional Control," *Annual Review of Sociology* 10 (1984): 1–20.

99. Scott Jashik, "State Funds for Higher Education Drop in Year, First Decline since Survey Began 33 Years Ago," *Chronicle of Higher Education* 38 (November 6, 1991): A1, A38.

100. Not all institutions proceeded in the same manner. Some universities developed alternative approaches to the reduction of the professional "periphery"—from across-the-board cuts to elimination of programs where the institution's comparative advantage was considered weak. See, e.g., Yale University, *Committee on Restructuring Yale College* (New Haven, Conn.: Yale University, January 1992).

101. According to public opinion surveys, fields like law and business had a worse reputation for high standards of "ethics and morality" and for contributing to the "general good of society" than did many of the fields threatened by university consolidations. On ethics, see Louis Harris and Associates, "Study for the American Institute of Certified Public Accountants," July 1986. On social contribution, see Gallup Organization, "Gallup Report Special Survey," January 1985.

102. Patricia Gumport, "The Contested Terrain of Academic Program Reduction," *The Journal of Higher Education* (in press). See also Patricia Gumport, "Tired Faculty: Reflections on Marginalization and Academic Identity," in William Tierney and Dan-

iel McLaughlin, eds., *Naming Silenced Lives: Personal Narratives and the Process of Educational Change* (New York: Routledge, 1993).

103. Mangan, "More Colleges Resort to Faculty and Staff Layoffs."

CHAPTER THREE

1. The lines of social structure that I discuss in this chapter are clearly overlapping in many specific instances. However, the overlap is far from perfect. Human service workers, for example, are primarily employed in the public sector. Yet a substantial minority of human service workers are not employed in the public sector. Using a multivariate framework is helpful under these circumstances.

2. I discuss the issue of how to conceptualize professional spheres in somewhat greater detail in my article, "Upper Professionals: A High Command of Commerce, Culture, and Civic Regulation," in John H. Mollenkopf and Manuel Castells, ed., *The Dual City: Restructuring New York* (New York: Russell Sage, 1991), 155–76.

3. These estimates were derived from an analysis of the General Social Survey cumulated over the years 1980–90.

4. For useful discussions of business services, see Matthew P. Drennan, "The Apple's Core: New York City's Export Industries," in Benjamin J. Klaibnar, ed., *New York City's Changing Economic Base* (New York: Pica Press, 1987), 23–32; and Thierry Noyelle and Anna B. Dutka, *International Trade in Business Services* (Cambridge, Mass.: Ballinger/American Enterprise Institute, 1988).

5. Noyelle and Dutka, *International Trade,* 10.

6. Ibid.

7. Virtually all architects, certified public accountants, and management consultants are employed in professional firm practices, as are 80 percent of corporate and tax lawyers. Business accountants are more evenly divided between corporate (54 percent) and professional firm (33 percent) employment, with a significant number also employed by government (13 percent). Three out of five management information specialists are employed by corporations. Estimates are from Barbara A. Curran and Clara N. Carson, *Supplement to the Lawyer Statistical Report: The U.S. Legal Profession in 1988* (Chicago: American Bar Association, 1990), 4 and *passim;* Abel, *American Lawyers,* 169; U.S. Department of Commerce, Bureau of the Census, *Occupation by Industry, 1980 Census of the Population* (Washington, D.C.: Government Printing Office, 1984).

8. Employment in small-to-medium size professional firms is the decided norm in the business service sphere. In the late 1980s, 95 percent of accounting firms, 93 percent of management consulting firms, 90 percent of advertising firms, and 85 percent of computer service firms had fewer than twenty employees, as did at least 80 percent of corporate and business law firms. These estimates are based on figures from the U.S. Department of Commerce, Bureau of the Census, *1987 Census of Service Industries: Establishment and Firm Size* (Washington, D.C.: Government Printing Office, 1987), table 2a; Abel, *American Lawyers,* 181, 203–4; and Curran and Carson, *Supplement to the Lawyer Statistical Report,* 12.

9. Some so-called "boutique" firms work on very specialized problems for clients of many different types. Boutiques are one common form of spin-off from large firm practice. See Abel, *American Lawyers,* 185, 222.

10. See, e.g., American Institute of Architects, *Architecture Fact Book* (New York: AIA, 1990), 22–24.

11. According to Richard Abel, the effect of further concentration and bureaucratization in law "will be to transform the professional firm into a capitalist multiservice corporation, characterized by hierarchy, bureaucracy, the extraction of extra value from workers by partners, and even the progressive separation of ownership from daily control [through the hiring of nonlawyer business managers] (Abel, *American Lawyers*, 244).

12. The largest firms now devote 40 to 50 percent of their work to nonaudit business services, and five of the top ten management consulting "firms" are, in fact, the management advisory service divisions of leading accounting firms. See Noyelle and Dutka, *International Trade*, 32. See also Previts, *Scope of CPA Services;* Olson, *Accounting Professions' Years of Trial;* and Harold E. Arnett and Paul Danos, *CPA Firm Viability: Environmental Factors Affecting Firms of Various Sizes and Characteristics* (Ann Arbor: University of Michigan Graduate School of Business Administration, 1979).

13. Noyelle and Dutka, *International Trade*, 34–39.

14. These income figures for partners in large legal firms are based on 1986 data. See Abel, *American Lawyers*, 191–203.

15. U.S. Department of Labor, *Occupational Projections and Training Data, 1990 Edition* (Washington, D.C.: Government Printing Office, 1990), 20–21.

16. American Association of Engineering Societies, *Professional Income of Engineers, 1990* (Washington, D.C.: AASE, 1990); American Association of Engineering Societies, *Professional Income of Engineers, 1991* (Washington, D.C.: AASE, 1991). This data is based on a survey of establishments and may underestimate small establishments. The 1991 study showed over 69 percent of engineers working for large companies (over 5,000 employees). Data kindly provided by Dick Ellis of the Engineering Manpower Commission.

17. Data for physicists from American Institute of Physics, *1987–88 Survey of Physics and Astronomy Bachelor's Degree Recipients* (Washington, D.C.: AIP, 1989); and American Institute of Physics, *1987 Salaries Society Membership Survey* (Washington, D.C.: AIP, n.d.). Data for chemists from American Chemical Society, *Salaries 1990* (Washington, D.C.: ACS, 1990). Data for geoscientists from American Geological Institute, *North American Survey of Geoscientists* (Alexandria, Va.: AGI, 1988). Data for engineers from Abbott Langer and Associates, *Compensation of Industrial Engineers*, 11th ed. (Crete, Ill.: Abbott Langer, 1989); Institute of Electrical and Electronics Engineers, IEEE U.S. Membership *Salary and Fringe Benefit Survey, 1987* (New York: IEEE-USA, 1987); and National Research Council, *Summary Report 1989* (Washington, D.C.: NRC, 1989).

18. See, e.g., Institute of Electrical and Electronics Engineers, *U.S. Membership Survey, 1987*, 13.

19. National Center for Educational Statistics, U.S. Department of Education, *Digest of Educational Statistics* (Washington, D.C.: Government Printing Office, 1991), 166. Faculty includes senior instructional staff only, that is, excluding graduate students but including lectors and instructors. Undergraduate enrollments include both four-year and two-year college students. For historical data, see also U.S. Bureau of the Census, *Historical Statistics of the United States: Colonial Times to 1970* (Washington, D.C.: U.S. Government Printing Office, 1975), 383.

20. Westat, Inc., *A Sourcebook of Arts Statistics* (Rockville, M.D.: Westat, Inc., 1990), 269, 276, 280.

21. Ibid., 473–74.

22. Ibid., 265.

23. Ibid., 135.

24. Ibid., 157–58.

25. Ibid., 170, 172–75.

26. Not all of the culture industries have increased as a proportion of GNP. Motion pictures declined from 0.6 in 1947 to 0.24 in 1987. Printing and publishing declined slightly from 1.36 in 1947 to 1.29 in 1987. Radio and television and recording expenditures were the largest gainers over the period, with radio and television increasing from 0.09 to 0.28 percent of GNP in the period (ibid., 12–17).

27. On professors, see Everett Carll Ladd, Jr., and Seymour Martin Lipset, *The Divided Academy* (New York: W. W. Norton, 1975); and Barbara K. Hofer and Donald R. Brown, "The Relative Importance of Research and Undergraduate Teaching," *CRLT Occasional Papers* 5 (Ann Arbor: University of Michigan, Center for Research and Learning and Teaching, 1992).

28. David H. Weaver and G. Cleveland Wilhoit, *The American Journalist: A Portrait of U.S. News People and Their Work* (Bloomington: Indiana University Press, 1986), chap. 3; S. Robert Lichter, Stanley Rothman, and Linda S. Lichter, *Media Elite* (New York: Hastings House, 1986), chap. 2.

29. Freelance writers operate on the market, but, by virtue of the nature of that market, many are nevertheless primarily oriented to educated elites and, therefore, close to the largely nonprofit "high culture" sphere. See Nicholas Zill and Marianne Winglee, *Who Reads Literature?* (Cabin John, Md.: Seven Locks Press, 1990).

30. In contrast to the visual arts, the degree of unconstrained entrepreneurial interest in monied elites appears to be somewhat reduced in the upper reaches of architecture, perhaps because academic gatekeepers play a more important role in creating reputations, and because academic study is more demanding than it typically is in the other visual arts. See Magali Sarfatti Larson, George Leon, and Jay Bolick, "The Professional Supply of Design," in Judith R. Blau et al., eds., *Professionals and Urban Form* (Albany: State University of New York Press, 1983), 251–79.

31. The trend in the 1980s was toward devolution of some government functions, particularly in social welfare, to the state and local levels. See U.S. Department of Commerce, *1987 Census of Governments, Compendium of Public Employment,* vol. 3, no. 2 (Washington, D.C.: Government Printing Office, 1991), vi–vii.

32. Expenditure data is available only for all levels of government combined. In the commerce and public safety category, I include spending on national defense and international relations, police, fire, corrections, legal administration, space research, highways, air transport, water transport, and other transportation. In the social welfare category, I include spending on education, libraries, public welfare, hospitals, health, social security administration, veterans' benefits, housing and community development, and insurance trusts. Comparisons with the 1972 Census of Governments, at a time of high levels of perceived governmental activism, suggest *negligible* shifts in distribution of expenditures between these two functional categories in the years between 1971–72 and 1986–87.

33. U.S. Department of Commerce, *1987 Census of Governments,* vol. 3, no. 2, 6.

34. U.S. Department of Commerce, *1987 Census of Governments,* vol. 3, no. 2.

35. Between 1982 and 1987, the number of federal employees per 10,000 people

decreased by 1.7 percent, and the number of state and local government employees per 10,000 people increased by 2.1 percent (ibid., v–vi).

36. See the discussion in Chapter 7.

37. For data on these trends, see Schlozman and Tierney, *Organized Interests in American Society*, 7.

38. Daniel Bell, "The New Class: A Muddled Concept" in Bruce-Briggs, *New Class?*, 188.

39. Thomas M. Stanback, Jr. *Services, The New Economy* (Totowa, N.J.: Allanheld, Osmun, 1981), 7.

40. Most estimates suggest that legal work is divided nearly equally between work for businesses and work for individuals. If one limits the human services component to services related to "personal plight," the proportion dips to approximately 18 percent of total lawyer effort. As Richard Abel notes, even this proportion is somewhat misleading because the time invested by lawyers serving corporations should be multiplied by the greater productivity available to them due to superior support, supplies, office equipment, etc. See Abel, *American Lawyers*, 203–4.

41. Two-thirds of doctors and psychiatrists and over 90 percent of dentists have office-based practices. The remainder of doctors are distributed between hospital-based practices and other salaried settings, including health maintenance organizations and government clinics. Bureau of Labor Statistics, *Occupational Outlook Handbook, 1990 91 Edition*, 54. Salaried employment, however, is on the rise, and it is likely that the great majority of physicians will be employed as salaried workers in managed care systems by the next decade. Nancy Ames and Mariane C. Fahs, "HMOs: An Answer to Fee-for-Service," *Mount Sinai Journal of Medicine* 55 (1988): 117–25.

42. According to recent estimates, some 80 percent of Americans had at least some health insurance in the early 1990s.

43. Before the push for health care reform in 1993–94, analysts projected that medical expenditures would grow to 15 percent of GNP in the United States by the year 2000. For a good brief overview of the medical care sector as of the late 1980s, see Ames and Fahs, "HMOs." For the historical development of the American medical care sector, see Starr, *Social Transformation of American Medicine*.

44. Richard P. Nathan, Fred C. Doolittle, and Associates, *Reagan and the States* (Princeton, N.J.: Princeton University Press, 1987), espec. chaps. 1, 3, and 15. Thirty-eight states raised taxes in 1983 alone to counter federal cutbacks, and real state spending rose at a significant rate throughout the 1984–86 period (ibid., 14).

45. Paul E. Peterson and Mark Rom, "Lower Taxes, More Spending, and Budget Deficits," in Charles O. Jones, ed., *The Reagan Legacy* (Chatham, N.J.: Chatham House, 1988).

46. Nathan, Doolittle, and Associates, *Reagan and the States*, 96–112.

47. Peterson and Rom, "Lower Taxes," 223. See also Wallace C. Peterson, *Transfer Spending, Taxes, and the American Welfare State* (Boston: Kluwer Academic Publishers, 1991), 95–132.

48. The Conference Board, "Business Expectations for the Next Four Years," *Chief Executive Opinion* 8 (New York: The Conference Board, 1993).

49. See Brint, "Upper Professionals," 160–61 and the studies cited therein.

50. Robert Zussman, *Mechanics of the Middle Class: Work and Politics among American Engineers* (Berkeley: University of California Press, 1985), 223–24.

51. The characteristic closeness of scientists and engineers to management shows

228

up also in patterns of social identification. Corporate scientists and engineers are much more likely than other professionals to include middle managers as belonging to "the same social class" as themselves. Brint, "The Occupational Class Identifications of Professionals," 45. For data on rates of mobility into management, see American Society for Engineering Education, *Future Directions for Engineering Education* (Cambridge, Mass.: Massachusetts Institute of Technologys, School of Engineering, 1975).

52. Veblen, *Engineers and the Price System.* For a penetrating critique, see Daniel Bell, "Veblen and the Technocrats," in Bell, *The Winding Passage* (New York: Basic Books, 1980), 69–90.

53. Throughout history, during periods of value integration or political authoritarianism, culture producers have been notable mainly for their high levels of conformity with the established order. The writers and thinkers of the Age of Augustus, of Pope Gregory VII, of the Meiji Restoration, or of Stalin's Russia are hardly renowned for their "adversarial" ideas. It is only in secular, liberal, and pluralist societies that some degree of critical tension appears to be more common. For a view based on comparative-historical analysis, see Lenski, *Power and Privilege,* 256–66.

54. See, e.g., Lipset and Dobson, "The Intellectual as Critic and Rebel"; Charles Kadushin, *The American Intellectual Elite* (Boston: Little-Brown, 1974); Ladd and Lipset, *Divided Academy;* Seymour Martin Lipset, "The Academic Mind at the Top: Political Behavior and Values of Faculty Elites," *Public Opinion Quarterly* 46 (1982): 143–68; S. Robert Lichter and Stanley Rothman, "Media and Business Elites," *Public Opinion* (October–November 1981): 42–46ff.; and Stanley Rothman and S. Robert Lichter, "What are Moviemakers Made Of?," *Public Opinion* (December–January 1984): 14–18.

55. Kevin Phillips, *The Emerging Republican Majority* (New Rochelle, N.Y.: Arlington House, 1969), espec. chaps. 1 and 6. See also Jeanne J. Kirkpatrick, *The New Presidential Elite* (New York: Russell Sage, 1976), 239–57; and P. J. O'Rourke, *Parliament of Whores* (New York: Atlantic Monthly Press, 1991).

56. Unpublished data derived from the Cumulative General Social Survey, 1974–88.

57. Morris Fiorina, *Divided Government* (Toronto: Maxwell Macmillan Canada, 1992), 35. For earlier data, see Paul T. David, *Party Strength in the United States, 1872–1970* (Charlottesville: University of Virginia Press, 1972).

58. See, e.g., Robert Goodman, *The Last Entrepreneurs* (Boston: South End Press, 1982).

59. David Osborne, *Laboratories of Democracy* (Boston: Harvard Business School, 1988), chaps. 2 and 8.

60. S. Robert Lichter and Stanley Rothman, "What Interests the Public and What Interests the Public Interests?," *Public Opinion* (April–May 1983): 44–48; David Vogel, "The Public Interest Movement and the American Reform Tradition," *Political Science Quarterly* 95 (1980–81): 607–27; and David Vogel, *Fluctuating Fortunes* (New York: Basic Books, 1989), chap. 5.

61. It appears that the "fate of idealism" is linearly related to the earnings curve of "human services occupations." New recruits to medicine and law tend to lose their idealism before they finish their professional training, while new recruits to other human service fields tend to require a year or two in the field. Service orientation, in this sense, is a compensatory device related to low income horizons. See Howard Becker, *Boys in White* (Chicago: University of Chicago Press, 1961); Dan Lortie,

Schoolteacher (Chicago: University of Chicago Press, 1975); and Michael Lipsky, *Street-Level Bureaucracy* (New York: Russell Sage, 1980), chap. 6.

62. Freidson, *Profession of Medicine,* chap 8.

63. Ibid., 168–78.

64. Ibid., chap. 3.

65. Everett Carll Ladd, Jr., "Pursuing the New Class: Social Theory and Survey Data," in Bruce-Briggs, *New Class?,* 115; Steven Brint, "The Political Attitudes of Professionals," *Annual Review of Sociology* 11 (1985), 402–3 and references cited therein; Derber, *Project on Professionals,* 58–69; and Derber, Schwartz, and Magrass, *Power in the Highest Degree,* 149.

66. For the classic statement, see Richard A. Musgrave and Peggy Musgrave, *Public Finance in Theory and Practice,* 3d ed. (New York: McGraw-Hill, 1980).

67. Paul J. DiMaggio and Helmut K. Anheier, "The Sociology of Non-Profit Organizations and Sectors," *Annual Review of Sociology* 16 (1990): 139–57.

68. Burton Weisbrod, *The Non-Profit Economy* (Cambridge, Mass.: Harvard University Press, 1988).

69. Hansmann has specified four conditions leading to "non-distribution of proceeds," all of which revolve around the amount or quality of information available for choice. See Howard Hansmann, "Economic Theories of Non-Profit Organization," in Walter W. Powell, ed., *The Non-Profit Sector: A Research Handbook* (New Haven, Conn.: Yale University Press, 1987).

70. Starr, *Social Transformation of American Medicine,* 235–89.

71. For a valuable discussion of the railroads, see Frank Dobbin, *Forging Industrial Policy: The United States, Britain, and France in the Railway Age* (Cambridge: Cambridge University Press, forthcoming).

72. See John D. Donahue, *The Privatization Decision: Public Ends, Private Means* (New York: Basic Books, 1989); John Kay, Colin Mayer, and David Thompson, *Privatisation and Regulation: The U.K. Experience* (Oxford: Clarendon Press, 1986); Ezra N. Suleiman and John Waterbury, *The Political Economy of Public Sector Reform and Privatization* (Boulder, Colo.: Westview Press, 1990).

73. In many areas where the possibilities for comparisons exist, it has been difficult to establish a clear private sector advantage. See the studies discussed in Donahue, *Privatization Decision;* and Kay, Mayer, and Thompson, *Privatisation and Regulation.* Nevertheless, the perception persists that the private sector is uniformly more efficient.

74. For principles bearing on the choice of privatization, see Donahue, *Privatization Decision,* 223; and Paul Starr, "The New Life of the Liberal State: Privatization and the Restructuring of State-Society Relations," in Suleiman and Waterbury, *Political Economy,* 22–54.

75. Robert Pear, "Bush to Make It Easier to Sell Public Property," *New York Times,* April 26, 1992, 28.

76. Starr, "New Life of the Liberal State," 45.

77. Calculated from Abel, *American Lawyers,* 300.

78. American Institute of Physics, *Employment Survey, 1989* (New York: AIP, 1990), 6–7. Data is based on recent graduates.

79. American Institute of Physics, *Society Membership Profile* (New York: AIP, 1989), 12.

80. Calculated from American Geological Institute, *Geoscience Employment and Hiring Survey 1990* (Alexandria, Va.: AGI, 1990), 7.

81. For schoolteachers, see U.S. Department of Education, *The Condition of Education, 1990* (Washington, D.C.: Government Printing Office, 1990), 13. For social workers, see U.S. Department of Labor, *Occupational Outlook Handbook 1990* (Washington, D.C.: Government Printing Office, 1990), 102.

82. James Hecimovich, *Planners' Salaries and Employment Trends* (Chicago: American Planning Association, 1989), 3–4.

83. U.S. Department of Labor, *Occupational Outlook Handbook 1990*.

84. Calculated from the General Social Survey, 1981–91. This distribution partly reflects the greater acceptability of the baccalaureate degree in the private sector as a qualification for mid-level employment.

85. See Wilensky, "The Professionalization of Everyone?," and Hall, "Professionalization and Bureaucratization."

86. Michael Macy, "New-Class Dissent among Social-Cultural Specialists," *Sociological Forum* 3 (1988): 325–56.

87. Burton A. Weisbrod, "Nonprofit and Proprietary Sector Behavior: Wage Differentials among Lawyers," *Journal of Labor Economics* 1 (1983): 246–63.

88. Charles Perrow, *Complex Organizations,* 3d ed. (New York: Random House, 1986), 232–35.

89. For evidence on the entire work force, see Randy Hodson, "Labor in the Monopoly, Competitive, and State Sectors," *Politics and Society* 8 (1978): 429–80.

90. Cf. Michèle Lamont, "Cultural Capital and the Liberal Political Attitudes of Professionals: Comment on Brint," *American Journal of Sociology* 92 (1987): 1501–5.

91. There is a voluminous literature on the Progressive period. Among the works that make a convincing case for efficiency-oriented ideals as one strand of this complex movement are the following: George B. Mowry, *The California Progressives* (Berkeley: University of California Press, 1951); Samuel P. Hays, *The Response to Industrialism, 1885–1914* (Chicago: University of Chicago Press, 1951); Robert H. Wiebe, *Businessmen and Reform: A Study of the Progressive Movement* (Cambridge, Mass.: Harvard University Press, 1962); Samuel Haber, *Efficiency and Uplift: Scientific Management in the Progressive Era* (Chicago: University of Chicago Press, 1964); James Weinstein, *The Corporate Ideal in the Liberal State, 1900–1918* (Boston: Beacon Press, 1968); Gabriel Kolko, *The Triumph of Conservatism: A Reinterpretation of American History, 1900–1916* (New York: Free Press, 1973); and Don S. Kirschner, *The Paradox of Professionalism: Reform and Public Service in Urban America, 1900–1940* (New York: Greenwood Press, 1986).

92. The idea for a "regulated, compensatory voucher program" came out of the nonprofit Center for the Study of Public Policy in Cambridge, Massachusetts, in the late 1960s. For a discussion of market-based approaches to "school choice," see John E. Chubb and Terry Moe, *Politics, Markets, and the Nation's Schools* (Washington, D.C.: Brookings Institution, 1990). Enterprise zones are a British idea, and they were advocated in this country most actively by Stuart Butler of the Heritage Institute. See his *Enterprise Zones: Greening the Inner Cities* (New York: Universe Books, 1981). Privatization of traditional government functions was promoted in the early 1970s by the nonprofit Committee for Economic Development. See Donahue, *Privatization Decision,* 131. For a review of entrepreneurialism in government, see David Osborne and Ted Gaebler, *Reinventing Government: How the Entrepreneurial Spirit Is Transforming the Public Sector* (Reading, Mass.: Addison-Wesley, 1992).

CHAPTER FOUR

1. For discussions of the effectiveness of different forms of psychotherapy, see, e g., William B. Stiles, David A. Shapiro, and Robert Elliott, "Are All Psychotherapies Equivalent?," *American Psychologist* 41 (1986): 165–80; and Alan E. Kazdin and Debra Bass, "Power to Detect Differences between Alternative Treatments in Comparative Psychotherapy Outcome Research," *Journal of Consulting and Clinical Psychology* 57 (1989): 138–47.

2. The major difference between professionals and other people in this respect is that, in the professions, these "human capital" and "social background" factors are sometimes magnified in importance. In the physical and applied sciences, for example, where the training is rigorous, degree differences tend to have greater effects on earnings than they do in many fields.

3. For a recent illuminating study, see Derek Bok, *The Cost of Talent: How Executives and Professionals Are Paid and How It Affects America* (New York: Free Press, 1993).

4. As an explanation for variations in earnings, occupation and industry-level differences are in many and perhaps most cases as important as the human capital differences between individuals. A well-controlled intraoccupational study conducted in 1986 under the auspices of the Institute of Electrical and Electronic Engineers indicates the relatively equal importance of individual-level and nonindividual-level factors on earnings for members of the association. See Institute of Electrical and Electronics Engineers, *U.S. Membership Survey,* (1987) 59–68. My thanks to Mr. W. Thomas Suttle, Associate Staff Director of the IEEE-USA, for making this study available to me.

5. The figures that I cite in this section are based on survey data and therefore have a standard error attached to them. Depending on the size of the standard error, the actual average income can be thousands or even tens of thousands of dollars different from the given average. Many professional occupations, particularly those employed primarily in the private sector, have high levels of dispersion around the median or mean income. Average earnings also do not include fringe benefits or "perks" that substantially raise the living standard for many professional people.

6. For lawyers, see Heinz and Laumann, *Chicago Lawyers,* 64–65, 177; and Abel, *American Lawyers,* 205–9ff.

7. Cf. Terence Johnson, *Professions and Power* (London: Macmillan, 1972), chap. 4.

8. For the reasons discussed above, law has the highest standard deviation in earnings of all professions. In no other occupation, as Richard Abel observes, do many members make fifty times what others make. See Abel, *American Lawyers,* 207. Dentistry and optometry also have high standard deviations of income. The survey figures I have for dentists show a standard deviation of nearly $57,000 on a mean of $87,410. This means that one-third of dentists earned more than $144,000 or less than $30,000 in 1988. See the American Dental Association, *The 1989 Survey of Dental Practice* (Chicago: ADA, 1989). For optometrists in 1990, the situation was even more extreme: a standard deviation of $68,000 on a mean of almost $75,000, meaning that one-third of optometrists earned more than $143,000 in 1990 or less than $7,000. These figures were kindly provided by the American Optometric Association.

9. American Medical Association, *Socioeconomic Characteristics of Medical Practice* (Chicago: AMA, 1991); Arthur Owens, "Earnings Make a Huge Breakthrough," *Medical Economics* (Sept. 3, 1990), 90–116.

10. American Medical Association, *Socioeconomic Characteristics*.

11. Given the tremendous dispersion in lawyer's salaries, few scholars of the American bar seem to think that the average salary is a useful statistic. My estimate is based on the discussion in Abel, *American Lawyers*, 167–200; on the U.S. Department of Labor's *National Survey of Professional, Administrative, Technical, and Clerical Pay, March 1989* (Washington, D.C.: Government Printing Office, 1989), which provides averages for the more peripheral salaried lawyers; and on the data in Richard H. Sander and E. Douglas Williams, "Why Are There So Many Lawyers?: Perspectives on a Turbulent Market," *Law and Social Inquiry* 14 (1989): 431–79.

12. American Dental Association, *1989 Survey*.

13. This estimate is based on figures for 1990 generously provided by Farrell Aron of the American Optometric Association.

14. Contrasts based on figures for professors provided by the College and University Personnel Association for 1988–89. See College and University Personnel Association, *1988–89 National Faculty Salary Survey by Discipline and Rank in Private Colleges and Universities* (Washington, D.C.: CUPA, 1989); and College and University Personnel Association, *1988–89 National Faculty Salary Survey by Discipline and Rank in Public Colleges and Universities* (Washington, D.C.: CUPA, 1989).

15. Of course, not all members of professional occupations where private practice is the norm actually work in private practice. Those who do earn substantially more on average than those who do not. The average doctor in private practice, for example, earns one-third more per year than the average salaried doctor. The average mid-career psychologist in private practice earns 50 percent more than the average full professor of psychology earns. Consulting scientists and engineers also tend to be at the high end of the salary spectrum of science and engineering. Data come from the following sources: American Medical Association, *Socioeconomic Characteristics*, 152; American Psychological Association, *1989 Salaries in Psychology* (Washington, D.C.: APA, 1989), tables 1 and 5; Institute of Electrical and Electronics Engineers, *U.S. Membership Survey, 1987*, 64–65; and Commission on Professionals in Science and Technology, *Salaries of Scientists, Engineers, and Technicians* (Washington, D.C.: CPST, 1990), 77, 115, 129, 132.

16. Data kindly supplied by the American Association of Medical Colleges.

17. Partners in management consulting, certified public accounting, and advertising firms also have significantly higher average incomes than senior professionals in any of the occupations predominantly employed on salary. U.S. Department of Labor, *Occupational Outlook Handbook* (Washington, D.C.: Government Printing Office, 1990), 13, 48, and 78. Throughout the "business services" sphere, firm size is strongly correlated with the incomes that partners can expect. See American Institute of Architects, *Architecture Factbook;* Abel, *American Lawyers*, 193–94; Arnett and Danos, *CPA Firm Viability*, 106.

18. American Institute of Architects, *Architecture Factbook*, 25.

19. For law, see Abel, *American Lawyers*, 190–200.

20. The standard deviation in optometry and dentistry is very large (see note 8, above). It is equally large in medicine, though given the high means, this represents comparatively lesser risk. See American Dental Association, *1989 Survey;* and Ameri-

can Medical Association, *Socioeconomic Characteristics*. Data on optometry are un-published results of a survey conducted by the American Optometric Association.

21. The exact figures are unavailable, but a comprehensive search in the medical literature found not a single reference to practice failure during the ten-year period 1983–92. Greater anxiety apparently exists in dentistry and psychotherapy, judging from the number of articles about the perils of private practice.

22. Approximately 80 percent of Americans have some form of health insurance. See the discussions in Zachary Y. Dyckman, *A Study of Physician Fees* (Washington, D.C.: Government Printing Office, 1978); Starr, *Social Transformation of American Medicine*, book 2, chap. 2; and Victor R. Fuchs, *The Health Economy* (Cambridge, Mass.: Harvard University Press, 1986), 69–107.

23. Arthur Stinchcombe, "Bureaucratic and Craft Administration of Production," *Administrative Sciences Quarterly* 4 (1959): 168–87; Oliver Williamson, "Economics of Organization: The Transaction Cost Approach," *American Journal of Sociology* 87 (1981): 548–77; and Robert G. Eccles, "Bureaucratic and Craft Administration Revisited," *Administrative Sciences Quarterly* 26 (1981): 449–61.

24. Studies of the distribution of in-house counsel, for example, suggest that employed lawyers are common in industries like finance, insurance, real estate, transportation, communications, and public utilities—all of which "generat[e] large numbers of fairly routine legal transactions" (Abel, *American Lawyers*, 169).

25. See American Geological Institute, *North American Survey*, 35; The Hay Group, *Hay Access Compensation Report, EDP Compensation Comparison, 1989* (Washington, D.C.: The Hay Group, 1989); Society of American Foresters, 1991 salary data kindly provided by P. Gregory Smith.

26. Among electrical and electronics engineers, for example, with all other significant factors held constant, location in these industries meant, on average, an increased annual salary between $2,000 and $5,000 (Institute of Electrical and Electronics Engineers, *U.S. Membership Survey, 1987*, 65). Aerospace was not quite as well-paying as the others. Similarly, Ph.D. chemists received their highest earnings in the electronics, pharmaceutical, and petroleum industries (American Chemical Society, *Salaries 1990*, 70). Salaries for television reporters average 50 percent more than salaries for print reporters, and salaries for Hollywood actors and writers are significantly higher than for actors and writers anywhere else. U.S. Department of Labor, *Occupational Outlook Handbook 1990–91*, 171, 182; Christopher H. Sterling and Timothy R. Haight, *Mass Media. Aspen Institute Guide to Communications Industry Trends* (New York: Praeger, 1979), 252.

27. Sterling and Haight, *Mass Media*, 251; Michael Duckworth et al., "The Bottom Line from the Top Down," *Columbia Journalism Review* (July–August 1990): 30–32. Additional information kindly provided by Ira D. Perry, Executive Director of the Society of Professional Journalists.

28. John Kenneth Galbraith, *The New Industrial State* (New York: Houghton-Mifflin, 1967), chap. 11.

29. Institute of Electrical and Electronics Engineers, *U.S. Membership Survey, 1987*, tables 4.1, 4.2.

30. Heinz and Laumann, *Chicago Lawyers*, 149–52.

31. See A. Michael Spence, *Market Signalling* (Cambridge, Mass.: Harvard University Press, 1974); Lester Thurow, "Education and Economic Equality," *The Public Interest* 28 (1972): 66–81; and Collins, *Credential Society*, chaps. 2–3.

234 • *N O T E S   T O   C H A P T E R   4* •

32. This theme unites laissez-faire economists, "resource and power-oriented" neo-Weberian sociologists, and ecologically oriented systems theorists. For the laissez-faire view, see Milton Friedman, *Capitalism and Freedom* (Chicago: University of Chicago Press, 1962), chap. 6. For the neo-Weberian perspective, see Collins, *Credential Society,* chap. 6; and Frank Parkin, *Marxism and Class Theory: A Bourgeois Critique* (New York: Columbia University Press, 1979), chap. 4. For a systems approach, see Abbott, *System of Professions,* chaps. 2–4.

33. See also Marsha Freedman, *Labor Markets: Segments and Shelters* (Montclair, N.J.: Allanheld, Osmun, 1976).

34. For psychiatrists, see AMA, *Socioeconomic Characteristics of Medical Practice* (Chicago: AMA, 1986). For clinical social workers during the same period, see Deborah Haas-Wilson, "Employment Choices and Earnings of Social Workers: Comparing Private Practice and Salaried Employment," *Inquiry* 26 (1986): 182–90.

35. The effectiveness of psychotherapy is a vexed issue on which a large body of not completely conclusive evidence exists. The best overview is American Psychiatric Association, *Psychotherapy Research: Methodological and Efficacy Issues* (Washington, D.C.: APA, 1982). See also the discussion in Abbott, *System of Professions,* 308–14.

36. When a firm is working as an independent auditor for one set of activities and as an obvious ally of management for another set of activities, it becomes difficult to maintain the fiction that independence is the key to the "professional standing" of accounting firms. This has led to a good bit of controversy and many scholastic discussions about "professional ethics." See, e.g., Previts, *Scope of CPA Services;* Olson, *Accounting Professions' Years of Trial;* and Arnett and Danos, *CPA Firm Viability.*

37. Paul Root Wolpe, "The Maintenance of Professional Authority: Acupuncture and the American Physician," *Social Problems* 32 (1985): 409–24.

38. In business management, 55 percent of undergraduates were enrolled in accredited programs in the late 1980s; in architecture, 61 percent. It appears that no professional accrediting body exists for computer and information science specialities. See American Association of Collegiate Schools of Business, *AACSB Goals* (St. Louis: AACSB, 1990); American Institute of Architects, *Architecture Factbook,* 39–43.

39. Data for engineering were kindly provided by Diane Shinberg of the Engineering Manpower Commission.

40. About 40 percent of engineers were registered in one or more jurisdictions in 1990. This figure was calculated from data on registered engineers kindly supplied by Roger B. Stricklin, Executive Director of the National Council of Examiners for Engineering and Surveying. According to data provided by the Institute for the Certification of Computer Professionals and the U.S. Labor Department, only six percent of the people who call themselves computer specialists were certified in 1989. Institute for the Certification of Computer Professionals, "The Test of Professional Success," (Des Plaines, Ill.: ICCP, 1990).

41. The Institute for Certification of Computer Professionals, for example, offered discounts in the late 1980s to institutions providing twenty-five or more applicants for the examinations with discount levels increasing in relation to the number of applicants.

42. The premier study of professional efforts to secure task area jurisdictions is Abbott, *System of Professions.*

43. American Geological Institute, *North American Survey of Geoscientists,* 7.

44. See, e.g., Elaine Sorenson, "The Wage Effects of Occupational Sex Composi-

tion: A Review and New Findings," in M. Anne Hall and Mark R. Killingsworth, eds., *Comparable Worth: Analyses and Evidence* (Ithaca: ILR Press, 1989), 57–79.

45. See Claudia Goldin, "Discussion," in Hall and Killingsworth, *Comparable Worth*, 83–89.

46. Calculated from American Federation of Teachers, *AFT 1990 Salary Survey* (Washington, D.C.: AFT, 1990), table 2–3.

47. For drafters and electronics technicians, see U.S. Department of Labor, *National Survey of Professional, Administrative, Technical, and Clerical Pay, March 1990* (Washington, D.C.: Government Printing Office, 1990). For nurses, see American Nursing Association, *Nursing and the American Nursing Association* (Kansas City, Mo.: ANA, 1991).

48. For pharmacists, see "New Trends in Pharmacy Profession," *Pharmacy Update* (July 16, 1990): 4–5; and "The Salary Race," *Hospital Pharmacist Report* (March 1991): 4ff.

49. For planners, see Hecimovich, *Planners Salaries and Employment Trends*, 11. For teachers, see National Education Association, *Status of the American Public School Teacher, 1989–90.* (Washington, D.C.: NEA, 1990). Social workers's recent salaries estimated on the basis of data from 1986–87, the most recent NASW survey. See National Association of Social Workers, *Salaries in Social Work, 1987* (Washington, D.C.: NASW, 1987).

50. Special Libraries Association, *Triennial Survey, 1986* (Washington, D.C.: SLA, 1986); and Association of Research Libraries, *ARL Annual Salary Survey* (Washington, D.C.: ARL, 1987), 12, 25.

51. Such a prospect is discussed in Abbott, *System of Professions*, chap. 9. For a skeptical reading about this possibility, see William J. Goode, "The Librarian: From Occupation to Profession?," *The Library Quarterly* 31 (1961): 306–20.

52. M. W. Maack, "Women Librarians in France," *Journal of Library History* 18 (1983): 407–49.

53. Joan Huber and William Form, *Income and Ideology: An Analysis of the American Political Formula* (New York: Free Press, 1973).

54. See, e.g., Bourdieu, *Outline of a Theory of Practice*, 58–71.

55. This is a theme associated with the work of Joseph Schumpeter. See his *Capitalism, Socialism, and Democracy* (New York: Harper and Row, 1942), 145–55. See also chapter 8 of this volume.

56. See, e.g., Jonathan Rieder, *Carnarsie: The Jews and Italians of New York against Liberalism* (Cambridge, Mass.: Harvard University Press, 1985).

57. The theme originates in Tocqueville. It is central to the thesis of Louis Hartz, *The Liberal Tradition: An Interpretation of American Political Thought since the Revolution* (New York: Harcourt Brace, 1955). For a recent discussion, see Michele Lamont, *Money, Morals, and Manners: The Culture of the French and the American Upper-Middle Class* (Chicago: University of Chicago Press, 1993).

CHAPTER FIVE

1. See, e.g., Gouldner, *Future of Intellectuals*, 19, 28–30.

2. Thomas L. Haskell, "Professionalism versus Capitalism," in Thomas L. Haskell, ed., *The Authority of Experts* (Bloomington: Indiana University Press), 217–20.

3. This idea is associated particularly with the work of Harold Garfinkel. See his *Studies in Ethnomethodology* (Englewood Cliffs, N.J.: Prentice-Hall, 1967), chaps. 1,

2, and 8. For elaborations, see Anthony Giddens, *The Constitution of Society* (Berkeley: University of California Press, 1984), chap. 2; and Paul J. DiMaggio and Walter W. Powell, "Introduction," in Walter W. Powell and Paul J. DiMaggio, eds., *The New Institutionalism in Organizational Studies* (Chicago: University of Chicago Press, 1991), 1–40.

4. See, e.g., Collins, *Credential Society,* chaps. 2–3.

5. For evidence that the idea of public service is rather insignificant to most professionals themselves, see, e.g., Hall, "Professionalization and Bureaucratization," espec. 97; and Derber, Swartz, and Magrass, *Power in the Highest Degree,* chap. 8. Other sources on professionals in applied science include Lotte Bailyn, *Living with Technology* (Cambridge: Mass.: MIT Press, 1978); Zussman, *Mechanics of the Middle Class;* and Theresa Sullivan and Daniel Cornfield, "Downgrading Computer Workers: Evidence from Occupational and Industrial Redistribution," *Sociology of Work and Occupations* 6 (1979): 184–203.

6. In the General Social Survey, from over the years 1974–88, 73 percent of social and cultural specialists, 70 percent of all salaried professionals, 60 percent of high-income managers, and 55 percent of blue-collar workers felt that "too little" was being spent on education.

7. Christopher Jencks et al., *Who Gets Ahead?* (New York: Basic Books, 1981).

8. Herbert Hyman and Charles Wright, *The Enduring Effects of Education* (Chicago: University of Chicago Press, 1979), chap. 4.

9. The evidence here is less good, but see, e.g., "Research Note," *Journal of Post-Secondary Education* 36 (January 1961): 64.

10. Steven Brint, "Stirrings of an Oppositional Elite?: The Social Bases and Historical Trajectory of Upper White Collar Liberalism and Dissent in the United States, 1960–1980" (Ph.D. diss., Harvard University, 1982), chaps. 6–7.

11. Ironically, the less educated have at times been more supportive of the idea of academic meritocracy as a valid means of measuring talent. See Orville G. Brim, Jr., *American Beliefs and Attitudes about Intelligence* (New York: Russell Sage, 1969).

12. In all of the better-known sociological studies of status attainment, the path coefficients between parental education, test scores, and educational attainment are higher than path coefficients between other variables in the model. See, e.g., Christopher Jencks et al., *Inequality* (New York: Basic Books, 1972); Robert M. Hauser and David L. Featherman, *The Process of Stratification: Trends and Analyses* (New York: Academic Press, 1977); David L. Featherman and Robert M. Hauser, *Opportunity and Change* (New York: Academic Press, 1978); and Christopher Jencks et al., *Who Gets Ahead?*

13. Data from Harvard University indicate that the percentage of newly admitted students from business-owner and corporation-executive backgrounds declined significantly between 1956 and 1978, from almost 30 percent of the total freshman class to 22 percent. At the same time, the percentage of new students from scientific-professional upper-middle-class professional backgrounds increased significantly from 20 percent to over one-third. This growth rate was faster than the rate of growth in these occupations over the same period. Registrar of Harvard University, *Report of the President of Harvard College and Reports of the Departments, 1955–56 through 1978–79* (Cambridge, Mass.: Harvard University News Office, 1956–1980). In recent years, well over half the students admitted to Harvard College have had fathers with graduate or professional degrees. See David Karen, "'Achievement' and 'Ascription' in Admission to an Elite College," *Sociological Forum* 6 (1991): 349–80.

14. See Vincent Tinto, "College Origins and Patterns of Status Attainment through Schooling among Professional and Business-Managerial Occupations," unpublished manuscript, Syracuse University, Graduate School of Education, March 1979.

15. For evidence that these expectations are, in fact, widespread, see the data on the Boston area professionals study, reported in Derber, *Report to Responding Organizations*. See also Freidson, *Professional Powers,* chaps. 6–8.

16. My interpretation here is based on, but is not identical to, the work of Melvin K. Kohn and his associates: Melvin K. Kohn, *Class and Conformity* (Homewood, Ill.: Dorsey, 1969); Melvin K. Kohn and Carmi Schooler, "Class, Occupation and Orientation," *American Sociological Review* 24 (1969): 783–91; Melvin K. Kohn and Carrie Schoenbach, "Class, Stratification, and Psychological Functioning," in Melvin K. Kohn and Carmi Schooler, eds., *Work and Personality* (Norwood, N.J.: Ablex Publishing, 1983), 154–90.

17. See, e.g., Charles Weaver, "Job Preferences of White Collar and Blue Collar Workers," *Academy of Management Journal* 18 (1975): 167–75; and James A. Davis, "Achievement Variables and Class Cultures," *American Sociological Review* 47 (1982): 569–86.

18. See Table 5.1 below.

19. Works cited are John Gardner, *Excellence* (New York: Harper and Row, 1961); Arthur Okun, *Efficiency and Equality: The Big Trade Off* (Washington, D.C.: Brookings Institution, 1975); Irving Kristol, *Two Cheers for Capitalism* (New York: Basic Books, 1978); and Lester Thurow, *The Zero-Sum Society* (New York: Basic Books, 1980), 191–214.

20. The formulations come from the following works: Robert B. Reich, *The Next American Frontier* (New York: Times Books, 1983), 1–12; Robert N. Bellah et al., *Habits of the Heart* (Berkeley: University of California Press, 1985); Orlando Patterson, *Ethnic Chauvinism* (New York: Basic Books, 1981); and Michael Schudson, "Delectable Materialism," *The American Prospect* 5 (Spring 1991): 26–35. For another significant recent example, see Alan Wolfe, *Whose Keeper?: Social Science and Moral Obligation* (Berkeley: University of California Press, 1989).

21. Richard Madsen, one of the coauthors of *Habits of the Heart,* observes that most speaking invitations following the publication of the book came from the liberal nonprofit sector, and particularly from liberal church groups. Madsen, personal communication.

22. See, e.g., the interpretation in Daniel Bell, *The Cultural Contradictions of Capitalism* (New York: Basic Books, 1976), part 1.

23. See, e.g., the interpretation in Ehrenreich, *Fear of Falling*, chap. 2. See also Paul Blumberg, *Inequality in an Age of Decline* (New York: Oxford University Press, 1980); and Katherine S. Newman, *Falling from Grace. The Experience of Downward Mobility in the American Middle Class* (New York: Free Press, 1988).

24. To some extent, the same principle holds also within companies; those who are occupationally engaged with the public—marketing professionals, in particular,—tend to be somewhat more liberal than those who are engaged only with the business and material sides of the organization. See Useem, *Liberal Arts and the Corporation.* By contrast, a more conservative spirit flourishes in most manufacturing firms, and, especially, in smaller companies, which face the rigors of competition most directly. See Collins, *Credential Society,* pp. 33–43; and Allan Barton, "Determinants of Economic Attitudes in the American Business Elite," *American Journal of Sociology* 91 (1985): 54–87.

238

NOTESNOTES TO CHAPTER 5 •

25. See, e.g., Joel Aberbach and Bert A. Rockman, "Clashing Beliefs within the Executive Branch: The Nixon Administration Bureaucracy," *American Political Science Review* 70 (1974): 456–68.

26. See the discussion in Zussman, *Mechanics of the Middle Class,* 223–24.

27. These occupations are drawn primarily from the spheres of "civic regulation" and "culture and communications" discussed in chapter 3. The spheres are so small that they must be collapsed to allow for meaningful statistical analysis.

28. Bruce M. Russett, "Political Perspectives of U.S. Military and Business Elites," *Armed Forces and Society* 1 (1974): 79–108. See also Bailyn, *Living with Technology,* 22–31.

29. For doctors, see J. B. Erdmann et al., *AAMC Longitudinal Study of Medical School Graduates of 1960* (Washington, D.C.: National Center for Health Services Research, 1979).

30. The domestic spending index, like the other indices, was based on items from the General Social Survey that loaded together when submitted to factor analysis. The domestic spending index included items asking whether too much, too little, or just the right amount was being spent on solving the problems of blacks, the cities, and on welfare programs. It also included items concerned with the responsibility of the government to help blacks, and on spending on the military as a negative factor. The support-for-welfare index included items concerning the responsibility of government to help the poor and the sick, whether government should require that people help themselves, and about support for existing welfare programs.

31. The organization variable was based on division between business services, manufacturing and trade, nonprofit services, and government. Income was divided by year into constant proportional divisions by low, middle, and high categories, thereby adjusting for inflation. It was not possible to obtain precisely equivalent proportions across years. The high categories were the top third to two-fifths; the medium categories were the middle two-fifths; and the low categories were the bottom fifth to one-quarter. The "social and cultural" professions included artists, writers, reporters, editors, professors, nonacademic social scientists, psychotherapists, government lawyers, government planners, and policy analysts. "Human service" professions included primary and secondary school teachers, librarians and counselors, social workers, clergy and religious workers, nurses, and health therapists. The "applied technical" professions included an amalgam of business service and applied science professions: nonuniversity scientists and engineers, computer and operations analysts, accountants, consultants, doctors, lawyers, and architects. Where ethos and function diverge, I made assignments on the basis of ethos rather than function. Doctors, for example, combine a scientific ethos with human services work, while librarians combine a human services ethos with cultural work.

32. The age variable divided people 35 years old or younger, 36–55, and 56 or older into young, middle-aged, and old categories. The education variable concentrated on degrees attained: less than B.A., B.A., and more than B.A. The religion variable separated Protestants, Catholics, Jews, and those who professed no religion. The religiosity variable was based on church and synagogue attendance. The variable separated those who attended weekly or more, nearly weekly, monthly, yearly, and never. The urbanism variable separated those living in the twelve largest SMSAs from those living in smaller cities, and the urban dwellers from those who lived in suburbs, towns, and rural areas. Race was divided into black, white, and other.

33. More detailed analyses are available on request.

34. A number of interaction terms were introduced into the analyses to test theoretical hunches, but none provided more than very marginal improvements in explanation.

35. Noyelle and Dutka, *International Trade*, 10.

36. Abel, *American Lawyers*, 181, 203–4; and Nathan Glazer, "Lawyers and the New Class," in B. Bruce-Briggs, ed., *The New Class?*, 89–100.

37. U.S. Department of Commerce, *Statistical Abstract of the United States, 1991* (Washington, D.C.: Government Printing Office, 1991), 591. Humanities are estimated as 1 percent or less of total federal research and development funds. The figures for the 1980s, by my estimate, run between 6.5 and 8 percent of federal funds going to social science and humanities research combined.

38. The various characterizations of "expressive values" mix together elements that had but a brief cultural moment (the reduced emphasis on materialism of the 1960s)— see, e.g., Daniel Yankelovich, *The New Morality* (New York: McGraw-Hill, 1974)— with other elements whose impact has been felt well beyond the spheres we associate with liberal professionals. These other elements include increasing interest in "self-fulfillment" as a life goal and changing sexual mores. See Garth D. Taylor and Tom W. Smith, "Public Opinion regarding Various Forms of Sexual Behavior," GSS Technical Report No. 10 (Chicago: National Opinion Research Center, 1978); and Daniel Yankelovich, *The New Rules* (New York: Basic Books, 1981), espec. 59–61. Some of the interest in "expressive values" as opposed to old-fashioned "materialism" seems to have diminished with the harder economic circumstances of the 1970s. See Paul Blumberg, *Inequality in an Age of Decline*. For the views of college students over a twenty-year period, see Astin et al., *American Freshman*.

39. Large sections of the liberal professional world—especially teachers and scholars, government and nonprofit sector bureaucrats—are thoroughly conventional in their consumption style, while large parts of the business community in the larger metropolitan areas are more free-wheeling, trend-conscious, youthful, and self-consciously unconventional. This is why the rule in advertising is that younger, urban, and higher-income people, whatever their occupational milieus, tend to consume products with a more youthful, convention-flaunting image. See William D. Wells, "Psychographics: A Critical Review," *Journal of Marketing Research* 12 (1975): 196–213; and Michael J. Weiss, *The Clustering of America* (New York: Harper and Row, 1988), 38–43, 287–91. For similar findings from France, see Pierre Bourdieu, *Distinction* (Cambridge, Mass.: Harvard University Press, 1984).

40. High education, relative youth, and work in cultural occupations are correlated both with arts participation and with political liberalism. At the same time, other correlates of arts participation, such as high income and gender, are not strongly correlated with political liberalism. See, e.g., Paul J. DiMaggio, Michael Useem, and Paula Brown, *Audience Studies of the Performing Arts and Museums* (Washington, D.C.: National Endowment for the Arts, 1978); Michael Hughes and Richard A. Peterson, "Isolating Cultural Choice Patterns in the U.S. Population," *American Behavioral Scientists* 26 (1983): 459–78; and John P. Robinson et al., *Public Participation in the Arts: Final Report* (Washington, D.C.: National Endowment for the Humanities, 1985). Data from the General Social Survey indicates that the 9 percent of Americans who say they are "members of literary, artistic, or discussion groups" are no more likely than other Americans to be Democrats, though they are slightly more likely than other Americans to say that their political views are "liberal" or "very liberal."

41. See, e.g., James A. Davis, *Undergraduate Career Decisions: Correlates of Occupational Choice* (Chicago: Aldine, 1965); James H. Barry, "The Social and Political Values of Knowledge-Based Elites in American Society" (Ph.D. diss., State University of New York, Buffalo, 1979); Brint, "Stirrings of an Oppositional Elite?," chap. 6; and Brint, "The Occupational Class Identifications of Professionals."

42. Rothman and Litcher, "What Are Moviemakers Made Of?," 16, 18. For a similar view, see Benjamin Stein, *The View from Sunset Boulevard* (New York: Basic Books, 1979).

43. See Charles Perrow, *Complex Organizations,* 3d ed. (New York: Random House, 1986); Erik Barnouw, *The Sponsor: Notes on a Modern Potentate* (New York: Oxford University Press, 1978); Richard A. Peterson and David G. Berger, "Cycles in Symbol Production: The Case of Popular Music," *American Sociological Review* 40 (1975): 158–73; Paul Hirsch, "Processing Fads and Fashions: An Organizational Set Analysis of Cultural Industry Systems," *American Journal of Sociology* 77 (1972): 639–59; and Todd Gitlin, *Inside Prime-Time* (New York: Pantheon Books, 1983).

44. The entertainment industry does not provide an exclusively bland and unproblematic picture of American society. But the industry does show a decided preference for "domesticating opposition, absorbing it into forms compatible with the core ideological structure." See Todd Gitlin, "Prime-Time Ideology: The Hegemonic Process in Television Entertainment," *Social Problems* 26 (1979): 251–66.

45. Michael Useem and S. M. Miller, "Privilege and Domination: The Role of the Upper Class in American Higher Education," *Social Science Information* 14 (1975): 115–45; Jerome Karabel and A. H. Halsey, *Power and Ideology in Education* (New York: Oxford University Press, 1978); and Collins, *Credential Society.*

46. The civil liberties index, like all indices, was composed of items that loaded together in factor analyses of the General Social Survey. The civil liberties index included questions on whether the following unpopular groups should be able to have their books in libraries and to have speakers address public gatherings: racists, atheists, communists, advocates of military rule, and homosexuals. The feminism index included questions on whether women should work only in the home, whether family should greatly outweigh other interests for women, whether government had a responsibility to improve the conditions for women, whether women should be more involved in the political arena, whether respondents would vote for a qualified woman candidate for president running as their party's nominee, whether a working woman hurts her children, and whether a woman should put her husband's career first. The racial attitudes index included questions about whether respondents approved of busing to promote integration, whether they felt the civil rights movement was "pushing too fast," whether they would work to integrate a social club to which they belonged, whether they favored open housing laws, whether differences between the races were due primarily to discrimination or other factors, and whether differences between the races were due primarily to education or other factors. The moral attitudes index was composed of items measuring respondents' attitudes toward premarital and extramarital sex, homosexuality, laws regarding pornography, marijuana, divorce, and abortion. The defense index consisted of items concerning respondents' relative level of confidence in the military, their views on appropriate levels of defense spending, and their evaluation of the communist system. The crime index included items measuring respondents' views on capital punishment and on whether the courts were too lenient with criminals.

47. On the relation of compositional change to political change, see the discussion in chapter 6.

48. On this point, cf. Hansfried Kellner and Peter L. Berger, "Lifestyle Engineering," in Hansfried Kellner and Frank W. Heuberger, eds., *Hidden Technocrats: The New Class and New Capitalism* (New Brunswick, N.J.: Transaction Books, 1992), 1–22.

49. Clem Brooks and Jeff Manza, "The American Middle Class and the Democratic Class Struggle, 1952–1992" (Unpublished ms., Department of Sociology, University of California, Berkeley, 1993).

CHAPTER SIX

1. For the abolitionists, see David Brion Davis, *Antebellum Reform* (New York: Harper and Row, 1967). For the Progressive Era, see Richard Hofstadter, *The Age of Reform: From Bryan to FDR* (New York: Knopf, 1955), chap. 6; Robert H. Wiebe, *The Search for Order, 1877–1920* (New York: Hill and Wang, 1967), chap. 5; and John Ehrenreich and Barbara Ehrenreich, "The Professional-Managerial Class," in Pat Walker, ed., *Between Labor and Capital* (Boston: South End Press, 1979), 5–49. For the New Deal, see Lewis Corey, *The Crisis of the Middle Class* (New York: Covici Frede, 1935); Harold Lasswell, *Politics: Who Gets What, When, How* (New Haven: Whittlesey House, 1936); and James Burnham, *The Managerial Revolution* (New York: John Day, 1941). For the New Frontier-Great Society, see Kristol, "About Equality" Gouldner, *Future of Intellectuals*; Cyril Leavitt, *Children of Privilege* (Toronto: University of Toronto Press, 1984); and Berger, *The Capitalist Revolution*.

2. Godfrey Hodgson, *America in Our Time* (Garden City, N.Y.: Doubleday, 1979), chap. 20.

3. See also Ehrenreich and Ehrenreich, "The Professional-Managerial Class"; Lipset, *Political Man*, 503–23; and Bill Martin and Ivan Szelenyi, "Beyond Cultural Capital: A Theory of Symbolic Domination." In Ron Eyerman et al., *Universities, Intellectuals, and the State* (Berkeley: University of California Press, 1987), 16–49.

4. Lipset, *Political Man*, 502–22. See also William Schneider, "Half a Realignment," *The New Republic*, December 3, 1984, 19–22.

5. See, e.g., Ladd, "Pursuing the New Class"; Lipset, *Political Man*, 503–23; Seymour Martin Lipset and William Schneider, *The Confidence Gap: Business, Labor and Government in the Public Mind* (New York: Free Press, 1983), 311–16; and Richard F. Hamilton and James Wright, *State of the Masses* (New York: Aldine, 1986), 412–20.

6. Ladd, "Pursuing the New Class."

7. For a comprehensive statistical analysis of trend lines in American public opinion over a forty-year period, see Tom W. Smith, "Liberal and Conservative Trends in the United States since World War II," *Public Opinion Quarterly* 54 (1990): 479–508.

8. A good compendium can be found in Philip E. Converse et al., *American Social Attitudes Data Sourcebook, 1947–1978* (Cambridge, Mass.: Harvard University Press, 1980).

9. Norman H. Nie, Sidney Verba, and John R. Petrocik, *The Changing American Voter* (Cambridge, Mass.: Harvard University Press, 1979), 234–42.

10. Ibid., 142–44; and John A. Fleishman, "Types of Political Attitude Structure: Results of a Cluster Analysis," *Public Opinion Quarterly* 50 (1986): 37–86.

11. See Steven Brint, "'New-Class' and Cumulative Trend Explanations of the Liberal Political Attitudes of Professionals," *American Journal of Sociology* 91 (1984): 68–69.

12. These data on "most important problems" were calculated from the American

National Election surveys. The same trends are found in the Gallup Poll series asking, "What is the most important problem facing the country today?" See figure 4.1 in Douglas A. Hibbs, Jr., *The American Political Economy* (Cambridge, Mass.: Harvard University Press, 1987), 128.

13. Philip E. Converse et al., "Continuity and Change in American Politics: Parties and Issues in the 1968 Election," *American Political Science Review* 63 (1969): 1083–1105.

14. John P. Robinson, "Public Reaction to Political Protest: Chicago 1968," *Public Opinion Quarterly* 34 (1970): 1–9.

15. Analyses of American attitudes about the war during this period can be found in Philip E. Converse and Howard Schuman, "Silent Majorities and the Vietnam War," *Scientific American* 222 (June 1970): 17–25; and Howard Schuman, "Two Sources of Antiwar Sentiment in America," *American Journal of Sociology* (1972): 513–36. See also Converse et al., "Continuity and Change in American Politics."

16. Data from the National Election series suggest that no more than 25–30 percent of voting-age Americans in the late 1960s and early 1970s felt even moderately warm toward the descriptive label "liberals."

17. These figures were compiled and plotted by Susan Kelley.

18. Seymour Martin Lipset and Everett Carll Ladd, Jr., "College Generations from the 1930s to the 1960s," *The Public Interest* 25 (1971): 99–113; M. Kent Jennings and Richard G. Neimi, "Continuity and Change in Political Orientations: A Longitudinal Study of Two Generations," *American Political Science Review* 69 (1975): 1316–35; and M. Kent Jennings and Richard G. Niemi, *Generations and Politics: A Panel Study of Young Adults and Their Parents* (Princeton, N.J.: Princeton University Press, 1981).

19. Lipset and Ladd, "College Generations"; M. Kent Jennings, "Residues of a Movement," *American Political Science Review* 81 (1987): 367–82; and Howard Schuman and Jacqueline Scott, "Generations and Collective Memories," *American Sociological Review* 54 (1989): 359–81.

20. Lipset and Ladd, "College Generations."

21. American Council on Education, *The American Freshman: National Norms for 1970* (Washington, D.C.: ACE, 1970).

22. Student attitudes were often more liberal than their self-professed ideologies. By 1973, between 60 to 75 percent of college students could be considered very liberal on sexual mores, depending on the specific issue discussed (Yankelovich, *The New Morality*, 90–94). Over 90 percent of young people interviewed by pollster Daniel Yankelovich in both 1969 and 1973 felt that businesses were "too concerned with profits and not enough with public responsibility" (122).

23. Derber, Schwartz, and Magrass, *Power in the Highest Degree*, chap. 16.

24. See, e.g., Richard Flacks, *Youth and Social Change,* (Chicago: Markham, 1971).

25. Converse, *American Social Attitudes Sourcebook*, 88, 392–93.

26. See Brint, "'New-Class' and Cumulative Trend Explanations"; and Macy, "New-Class Dissent among Social-Cultural Specialists."

27. Orlando Rodriguez, "Occupational Shifts and Educational Upgrading in the American Labor Force 1950–1970," *Sociology of Education* 51 (1978): 59.

28. For an analysis, see B. Bruce-Briggs, "Conclusion," in Bruce-Briggs, *New Class?*, 220–22.

29. Cf. Peter Steinfels, *The Neo-Conservatives* (New York: Simon and Schuster, 1979), 57; Everett Carll Ladd, Jr., and Seymour Martin Lipset, "Anatomy of a De-

cade," *Public Opinion* 3 (December–January 1980): 2–9; Daniel Patrick Moynihan, "Equalizing Education: In Whose Interest?: *The Public Interest* 29 (1972): 69–84; Robert Bartley, "Business and the New Class," in B. Bruce-Briggs, *New Class?*, 57–66; and Ladd, "Pursuing the New Class."

30. An example to help illustrate: let us say that social and cultural professionals grow by one million during a period of reform—from one million to two million. Let us say further that the rate of change among social and cultural specialists is a tripling of liberal sentiment during periods of reform, whereas the rate of change generally is a doubling of liberal sentiment. If at the beginning of the reform period 20 percent of social and cultural specialists are liberal, the total number of liberals in the category at the beginning of the period will be 200,000. By the end of the reform period, the total number of liberals will be 1.2 million (or 60 percent of two million people). This is a much larger pressure group than the original 200,000. It is also substantially larger than 800,000, the number that would occur if the conversion rate among social and cultural professionals were the same as that of the population at large.

31. Inflation increased from an annual rate of 1.2 percent in 1965 to 3.4 percent in 1969, and between 1970 and 1975 it rose to a mean of 6.6 percent per year. These figures are drawn from Jerome Himmelstein, *To the Right* (Berkeley: University of California Press), chap. 4. For other useful analyses of the political economy during the 1960s and 1970s, see Douglas A. Hibbs, Jr., *American Political Economy;* Douglas A. Hibbs, Jr., "On the Demand for Economic Outcomes: Macro-Economic Performance and Mass Political Support in the United States, Great Britain, and Germany," *Journal of Politics* 44 (1982): 426–63; Lipset and Schneider, *Confidence Gap;* Fred Block, *The Origins of International Monetary Disorder* (Berkeley: University of California Press, 1977); Robert Keohane, "The World Political Economy and the Crisis of Embedded Liberalism," in John H. Goldthorpe, ed., *Order and Conflict in Contemporary Capitalism* (New York: Oxford University Press, 1984); and David R. Cameron, "On the Limits of the Public Economy," *Annals of the American Academy of Political and Social Science* 459 (1982): 46–62.

32. For a useful overview, see Hibbs, *American Political Economy,* 72–74.

33. Cited in Lipset and Schneider, *Confidence Gap,* 181–82.

34. Ibid., 311–16.

35. The best sources on business attitudes during this period are Frederick P. Randall and Michael G. Duerr, *Private Enterprise Looks at Its Image* (New York: The Conference Board, 1974); and Leonard Silk and David Vogel, *Ethics and Politics: The Crisis of Confidence in American Business* (New York: Simon and Schuster, 1976), espec. 58, for a summary of the mood of American corporate leaders.

36. Himmelstein, *To the Right,* 135–36.

37. Ibid., 311–29.

38. Silk and Vogel, *Ethics and Politics,* 25.

39. See Arthur Miller, Jeffrey Brudney, and Peter Joftis, "Presidential Crises and Political Support: The Impact of Watergate on Attitudes toward Institutions" (Paper presented at the annual meeting of the Midwest Political Science Association, Chicago, 1975).

40. Hodgson, *America in Our Time,* chap. 21; David Vogel, "The Public Interest Movement and the American Reform Tradition"; Vogel, *Fluctuating Fortunes,* chap. 5; and Michael S. Greve and James Keller, "Funding the Left: The Sources of Support for 'Public Interest' Law Firms," Working Paper No. 9, Washington Legal Foundation, January 1987.

41. David Vogel, "How Business Responds to Opposition: Corporate Political

Strategies during the 1970s" (Paper presented at the annual meeting of the American Political Science Association, Washington, D.C., 1979); and Vogel, *Fluctuating Fortunes,* chap. 5.

42. For the movements of the period, see Hodgson, *America in Our Time;* and Vogel, *Fluctuating Fortunes.* For the Port Huron statement, see Charles Perrow, ed., *The Radical Attack on Business* (New York: Harcourt Brace Jovanovich, 1972), 14. King's remark is from *The Words of Martin Luther King* (New York: New Market Press, 1983), 19.

43. For evidence of increasing support for liberalism on social issues in the 1970s, see John P. Robinson and John A. Fleishman, "Ideological Trends in American Public Opinion," *Annuals of American Academy of Political and Social Science* 472 (1984): 55.

44. John L. Goodman, Jr., *Public Opinion during the Reagan Administration* (Washington, D.C.: Urban Institute, 1983); David Gergen, "Following the Leaders: How Ronald Reagan and Margaret Thatcher Have Changed Public Opinion," *Public Opinion* 8 (June–July 1985), 56; Hibbs, *American Political Economy,* 200–202; William Schneider, "The Divided Electorate," *National Journal,* October 29, 1983, 2203; and William Schneider, "The Voters' Mood in 1986," *National Journal,* December 7, 1985, 2759.

45. Lipset and Schneider, *Confidence Gap,* rev. ed., chap. 13; and William Schneider, "The Political Legacy of the Reagan Years," in Sidney Blumenthal and Thomas Byrne Edsall, eds., *The Reagan Legacy* (New York: Pantheon Books, 1988).

46. For conservative trends on issues involving sexual morality, see Robinson and Fleishman, "Ideological Trends," 55.

47. James A. Davis, "Conservative Weather in a Liberalizing Climate. Change in Selected NORC General Social Survey Items, 1972–1978," *Social Forces* 58 (1980): 1129–56.

48. John C. Pierce, Kathleen M. Beatty, and Paul R. Hagner, *The Dynamics of American Public Opinion* (Glenview, Ill.: Scott, Foresman, 1982), 213. For other data on tax sentiment during the period, see Lipset and Schneider, *Confidence Gap,* 342–46; and Robert Kuttner, *Revolt of the Haves* (New York: Simon and Schuster, 1980), 24–25.

49. On the California tax revolt, see Kuttner, *Revolt of the Haves;* and David O. Sears and Jack Citrin, *Tax Revolt: Something for Nothing in California* (Cambridge, Mass.: Harvard University Press, 1982).

50. Brint, " 'New-Class' and Cumulative Trend Explanations," 68–69.

51. Lipset and Schneider, *Confidence Gap,* 65, 155.

52. See, e.g., Hibbs, *American Political Economy,* chap. 5.

53. The best-known Democratic statement along these lines is Ben Wattenberg's *The Real Majority* (New York: G. P. Putnam, 1974). For an influential Republican statement, see Phillips, *Emerging Republican Majority.*

54. The mobilization of corporate business during the 1970s is discussed in the following works: Himmelstein, *To the Right,* chap. 4; Thomas Ferguson and Joel Rogers, *Right Turn;* (New York: Hill and Wang, 1986) Edsall, *New Politics of Inequality;* Sidney Blumethal, *The Rise of the Counter-Establishment* (New York: Times Books, 1986); Frances Fox Piven and Richard Cloward, *The New Class War* (New York: Pantheon, 1982); Dan Clawson, Alan Neustadl, and James Bearden, "The Logic of Business Unity: Corporate Contributions to the 1980 Congressional Elections," *American Sociological Review* 51 (1986): 797–811; and Joseph G. Peschek, *Policy Planning Organizations* (Philadelphia: Temple University Press, 1987).

55. In some urban centers, such as New York City, white professionals remained slightly less conservative than other whites, partly because of the intense racial politics affecting other whites and partly because their relative security allowed them to express a degree of reformist sentiment. See Brint, "Upper Professionals," 167–72.

56. "Opinion Roundup," *Public Opinion* (November–December 1988), 34.

57. Ibid.

58. James M. Fendrich, "Keeping the Faith or Pursuing the Good Life: A Study of the Consequences of Participation in the Civil Rights Movement," *American Sociological Review* 42 (1977): 144–57.

59. See Steven Brint and Susan Kelley, "The Social Bases of Political Beliefs in the United States: Interest, Culture, and Normative Pressures in Comparative-Historical Context," *Research in Political Sociology* 6 (1993): 277–317; and Frederick D. Weil, "The Variable Effects of Education on Liberal Attitudes: A Comparative-Historical Analysis of Anti-Semitism Using Public Opinion Survey Data," *American Sociological Review* 50 (1985): 458–74.

60. Noyelle and Dutka, *International Trade*, 10.

61. Kuttner, *Revolt of the Haves*, 28.

62. *Economic Report of the President, January 1987* (Washington, D.C.: Government Printing Office), 69–70; and Hibbs, *American Political Economy*, 287, 307–22.

63. David Stockman, *The Triumph of Politics: Why the Reagan Revolution Failed* (New York: Harper and Row, 1986); See also Michael S. Greve, "Why Defunding the Left Failed," *Public Interest* 69 (Fall 1987): 91–106.

64. Hibbs, *American Political Economy*, 284–87. The 1982 tax act repealed about half of the business tax reductions from the original 1981 Economic Recovery and Taxation Act.

65. For the largest number of professional workers, those in $20,000 to $50,000 range, the improvements were more modest—between 4 and a little over 5 percent. John Karl Scholz, "Individual Income Tax Provisions of the 1982 Tax Act," in Joseph Pechman, ed., *Setting National Priorities: The 1983 Budget* (Washington, D.C.: Brookings, 1982), 252, 255. The data is discussed in Hibbs, *American Political Economy*, 310–11.

66. Benjamin Ginsberg and Martin Shefter, "A Critical Realignment?: The New Politics, the Reconstituted Right, and the 1984 Election," in Michael Nelson, ed., *The Elections of 1984* (Washington, D.C.: Congressional Quarterly Press, 1985), 1–25. See also Schneider, "The Political Legacy of the Reagan Years."

67. While differences between professionals and business people are consistent, they are by no means as large as the 30 to 40 percent gaps that can be found between blue-collar workers and both professionals and managers on issues involving race, gender, and civil liberties.

68. Cf. Lamont, "Cultural Capital."

69. For one such case, see Michele Renee Salzman, "How the West Was Won: The Christianization of the Roman Aristocracy in the West in the Years after Constantine," *Collection Latomus. Studies in Latin Literature and Roman History*, 217 (1992): 451–79.

70. Some examples: The largest growth in geoscience comes from employment in petroleum engineering. See American Geological Institute, *Geoscience Employment and Hiring Survey* (Alexandria, Va.: AGI, 1990). In electrical and electronics engineering, the largest growth comes from the computer area. Institute of Electronics Engineers, *U.S. Membership Survey* (1991) (Washington, D.C.: IEEE-USA, 1991). In biology, the largest growth has come from biotechnology and genetic engineering. Even in

sociology, long-considered a discipline critical of "power elites," one of the major sites of growth has been in organization studies, often connected to business schools. Randall Collins, "Future Organizational Trends of the ASA," *Footnotes* (Washington, D.C.: American Sociological Association, 1989).

71. See, e.g., William J. Broad, "Ridden with Debt, U.S. Companies Cut Funds for Research," *New York Times,* June 30, 1992, C1.

72. Leon M. Lederman, *Science: The End of a Frontier?* (Washington, D.C.: American Association for the Advancement of Science, 1990).

73. Ibid.

74. American Psychological Association, Committee on Employment and Human Resources, "The Changing Face of American Psychology" *American Psychologist* 41 (1986): 1326.

75. Diana Crane, *The Transformation of the Avant-Garde* (Chicago: University of Chicago Press, 1987), chaps. 3, 4, 8. See also Janet Malcolm, "Profile: Ingrid Sischy (I)," *New Yorker,* October 20, 1986, 49–52ff.; Janet Malcolm, "Profile: Ingrid Sischy (II)," *New Yorker,* October 27, 1986, 47–48ff.; and Robert Hughes, *Nothing if Not Critical: Selected Essays on Art and Artists* (New York: Knopf, 1990).

76. Crane, *The Transformation of the Avant-Garde,* 141.

77. Similar movements have occurred, in a weaker way, in some other literary and artistic fields. For example, in architecture, aggressively market-oriented firms overshadow in earnings and often in prominence the more design-conscious firms. See Larson, Leon, and Bolick, "The Professional Supply of Design."

78. Van Gordon Sauter, quoted in David Shaw, "Trust in Media on Decline," *Los Angeles Times,* March 31, 1993, A17.

79. William Kovach, quoted in Shaw, ibid.

80. Ibid., A16.

CHAPTER SEVEN

1. For Saint-Simon's advocacy of technocracy, see F. M. H. Markham, *Henri Comte de Saint-Simon: Selected Writings* (Oxford: Oxford University Press, 1952). For the doctrinal statement of the American technocratic movement, see Howard Scott, *Introduction to Technocracy* (Vancouver: Technocracy, Inc., 1936); and William E. Akin, *Technocracy and the American Dream: The Technocrat Movement, 1900–1941* (Berkeley: University of California Press, 1977). For some recent American statements, see Daniel Patrick Moynihan, "The Professionalization of Reform," *The Public Interest* 1 (1965): 6–16; Zbigniew Brzezinski, *Between Two Ages: America's Role in the Technetronic Era* (New York: Viking Press, 1970); and Bell, *Coming of Post-Industrial Society.* For a useful survey of technocratic thought, see Robert D. Putnam, "Elite Transformation in Advanced Industrial Societies: An Empirical Assessment of the Theory of Technocracy," *Comparative Political Studies* 10 (1977): 383–412.

2. Michael J. Malbin, *Unelected Representatives: Congressional Staff and the Future of Representative Government* (New York: Basic Books, 1980), 10.

3. Ibid., chap. 2. The precise rate of change is impossible to determine since good breakdowns of staff categories do not exist in the available historical statistics.

4. The figures are adapted and extrapolated from Malbin, ibid.; Steven Kelman, *Making Public Policy* (New York: Basic Books, 1987), 55; and Stephen Hess, *Organizing the Presidency* (Washington, D.C.: Brookings Institution, 1988), 225.

5. Kelman, *Making Public Policy,* 81; Hess, *Organizing the Presidency,* 225.

6. Kelman, *Making Public Policy,* 81. For earlier evidence, see Kenneth Prewitt and William McAllister, "Changes in the American Executive Elite, 1930–1970," in Hans Eulau and M. M. Czudnowski, eds., *Elite Recruitment in Democratic Politics* (Beverly Hill, Calif.: Sage Publications, 1976), 105–32.

7. Kelman, *Making Public Policy.*

8. Bell, *Coming of Post-Industrial Society,* 29.

9. Ibid., 32–35. For a study of one of the most important of the predominantly government-funded "think tanks," see Bruce L. R. Smith, *The RAND Corporation: Case Study of a Non-Profit Advisory Corporation* (Cambridge, Mass.: Harvard University Press, 1961).

10. Henry Kissinger, *American Foreign Policy* (New York: W. W. Norton, 1969), 20–21.

11. Malbin, *Unelected Representatives,* 247.

12. Hedrick Smith, *The Power Game* (New York: Random House, 1988), 293.

13. Ibid., 317.

14. Theda Skocpol, "Bringing the State Back In," in Peter B. Evans, Dietrich Rueschemeyer, and Theda Skocpol, eds., *Bringing the State Back In* (Cambridge: Cambridge University Press, 1985), 3–43, espec. 23–24. See also Robert H. Salisbury, "Why No Corporatism in the United States?," in Philippe Schmitter and Gerhard Lembruch, *Patterns of Corporatist Intermediation* (Beverly Hills, Calif.: Sage Publications, 1979), 213–30; Ronald Aberbach, Robert D. Putnam, and Bert A. Rockman, *Bureaucrats and Politicians in Western Democracies* (Cambridge, Mass.: Harvard University Press, 1981) 94–100, 228–29; and Graham K. Wilson, "Why Is There No Corporatism in the United States?," in Gerhard Lembruch and Philippe Schmitter, *Patterns of Corporatist Policy-Making* (Beverly Hills, Calif.: Sage Publications, 1982), 219–36.

15. David A. Rhode and Kenneth A. Shepsle, "Democratic Committee Assignments in the House of Representatives: Strategic Aspects of a Social Choice Process," *American Political Science Review* 67 (1973): 889–905; Richard F. Fenno, Jr., "The Internal Distribution of Influence: The House," in David B. Truman, ed., *The Congress and America's Future,* 2d ed. (Englewood Cliffs, N.J.: Prentice-Hall, 1973). For an overview of the stratification and segmentation structure in Congress, see Roger H. Davidson and Walter J. Oleszek, *Congress and Its Members* (Washington, D.C.: Congressional Quarterly Press, 1981); and Randall B. Ripley, *Congress: Process and Policy,* 3d ed. (New York: W. W. Norton, 1983).

16. Kelman, *Making Public Policy,* 63.

17. Edward O. Laumann and David Knoke, *The Organizational State* (Madison: University of Wisconsin Press, 1987), 375–80.

18. Ibid., 375.

19. Ibid., 393–97.

20. Ibid., 393–99.

21. Wilson's framework is discussed in several of his works, including the following: *Political Organizations* (New York: Basic Books, 1973), chap. 15; "The Politics of Regulation," in James Q. Wilson, ed., *The Politics of Regulation* (New York: Basic Books, 1980); and *American Government: Institutions and Policies,* 2d ed. (Lexington, Mass.: D. C. Heath, 1983), chap. 14. See also the critical discussion in Schlozman and Tierney, *Organized Interests,* 82–85.

22. For a particularly well-reported example of this process, see Eric Redman, *The Dance of Legislation* (New York: Simon and Schuster, 1973). It is also true that issues

have a way of never being settled. Once a battle is lost, groups pressing a particular issue will look opportunistically for a vehicle through which they can reinsert the issue into the policy-making agenda. See, for example, John Kingdon, *Agendas, Alternatives, and Public Policies* (Boston: Little, Brown, 1984).

23. See Aberbach, Putnam, and Rockman, *Bureaucrats and Politicians*, 228–29; Salisbury, "Why No Corporatism in America?"; and Wilson, "Why Is There No Corporatism in the United States?"

24. Aberbach, Putnam, and Rockman, *Bureaucrats and Politicians*, 229.

25. Ibid., 99–100.

26. Ibid., 228.

27. The exceptionalism of the American pattern is confirmed by the self-characterizations of bureaucrats and politicians in several of the liberal democracies. See ibid., 94–100, particularly table 4–3.

28. Laumann and Knoke, *Organizational State*, 382.

29. The results of the study are reported in somewhat greater detail in Steven Brint, "Rethinking the Policy Influence of Experts: From General Characterizations to Analysis of Variation," *Sociological Forum* 5 (1990): 361–85.

30. John F. Padgett, "Hierarchy and Ecological Control in Federal Budgetary Decision-Making," *American Journal of Sociology* 87 (1981): 75–129.

31. See, in particular, Dorothy Nelkin, "The Political Impact of Technical Expertise," *Social Studies of Science* 5 (1975): 35–54; Sanford A. Lakoff, "Scientists, Technologists, and Political Power," in Ina Spiegel-Rosing and Derek de Solla Price, eds., *Science, Technology and Society* (Beverly Hills, Calif.: Sage Publications, 1977), 355–91; Dorothy Nelkin, "Technology and Public Policy," in Spiegel-Rosing and de Solla Price, *Science, Technology and Society*, 392–442; Dorothy Nelkin, *The Creation Controversy: Science or Scripture?* (New York: W. W. Norton, 1982); Magali Sarfatti Larson, "The Production of Expertise and the Constitution of Expert Power," in Haskell, *Authority of Experts*, 28–80; Dorothy Nelkin, ed., *Controversy: The Politics of Technical Decisions* (Beverly Hills, Calif.: Sage Publications, 1984); and Freidson, *Professional Powers*, chap. 9.

32. Freidson, *Professional Powers*, 142.

33. Sanford A. Lakoff, ed., *Knowledge and Power: Essays on Science and Government* (New York: Free Press, 1966); Daniel Patrick Moynihan, *The Politics of a Guaranteed Income* (New York: Random House, 1973); Lakoff, "Scientists, Technologists, and Political Power"; Nelkin, *Controversy*; Freidson, *Professional Powers*, chap. 9. The same is true when expert opinion is divided. See Allan Mazur, "Disputes between Experts," *Minerva* 11 (1973): 243–62.

34. Thomas E. Cronin and Norman C. Thomas, "Federal Advisory Processes: Advice and Discontent," *Science* 171 (1971): 771–79; and Joel Primack and Frank von Hippel, *Advice and Dissent: Scientists in the Political Arena* (New York: Basic Books, 1974).

35. Lakoff, "Scientists, Technologists, and Political Power"; Nelkin, "Technology and Public Policy"; and Larson, "The Production of Expertise."

36. Lakoff, "Scientists, Technologists, and Political Power."

37. Daniel Kevles, "Scientists, the Military, and the Control of Post-War Defense Research: The Case of the Research Board for National Security, 1944–46," *Technology and Culture* 16 (1975): 20–47.

38. Nelkin, *Creation Controversy*.

39. Lakoff, "Scientists, Technologists, and Political Power," 371.

40. Most of the leading students of governmental process have come to agree with this conclusion about the incrementally growing influence of staff. See, e.g., Kelman, *Making Public Policy*, chap. 5; and James Q. Wilson, *Bureaucracy: What Government Agencies Do and Why They Do It* (New York: Basic Books, 1989), chap. 14.

41. Malbin, *Unelected Representatives*, 243–44.

42. Kelman, *Making Public Policy*, 56.

43. Another source of staff influence is the degree of permeability of the boundary protecting agencies from outside pressures. Staff experts in the State Department may tend to have relatively greater influence than staff experts in the Occupational Safety and Health Administration, because access to policy makers is more limited in the former than the latter. See Kelman, *Making Public Policy*, 104–5; and Theda Skocpol and Kenneth Finegold, "State Capacity and Economic Intervention in the Early New Deal," *Political Science Quarterly* 97 (1982): 255–78.

44. Expert-dominated policy making on significant issues does sometimes occur in *politicized* settings, but, outside the economic policy domain, these are rare events and they depend on the implicit support of at least one powerful political leader (usually the president or governor) and the disinclination of others to mount a contest. For an apt example, see Edward C. Banfield, "Making a New Federal Program: Model Cities, 1964–68," in Alan P. Sidler, ed., *Policy and Politics in America* (Boston: Little, Brown, 1973), 125–58.

45. Because professional influence appears to be greatest where conflict is least apparent, the decision-based methodology, on which most studies are based, may be especially limited for investigating expert influence. For critiques of decision-based methodologies in political studies, see Peter Bachrach and Morton S. Baratz, *Power and Poverty* (New York: Oxford University Press, 1970); Matthew Crenson, *The Unpolitics of Air Pollution* (Baltimore: Johns Hopkins University Press, 1971); and John Gaventa, *Power and Powerlessness* (New York: Oxford University Press, 1980), chap. 1.

46. Steven Brint and Jerome Karabel, *The Diverted Dream: Community Colleges and the Promise of Educational Opportunity in America, 1900–1980* (New York: Oxford University Press, 1989), part 1.

47. Among the standard works are Hofstadter, *Age of Reform*, chap. 6; and Wiebe, *Search for Order*, chap. 5. See also Haskell, "Professionalism versus Capitalism," 179–86.

48. Terence C. Halliday, *Beyond Monopoly: Lawyers, State Crises, and Professional Empowerment* (Chicago: University of Chicago Press, 1987), chap. 10.

49. See the discussion in Donahue, *The Privatization Decision*.

50. Halliday, *Beyond Monopoly*, chap. 10.

51. Schlozman and Tierney, *Organized Interests*, 82–85.

52. On this point, see Theodore Lowi, *The End of Liberalism: The Second Republic in America*, 2d ed. (New York: W. W. Norton, 1979); and Halliday, *Beyond Monopoly*.

53. Hedrick Smith cites the opposite case of loopholes being closed from many special business interests in the 1985 tax reform bill, which was decisively influenced by congressional staff experts. See Smith, *Power Game*, 272–79.

54. For a discussion of the IQ test, see N. J. Block and Gerald Dworkin, "IQ, Heritability, and Inequality," in Block and Dworkin, eds., *The IQ Controversy* (New York: Pantheon, 1976); 410–542; and Michael Schudson, "Organizing the Mer-

itocracy: A History of the College Examination Boards," *Harvard Educational Review* 42 (1972): 34–69. For rationalization efforts based on alternative theories of intelligence, see Howard Gardner, *Frames of Mind: The Theory of Multiple Intelligences* (New York: Basic Books, 1983); and Robert J. Sternberg, *The Triarchic Mind: A New Theory of Human Intelligence* (New York: Viking, 1988).

55. Lenore Weitzman, *The Divorce Revolution: The Unexpected Social and Economic Consequences for Women and Children in America* (New York: Free Press, 1985); and Herbert Jacob, *Silent Revolution: The Transformation of Divorce Law in the United States* (Chicago: University of Chicago Press, 1988).

56. Luker, *Abortion*, chap. 2.

57. Frank G. Houdek, *The Freedom of Information Act: A Comprehensive Bibliography of Law-Related Materials,* 3d ed. (Austin: University of Texas Press, 1985).

58. Richard K. Scotch, *From Good Will to Civil Rights* (Philadelphia: Temple University Press, 1984).

59. Terence C. Halliday, "The Idiom of Legalism in Bar Politics; Lawyers, McCarthyism, and the Civil Rights Era," *American Bar Foundation Research Journal* 4 (1982): 911–89.

60. See, e.g., Bledstein, *Culture of Professionalism*, chap. 9.

61. Christopher Lasch, *Haven in a Heartless World* (New York: Basic Books, 1979), chap. 6.

62. Dick Netzer, *The Subsidized Muse* (Cambridge: Cambridge University Press, 1978).

63. See Edward A. Shils, "Deference," in John A. Jackson, ed., *Social Stratification* (Cambridge: Cambridge University Press, 1968), 104–32. Cf. Halliday, "Knowledge Mandates."

64. From the point of view of political and economic elites, who are the key evaluators, natural scientists, for example, often appear unwilling to credit political realities and are inclined instead to take uncompromising positions on the basis of scientific truth as currently understood. See the references in note 31 above. Other professional occupations may be regarded as unfit to play a major role in social regulation, either because they represent a knowledge base that is too much tied from the point of view of elites to "special interests" (e.g., labor intellectuals and social workers), or simply because they are too distant from the centers of political and economic power in society (e.g., artists and writers).

65. See, in particular, Tyack, *The One Best System;* Collins, *Credential Society,* chap. 7; Tyack and Hansot, *Managers of Virtue;* and Brint and Karabel, *Diverted Dream,* chaps. 2–3.

66. Sandra Wong, "Evaluating the Content of Textbooks: Public Interests and Professional Authority," *Sociology of Education* 64 (1991): 11–18.

67. See, e.g., David J. Rothman, *The Discovery of the Asylum* (Boston: Little, Brown, 1971); and Andrew T. Scull, *Museums of Madness* (London: Allen-Lane, 1979).

68. See, e.g., Lasch, *Haven in a Heartless World;* William Ray Arney and Bernard J. Bergen, *Medicine and the Management of Living* (Chicago: University of Chicago Press, 1984); and Leslie Rado, "Death Redefined: Social and Cultural Influences on Legislation," *Journal of Communications* 31 (1981): 41–47.

69. Albert O. Hirschman, "How Keynes was spread in America," *Challenge* 31 (1988): 4–7.

70. Robert Gordon, "The Consumer Price Index: Measuring Inflation and Causing It," *The Public Interest* 63 (1981): 112–34. For other examples of the sociological importance of economic statistics, see Paul Starr and William Alonso, eds., *The Politics of Numbers* (New York: Russell Sage, 1987), part 1.

71. In Weber's famous passage: "For of the last stage of . . . cultural development, it might well be truly said: 'Specialists without spirit, sensualists without heart; this nullity imagines that it has attained a level of civilization never before achieved'" (Max Weber, *The Protestant Ethic and the Spirit of Capitalism* [New York: Charles Scribner and Sons, 1958], 182). Here Weber's views (originally published in 1904–5) seem to me to reflect the specific circumstances of Wilhelmine Germany, and particularly the conflicts between the status culture of the old professoriat and the new bureaucratic specialists.

72. Kelman, *Making Public Policy,* 109–12.

73. Kelman, *Making Public Policy,* 110.

74. Hall, "Professionalization and Bureaucratization."

75. For the difference that patrimonially oriented cultural traditions can make, cf. Miguel Centeno, "From Corporatism to Planning: Institutional Patterns of Policy Making in Mexico" (Paper presented at the annual meeting of the American Sociological Association, Washington, D.C., August, 1990).

76. This example is drawn from Abbott, *System of Professions,* 37.

77. Wilson, *Bureaucracy,* 179–80.

78. See also Alicia H. Manuel, ed., *Lessons from the Income Maintenance Experiments: Proceedings from a Conference Sponsored by the Federal Reserve and the Brookings Institution* (Washington, D.C.: Federal Reserve and Brookings Institution, 1986).

79. Garry Wills, "A Tale of Three Cities," *New York Review of Books* March 28, 1991, 14.

80. Charles E. Lindblom has been a pioneer in thinking through the strengths and weaknesses of scientific expertise as one among several modes of social problem solving. The key works are Charles E. Lindblom and David Braybrooke, *A Strategy of Decision* (New York: Free Press, 1963); Charles E. Lindblom and David K. Cohen, *Usable Knowledge* (New Haven, Conn.: Yale University Press, 1979); and Charles E. Lindblom, *Inquiry and Change* (New Haven, Conn.: Yale University Press, 1990). See also Carol H. Weiss, ed., *Using Social Research for Public Policy Making* (Lexington, Mass.: D.C. Heath, 1977).

81. When surveyed, most experts can provide a rational defense of values and the goals of the policies they advocate. See Aberbach, Putnam, and Rockman, *Bureaucrats and Politicians,* chap. 5, espec. 134–41.

82. Cf. Jeffrey Pressman and Aaron Wildavsky, *Implementation* (1973; reprint, Berkeley: University of California Press, 1984); and Gordon Chase, "Implementing a Human Services Program: How Hard Will It Be?," *Public Policy* 27 (1979): 385–436.

83. Paul J. DiMaggio, "Constructing an Organizational Field as a Professional Project; U.S. Art Museums, 1920–1940," in Powell and DiMaggio, *The New Institutionalism in Organizational Studies,* 267–92.

84. For more radical views on the organization of power in the advanced societies, see Ralph Miliband, *The State in Capitalist Society* (New York: Basic Books, 1969); James O'Connor, *The Fiscal Crisis of the State* (New York: St. Martin's Press, 1973);

and Martin Carnoy, *The State and Political Theory* (Princeton, N.J.: Princeton University Press, 1984).

85. Brint and Karabel, *Diverted Dream,* chap. 8.

86. See, e.g., G. William Domhoff, *Who Really Rules? New Haven and Community Power Re-Examined* (New Brunswick, N.J.: Transaction Books, 1978); Manuel Castells, *The Economic Crisis and American Society* (Princeton, N.J.: Princeton University Press, 1980); and John H. Mollenkopf, *The Contested City* (Princeton, N.J.: Princeton University Press, 1983).

CHAPTER EIGHT

1. Lewis A. Coser, *Men of Ideas* (New York: Free Press, 1965), viii.

2. Edmund Burke, *Reflections on the Revolution in France* (1790; reprint, Garden City, N.Y.: Doubleday, 1960).

3. See Alexis de Tocqueville, *The Old Regime and the French Revolution* (1856; reprint, Garden City, N.Y.: Doubleday, 1955), 147; Max Weber, *The Sociology of Religion* (1922; reprint, Boston: Beacon Press, 1963), chap. 7; Schumpeter, *Capitalism, Socialism, and Democracy,* chap. 13; and Raymond Aron, *The Opium of the Intellectuals* (1955; reprint, Garden City, N.Y.: Doubleday, 1957).

4. Lionel Trilling, *Beyond Culture* (New York: Viking Press, 1965), xii–xiii.

5. Podhoretz, "Adversary Culture and the New Class," 21, 25.

6. Ibid., 25.

7. Bell, *Coming of Post-Industrial Society,* 214.

8. In the mid-1970s, the idea of an "adversary culture" of intellectuals entered popular discourse as a staple of conservative commentary concerning the potential threat of a government-oriented "new class." See Brint, "Stirrings of an Oppositional Elite?," chap. 1. For examples of the continued usage of the idea in the 1980s, see Blumenthal, *Rise of the Counter-Establishment,* 7; and Peggy Noonan, *What I Saw at the Revolution* (New York: Random House, 1990), 12–16.

9. Ladd and Lipset, *Divided Academy,* chaps. 3–7.

10. Ladd and Lipset summarized the findings of their second study of the professioriat in a series that ran in the *Chronicle of Higher Education* from September 15, 1975, to May 31, 1976. The quote is from the article of October 20, 1975.

11. Kadushin, *American Intellectual Elite,* 263–89.

12. Ibid., 279.

13. Not surprisingly, the quarter of the sample of intellectuals with regular lines of access to men of power were particularly unlikely to participate in protest. Only a handful of these well-connected intellectuals said they had participated in demonstrations. Ibid., 318.

14. Kirkpatrick Sale, *SDS* (New York: Random House, 1973).

15. Michael Miles, *Radical Probe: The Logic of Student Rebellion* (New York: Atheneum, 1973), 3–22.

16. For one statement of concern about the student left, perhaps more impassioned than most, see Daniel Bell, "Quo Warranto: Notes on the Governance of Universities in the 1970s," *Public Interest* 19 (1970): 53–68.

17. The period of greatest productivity is bounded by Edward A. Shils's "The Intellectuals and the Powers" (*Comparative Studies in Society and History* 1 [1958]: 5–73) and Lewis Coser's *Men of Ideas* (1965). For other useful works on intellectuals by mid-century writers, see Henry A. Kissinger, "The Policy-Maker and the Intellec-

tual," *The Reporter*, March 5, 1959, 30–35; Lipset, *Political Man*, chap. 10; and Hofstadter, *Anti-Intellectualism in American Life*. Other significant works of scholarship and commentary from the period include Marcus Cunliffe, "The Intellectuals: The United States," *Encounter* 4 (May 1955): 23–33; Merle Curti, *The American Paradox: The Conflict of Thought and Action* (New Brunswick, N.J.: Rutgers University Press, 1956); Raymond Williams, *Culture and Society;* Arthur M. Schlesinger, Jr., et al., "American Intellectuals: Their Status and Politics," *Daedalus* 88 (1959): 487–98; Daniel Bell, *The End of Ideology* (Glencoe, Ill.: Free Press, 1960); George B. de Huszar, ed., *The Intellectuals: A Controversial Portrait* (New York: Free Press, 1960); David E. Apter, ed., *Ideology and Discontent* (London: Free Press of Glencoe, 1964); and Daniel Lerner and Harold Lasswell, *World Revolutionary Elites* (Cambridge, Mass.: MIT Press, 1965).

18. Shils, "Intellectuals and the Powers," 13.

19. See, e.g., Hofstadter, *Anti-Intellectualism in American Life;* Lipset, *Political Man*, chap. 10; and Coser, *Men of Ideas*. Lipset also connected intellectual criticism to the sociological idea of status inconsistency.

20. Shils, "Intellectuals and the Powers," 15–19.

21. See Edward A. Shils, "The End of Ideology?," *Encounter* 5 (November 1955): 52–58; Lipset, *Political Man*, chap. 13; and Bell, *End of Ideology*, 369–73.

22. Lipset, *Political Man*, 439–44.

23. Ibid., 441.

24. Coser makes only a passing reference to this fourth group of intellectuals in the chapters illustrating his typology. See Coser, *Men of Ideas*, 136. Some historical forerunners of these academic intellectual experts are also discussed in part 1 of the book.

25. See, e.g., Bruce Robbins, ed., *Intellectuals: Aesthetics, Politics, Academics* (Minneapolis: University of Minnesota Press, 1990).

26. Cf. Roger Kimball, *Tenured Radicals: How Politics Has Corrupted Our Higher Education* (New York: Harper Collins, 1990). In this vein, see also Dinesh D'Souza, *Illiberal Education: The Politics of Race and Sex on Campus* (New York: Free Press, 1991).

27. Richard F. Hamilton and Lowell L. Hargens, "The Politics of the Professors: Self-Identifications, 1969–84," *Social Forces* 71 (1993): 603–27. Journalists, another group often associated with intellectual culture, also moved to the right during the 1970s and early 1980s. See Weaver and Wilhoit, *American Journalist*, chap. 1.

28. Professors were much less likely in the 1980s than they had been in the 1960s and 1970s to think that standards should be changed in order to attract more minority faculty. This position was, interestingly, particularly changed among self-described "left" identifiers. Hamilton and Hargens, "The Politics of the Professors," 620.

29. Carolyn J. Mooney, "Study Finds Professors Are Still Teaching the Classics, Sometimes in New Ways," *Chronicle of Higher Education* November 6, 1991, A1, A22. This study of 571 English literature professors on 350 campuses found that professors used a variety of theoretical approaches to the understanding of texts. These included: "history of ideas" (76 percent), "new criticism" (close textual analysis) (64 percent), feminist theory (61 percent), reader-response theory (44 percent), "new historicism" (40 percent), psychoanalytic theory (38 percent), Marxist approaches (28 percent), and "post-structuralism" (including deconstruction) (21 percent). Professors at leading research universities were more likely to use the newer theoretical approaches than were other professors. In courses on nineteenth-century America,

Whitman, Emerson, Melville and Twain continued to be most popular. In courses on nineteenth-century England, Dickens, Eliot, and Hardy continued to be emphasized.

30. Hamilton and Hargens, "The Politics of the Professors," 615–17.

31. Ibid., 616–17.

32. Ibid., 609–12.

33. Surveys were sent to the following writers, thinkers, and editors: David E. Apter, James Atlas, Daniel Bell, Thomas Bender, Leon Botstein, Robert Boyers, Peter Brooks, Robert Brustein, William F. Buckley, Lewis A. Coser, Don DeLillo, Barbara Ehrenreich, Whitney Ellsworth, Kai Erikson, James Fallows, Barbara Fields, Henry Louis Gates, Jr., Peter Gay, Todd Gitlin, Nathan Glazer, Ellen Goodman, Stephen Jay Gould, Gerald Graff, Francine du Plessix Gray, Robert Heilbroner, Caroline Heilbrun, Gertrude Himmelfarb, E. D. Hirsch, Stanley Hoffmann, John Hollander, Gerald Holton, Irving Louis Horowitz, Irving Howe, Russell Jacoby, Nan Keohane, Daniel Kevles, Roger Kimball, Michael Kinsley, Jeanne J. Kirkpatrick, Irving Kristol, Robert Kuttner, Joseph LaPalombara, Christopher Lasch, Nicholas Lemann, Mark Lilla, Alastair MacIntyre, Terry McMillan, Norman Mailer, David Mamet, Stephen Marcus, James Merrill, W. S. Merwin, Toni Morrison, Bill Moyers, Victor Navasky, Michael Novak, Martha Nussbaum, Joyce Carol Oates, Cynthia Ozick, Orlando Patterson, Charles Peters, Diane Ravitch, Robert Reich, Richard Rorty, Oliver Sacks, Edward Said, Daniel Schorr, John Searle, Barbara Herrnstein Smith, Susan Sontag, Thomas Sowell, Paul Starr, Catherine Stimpson, Lester Thurow, Alan Trachtenberg, John Updike, Derek Walcott, Michael Walzer, Cornel West, Leon Wieseltier, George F. Will, James Wolcott, Alan Wolfe, C. Vann Woodward, and Dennis Wrong.

34. The sample universe included every article and review over the three years for the quarterlies; articles and reviews in every other issue for the monthlies; articles and reviews every third issue for biweeklies; and articles and reviews in issues at six-week intervals for the weeklies. Some oversampling of particular periodicals (The *Atlantic, Commentary,* the *New Yorker,* and the *Public Interest*) was necessary to correct for differences in the average number of articles per issue and for the relative prominence of the periodicals.

35. The following graduate students from Yale University participated in the project as coders: Iverson Griffin (Sociology), Leif W. Haase (American Studies), Francesca Polletta (Sociology), Bill Preston (Political Science), Corey Robin (Political Science), and Dan Ryan (Sociology). Charles Kadushin provided helpful and generous consultation at the time of the design of the project.

36. Coders were provided with a glossary of terms to aid in coding decisions. Before beginning their formal coding, coders were asked to practice on several sample articles. These articles were discussed in group meetings or individually with me for errors and biases. Throughout the project, I consulted with coders and coders consulted with each other on difficult decisions. Coding issues were noted on article write-ups, and each of the coders also wrote a memo discussing the problems they encountered and their observations about the project. I spot-checked 20 percent of the coded articles.

37. The issues raised by subtextual reading can be seen in one article on the troubled and violent transition of Uruguay from democracy to dictatorship. This article may suggest an implicit comparison with the United States. Uruguay is described as economically weakened, reliant on monetarism for its economic policy, and committed to union busting and other attacks on labor. One Uruguayan intellectual is quoted as saying, "It can happen anywhere." Article 1873, "A Reporter at Large," *New Yorker* (April 3, 1989). I am grateful to Leif Haase for suggesting this example.

38. Article 1497, "Dickens: A Biography," *New York Review of Books* (January 19, 1989).

39. Article 1889: "A Reporter at Large," *New Yorker* (July 17, 1989).

40. One article fits this description of examining manmade or natural phenomena for their larger import: Article 0765, "Notes: Oh, Well," *Atlantic* (July 1987), an article about the disappointing results of time capsule openings.

41. Three articles did take up perennial issues in the study of man through the medium of character study. Interestingly, all three concerned the themes of ambivalent identifications, trust, and betrayal. These were: Article 1515, "Chicago Blues," *New York Review of Books* (March 16, 1989); Article 1836, "Annals of War," *New Yorker* (July 4, 1988); and Article 1869; "Reflections: The Journalist and the Murderer," *New Yorker* (March 13, 1989).

42. We found only one sustained close reading in the sample: Article 0908, "Kundera's Quartet," *Salmagundi* (Spring/Summer 1988).

43. Article 0192, "Female-Headed Households," *Public Interest* (Fall 1987).

44. Article 0647, "Soviet and Chinese Economic Reform," *Foreign Affairs* (Winter 1988).

45. Article 0222, "Taking Drugs Seriously," *Public Interest* (Summer 1988).

46. Article 1531, "Watching Television," *New York Review of Books* (April 1, 1989).

47. Article 1212, "The President Who Oppressed Himself," *New York Times Book Review* (April 9, 1989).

48. Article 1836, "Annals of War," *New Yorker* (July 4, 1988).

49. Article 1203, "A Fair Shake," *New York Times Book Review* (April 9, 1989).

50. Article 1562, "The Last Lion," *New York Review of Books* (June 15, 1989).

51. Article 1971, "Minority Report," *Nation* (February 20, 1988).

52. Article 1867, "The Art World," *New Yorker* (February 20, 1989).

53. Article 0191, "Workfare," *Public Interest* (Fall 1987).

54. Article 0343, "Constitution III," *New Republic* (June 29, 1987).

55. Article 0278, "Problems and Non-Problems," *Public Interest* (Fall 1989).

56. Article 0222, "Taking Drugs Seriously," *Public Interest* (Summer 1988).

57. Article 0363, "Science and Society," *New Republic* (December 12, 1987).

58. Article 0178, "Elder Abuse," *Public Interest* (Summer 1987).

59. Article 0492, "Case Closed," *New Republic* (January 9, 1989).

60. Article 0809, "Borders and Quotas," *Public Interest* (Summer 1989).

61. Article 0346, "The Untouchables," *New Republic* (June 29, 1987).

62. Article 0630, "The Cuban Missile Crisis Revisited," *Foreign Affairs* (Fall 1987).

63. Article 0760, "The Making of a Classic," *Atlantic* (May 1987).

64. Article 1719, "Art, Kitsch, and Politics," *Commentary* (May 1988).

65. Article 1964, "The Remington Murder," *Nation* (January 9, 1989).

66. Article 1080, "The King of Kiss and Tell," *New York Times Book Review* (January 10, 1988).

67. Article 0173, "Keynes," *Public Interest* (Spring 1987).

68. Article 0409, "Southern Uncomfort," *New Republic* (February 29, 1988).

69. Article 0267, "AIDS Prevention," *Public Interest* (Summer 1989).

70. Article 0420, "Rent Control," *New Republic* (April 11, 1988).

71. Article 0435, "Bulldog Bull," *New Republic* (May 23, 1988).

72. When the culture of particularizing refinement has been examined by sociologists, it has often been examined in the context of social stratification. Consequently,

there is a distinct tendency in sociology to simply relabel the culture of particularizing refinement as an element of status group closure in the upper classes. See, e.g., Bourdieu, *Distinction,* chap. 5.

73. For a defense of the values of ideology, properly understood, see Alvin Gouldner, *The Dialectic of Ideology and Technology* (New York: Seabury Press, 1976), chap. 2.

74. Some of the same requirements are found in academe, but not the requirement to be "interesting." The investigation of truly esoteric problems and the outcomes of replication or refinement are acceptable in academe, but not in the consumer market. The isolated scholar is perhaps freer to continue to hold idiosyncratic or clearly dissenting views than are those who write for the larger markets of educated general readers. Cf. Jacoby, *The Last Intellectuals: American Culture in the Age of Academe* (New York: Basic Books, 1987).

75. I am grateful to Ann Swidler for this observation.

76. See, e.g., Jacoby, *Last Intellectuals;* Zygmut Baumann, *Legislators and Interpreters: On Modernity, Post-Modernity, and Intellectuals* (Ithaca, N.Y.: Cornell University Press, 1987); and Thomas Bender, *Intellect and Public Life: Essays on the Social History of Academic Intellectuals in the United States* (Baltimore: Johns Hopkins University Press, 1993).

77. Cf. Talcott Parsons, "The Intellectual: A Social Role Category," in Philip Rieff, ed., *On Intellectuals* (Garden City, N.Y.: Doubleday, 1969), 22; and Hofstadter, *Anti-Intellectualism,* 395.

78. See, e.g., Cameron, "On the Limits of the Public Economy" and Keohane, "The World Political Economy and the Crisis of Embedded Liberalism."

79. See, e.g., Noonan, *What I Saw at the Revolution,* 53.

80. Arlie Hochschild, *The Second Shift: Working Parents and the Revolution at Home* (New York: Viking Press, 1989).

81. Nathan Glazer, *Affirmative Discrimination: Ethnic Inequality and Public Policy* (New York: Basic Books, 1975).

82. E. D. Hirsch, *Cultural Literacy* (Boston: Houghton-Mifflin, 1987).

83. Paul Kennedy, *The Rise and Fall of the Great Powers* (New York: Random House, 1987).

84. See Howard Schuman, Charlotte Steeh, and Lawrence Bobo, *Racial Attitudes in America: Trends and Interpretations* (Cambridge, Mass.: Harvard University Press, 1985).

85. William A. Gamson and Andre Modigliani, "The Changing Culture of Affirmative Action," in Richard D. Braungart, ed., *Research in Political Sociology* 3 (1987): 137–77. See also William A. Gamson, *Talking Politics* (Cambridge: Cambridge University Press, 1992), 43–51.

CHAPTER NINE

1. There is now an enormous literature on the development of professions in Europe. For an overview of some of the more important of the recent literature, see Michael Burrage, "Introduction: The Professions in Sociology and History," in Michael Burrage and Rolf Torstendahl, eds., *Professions in Theory and History* (London and Newbury Park, Calif.: Sage Publications, 1990), 1–23.

2. For discussions of the Anglo-American and Continental patterns of organization, see Ben-David, *Centers of Learning,* chap. 1; Freidson, *Professional Powers,* chap.

257

2; Randall Collins, "Changing Conceptions in the Sociology of the Professions," in Rolf Torstendahl and Michael Burrage eds., *The Formation of Professions* (London and Newbury Park, Calif.: Sage Publications, 1990); and Burrage, "Introduction."

3. Ben-David, *Centers of Learning*, 15.

4. Freidson, *Professional Powers*, 34.

5. Jurgen Kocka, "'Burgertum' and Professions in the Nineteenth Century: Two Alternative Approaches," in Burrage and Torstendahl, *Professions in Theory and History*, espec. 71–73.

6. Ibid.

7. Freidson, *Professional Powers*, 46. On the industrial staff in France, see Luc Boltanski, *The Making of a Middle Class: Cadres in French Society* (Cambridge: Cambridge University Press, 1987).

8. Kocka, "'Burgertum' and Professions in the Nineteenth Century," 70–71.

9. See, e.g., J. P. de Crayencour, *Professions in the European Community* (Brussels: European Perspectives, 1982); Commission of the European Communities, *A Common Market for Services* (Brussels: Office for Official Publications of the European Community, 1989). Cf. Noyelle and Dutka, *International Trade*.

10. Because of the limitations of the international data, I sometimes could not construct refined categories. The occupation variable separated social and cultural professionals from technical professionals and from managers. The social and cultural professionals included artists, writers, social scientists, planners, professors, journalists, editors, teachers, social workers, and clergy. The technical professionals included scientists, engineers, doctors, lawyers, accountants, marketing specialists, and computer specialists. Managers included all business and farm owners and salaried managers. The public sector variable was missing for Italy. The public sector for Austria was coded from industrial classifications. High levels of education were coded from the highest level of schooling attained to obtain similar relative proportions: for Australia, diploma or bachelor's degree and higher; for Austria, gymnasium matura or university; for West Germany, abitur or university; for Great Britain, higher education certificate, diploma, or degree; for Italy, university attendance or graduation; for the U.S., bachelor's degree or higher. Urban residence was coded from separate country categorizations: for Australia, 100,000 and above; for Austria, 50,000 and above; for Great Britain, "big city" or "suburbs or outskirts of city"; for Italy, 30,000 and above; for the U.S., city or suburbs of city, 250,000 and above. Family income was divided proportionately into three categories: highest 40 percent; middle 40 percent; lowest 20 percent. Age was represented in six categories from under 25 as the lowest to 65 and older as the highest. Religiosity was based on church or synagogue attendance, coded in five categories, ranging from weekly or more to never.

11. These analyses are discussed in greater detail in Steven Brint, "The Social Bases and National Context of Middle-Class Liberalism and Dissent in Western Societies," unpublished paper, Department of Sociology, Yale University, 1989.

12. In reading the results of the analysis of the ISSP 1985 data, it is important to keep in mind that by 1985 the ruling socialist parties of Europe had given up their policies of nationalization and had moved toward growth rather than redistribution as their major policy aim. These policy choices were reinforced in some cases by the beginnings of reform in Eastern Europe. It is possible that the greater moderation of the European labor and socialist parties during this period encouraged a greater degree of support for them on the part of the middle classes generally. See Seymour Martin Lipset, "No Third Way: A Comparative Perspective on the Left," in Daniel

Chirot, ed., *The Crisis of Leninism and the Decline of the Left* (Seattle: University of Washington Press, 1991), 183–232; and the articles in John H. Goldthorpe, ed., *Consensus and Conflict in Modern Capitalism* (New York: Oxford University Press, 1984).

13. For theoretical suggestions, see also Alain Touraine, *The Voice and the Eye* (New York: Random House, 1981), chap. 1; and Claus Offe, *Disorganized Capitalism* (Cambridge, Mass.: MIT Press, 1985), chap. 5.

14. Touraine, *Voice and the Eye,* chap. 1.

15. In the ISSP data the broader professional stratum is at least as liberal as the social and cultural segment in three of the national samples: Austria, West Germany, and (surprisingly) the United States. The U.S. case is perplexing, since it departs from previous American findings. Some two-fifths of the small (N = 54) American sample of nonbusiness professionals is composed of elementary school teachers, a not very liberal group. Thus, sample size and variation may help to explain the anomaly of the American case.

16. The Egalitarian Attitudes index, like all other indices, was created from items that loaded together on factor analyses of the ISSP. It included items asking respondents whether the rich should pay a higher or lower proportion of their income in taxes; whether government should be responsible for reducing income inequalities; whether government should be responsible for providing jobs for the unemployed; whether corporations have too much power in society; and whether government should be responsible for providing decent jobs for those in need. The Business Regulation scale included items asking respondents whether business should pay more or less tax; whether corporations have too much power in society; whether government should reduce regulation of business; and whether government has too little power in society. The Government Ownership scale included items asking respondents about what role government should play in either owning, regulating, or staying out of the steel, banking, auto, mass transit, and electrical utilities industries. The Social Spending index included items asking respondents how much government should spend on benefits for the unemployed; how much government should spend on the aged; whether government should rescue declining industries to protect workers' jobs; how much government should spend on the nation's health; whether government spending should be cut; and how much government should spend on improving the nation's educational system. The Labor index included items asking respondents whether government was responsible for providing decent jobs for the unemployed; whether government was responsible for protecting the unemployed; whether unemployment or inflation was the highest economic priority; whether corporations had too much power in society; and whether labor unions had too little power in society. Party identifications are discussed in note 18.

17. This Middle-Class Spending index included items asking respondents how much the government should spend on the environment, the arts, education, and defense (as a negative factor). The Civil Liberties index included items that asked respondents whether racists and revolutionists should be able to hold meetings, publish books, and teach. The Protest index included items asking respondents whether it was acceptable for dissidents to organize a national strike; whether it was acceptable for dissidents to organize mass protest demonstrations; whether revolutionists should be able to meet, publish books, and teach; and whether people should be able to follow their conscience in disobedience of law. The Independence Training index included items asking respondents how important it was for the schools to teach discipline, respect for authority, and job training. The Humanist Culture index included items

asking respondents how important it was for the schools to teach literature and the arts, science and technology, judgment, and concern for minorities and the poor.

18. Communist, Socialist, Social Democratic, Labour, Green, Australian Liberal, and American Democratic parties were categorized as Left Parties. Conservative, Christian Democratic, Nationalist, and American Republican parties were categorized as Right Parties.

19. Information was not available on all of the dependent variables for all of the countries. Data was not collected in Italy on party identifications, and data was not collected in Austria that allowed for the creation of the independence training and humanist culture scales. These are not counted in the calculations of Table 9.3.

20. Controlling for the other significant variables, the gender variable added very little to the explanation of the economic scales. Indeed, in four out of five cases, women were more rather than less conservative. It may be that women's concerns about security still overshadowed their weaker average market situation as an influence on their political thought.

21. The proportion of correct to possible predictions was as follows: Australia (51 percent), U.S. (39 percent), Great Britain (27 percent), Italy (27 percent), Australia (24 percent), and West Germany (23 percent). The average adjusted R^2, using just the main variables on the eleven scales, was as follows: Australia (.12), U.S. (.09), Austria (.08), Great Britain (.06), Italy (.05), and West Germany (.04).

22. Michele Kiang, "The New Class in Singapore," unpublished paper, Department of Sociology, Columbia University, 1990.

23. Data is far from complete here, but see Everett C. Ladd, Jr., and Charles Hadley, *Party Systems in American Politics* (New York: W. W. Norton, 1976), 98–111.

24. Michael Keren, "Intellectuals and the Open Society in Israel," in Alain Gagnon, ed., *Intellectuals in Liberal Democracies* (New York: Praeger, 1987), 143–53.

25. See Sidney Verba et al., *Elites and the Idea of Equality* (Cambridge, Mass.: Harvard University Press, 1987), chap. 9; and Ikuo Kabashima and Jeffrey Broadbent, "Keeping the LDP on a Tight Rein: Japan's New Middle Class and Voter Rationality under a Dominant Regime," unpublished paper, Department of Sociology, University of Michigan, 1985.

26. Strong country effects were also found in a separate analysis of the European Values Study of 1981. See Brint, "Social Bases and National Contexts."

27. Ibid.

28. The English reaction on civil liberties and other social issues would also appear to be more a temporal phenomenon than a deep structural influence—in this case, having to do with dissatisfaction over labor unrest and also the conservatizing effect of the Thatcher government.

29. See Frederic Spotts and Theodore Weiser, *Italy: A Difficult Democracy* (Cambridge: Cambridge University Press, 1986), chap. 14; and Joseph LaPalombara, *Democracy, Italian Style* (New Haven, Conn.: Yale University Press, 1987), chap. 10.

30. Weil, "The Variable Effects of Education on Liberal Attitudes."

31. Stanley Lieberson, "Small N's and Big Conclusions: An Examination of the Reasoning in Comparative Studies based on a Small Number of Cases," *Social Forces* 70 (1991): 307–20.

32. Ron Eyerman, "Rationalizing Intellectuals," *Theory and Society* 14 (1985): 803.

33. Ibid., 803–4.

34. Ezra N. Suleiman, *Elites in French Society* (Princeton, N.J.: Princeton Univer-

sity Press, 1978), 162. Cf. Vincent Wright, *The Government and Politics of France*, 3d ed. (New York: Holmes and Meier, 1989), 129. For Wright's detailed critique of the technocracy theory as it applies to France, see chap. 6.

35. See, e.g., Jean Meynaud, *Technocracy* (New York: Free Press, 1968); Jacques Ellul, *The Technological Society* (New York: Knopf, 1964); and Suleiman, *Elites in French Society.*

36. Touraine, *Voice and the Eye,* chaps. 1, 5.

37. Sidney Tarrow, *Between Center and Periphery* (New Haven, Conn.: Yale University Press, 1977), 248.

38. Suleiman, *Elites in French Society,* 280.

39. Patricia E. Craig, "The Spanish Socialist Workers' Party: Ideology and Organization in a Contemporary Social Democratic party," (Ph.D. diss., Yale University, 1993).

40. Stein Berglund and Pertti Personen, "Political Party Systems," in Erik Allardt et al. eds., *Nordic Democracy* (Copenhagen: Det Danske Selskab, 1981), 80–126.

41. See, e.g., Eyerman, "Rationalizing Intellectuals."

42. See David R. Cameron, "The Expansion of the Public Economy: A Comparative Analysis," *American Political Science Review* 72 (1978): 1243–61; Peter Katzenstein, *Small States in World Markets* (Ithaca, N.Y.: Cornell University Press, 1985); and Hugh Heclo and Henrik Madsen, *Party and Politics in Sweden* (Ithaca, N.Y.: Cornell University Press, 1987).

43. Walter Korpi, *The Democratic Class Struggle* (London: Routledge and Kegan Paul, 1983); and Heclo and Madsen, *Party and Politics in Sweden.*

44. This spirit of "saklighet" is discussed in Henry Milner, *Sweden: Social Democracy in Practice* (Oxford: Oxford University Press, 1982), chap. 2.

45. These institutions are discussed in particularly illuminating detail in Heclo and Madsen, *Party and Politics in Sweden.*

46. Cameron, "The Expansion of the Public Economy."

47. Gösta Esping-Andersen, *Politics against Markets* (Princeton, N.J.: Princeton University Press, 1984).

48. Neil Elder, *Government in Sweden: The Executive at Work* (Oxford: Pergamon Press, 1970), chap. 9.

49. Ibid.

50. Heclo and Madsen, *Party and Politics in Sweden;* Per Laegreid and Johan P. Olsen, "Top Civil Servants in Norway: Key Players—On Different Teams," in Ezra Suleiman, ed., *Bureaucrats and Policy-Making* (New York: Holmes and Meier, 1984), 206–41.

51. Of course, in many respects, this is the legacy of the French Revolution and even, as Tocqueville pointed out, of the absolutism that so aroused Jacobin resistance. But Napoleon did provide the legal binding that allowed the Jacobin spirit to take a more permanent form. See Suleiman, *Elites in French Society,* chaps. 1–2.

52. Ibid., 12.

53. Ibid., 280.

54. Ibid., espec. chaps. 5–7.

55. Vincent Wright, quoted in Aberbach, Putnam, and Rockman, *Bureaucrats and Politicians and Western Democracies,* 250.

56. See Ezra N. Suleiman, "From Right to Left: Bureaucracy and Politics in France," in Suleiman, *Bureaucrats and Policy-Making,* 107–55.

57. See Peter A. Hall, *Governing the Economy: The Politics of State Intervention in Britain and France* (New York: Oxford University Press, 1986), 244.

58. Ibid., 247.

59. Gerhard Lembruch, "Concentration and the Structure of Corporatist Networks," in Goldthorpe, *Order and Conflict*, 60–80.

60. See Robert Putnam, "The Political Attitudes of Senior Civil Servants in Britain, Germany, and Italy," in Mattei Dogan, ed., *The Mandarins of Western Europe* (New York: Wiley, 1975) 87–127; Aberbach, Putnam, and Rockman, *Bureaucrats and Politicians in Western Democracies;* and, for a historical view, R. K. Kelsall, *The Higher Civil Servants in Britain* (London: Routledge and Kegan Paul, 1955).

61. Richard Rose, "Higher Civil Servants in Britain," in Suleiman, *Bureaucrats and Policy-Making*, 142–46.

62. Ibid., 142.

63. Aberbach, Putnam, and Rockman, *Bureaucrats and Politicians in Western Democracies*, 228–37.

64. See Dennis Kavanagh, *Thatcherism and British Politics* (Oxford: Oxford University Press, 1987), chaps. 9–10; and Peter Riddel, *The Thatcher Decade* (London: Basil Blackwell, 1989), chap. 9.

65. Putnam, "The Political Attitudes of Senior Civil Servants," 110.

66. See, e.g., ibid.; and Sabino Cassesse, "The Higher Civil Service in Italy," in Suleiman, *Bureaucrats and Policy-Making*, 35–71.

67. LaPalombara, *Democracy, Italian Style*, 217.

68. See, among many others, Timothy Garton Ash, *Magic Lantern: The Revolution of '89, Witnessed in Warsaw, Budapest, Berlin and Prague* (New York: Random House, 1990); and Daniel Chirot, "What Happened in Eastern Europe in 1989," in Chirot, *Crisis of Leninism*, 3–32.

69. Cameron, "On the Limits of the Public Economy"; Keohane, "The World Political Economy and the Crisis of Embedded Liberalism"; Hall, *Governing the Economy;* and Lipset, "No Third Way."

70. Craig, "The Spanish Socialist Workers' Party," chap. 3.

71. On the purported shift from "industrial" to "post-industrial" social movements, see Alberto Melluci, *Lotte Sociali e Movimento* (Milan, 1974); Touraine, *Voice and the Eye*, chap. 1; and Ronald Inglehart, *Culture Shift in Advanced Industrial Society* (Princeton, N.J.: Princeton University Press, 1990).

72. Maurice Pinard and Richard Hamilton, "Intellectuals and the Leadership of Social Movements," *Research in Social Movements, Conflicts and Change* 11 (1989): 73–108.

73. Hanspeter Kriesi, "New Social Movements and the New Class in the Netherlands," *American Journal of Sociology* 94 (1989): 1078–1116.

74. Ferdinand Mueller-Rommel, "The Greens in Western Europe: Similar, But Different," *International Political Science Review* 6 (1985): 483–99.

75. Wolfgang Ruedig, "Peace and Ecology Movements in Western Europe," *West European Politics* 11 (1988): 29. See also Herbert Kitschelt and Staff Hellemans, *Beyond the European Left: Ideology and Political Action in the Belgian Ecology Parties* (Durham, N.C.: Duke University Press, 1990). I am grateful to John Torpey for calling these works to my attention and for access to his unpublished review of the literature on Green party support in Europe.

76. Samuel H. Barnes, Max Kaase, Klaus R. Allerbeck et al., *Political Action: Mass*

Participation in Five Western Democracies (Beverly Hills, Calif.: Sage Publications, 1979); Phillipe C. Schmitter, "Interest Intermediation and Regime Governability in Contemporary Western Europe and North America," in Suzanne Berger, ed., *Organizing Interests in Western Europe* (Cambridge: Cambridge University Press, 1981), 285–327; and Russell Dalton, *Citizen Politics in Western Democracies* (Chatham, N.J.: Chatham Publishers, 1988), chap. 4.

77. Dalton, *Citizen Politics in Western Democracies,* chap. 4.

78. Using a measure based on the total frequency of riots, antigovernment demonstrations, and political strikes, the political scientist Phillipe Schmitter ranked fifteen countries by level of "unruliness" in the 1957–67 period—a period of significant civil strife. Schmitter, "Interest Intermediation," 297–305.

79. Eric Nordlinger, *Soldiers in Politics* (Englewood Cliffs, N.J.: Prentice-Hall, 1971), chap. 3.

80. LaPalombara, *Democracy, Italian Style,* 178.

81. See Schmitter, "Interest Intermediation."

82. For discussion of the peace institutes and their relation to governmental sponsorship, see Jeffrey Herf, "War, Peace, and the Intellectuals," *International Security* 10 (1986): 172–200.

CHAPTER TEN

1. Emile Durkheim, *Professional Ethics and Civic Morals*. trans. Cordelia Brookfield (London: Routledge and Kegan Paul, 1957). The book is based on Durkheim's lectures at the faculty of law in Istanbul in 1898–99.

2. For an excellent summary of the broader set of ideas of which Durkheim's were a part, see Haskell, "Professionalism versus Capitalism."

3. Discussion of professions are connected in this way to the literature on the voluntary sector as an alternative to markets and states. See, e.g., Robert Wuthnow, ed., *Between States and Markets: The Voluntary Sector in Comparative Perspective* (Princeton, N.J.: Princeton University Press, 1991).

4. Eliot Freidson, "Are Professions Necessary?," in Haskell, *Authority of Experts,* 3–28.

5. See Lortie, *Schoolteacher,* 109–86; and Burton R. Clark, *The School and the University* (Berkeley: University of California Press, 1985), 290–323.

6. Heiner and Mitchell L. Stevens, "Social Work, Medical Work, and an Organizational Model of Caring" (Paper presented at the Annual Meeting of the American Sociological Association, Miami, 1993).

7. Abel, *American Lawyers,* 234–36; Noyelle and Dutka, *International Trade,* 10–12.

8. For numerous examples, see Abbott, *System of Professions.*

9. Abel, *American Lawyers,* 185, 222.

10. Crane, *Transformation of the Avant-Garde,* chaps. 1, 7.

11. See, e.g., Brint and Karabel, *Diverted Dream;* John Mohr, "People, Categories, and Organizations: Making Sense out of Poverty in New York City, 1888–1917" (Paper presented at the American Sociological Association Meeting, Pittsburgh, 1992); and DiMaggio and Anheir, "Sociology of the Non-Profit Sector."

12. Bourdieu, *Outline of a Theory of Practice,* 30–71. See also Bourdieu, *Distinction,* espec. part 3.

13. Brint, "Upper Professionals."

14. See, in particular, Shils, "Intellectuals and the Powers." See also Gouldner, *Dialectic of Ideology and Technology;* and Gouldner, *Future of Intellectuals.*

15. Hamilton and Wright, *State of the Masses,* chap. 3.

16. Francis Fukuyama, *The End of History and the Last Man* (New York: Free Press, 1992).

17. See, e.g., Lionel Trilling, *The Liberal Imagination: Essays on Literature and Society* (New York: Harcourt Brace Jovanovich, 1950).

18. Helen Vendler, "Anxiety of Innocence," *New Republic,* November 22, 1993, 34.

19. Ibid., vii–xiv.

20. For an interesting recent discussion, see Wolfe, *Whose Keeper?,* introduction and chaps. 7–9.

Bachrach, Peter, 249n.45
Bailyn, Lotte, 236n.5
Banfield, Edward C., 249n.44
Baratz, Morton S., 249n.45
Barber, Bernard, 214n.15
Barnes, Samuel H., 261n.76
Barnouw, Erik, 240n.43
Barry, James H., 240n.41
Bartley, Robert, 243n.29
Barton, Allan H., 237n.24
Bass, Debra, 231n.1
Bauman, Zygmut, 256n.76
Bearden, James, 244n.54
Beatty, Kathleen M., 244n.48
Becker, Howard S., 216n.7, 228n.61
Bell, Daniel, 3, 40, 54, 130, 155, 213nn. 2, 9, and 10, 222nn. 85 and 86, 227n.38, 228n.52, 237n.22, 246n.1, 247nn. 8 and 9, 252nn. 7 and 16, 253 nn. 17 and 21, 254n.33
Bellah, Robert N., 237n.20
Ben-David, Joseph, 175, 219n.52, 256n.2, 257n.3
Bender, Thomas, 254n.33, 256n.76
Bergen, Bernard J., 250n.68
Berger, David G., 240n.43
Berger, Peter L., 213n.9, 241nn. 48 and 1
Berger, Suzanne, 262n.76
Berglund, Stein, 260n.40
Berlant, Jeffrey, 222n.82
Blair, Roger D., 219n.50
Blau, Judith R., 226n.30
Bledstein, Burton, 213n.9, 215n.26, 219nn. 46, 53, 54, and 55, 222nn. 75 and 76, 250n.60
Block, Fred, 243n.31
Block, N. J., 249n.54
blue-collar workers, 4, 208–209; declining social and political influence of, 208–209; politics of, 86–88, 245n.67; political profile compared with other key strata in American society, 7, 82–84, 176. *See also* labor unions
Blumberg, Paul, 237n.23, 239n.38
Blumenthal, Sidney, 244nn. 45 and 54, 252n.8
Bobo, Lawrence, 256n.84
Bok, Derek, 231n.3
Bolick, Jay, 226n.30, 246n.77
Boltanski, Luc, 257n.7
Botstein, Leon, 254n.33
Bourdieu, Pierre, 4, 213n.9, 215n.31, 235n.54, 239n.39, 256n.72, 262n.12

"boutique firms," 206, 224n.9
Bowen, William G., 223n.95
Boyers, Robert, 254n.33
Braungart, Richard, 256n.85
Braybrooke, David, 251n.80
Brim, Orville G., 236n.11
Brint, Steven, 222n.81, 223n.97, 224n.2, 227n.49, 228n.51, 229n.65, 236n.10, 240n.41, 241n.11, 242n.26, 244n.50, 245nn. 55 and 59, 248n.29, 249n.46, 252nn. 85 and 8, 257n.11, 259nn. 26 and 27, 262nn. 11 and 13
Broad, William J. 246n.71
Broadbent, Jeffrey, 259n.25
Brooks, Clem, 241n.49
Brooks, Peter, 254n.33
Brown, Donald R., 226n.27
Brown, Paula, 239n.40
Bruce-Briggs, B., 216n.42, 227n.38, 229n.65, 239n.36, 242n.28
Brudney, Jeffrey, 243n.35
Brustein, Robert, 254n.33
Brzezinski, Zbigniew, 246n.1
Buckley, William F., 155, 254n.33
Burgess, John M., 220n.58
Burke, Edmund, 150, 252n.2
Burke, Kenneth, 168
Burnham, James, 241n.1
Burrage, Michael, 256n.1, 257nn. 2 and 5
business accountants, 47–48, 224n.7
business owners and executives, 3, 5, 12, 85–88, 104, 111–13, 116–19, 120–23, 223n. 101, 244n. 51, 245n.67; and "attitude gap," 113, 121–23, 245n.67; compositional changes among, 121–23; organization of, 116–17, 244n.51; politics of, 5, 86–88, 104, 111–13, 116–17; public opinion about, 111–12, 223n.101; similarities to professionals, 12, 85, 118–19. *See also* managers; professional training in business
Business Roundtable, 116
business services sphere, 9, 46–48, 55; dominant ethos in, 55; earnings in, 48; economic growth of, 9, 48; entrepreneurial outlook in, 48; organizational distribution in, 48; politics of professionals in, 55; size of, 47; sources of growth of 46–48, 118. *See also* spheres of social purpose
Butler, Stuart, 230n. 92

California Master Plan, 141
Calvert, Monte A., 221n.72

McNamara, Robert, 146
McNeill, William, 217nn. 24 and 25
Medical Act of 1858, 32, 218n.39
medicine, 9, 27, 31–32, 54, 205–206. *See also* doctors
Melluci, Alberto, 261n.71
meritocracy, 83, 104, 142, 236nn. 11, 12, and 13. *See also* higher education; professional culture
Merrill, James, 254n.33
Merwin, W. S., 254n.33
Metzger, Walter P., 214n.14, 220n.54
Meynaud, Jean, 193, 260n.35
middle class, 25, 198–201. *See also* professional stratum
Miles, Michael, 252n.15
Miliband, Ralph, 251n.84
military officers, 28–29, 52, 66, 136
Mill, John Stuart, 207, 218n.32
Miller, Arthur, 243n.39
Miller, S. M., 240n.45
Millerson, Geoffrey, 214n.15, 217nn. 13, 14, 15, 16, 17, and 28, 219n.51, 220n.52
Mills, C. Wright, 213n.8
Mills, Donald L., 214n.15
Milner, Henry, 260n.44
Modigliani, Andre, 256n.85
Moe, Terry, 230n.92
Mohr, John, 262n.11
Mollenkopf, John H. 224n.2, 252n.86
Mooney, Carolyn J. 253n.29
Morison, Samuel Eliot, 220n.55
Morrison, Toni, 155, 254n.33
Mowry, George B., 230n.91
Moyers, Bill, 254n.33
Moynihan, Daniel Patrick, 213n.9, 243n.29, 246n.1, 248n.33
Mueller-Rommel, Ferdinand, 261n.74
"multiservice oligopolies," 206, 225n.11
Musgrave, Peggy, 229n.66
Musgrave, Richard A., 229n.66
Myrdal, Gunnar, 153, 192

Nathan, Richard P., 227nn. 44 and 46
Nation, 155–57
National Center for Educational Statistics, 225n.19
National Association of Social Workers, 235n.49
National Education Association, 235n.49
National Review, 155
natural scientists, 28, 48–50, 62; earnings of, 71, 73–75; emergence of, 28–29; em-

ployment of, 48–50, 62, 245n.70; and erosion of professional autonomy, 125; limited influence on public policy of, 136–37, 250n.64; as model for professionalizing occupations, 35; numbers of, 62; sectoral distribution of, 62; and university incorporation, 35. *See also* applied science sphere
Navasky, Victor, 254n.33
Nelkin, Dorothy, 248nn. 31, 32, 35, and 38
Nelson, Michael, 245n.66
neo-corporatism, 194, 197, 200
Netzer, Dick, 250n.62
Neustadl, Alan, 244n.54
"new class" theory, 4, 13, 18–19, 64, 85, 96, 104–105, 123, 177, 192, 206–207, 210, 252n.8
New Criterion, 156–57
New Deal, 54, 130, 153, 172
New Left, 152, 171
New Politics movement, 106
New Republic, 155–56
"New York Intellectuals," 154
New York Review of Books, 155–56
New York Times Book Review, 155–56
New Yorker, 155–56
Newman, Katherine S., 237n.23
Nie, Norman H., 241nn. 9 and 10
Nieman Foundation (Harvard University), 125–26
Niemi, G. Richard, 242nn. 18 and 19
Nixon, Richard M., 130
Noble, David F., 214n.19
Noonan, Peggy, 252n.8, 256n.79
Nordlinger, Eric, 262n.79
Novak, Michael, 254n.33
Noyelle, Thierry, 224nn. 4, 5, and 6, 225nn. 12 and 13, 238n.35, 245n.60, 257n.9, 262n.7
nurses, 54, 73–74, 78–79, 203
Nussbaum, Martha, 254n.33

Oakeshott, Michael, 41, 222n.87
Oakley, Francis, 223n.95
Oates, Joyce Carol, 254n.33
Oberschall, Anthony, 220n.60
occupational centrality in social regulation, 142–43, 250n.64
occupational prestige, 38, 41–42, 222nn. 74, 89, and 90
"occupational professionalism," 30–31
occupational structure, 110
O'Connor, James, 251n.84